Capital Punishment's Collateral Damage

Capital Punishment's Collateral Damage

Robert M. Bohm

PROFESSOR OF CRIMINAL JUSTICE
UNIVERSITY OF CENTRAL FLORIDA
ORLANDO, FLORIDA

CAROLINA ACADEMIC PRESS
Durham, North Carolina

Library of Congress Cataloging-in-Publication Data
Bohm, Robert M.
  Capital punishment's collateral damage / Robert M. Bohm.
      p. cm.
  Includes bibliographical references and index.
  ISBN 978-1-61163-209-5 (alk. paper)
  1. Capital punishment--United States. I. Title.

  HV8699.U5B64 2012
  364.66--dc23   2012023669

Carolina Academic Press
700 Kent Street
Durham, North Carolina 27701
Telephone (919) 489-7486
Fax (919) 493-5668
www.cap-press.com

Printed in the United States of America

Contents

Capital Punishment's Collateral Damage

Introduction

The literature on capital punishment is voluminous. For nearly 250 years, scholars have discussed and debated such issues as its deterrent effect (or lack thereof); retributive and religious arguments; costs; administration, including miscarriages of justice and whether it is imposed in an arbitrary and discriminatory manner; and whether methods of execution are cruel and unusual. Conspicuously missing from this literature is the human element, the impact of capital punishment on the lives of those who are involved in the process by calamity, duty, or choice.

This book seeks to rectify that omission by allowing the participants in this ritual of death to describe in their own words their role in the process and, especially, its effects on them.[1] In this way, we can begin to understand the reach of capital punishment beyond just the victim and the perpetrator. We can begin to understand the collateral damage of capital punishment.

Before turning to the participants, however, this introduction addresses a few preliminary matters. The first is an overview of the modern death penalty's creation; the second is a detailed description of the capital punishment process. Along the way, key terminology is defined. For now, note that the terms *death penalty* and *capital punishment* are used interchangeably. Also, when referring to capital offenders, masculine pronouns are used because in the United States, the death penalty is reserved almost exclusively for men. During the modern death penalty era, explained below, women have constituted fewer than one percent of all those executed and fewer than two percent of all those on death row. Women commit no more than ten percent of all murders, but the percentage of women whose murders are death-eligible is unknown. Finally, except where indicated otherwise, all direct quotes not followed by a source citation are from interviews conducted by the author or from written responses to survey questions posed by the author.

The Modern Death Penalty

The modern death penalty era began in 1976, when the U.S. Supreme Court approved new "guided-discretion" death penalty statutes in the cases of *Gregg v. Georgia*,[2] *Jurek v. Texas*,[3] and *Proffitt v. Florida*[4] (hereafter referred to as the "*Gregg* decision"). Just four

---

1. This book is an unabridged and updated version of a book that was originally published in 2010 under the title of *Ultimate Sanction: Understanding the Death Penalty Through Its Many Voices and Many Sides*.
2. 428 U.S. 153.
3. 428 U.S. 262.
4. 428 U.S. 242.

years earlier, in the landmark cases of *Furman v. Georgia*, *Jackson v. Georgia*, and *Branch v. Texas* (hereafter referred to as the "*Furman* decision"[5]), the Supreme Court for the first and only time in American history struck down the death penalty, holding that the capital punishment statutes in the three cases were unconstitutional because they gave the jury complete discretion to decide whether to impose the death penalty or a lesser punishment in capital cases. Although nine separate opinions were written—a very rare occurrence—the majority of five justices (William O. Douglas, William J. Brennan, Potter Stewart, Byron R. White, and Thurgood Marshall) pointed out that the death penalty had been imposed arbitrarily, infrequently, and often selectively against minorities. The majority agreed that the statutes provided for a cruel and unusual punishment in violation of the Eighth and Fourteenth Amendments. A practical effect of the *Furman* decision was the Supreme Court's voiding forty death penalty statutes and the sentences of more than six hundred death row inmates in thirty-two states.[6]

In *Gregg*, the Court approved, by a 7-to-2 vote (Justices Marshall and Brennan dissented), guided-discretion statutes that set standards for juries and judges to use when deciding whether to impose the death penalty. The Court's majority concluded that the guided-discretion statutes struck a reasonable balance between giving the jury some direction and allowing it to consider the defendant's background and character and the circumstances of the crime. Following a decadelong moratorium, the first person executed under the new guided discretion statutes was Gary Gilmore, who, on January 17, 1977, was executed in Utah by firing squad.

The Capital Punishment Process

Few people comprehend how complex, costly, and time-consuming the capital punishment process can be. As Supreme Court Justice William Brennan first articulated in *Furman*, and as has been repeated in numerous court decisions ever since, "death is different." According to Justice Brennan, the death penalty is "an unusually severe punishment, unusual in its pain, in its finality, and in its enormity."[7] In his concurring opinion, Justice Potter Stewart augmented his colleague's description: "[T]he penalty of death differs from all other forms of criminal punishment, not in degrees but in kind. It is unique in its total irrevocability. It is unique in its rejection of rehabilitation of the convict as a basic purpose of criminal justice, and it is unique, finally, in its absolute renunciation of all that is embodied in our concept of humanity."[8] Because "death is different," capital cases are handled differently than other felony cases. The due process procedures used in capital cases, for example, are so different from the due process procedures used in other felony cases that they have been given the clever label of "super due process."[9]

---

5. All three cases were consolidated under 408 U.S. 238.

6. Bob Woodward and Scott Armstrong (1979) *The Brethren: Inside the Supreme Court*. New York: Simon and Schuster, p. 220.

7. *Furman v. Georgia*, op. cit., pp. 287-289.

8. Ibid., p. 306.

9. Margaret Jane Radin (1980) "Cruel Punishment and Respect for Persons: Super Due Process for Death," *Southern California Law Review* 53:1143-1185.

Elements of Super Due Process

The principal elements of super due process are *bifurcated trials*; sentencing guidelines that require jurors to weigh aggravating and mitigating factors; *automatic appellate review*; and *proportionality review*. A bifurcated trial is a two-stage trial with separate guilt and penalty phases, unlike other felony trials in which the guilt and penalty phases are joined. During the *guilt phase*, the only question considered by the jury is whether the defendant is guilty or not guilty. During the *penalty phase*, the only question considered by the jury is whether the guilty defendant should be sentenced to death or, in most jurisdictions, life imprisonment without opportunity for parole.

Sentencing guidelines, which are provided in guided-discretion death penalty statutes, set standards for judges and juries to use in determining whether death is the appropriate penalty in capital cases. In *Gregg*, the Court's majority concluded that the sentencing guidelines would sufficiently circumscribe what had previously been a jury's unfettered sentencing discretion by giving the jury some direction and allowing it to consider the defendant's background and the character and the circumstances of the crime. All death penalty statutes list specific aggravating factors, which are weighed against mitigating factors. The mitigating factors may or may not be listed in the statute. To charge a suspect with a death-eligible offense in all death penalty states, the prosecutor must be able to prove, generally beyond a reasonable doubt, at least one aggravating factor.

Aggravating factors (also referred to as *aggravating circumstances* or *special circumstances*) are facts or situations that increase the blameworthiness of a criminal act. There are three broad types of aggravating factors: those that focus on offender characteristics; those that focus on the manner in which the murder was committed; and those that focus on victim characteristics. Specific examples of aggravating factors include evidence of premeditation and planning, torture, and creating a great risk of death to many people. Death penalty states vary in the number of aggravating factors listed in their statutes. Connecticut, Kansas, Kentucky, Mississippi, and Oklahoma have the fewest, with eight; California and Delaware have the most, with twenty-two. The average number of aggravating factors is thirteen, but the trend is toward an increase in the number of statutory aggravating factors.[10] Aggravating factors differ widely in their significance; therefore, their content is more important than how many there are in determining the number of death–eligible offenses. The purpose of aggravating factors is to narrow death eligibility.

Mitigating factors (also referred to as *mitigating circumstances* or *extenuating circumstances*) are facts or situations that do not justify or excuse a capital crime but reduce the degree of a defendant's blameworthiness and thus may reduce his punishment. Examples of mitigating factors are immaturity, no record of prior criminal activity, and being under the influence of another person. The Supreme Court has ruled that during the penalty phase of a bifurcated trial, judges and juries must consider any mitigating factors that a defense

---

10. Timothy P. Colyer and Robert M. Bohm (2012) "You're Killing Me: A Review of State and Federal Death Penalty Statutes." *The Criminal Law Bulletin* 48 (forthcoming); Tracy L. Snell (2006) "Capital Punishment 2005," U.S. Department of Justice, *Bureau of Justice Statistics Bulletin* (December), p. 2, Table 1; James R. Acker and Charles S. Lanier (2003) "Beyond Human Ability? The Rise and Fall of Death Penalty Legislation," pp. 85–125 in J. R. Acker, R. M. Bohm, and C. S. Lanier (eds.) *America's Experiment with Capital Punishment: Reflections on the Past, Present and Future of the Ultimate Penal Sanction*, 2nd Ed. Durham, NC: Carolina Academic Press.

attorney presents, whether they are listed in a death penalty statute or not, as long as they are supported with evidence. The primary purpose of a judge or jury's consideration of mitigating factors is to temper with mercy the desires for retribution and punishment. The consideration of mitigating factors is predicated on the belief that not all people who kill deserve the death penalty.

Under guided-discretion statutes, jurors must find at least one aggravating factor before the death penalty may be considered. If jurors find one or more aggravating factors, they are weighed against any mitigating factors. If the aggravating factors outweigh the mitigating factors, then the sentence is death. If the mitigating factors outweigh the aggravating factors, the sentence is life imprisonment without parole. If the aggravating and mitigating factors are of equal weight, a death sentence may be imposed. Weighing aggravating versus mitigating factors is not intended as a simple exercise in addition and subtraction. Jurors are not supposed to count the number of aggravating factors and then subtract them from the number of mitigating factors, or vice versa. Not all factors necessarily count equally. It is conceivable that a single aggravating factor could outweigh several mitigating factors, or the opposite could be true.

A third element of super due process is *automatic appellate review* (also called *direct appeal*). Although states are not constitutionally obligated to provide automatic appeal, nearly all jurisdictions with capital punishment statutes require automatic review of conviction and/or death sentence by the state supreme court, regardless of the defendant's wishes.

Finally, some states provide *proportionality review*, although the Supreme Court does not require it. Proportionality review is a process whereby state appellate courts compare the sentence in the case being reviewed with sentences imposed in similar cases in the state. Its purpose is to identify disparities in sentencing.

Although all death penalty statutes in the United States have super due process elements, no two statutes are exactly the same. Thus, the United States actually has thirty-five different death penalty jurisdictions (as of August 2012) — 33 states, the U.S. government, and the U.S. military.

Investigation and Arrest

The capital punishment process begins when a potentially capital crime — nearly always a murder with at least one aggravating factor — has been reported to the police. The investigation of potentially capital crimes tends to be more rigorous than the investigation of other felonies. When the crime may be a capital offense, forensic experts generally examine the crime scene more carefully. Investigation of the case frequently continues through trial and can take three to five times longer than for other felonies, primarily because the prosecution as well as the defense must prepare for both stages of the bifurcated trial.[11] Because defense counsel may present any relevant mitigating evidence during the penalty phase of a capital trial as long as it is supported by evidence, a thorough investigation

---

11. Robert L. Spangenberg and Elizabeth R. Walsh (1989) "Capital Punishment or Life Imprisonment? Some Cost Considerations." *Loyola of Los Angeles Law Review* 23:45–58, p. 49; Margot Garey (1985) "The Cost of Taking a Life: Dollars and Sense of the Death Penalty." *University of California, Davis Law Review* 18:1221–1273, p. 1252; Justin Brooks and Jeanne Huey Erikson (1996) "The Dire Wolf Collects His Due While the Boys Sit by the Fire: Why Michigan Cannot Afford to Buy into the Death Penalty." *Thomas M. Cooley Law Review* 13:877–905, p. 893.

of possible mitigating factors is time-consuming and expensive. If an investigation is successful, a suspect is arrested. (Homicide detectives and other investigative personnel are the subjects of chapter 1.)

Booking and Charging

Once a suspect has been identified and arrested, his Miranda rights are supposed to be read to him — the most important of these, arguably, being the right to the effective assistance of counsel. After being made aware of his rights, the suspect is transported to the police station to be booked. *Booking* is the process in which suspects' names, the charges for which they were arrested, their fingerprints, and perhaps their photographs are entered on the police blotter. The phone call routinely afforded arrested suspects at the police station is for the specific purpose of obtaining counsel. If a suspect cannot afford an attorney and is accused of a capital crime (or any crime for which conviction could warrant imprisonment), the state is required to provide an attorney at the state's expense. In many jurisdictions, a capital defendant is entitled to two attorneys at trial. (Defense attorneys are the subject of chapter 4.)

Following booking, a prosecutor is asked to review the facts of the case and decide whether a suspect should be charged with a crime or crimes. Sometimes prosecutors review a case prior to the arrest, in which case the *indictment*, or *information* (discussed below), serves as the basis for an arrest warrant that a judge issues upon a prosecutor's request. As a result of the review, the prosecutor may tell the police that they do not have a case or that the case is weak, requiring further investigation and additional evidence. However, if the prosecutor decides that a suspect is *chargeable*, he or she prepares a charging document. The crime(s) with which the suspect is charged may or may not be the same crime(s) for which he was arrested originally. For example, the police may arrest a suspect on a charge of first-degree murder, but after reviewing the evidence, the prosecutor may change it to second-degree murder or perhaps first-degree manslaughter. (Chapter 2 examines prosecutors.)

Grand Jury Indictment and Information

If the prosecutor believes there is evidence to convict the suspect of the crime, and the crime is an aggravated murder (or other capital offense), then the prosecutor will seek an indictment for capital murder in jurisdictions that employ grand juries. In those jurisdictions that do not use grand juries, formal charges are filed through an information.

A *grand jury* is generally a group of twelve to twenty-three citizens who meet in closed sessions to determine whether there is *probable cause* to believe that the suspect is guilty of the charge(s) brought by the prosecutor. Before appearing in front of a grand jury, the prosecutor drafts an indictment, which is a document outlining the charge(s) against a suspect. Because the grand jury has to determine only whether there is probable cause that a suspect committed the crime(s) with which he is charged, only the prosecution's evidence and witnesses are heard. Probable cause, in this context, is the amount of proof necessary for a reasonably intelligent person to believe that a crime has been committed. In most jurisdictions, neither the suspect nor the suspect's counsel has a right to be present during grand jury proceedings. Furthermore, during these proceedings, unlike in criminal trials, prosecutors are allowed to present *hearsay evidence*, which is information learned from someone other than the witness who is testifying. They also may use illegally obtained evidence because the *exclusionary rule* does not apply to grand jury proceedings. (The exclusionary rule requires that illegally seized evidence be excluded from criminal trials.) Prosecutors can subpoena witnesses to testify. A witness who refuses to testify can be held in contempt and can be jailed until he or she provides the requested information. After hearing the prosecutor's evidence and witnesses, the grand jury makes its probable cause determination and, usually on a majority vote, either indicts (issues a *true bill*) or fails to indict (*no bill*). In most jurisdictions, if the grand jury fails to indict, then the prosecution must be dropped. However, in some jurisdictions, the case can be brought before another grand jury.

An information—an alternative to a grand jury indictment—is a document that outlines the formal charge(s), the law or laws that have been violated, and the evidence to support the charge(s).

Initial Appearance

After the charge(s) have been filed, suspects—now defendants—are brought before a lower court judge for an *initial appearance*, where they are given formal notice of the charge(s) against them and advised of their constitutional rights (for example, the right to counsel). If suspects are arrested without a warrant, as is most often the case, they must generally be released from custody if they do not have an initial appearance within forty-eight hours of their arrest. The one exception to this requirement concerns suspects arrested on a Friday night and not brought before a judge until Monday morning. Consequently, suspects arrested without a warrant frequently have an ititial appearance before formal charges have been filed, in which case a judge must determine only whether the police had probable cause to make the arrest.

Also during the initial appearance, a bond hearing is held. *Bond*, or *bail*, is usually a monetary guarantee deposited with the court that is supposed to ensure that the suspect or defendant will appear at a later stage in the criminal justice process. In other words, bond or bail allows suspects or defendants to remain free while awaiting the next stage in the adjudication process. If bond is denied, which is likely with potentially capital crimes, the suspect is incarcerated to await either a preliminary hearing in those jurisdictions that provide for them or an arraignment in those that do not provide preliminary hearings or in cases in which a preliminary hearing is waived.

Preliminary Hearing

If the prosecutor has not taken the case directly to a grand jury in grand jury states, the next stage is a *preliminary hearing*. The purpose of the preliminary hearing, which is used in about half of all states, is for a judge to determine whether there is probable cause to support the charge(s) imposed by the prosecutor.

A preliminary hearing is similar to a criminal trial in that defendants can be represented by legal counsel and can call witnesses on their behalf. It differs in that the judge must determine only that there is probable cause that the defendant committed the crime(s) with which he is charged. At criminal trials, guilt must be determined beyond a reasonable doubt. Also, at preliminary hearings, unlike in criminal trials, defendants have no right to be heard by a jury.

If the judge determines that there is probable cause that a defendant committed the crime(s) with which he is charged, then the defendant is bound over for possible indictment in states with grand juries or for arraignment on an information in states without grand juries. Sometimes prosecutors delay preliminary hearings to await a grand jury action to avoid disclosing evidence in open court that might help defense attorneys at trial.

Although judges at preliminary hearings are supposed to examine the facts of the case before making a probable cause determination, in practice they seldom do. In big cities, judges generally do not have the time to inquire into the facts of a case. Consequently, at most preliminary hearings, judges simply assume that if a police officer made an arrest, and a prosecutor charged the defendant with a crime(s), then there must be probable cause that the defendant did, in fact, commit the crime or crimes. Few cases are dismissed for lack of probable cause at preliminary hearings. Not suprisingly, then, defendants frequently waive the right to a preliminary hearing.

Arraignment

The primary purpose of an *arraignment* is to hear the formal information or indictment and to allow the defendant to enter a plea. The two most common pleas are *guilty* and *not guilty*. Capital defendants seldom plead guilty. In some states, defendants can stand mute or can plead not guilty by reason of insanity. Standing mute at arraignment is interpreted as pleading not guilty. In states that do not accept a plea of not guilty by reason of insanity, defendants plead not guilty and assume the burden of proving insanity at trial.

At arraignment, the judge also determines whether a defendant is competent to stand trial. Defendants can seek a delay before trial to consult further with their attorneys. A defendant who does not already have an attorney can ask that one be appointed. Defendants sometimes attempt to have their cases dismissed at arraignment. For example, they may assert that the state lacks sufficient evidence or that improper arrest procedures were used. If the case is not dismissed, and the defendant pleads not guilty, a trial date is set.

Trial

One of the distinctive features of American criminal justice is trial by a jury of one's peers. The principal purpose of *jury trials*—and of criminal trials without juries—is to discover the truth of whether defendants are guilty or innocent of the crimes with which they are charged. The process by which truth is sought is an adversarial one regulated by specific procedures and rules. The adversaries in a criminal trial are the state (represented by the prosecutor) and the defendant (usually represented by defense counsel). The burden of proof is on the prosecution to show, beyond a reasonable doubt, that the defendant is guilty. The goal of defense counsel is to discredit the prosecution's case and to create reasonable doubt about the defendant's guilt. It is the responsibility of the jury (in jury trials) or the judge (in trials without juries) to determine and assign guilt.

Only about five percent of criminal cases ever reach trial; the vast majority are resolved through *plea bargaining*. Plea bargaining refers to the practice whereby the prosecutor, the defense attorney, the defendant, and, in some jurisdictions, the judge agree on a specific sentence to be imposed if the accused pleads guilty to an agreed-upon charge or charges instead of going to trial. Because "death is different," death penalty cases go to trial ten times more often than do other felony cases.[12]

Still, plea bargaining plays a prominent role in death-eligible cases. For example, prosecutors frequently waive the death penalty if defendants agree to accept lengthy prison sentences or life imprisonment without opportunity of parole as part of a negotiated plea bargain. Used this way, the death penalty gives prosecutors leverage during plea negotiations, and places defendants in a difficult situation. If they plead guilty, they spend the rest of their lives (or most of their lives) in prison; if they go to trial, they may be aquitted, or they may be sentenced to death. The decision is made more difficult by knowledge that, all too often, innocent people are wrongly convicted and sentenced to death.

Since 1973, 140 inmates in twenty-six states have been released from death row because of evidence of their innocence.[13] No one knows how many innocent death row inmates have been executed. Thus, making the wrong choice can have deadly consequences, as the case of John Spenkelink, the second person executed under post-*Furman* statutes, illustrates. Had Spenkelink plea bargained and accepted the uncontested second-degree murder conviction offered to him by the state of Florida, he already could have been paroled on the date he was executed.[14]

Jury Selection

Before a capital trial begins, several preliminary matters must be addressed. The first is usually jury selection. Capital trials require twelve jurors, unlike some other felony trials, which require as few as six. The selection of a jury begins with a master list of all eligible jurors. From the master list, a sufficient number of eligible jurors is randomly chosen to make up the *jury pool*, or *venire*. Those chosen are summoned for service by the sheriff. However, not all those summoned will actually serve on the venire. Potential jurors must generally be U.S. citizens, residents of the locality of the trial, of a certain minimum age, and able to understand English. Convicted felons and mentally ill persons are almost always excluded. Most jurisdictions also require that jurors be of "good character" and be "well-informed," which eliminates other potential jurors. In addition, members of certain professions often escape jury service because their services are considered indispensable or because they are connected to the criminal justice process. These include doctors, lawyers, teachers, some elected officials, military personnel on active duty, and law enforcement personnel. Many jurisdictions allow citizens to be excused from jury service if it would cause them physical or economic difficulties. Consequently, only about twenty-five percent of adult Americans have ever served on juries. A "jury of one's peers," then, is really a jury of people who are eligible and, in many cases, willing to serve.

For noncapital felony trials, as many as thirty people are randomly selected from the venire by the court clerk for the jury panel from which the actual trial jury is selected.

---

12. Spangenberg and Walsh, ibid.; Garey, ibid., p. 1247, n. 114.
13. Death Penalty Information Center at www.deathpenaltyinfo.org (accessed August 25, 2012).
14. Hugo Adam Bedau (ed.) (1982) *The Death Penalty in America*, Third Edition. New York: Oxford University Press, p. 190.

However, for capital trials, the court clerk typically selects one hundred or more people for the jury panel.

To ensure a fair trial, potential trial jurors go through *voir dire*, a process in which persons who might be biased or unable to render a fair verdict are screened out. In most jurisdictions, a first step in this process is for potential jurors to fill out a lengthy questionnaire. Typical questions include: "Do you have any moral, religious, or personal beliefs that would prevent you from sitting in judgment of another person?" "What do you consider the main purpose of the death penalty?" "Do you believe the death penalty is a necessary punishment in our society?"[15]

During voir dire, the defense, the prosecution, and the judge question jurors about their backgrounds and knowledge of the case and the defendant. Many death penalty jurisdictions require that jurors not only be questioned individually but also that they remain sequestered until the full jury is selected or until they are dismissed. Jury sequestration is the isolation or segregation of jurors to prevent them from being exposed to biasing information. (Some juries also are sequestered when attempting to reach a verdict.) In many jurisdictions, defendants are allowed to waive the requirements that jurors be questioned individually and/or be sequestered.

If it appears that a juror might be biased or unable to render a fair verdict, the juror can be challenged *for cause*—that is, for a specific reason—by either the defense or the prosecution. If the judge agrees, the juror is dismissed from jury service. In death penalty trials, potential jurors can be excluded for cause if they are opposed to the death penalty regardless of circumstances. This process is referred to as *death qualification*. Thus, a jury of one's peers in capital trials is a jury of people who are eligible; in many cases, willing to serve; and not adverse to imposing the death penalty if the circumstances warrant it. Generally, there is no limit to the number of jurors that can be eliminated for cause. In practice, however, few potential jurors are eliminated for cause, except in high-profile trials.

Another way that either the defense or the prosecution can eliminate potential jurors from jury service is by the use of *peremptory challenges*, which allow either prosecutors or defense attorneys to excuse jurors without having to provide a reason. Peremptory challenges are frequently used to eliminate jurors whose characteristics place them in a group likely to be unfavorable to the case of either the prosecution or the defense. For example, in death penalty cases, prosecutors often use their peremptory challenges to eliminate people of color and women because, statistically, people of color and women are less likely to favor capital punishment. However, prosecutors must be careful in their use of peremptory challenges for such purposes because the Supreme Court has forbidden the use of peremptory challenges to exclude potential jurors solely on account of their race or gender. The number of peremptory challenges is limited by statute. In most jurisdictions, the prosecution is allowed from six to eight peremptory challenges and the defense from eight to ten.

Voir dire typically continues until fourteen jurors have been selected: twelve regular jurors and, usually, two alternates who can replace jurors unable to continue because of illness, accident, or personal emergency. The voir dire process may take an hour or two or, in rare cases, months. (Jurors are the subject of chapter 7.)

---

15. Robert Jay Lifton and Greg Mitchell (2002) *Who Owns Death? Capital Punishment, the American Conscience, and the End of Executions.* New York: Perennial, pp. 139-40.

Motions

A second preliminary matter that typically must be addressed prior to trial is the filing and disposing of *motions*: court applications requesting a judge to order a particular action. (Motions also can be made during and after a trial.) Defense counsel has both a professional and ethical obligation to represent his or her client's interests by filing nonfrivolous motions that, at minimum, create and preserve the defendant's record for appeal. The prosecution must respond to the motions as well as file its own. Typical motions filed in capital cases involve voir dire, jury composition, change of venue, challenges to the death-qualification process, and challenges to the death penalty's constitutionality in general and to the state's death penalty statute in particular. Those motions are in addition to more standard ones such as having a confession ruled inadmissible because of Miranda violations. It is estimated that two to six times more motions are filed in death penalty cases than in other felony cases.[16]

The Guilt Phase

After the jury has been sworn in, and the court clerk has read the criminal charge or charges, the prosecution begins the trial with an opening statement outlining its case. Next is the opening statement by the defense. In some jurisdictions, though, the defense is allowed to defer its opening statement until after the prosecution has presented its case or to not make an opening statement at all.

The prosecution then submits its evidence and questions its witnesses. The prosecution must establish beyond a reasonable doubt each element of the crime. The specific elements of a capital crime are provided in state and federal statutes. Some of these include *actus reus* (criminal conduct), *mens rea* (criminal intent), and concurrence (the criminal conduct and the criminal intent must occur together). If the defense believes that the prosecution has failed to make its case, then the defense may choose to "rest"—that is, to not defend its client against the charge or charges. At this point, the defense in most states is allowed to request a *directed verdict,* or to make a motion for dismissal. If the judge agrees with the defense that the prosecution's evidence is insufficient for conviction, he or she can either direct the jury to acquit the defendant or "take the case from the jury" and grant the motion for dismissal. If the defense does not seek a dismissal or if it is not granted, the defense follows the prosecution with its witnesses and any contrary evidence. Then the prosecution and the defense take turns offering rebuttals to the other side's evidence, cross-examining witnesses, and reexamining their own witnesses. Following the rebuttal period, the prosecution summarizes its case. The defense then summarizes its case and makes its closing statement. The closing statement by the prosecution ends the adversarial portion of the trial.

Normally, after the closing statement by the prosecution, the judge instructs, or *charges,* the jurors concerning the principles of law they are to utilize in determining guilt or innocence. The judge also explains to the jury the charges, the rules of evidence, and the possible verdicts. In some jurisdictions, the judge summarizes the evidence presented from notes taken during the trial. (Trial judges are the subject of chapter 6.)

---

16. Garey, op. cit.; Spangenberg and Walsh, op. cit.

Jury Deliberation

The jury deliberates until it reaches a verdict. In a room with complete privacy, the jury elects from its members a foreperson to preside over the subsequent deliberations. Jurors are not allowed to discuss the case with anyone other than another juror. In some cases, a jury is sequestered at night in a hotel or motel to prevent any chance of outside influence.

To find a defendant guilty as charged, the jury must be convinced "beyond a reasonable doubt" that the defendant has committed the crime. Some juries reach a verdict in a matter of minutes; some juries take weeks or more. In the federal courts and in nearly every state, a unanimous verdict is required. If, after serious deliberation, even one juror cannot agree with the others on a verdict, the result is a *hung jury*. Even in jurisdictions that do not require a unanimous verdict, such as Florida, a hung (deadlocked) jury results when a jury cannot reach a verdict by the required voting margin.

Judges hate hung juries. Not only do they fail to produce a decisive trial outcome— either a conviction or an acquittal—but also they result in a huge waste of time and money for all parties involved. If the jury remains deadlocked, the judge declares a mistrial, and the prosecutor must decide whether to retry the case. Hung juries occur infrequently.

After the verdict has been read in the courtroom, either the defense or the prosecution may ask that the jury be polled individually, with each juror stating publicly how he or she voted. If the jury finds the defendant not guilty, the defendant is released from the jurisdiction of the court and is a free person. If the jury finds the defendant guilty as charged, as is most often the case, the guilt phase of the bifurcated trial is concluded, and the penalty phase begins. In recent years, Virginia, Alabama, Mississippi, and Lousiana juries have found defendants guilty in 75 percent to more than 90 percent of capital trials; juries have found defendants guilty in about 99 percent of recent capital trials in the Texas cities of Houston, Dallas, and San Antonio.[17]

The Penalty Phase

The object of the penalty phase of a bifurcated-capital trial is for the jury to determine whether the sentence will be death or, in nearly all jurisdictions, life imprisonment without opportunity of parole. Those are the only two options. In the penalty phase, evidence may be introduced, witnesses may be called to testify, and victims' family members may make *victim-impact statements*, which are descriptions of the harm and suffering that the crime has caused the victims' survivors. (Victims' family members are examined in chapter 3.) Some states require the selection of a separate jury for the penalty phase. In short, all of the due process procedures that applied to the guilt phase apply to the penalty phase as well. It is during the penalty phase that a persuasive presentation of mitigating evidence may mean the difference between life and death.

As noted previously, if jurors find one or more aggravating factors, they are weighed against any mitigating factors. If the aggravating factors outweigh the mitigating factors,

---

17. David R. Dow, (2002a) "The Problem of Innocence," pp. 1-8 in D. R. Dow and M. Dow (eds.) *Machinery of Death: The Reality of America's Death Penalty Regime.* New York: Routledge, p. 4.

then the sentence is death. If the mitigating factors outweigh the aggravating factors, the sentence is life imprisonment without parole. If the aggravating and mitigating factors are of equal weight, a death sentence may be imposed.

Appeals

The first and only appeal required by most death penalty states is the automatic or direct appeal, which occurs regardless of the defendant's wishes. Most jurisdictions provide either one or two new attorneys for the automatic appeal. In official court proceedings at this point, the defendant is called the *appellant*, and the state is called the *respondent*. The trial record—including all of the papers filed in the trial court, the evidence presented at trial, and the trial transcript—is amassed and typically filed in the state supreme court. The appellant's lawyer then files a *brief*, which describes the error or errors that occurred at trial and argues that the appellant's conviction and/or death sentence should be reversed. The state attorney general's office then files the state's brief, responding to the claims in the appellant's brief. The appellant has an opportunity to respond to the state's brief. This is followed by oral argument before the state supreme court.

In some states, the duties of the reviewing court are specified by statute, while in other states they are not. In Florida, the only issue addressed on direct appeal is whether the trial judge made any errors. Not considered at direct appeal to the Florida Supreme Court are issues of prosecutorial misconduct, attorney ineffectiveness, and claims of innocence, for example, which can be raised at other post-conviction proceedings.[18]

Next the state supreme court reviews the written and oral arguments presented. Generally, within a few months, it issues a written opinion addressing each of the appellant's claims and either affirms or reverses the conviction and/or death sentence. As part of the automatic appeal, some states also provide proportionality review, although, as noted, the Supreme Court does not require it. If either the conviction or the sentence is reversed on appeal, which occurs in fewer than 10 percent of all cases and less than two percent of cases in Texas and Virginia[19]—the two states with the most executions in the modern death penalty era—then the case is sent back to the trial court for additional proceedings or for retrial. It is possible that the death sentence may be reimposed as a result of this process. If the state supreme court affirms the conviction and sentence, which occurs in more than 90 percent of all cases and more than 98 percent of the cases in Texas and Virginia,[20] the appellant may then petition the U.S. Supreme Court for a *writ of certiorari*.[21] This is an order from a higher court to a lower court, whose decision is being appealed, to forward the case records for review.

The U.S. Supreme Court is limited by law and custom in the types of cases for which it issues writs of certiorari. The Court will issue a writ only if the case involves a substantial

---

18. Angela Mae Willis (2008) "Time on Florida's Death Row: A Theory of 'Benign Neglect,'" Unpublished Master's Thesis, Department of Criminal Justice and Legal Studies, University of Central Florida.

19. David R. Dow (2002b) "How the Death Penalty Really Works," pp. 11-35 in D. R. Dow and M. Dow (eds.) *Machinery of Death: The Reality of America's Death Penalty Regime.* New York: Routledge, p. 14.

20. Ibid.

21. Much of the material on automatic appellate review is from Office of Victim's Services, California Attorney General's Office, Bill Lockyer, Attorney General, *A Victim's Guide to the Capital Punishment Process* at http://ag.ca.gov/publications/pdf/deathpen.pdf (accessed July 17, 2008).

federal question as defined by the appellate court. A substantial federal question pertains to an alleged violation of either the U.S. Constitution or federal law. (On *collateral review*, see below, the Court will also issue a writ only if the appellant has exhausted all other avenues of appeal.) When the Supreme Court decides a case it has accepted on appeal, it can do one of the following:

- affirm the verdict or decision of the lower court and let it stand;

- modify the verdict or decision of the lower court, without totally reversing it;

- reverse the verdict or decision of the lower court, requiring no further court action;

- reverse the verdict or decision of the lower court and remand the case to the original trial court for either retrial or resentencing.

Appeals to the U.S. Supreme Court are heard at the discretion of the Court, in contrast to appeals to the U.S. circuit courts, which review cases as a matter of right. In most years, the Supreme Court opts not to review nearly 99 percent of the cases appealed to it.[22] If the Court elects not to review a case, the case is considered final, which means, among other things, that the death row inmate no longer has a constitutional right to be represented by counsel.[23]

In addition to the automatic or direct appellate review, capital defendants have access to a dual system of collateral review. In other words, capital defendants may contest their convictions and sentences through both state and federal postconviction proceedings. Including the automatic appeal, as many as nine or ten possible levels of review are available. However, these reviews are heard at the discretion of the courts; that is, the courts do not have to grant the death row inmate permission to be heard. And, as noted, the death row inmate has no constitutional right to the assistance of counsel for any of these reviews. (Nevertheless, counsel is generally provided.)

Some death row inmates whose appeals have been denied by the U.S. Supreme Court may still try to have the Supreme Court review their cases on constitutional grounds by filing a writ of *habeas corpus*: a court order directing a law officer to produce a prisoner in court to determine whether he or she is being legally detained or imprisoned. Unlike the situation for state postconviction proceedings, the federal government requires legal representation for capital defendants pursuing federal habeas corpus appeals. The most common claim on habeas review is that the death row inmate's trial or appellate attorneys were ineffective.[24] (Postconviction counsel and appellate judges are the subjects of chapters 8 and 9, respectively.)

Death Row Imprisonment

Under current practices, convicted capital offenders serve a long prison term on death row (averaging more than fourteen years) before being executed — if they are ever executed. (Death row inmates have a much greater chance of reversal than execution.)[25] Some death row inmates have been on death row for more than thirty

---

22. See, for example, Supreme Court of the United States, "2006 Year-End Report on the Federal Judiciary" at www.supremecourtus.gov/publicinfo/publicinfo.html.

23. Dow (2002b), op. cit., p. 15.

24. Ibid., p. 16.

25. *The Death Penalty in 2008: Year End Report* (December 2008), Death Penalty Information Center at www.deathpenaltyinfo.org/2008YearEnd.pdf (accessed August 18, 2009).

years. While on death row, the only human beings with which the inmates have daily contact are the prison's correctional officers. (Death row corrections officers are the subject of chapter 11.)

Conditions on death rows vary, but no where can they be considered comfortable. Indeed, the U.S. Supreme Court has ruled in *Rhodes v. Chapman* (1981)[26] that "the Constitution does not mandate comfortable prisons." According to the Court, conditions may be "restrictive and even harsh." To rise to the level of an Eighth Amendment violation, prison conditions must "involve the wanton and unnecessary infliction of pain." In two cases decided by federal appellate courts in 2004, death row conditions were challenged on Eighth Amendment grounds. The first case, *Gates v. Cook,*[27] addressed death row conditions at the Mississippi State Penitentiary in Parchman. In the class action suit, it was claimed that "prisoners housed on Death Row are knowingly and deliberately subjected to profound isolation, lack of exercise, stench and filth, malfunctioning plumbing, high temperatures, uncontrolled mosquito and insect infestations, a lack of sufficient mental health care, and exposure to psychotic inmates in adjoining cells."

The trial court concluded that the aforementioned conditions constituted Eighth Amendment violations and ordered injunctive relief (a court order commanding or preventing an action). The appeals court affirmed three of the injunctions and issued three orders:

1. If inmates are moved from cell to cell on death row, prison officials must ensure that the cell to which an inmate is moved is clean prior to the move.

2. Adequate cleaning supplies and equipment must be provided inmates in order that they may clean their cells at least weekly.

3. Prison officials must comply with professionally recognized medical and mental health standards, such as giving each inmate on death row a yearly comprehensive mental health examination in private.

In the other case, the class action suit, *Chandler v. Crosby,*[28] the U.S. Circuit Court of Appeals for the Eleventh Circuit ruled against 365 Florida death row inmates at Union Correctional Institution in Raiford. The inmates claimed that high temperatures in their cells during the summer months, combined with high humidity and inadequate ventilation, amounted to cruel and unusual punishment in violation of the Eighth Amendment. To deal with the heat, inmates would stand in toilets, drape themselves in wet towels, and sleep naked on the concrete floors. The court held that "while no one would call the summertime temperatures at the Unit pleasant, the heat is not unconstitutionally excessive ... [and is] to be expected in a residential setting in Florida in a building that is not air-conditioned."

The Death Warrant

In all death penalty jurisdictions, a death, or execution, warrant authorizes a warden or other prison official to carry out a death sentence; typically it also sets the date and place for execution. Usually a death warrant is issued by a state's governor or, in federal death penalty cases, the president of the United States. In Texas, a district court judge sets the execution date. (The role of governors is discussed in chapter 13.)

---

26. 452 U.S. 337.
27. 376 F.3d 323 (5th Cir. 2004).
28. 379 F.3d 1278 (11th Cir. 2004).

A death warrant commonly lists the execution as a homicide and absolves the executioner of criminal responsibility. The length of time before a death warrant expires and has to be reissued varies from a few days to several months. Florida, for example, no longer issues multiple death warrants (after previous warrants expire) as other states do; instead it issues one death warrant and multiple execution dates as needed.

Deathwatch

After prison officials receive the death warrant, a condemned inmate and all his belongings generally are moved from his death row cell to the deathwatch cell or holding cell. Depending on the state and the execution date, the move may be made as early as immediately after the death warrant is received and read to the inmate, as late as twenty-four hours before the execution, or anytime in between. In some states, inmates are given the choice of moving immediately to the holding cell or delaying the move until prison officials say it is time. Inmates will be moved immediately when their security is in jeopardy, for example—if they appear suicidal—or if it is believed that another inmate aims to preempt the execution by killing the condemned inmate.

During the deathwatch, a corrections officer is stationed either in the holding cell with the inmate or right outside the holding cell twenty-four hours a day. (Some states assign two or three officers to the holding cell.) A deathwatch officer's primary goal is to keep the inmate calm and under control. The officer keeps a detailed log of all the inmate's actions. The inmate is allowed to make collect phone calls if prison officials approve them. The holding cell usually is equipped with a television and a VCR, and most inmates pass the time watching movies on video. In some states, an inmate on deathwatch (at least those who are there for relatively short periods of time) can also get free items from the commissary. Popular items are soft drinks, snacks, and cigarettes. Many states maintain a liberal visitation policy during the deathwatch. For security purposes, the inmate generally is allowed only two visitors at a time. Besides his attorneys, family, and friends, the inmate may be visited by ministers or religious advisers. (Offender's family members are the subject of chapter 5.) As for the length of visits, many prison officials try to be flexible. This is especially true the day of the execution.

Executions

The death warrant does not specify the actual time of execution, which is left to the warden's discretion. However, executions typically have been conducted at 12:01 a.m. The reason is fivefold: it has become the traditional time for executions; it provides extra security (at that time of night, all inmates are locked down); the early hour deters some demonstrators; adverse publicity is reduced because the execution takes place after the eleven o'clock TV news and past the deadline for the morning newspapers; and it allows the state a full twenty-four hours to carry out the death sentence. Between 1977 and 1995, more than eighty percent of all executions took place between 11 p.m. and 7 a.m., and half of those were scheduled for between midnight and 1 a.m.[29] Sometimes events such as a stay of execution require the execution to be conducted at a later time.

---

29. Lifton and Mitchell, op. cit., p. 178.

Recently, some states, most notably Texas and Florida, have changed the time of their lethal injection executions to 6 p.m. to better accommodate the work schedules of prison personnel, judges, attorneys, witnesses, and journalists. Having executions at 6 p.m. also reduces the need for overtime pay for prison personnel and execution team members. Another possible reason for the earlier execution times in some states is that "executions have now become so routine in certain states, and meet so little public protest, that prison officials have little reason to hide, or appear to hide, them in the middle of the night."[30]

On execution day, the prison is gradually closed, and only those people who are directly involved with the execution or have a work assignment are allowed on the institution grounds. A briefing is held for personnel involved with the execution. (Execution team members, including prison chaplains, are examined in chapter 11.) The execution equipment is checked and rechecked. The inmate receives his last meal. Usually, a few hours before the execution, the inmate is offerred a sedative. The press and state witnesses are briefed on what to expect.

Approximately thirty minutes before the execution, the inmate is brought into the execution chamber and strapped down to the gurney. An intravenous line, or IV, is placed in the inmate's arm (sometimes in both arms), and he is connected to a heart monitor. Witnesses are escorted into the witness room or rooms. (Witnesses are the subject of chapter 12.) The inmate is allowed to make a final statement. The warden checks with the governor's office and the state attorney general's office to make sure the execution should proceed. (Prison wardens are the subject of Chapter 10, and governors are examined in Chapter 13.) If there are no last-minute stays, the warden reads the death warrant and gives the order to commence the execution.

Lethal injection is now the sole or principal method of execution in all executing jurisdictions in the United States. However, there is no uniform policy for conducting lethal injections. There are differences in details such as procedure, the number amount of drugs used, who performs the injections, how well the executioners are trained, and how much the executioners are paid. Nevertheless, most states, until very recently, used a three chemical combination consisting of sodium thiopental or sodium pentothal, pancuronium bromide (Pavulon), and potassium chloride.

Sodium thiopental, or sodium pentothal, an anesthetic commonly used in surgery, is an ultrashort–acting barbiturate that induces a deep sleep and loss of consciousness in about twenty seconds. Pancuronium bromide is a total muscle relaxant; in sufficient dosages, it stops breathing by paralyzing the diaphragm and lungs. The third drug, potassium chloride, induces cardiac arrest and stops the inmate's heartbeat permanently. The order in which the chemicals are administered is critical. Between the injection of each chemical, the IV line is flushed with a saline solution.

Recently, because of supply problems, some states, such as Oklahoma, Texas, and Ohio, have substituted the barbiturate pentobarbital for sodium thiopental in their execution processes. Pentobarbital is most commonly used in euthanizing animals.

Theoretically, death by lethal injection should be a more humane method of execution than any of the other methods then or now in use. Other methods of execution that may be used under rare circumstances (and have been used in the past) are hanging, firing squad, electrocution, and lethal gas. The popular image of a lethal-injection execution is one in which the condemned inmate painlessly falls asleep (forever) on a hospital gurney. The reality, however, is sometimes different. For example, in 2006,

---

30. Ibid., pp. 179-80.

Angel Nieves Diaz was executed by lethal injection in Florida. He took 34 minutes to die and was seen to be struggling for breath, moving, attempting to speak, and grimacing in pain for the first 24 minutes of the procedure. At his autopsy, the medical examiner discovered eleven- and twelve-inch blisters on his right and left arms. The problem was that when the execution technician inserted the IV, he pushed the needle through the vein into the surrounding soft tissue. Because this mistake delayed the absorption of the lethal chemicals, Mr. Diaz was administered a second dose. The longest previous Florida lethal injection execution lasted 17 minutes before death was pronounced.[31] Typically, death occurs in approximately four and one-half minutes after the first chemical has been injected.

A doctor who has been watching the heart monitor examines the inmate and pronounces him dead. The witnesses then are escorted out of the witness room(s), but before the official witnesses are dismissed, they are required to sign a notarized return warrant of execution, which attests to the execution having taken place. The inmate is disconnected from the IV, and the coroner comes in and takes the corpse.

Other Participants

Death penalty cases affect far more people than just the perpetrator and his victim. This book looks at a number of participants involved in death penalty cases, including detectives, legal counsel, and family members. Other participants who are not examined in this book include:

- jail administrators and jail correctional officers, who are in charge of the custody of capital defendants, while they are awaiting trial, being tried, and awaiting transfer to death row;
- experts, who do research for motions and may testify in court;
- witnesses, who also testify;
- executioners, whose identities are kept secret;
- physicians or other medical personnel, who insert IVs and pronounce death;
- other court participants such as court administrators, bailiffs, and court stenographers;
- pardon board members, who in some states, are involved in clemency decisions;
- legislators, who ultimately are responsible for the continued existence of capital punishment in the United States.

Other, indirect participants could be added to this list if one wanted to cast the net even wider. Each participant has his or her own view of a particular case and of the system. This book will examine a few of those views as part of the ongoing debate about capital punishment.

---

31. Gavin Lee (2008) "A Painless Cocktail? The Lethal Injection Controversy," pp. 93-110 in R. M. Bohm (ed.) *The Death Penalty Today*. Boca Raton, FL: CRC Press, pp. 103-105.

Chapter 1

Homicide Detectives and Other Investigative Personnel

Homicide detectives occupy a prestigious position in any law enforcement agency, but they pay a high price for the honor. The job is difficult, dangerous, frustrating, stressful, physically demanding, emotionally challenging, and all-consuming. They work under a constant fear of "screwing up." Normal family lives are impossible, spouses and children must be understanding.

Homicide detectives have done their jobs well when a suspect has been successfully arrested, charged, and convicted. However, in general, homicide detectives are only moderately successful in solving murders. Given the pressures they face, some screw up—and they do so with some regularity. When they are unable to solve a murder within a reasonable amount of time, homicide detectives sometimes cut corners and jump to conclusions. They, or others who aid them, such as police crime laboratory technicians, may even go so far as to lose, destroy, or manufacture evidence against a suspect.

Not surprisingly, most homicide detectives are ardent proponents of capital punishment. This chapter looks at homicide detectives and other investigative personnel and their roles in the capital punishment process.

The Sharp Guys

In most communities, soon after a homicide has been reported to the police, detectives will be dispatched to the crime scene to investigate. If they are successful, they will identify the killer, make an arrest (although, frequently, other police officers will make the arrest), and gather enough evidence to secure a conviction. The homicide detective generally is considered the most prestigious nonmanagement police department position. As one homicide detective explained:

> There's a pecking order in any investigative field you're in. I don't care where it is. It's not that nobody cares about the property detectives, but everyone knows who the sharp guys are. If you can transfer to homicide and you don't do as well as expected, you won't be there long. It's not a place where they keep people who aren't productive. It's a highly sought after spot. It's tough to get into.

Becoming a homicide detective is a lengthy process. In most departments, candidates first must serve as uniformed patrol officers for approximately two to four years. Then, when the investigation unit posts openings, experienced patrol officers may apply for detective positions. This usually entails submitting a resume through the chain of command.

In some departments, officers also are interviewed and may have to pass an exam. They are not likely to be selected as a detective if they did not excel as a patrol officer. If selected, they will not be assigned to the homicide unit at first. They generally will be assigned to the property crimes unit for one to two years. If they do well in the property crimes unit, their next assignment is likely to be in the crimes against persons unit, where they will investigate sex crimes, robberies, and assaults and batteries for another two to four years. Only then, if they have done well in that assignment, will they be considered for the homicide unit.

Being a homicide detective has a number of perceived advantages over being a patrol officer. Among those advantages are the following, in no particular order:

- Homicide detectives do not have to wear uniforms.
- Homicide detectives have anonymity during work hours if they choose it.
- Homicide detectives have offices and desks.
- Homicide detectives enjoy the prestige associated with the position.
- In many agencies, homicide detectives receive higher compensation and hold a higher rank. (Though in some agencies, the homicide detective is no different than the patrol officer in terms of rank and pay.)
- Perhaps most important, homicide detectives enjoy more freedom than patrol officers from the police radio, geographical boundaries, and close supervision.

For these reasons, many police officers aspire to the position of homicide detective. Some of the disadvantages of being a homicide detective are described later in the chapter.

Ordinarily, homicide investigations are conducted by plainclothes detectives, although small and medium-sized agencies may require patrol officers or a patrol supervisor to follow up. Some departments have specialized homicide units, while other departments utilize a *major crimes unit* to investigate homicides and other serious felonies. Detectives typically work in pairs, but some departments assign more than two detectives to investigate a case.

In homicide investigations, like in the investigation of other crimes, detectives typically have a number of responsibilties, including:

- locating witnesses and suspects;
- arresting criminals (in some departments *felony squads* make arrests);
- collecting, preserving, and analyzing evidence;
- interviewing witnesses;
- interrogating suspects;
- writing reports;
- preparing cases and testifying in court.

Given the complexities of homicide investigations, one would expect homicide detectives to receive specialized training, but, generally, that is not the case. As noted above, they already will have had years of experience on the street and in investigating other types of crimes, but they will not have had experience investigating homicides. A homicide detective described the typical situation:

> So you're going to go there with the idea that there's no training. You come in there you're supposed to be hitting the ground. You learn some finer points you

might not learn in other investigative fields, like the morgue and some forensic issues, but you're expected to hit the ground running and you're expected to do a good job and if you don't you won't last long.

Do Not Screw Up!

Doing a good job does not necessarily mean solving a large number of crimes. As a homicide detective explained:

> Solving crimes isn't necessarily indicative of your work effort. People know what you're doing, and the word gets out. There are detectives whose solve rate is not that high, but you know they're hustling. They're doing everything they can possibly do, doing the best job they can. It's just nothing is cracking. People know that; they know who the hustlers are.

The key, according to one homicide detective, is to not make mistakes: "People are rated internally on how much they screw up. That's putting it as simply as you possibly can. If you don't screw up, you're known to be pretty good at what you do. If you screw it up all the time, you're probably going to be working somewhere else."

Homicide detectives have the cards stacked against them most of the time. In fact, the chances of solving the crime are not great. Nationwide, the police are able to *clear* only about 60 percent of all murders reported to them annually. (Note that only about 20 percent of murders are capital murders, and the percentage of capital murders cleared is unknown. For purposes of this discussion, the terms *homicide* and *murder* are used interchangeably, although, technically, a murder is a felonious homicide.) Clearing a crime (or the *clearance rate*) refers to the police arresting a suspect, charging him with an offense, and then turning him over to the court for prosecution. Clearances may pertain to offenses that occurred in previous years.[1]

When asked about their clearance rates, one homicide detective believed his was 68 percent, while another said his was 60 percent. A third homicide detective boasted that his clearance rate was in the high 90s, but he was quick to add that it was not because he was better than anyone else; rather, he said he was real lucky. While on call, cases are assigned on a rotating basis, and he did not get many unsolvable ones. The cases that are cleared by arrest, he noted, typically solve themselves. For example, as often can happen in a domestic violence case, the wife is found dead on the floor with her husband standing over her with a gun in his hand.

When homicide detectives are called to a crime scene to investigate a murder, they never know for sure whether they will be investigating a capital crime. Of course, in some cases the capital or aggravating aspects of the crime are apparent (a brutal torture murder, for example), but that does not mean a prosecutor will charge the offender with a capital crime. In fact, homicide detectives are familiar with murderers whom they believe deserved the death penalty but were not charged with a capital crime, as well as murderers they believe did not deserve the death penalty but were charged with a capital crime. The

---

1. Federal Bureau of Investigation, "Clearances" at www.fbi.gov/ucr/cius2006/offenses/clearances/index.html

overriding goal of the homicide detective is always to discover who committed the murder; theoretically, it does not really matter whether the murder ends up being a capital crime.

Nevertheless, as one homicide detective admitted: "When I know it's a death penalty case ... there is extra scrutiny that goes into it. There's extra ... you're a little more meticulous. You might talk to one more person than you normally would. There are differences, I think. You really should treat every case like it's going to be a death penalty case." He gave an example of what he meant by being "a little more meticulous":

> [My partner] and I worked on a murder of an elderly woman.... Right off the bat, patrol officers are pulling in there with their laptops, showing us photos of people they think might be involved. They're providing us with names and addresses and everything else. It turns out those guys had nothing to do with the crime. We were able to make an arrest within a week, I think, of it happening. Anyway, we made an arrest based on some tips and others things, and the guy confessed. But, in that particular case, we did decide to go ahead and follow up on the other guys to make sure they had an alibi. One of them was in jail so that was perfect. In some cases, you might not. You might say, "I've already got my guy; he confessed." And everything is good with it. In some cases, if you know it's not a death penalty case, there's a good chance that you might get asked about it, but it won't be scrutinized by somebody down the line in the appellate court or appellate process or whatever. In that [presumed death penalty] case, we make sure those guys weren't involved and document it.

He provided another example involving the collection of DNA evidence: "I know that you get tons of samples from the scene, and in a lot of homicides, you might submit twenty samples to the lab to be examined. But in a death penalty case, you might send more because you're going to get asked about them later. It's going to come up."

A Frustrating Business

Because of limited investigative resources—time, money, and equipment—homicide detectives do not treat all murders the same. A victim's status in the community usually determines the level of investigation. As one detective put it, the murder of a mayor's daughter will always have priority over the murder of a transsexual crack whore. He described the situation this way: A transsexual crack whore was murdered in a hotel room. The cause of death was a drug overdose. Some people in the room contributed to her death. He then asked, "So do we track these people down and try to prosecute them, or do we move on to the next one?" The detective was quick to add that he was not referring to limitations on forensics. He stated that forensics "comes after everything. They do an outstanding job." He only meant that a detective's caseload can get "insurmountable." He related, "You can only work so many thirty-six hour days. You can't keep that pace up. So you only have so many hours you can give to a case." Detectives generally determine their own priorities. As a detective noted, "You don't have to be a highly experienced homicide detective to know which cases are priority and which ones are not."

Financial considerations, too, can affect homicide cases, especially when budgets are tight. As one detective stated:

Recently, I don't know how many times we should have traveled somewhere to be sitting like we're sitting now [conducting an interview]. I don't know about you, but I don't like to interview people over the telephone. It's crazy, especially if they're a suspect in the crime. From other agencies, I don't know those guys [law enforecement officers] from Alabama. I don't know if they're going to interview this guy effectively for me. There have been times when they [the department] won't send us because of money.

Another detective provided this example of financial considerations hindering an investigation:

[W]e lost a critical piece of evidence in a case which could have been a capital case because of a financial consideration. I found something out in a case, and we needed to fly out then. It was a Saturday, and we needed to go right then to Gulfport, Mississippi. And they said, "No you can't go. You need to get somebody in Gulfport to do it." So come Monday, we did, and then some other information came up. We did try and get somebody from Gulfport to do our work for us, and they did end up setting us up later on. It ended up the evidence was lost because we didn't [go immediately]. It may be as serious as it may cost the case. I don't know if it was financial; I know it was more expensive [to fly us out].

Pressures to Solve the Case

Rarely are homicide detectives pressured by others to solve a crime, although they frequently put pressure on themselves. As one homicide detective recounted:

Everybody is well aware of the fact that homicide detectives are most often the crème de la crème of your investigators. These aren't the guys that can't make it as property detectives or persons detectives. These are people who want to be in homicide, and they get there because they are good at what they do. And everyone knows you are doing the best you can possibly do. Look at the guys working the [the name of a recent high-profile murder victim] case right now. You know those guys are knocking themselves out. Nobody is telling them, "Look, you guys need to do a better job, you gotta do more." They know what they gotta do, and they're doing it, and no one is pressuring them. They see that there's a camera outside the building everyday when they leave.

Another homicide detective provided a similar response: "[M]ost of the pressure for solving the cases comes from me. I don't want to be sixty percent [referring to his clearance rate], you know? I want to solve all my cases. It's more a matter of pride." He added, "[I]f you are in homicide for the right reasons, it's going to bother you that you haven't solved it, more than your bosses or the families." For added motivation, he keeps visual reminders of some of his unsolved cases:

I have pictures of four of my unsolved cases [at my desk].... A couple of them weren't doing what they should be doing. I asked their parents to send me pictures of them as a kid to remind [me] that they weren't always a drug dealer. They were somebody's kid. As fathers ourselves ... I don't know why I do that to myself, but I do. I have pictures. And the reason I think I do ... [a victim's father] whose daughter was killed back in 1985. I was assigned her cold case, and he came up to the station one day, he gave me a huge picture of her and asked me to put it on my desk, and it does: It sits there on my desk.

He then admitted, "You do feel pressure from the families. There's a lot of nice people out there that have lost their sons and daughters, even if they weren't doing the right things at the time. They're still somebody's son or daughter."

Sometimes there are other external pressures to solve a crime. A detective mentioned a woman whose boyfriend had been killed two or three years ago: "He was just shot dead in a parking lot. That was my only 2006 unsolved case. This guy's girlfriend calls me all the time. She asks if anything is going on. 'Anything new?' 'No, sorry.' We don't ever close them, so they're going to ask…. It's tough. There's no closure." Another homicide detective experienced external pressures in a high-profile missing person's case he was assigned to work. When asked where the pressure comes from, he said, "Most of it comes from everybody that's involved. It starts with the … family. Great people; I'm friends with them. I know that's one of the things you're not supposed to do. But it's kind of hard when I talk to her dad everyday…. Almost every single day. Like on the weekends, we talk a lot." The detective had been working on the case for three years but had been put on it full-time "just" six months ago. He explained why he was put on the case full-time:

> We had over one thousand tips, and many of them hadn't really been followed up. Part of my job was to get these huge boxes of *Crimeline* tips, *America's Most Wanted* [tips], directly to the station. All kinds of different ways. They're going into this LEADS tracking system that [the state department of law enforcement] has. They're going through every one. Up until recently, we thought we were making some incredibly good progress but had a big disappointment. We were zeroing in on somebody who looked awesome on paper and recently cleared the guy. But he didn't do it … so.

He noted that in this case, the pressure he was receiving was "not just from the family, but from [his] bosses higher up," who required him to write a weekly summary of his activities. "All that's public record," he points out. "So I have to somehow write down what I did without really writing what I did. Just so my boss … can know what's going on." Then he divulged why he really had to keep the weekly summary, and the major source of the pressure he was feeling: "Really to justify to my coworkers why I'm not in the homicide rotation. Because those guys are working their asses off, and I'm not on call like everybody else. My pressure, too, is to hurry up and finish so that my coworkers don't hate my guts for not carrying my share of the load."

The most important aspect of investigating a homicide and generally the most stressful for the detective, as noted previously, is not to screw up. According to one detective:

> The nightmare of … screw[ing] something up. I mean, I couldn't even explain to you adequately how serious and how important it is that you don't screw this up. If you screw up a Miranda on a property case, you lost a guy's couch. You screw up a murder on a capital murder case, you potentially lost your suspect and your case. Some of the legal aspects are so important. You better know Miranda, you better know search and seizure, you better know custodial and non-custodial interviews. You better know it all. And you don't have any time for research. It always weighed on me tremendously. This has to be perfect. There's no room to screw it up … you have no room for error. It's a very high-pressured situation to get yourself into.

Another detective was more specific and maintained that arresting the right person is the most important aspect of investigating a homicide. "Obviously you'd rather not arrest anybody for anything than put the wrong person in jail," he explained. "In the examples that I can come up with, I've seen people in the past arrested on photo lineup IDs alone. And to me that's very, very risky because you're relying on an eyewitness. If you don't have the necessary elements, you just don't put them in jail. It's just the way it goes." A third detective put it more succinctly: "Ultimately, our name goes on that. So if you don't believe that that case can be proven beyond a reasonable doubt, you shouldn't put your name on it."

Notifying the next of kin in a homicide can be another stressful aspect of the homicide detective's job:

> Of all the dirty tasks that go with the dirty work of chasing a killer, notifying the next of kin is the job that homicide detectives hate most. It's worse than getting up at 3 a.m. on a February night to slog through a field of freezing mud toward a body that needed burying two days ago. Worse than staring into the flat cold eyes of a teenager who bragged about dragging a man through the streets to his death. Worse than visiting every sleazy dive in town until you finally find the one person who can put the murderer away and having that person say as cool as a debutante with a full dance card, "I don't want to get involved."[2]

However, notifying the next of kin may be harder for rookie homicide detectives than for more experienced ones. An experienced homicide detective explained:

> Yeah, the first few of those are tough because nobody likes to deal with emotions, but when you are a homicide detective, you deal with emotions all the time. So a grieving family is not a really difficult thing to deal with. If you do it often enough, it doesn't matter anymore. Well, you can do it with all the grace and finesse and passion. I would have to say as many times as I've done it, you wanna get going and get things together, that if there's any evidence in that house that you might get a lead on, that takes priority. So let's get this death notification and see what we can get out of it. You ask if you can search their son's room. Giving a family death notification—after awhile, it just became part of the investigative process.

Perhaps the most difficult aspect of investigating a homicide is the lack of physical evidence—"if you have nothing." As one detective commented:

> I only have two unsolved homicides in my six years working [as a homicide detective] with the sheriff's office. In one of the cases we got to the parking lot and there's an African-American male with a bullet hole through him. No shell casing, no gun, no suspects, no people, no cars, nothing. All you have is a body with a hole through it. He's dead, so he can't talk to you. So you have nothing to go on. You can post your signs, you can ask *Crimeline*, and throw all that money around. [However, in this case] we did not get one call. So, that's frustrating. Because the only thing you have is the information that you receive and the investigative leads you have. You can't fabricate stuff. You can't create things. That's frustrating when you got a guy out there, and you can't do a damn thing for him.

For another detective, organizing and presenting the case is the most difficult aspect of investigating a homicide:

---

2. Christine Wicker (1996), "Death Beat," in Keith N. Haley and Mark A. Stallo, *Texas Crime, Texas Justice*. New York: McGraw-Hill.

> Sometimes we call ourselves glorified secretaries because we just gather information and put it all together to make it make sense. We start with a notepad.... Then it grows into a manilla folder, and then an accordian file, and several accordian files, and then these big binders. It's amazing all this work that goes into it. Organizing everyone's input. The sergeant at the scene has input. The first officer you talk to. The crime scene techs. Everybody gives you a report of what they did. And if they don't, you need to get it. And it goes right up until deposition. You have to study. Of course for trial, you have to study.... you'll go lock yourself in your kitchen for three days to study. And I did for that particular trial.... The most difficult thing is getting things organized and presenting it to where it makes sense. Getting that report put together to where it falls into place. Having all your information there. You're dealing with labs and crime scene techs and officers that are doing supplements for you who may not want to and all that.

For an obviously frustrated detective, the most difficult aspect is institutional, by which he meant dealing with the chain of command:

> For me it's institutional; where you have people that are in your chain of command that have never worked a homicide, let alone a capital homicide. Who have never been on the witness stand, putting that pressure on them. Telling them where your priorities should be.... You get people that will come in and say, you know, stop doing this and do this. If you have an unknown suspect, this happens a lot, too. People think they have the tip that's going to solve the case, and if you don't stop what you're doing right now to take care of this, you're an idiot. You're messing the thing up. Or people get trapped into a suspect looking good on paper and then thinking that this person did it. And if you can't prove that they did it, you're an idiot. The hardest part is the institutional part. Just kind of keeping focused on what you're supposed to do and not getting too bogged down.

The detective gave another example of what he considered an institutional problem; again one that involved meddling by his supervisors:

> One of the big frustrations for me right now with our cases is that, with the homicide rate the way it is, the very first thing that we get asked about from people that are heads of the agencies, what was the guy's [the victim's] criminal history? They want to put out as soon as possible that this wasn't some innocent victim.... I had a homicide in January where the guy came down from [names a city] to do a drug deal and got murdered. They couldn't wait to release that he had just gotten out of prison for cocaine trafficking. That case dried up in a hurry. One: anyone who might have seen it says, "Well I'm not getting involved in some drug murder." And two: people who might be able to find them, "Well the guy was a drug dealer. The guy had what's coming to him." It kills an investigation, 'cause they want to put out there, "If you're not a drug dealer, you won't be killed."

He continued:

> I was telling [my partner] not too long ago, if I want to do something at work, I have to ask five people. Really. I've got that many bosses, and that's just within the police department. We were talking about supervisors—we shouldn't even limit it to supervisors trying to direct us. We've got people much higher on the chain who really have no knowledge other than shuffling papers and making financial decisions about murders telling us what to do.

His partner added:

> We have a sergeant, a lieutenant, a captain, a deputy chief, and then we have the chief. That's how many people we are below. If you get any person in that chain that thinks they know more than you … and you know, odds are, that's going to happen. And if you get a high-profile case, they're going to want to get involved and make decisions and tell you what to do. I know I should be doing other things but can't because this jackass wants me to talk to somebody who knows nothing about the case and waste my time.

Another homicide detective simply stated that the worst part of the job was all the "investigative suggestions" he received "along the way."

One might think that working with dead people would be difficult for a homicide detective, but apparently it is not very difficult for experienced homicide detectives:

> The first couple are tough, but once you get it down, it's no more than … how do you deal with dead people? Dead people are no more than horizontal evidence. So it doesn't matter anymore. Some of the most shocking things that have occurred to me are people who I've met in the morgue in death are people that I knew in real life. You're looking at them going, you know you're not supposed to be doing that, you're supposed to be up. So dead people were nothing more than horizontal evidence, and that's how you treat them.

Another homicide detective cited the the time commitment as the worst part of his work:

> We all signed up for that when we became homicide detectives. And you know you're going to be away from your family a lot. Especially when it's not solved yet. You'll have your pager. The only time I don't have my pager on my side is when I'm in the shower or swimming. It's different. It's really tough on your family life. [With] capital cases … you're going to have a lot more work to do.

Investigators know that time is always at a premimum. Different cases consume different amounts of time, but homicide cases often are the most time-consuming. Homicide investigations can last a short time, as in the domestic violence case described above, or six months or longer. Of course, some homicides are never solved. As one detective described it, "You get past the first thirty-six hours, now you're just working as the leads come in. Then you try to generate your own leads. But you'll work a good case for six months before you finally make an arrest. You try to do it as fast as you can because a lot of these people are flight risks.… It doesn't always work that way." In some departments, cases are handed off to the next shift. In other departments, though, a case belongs to the detectives who originally were assigned it until the case is resolved one way or another. That means having to cancel vacations, if necessary, and missing other events and family obligations.

Side Effects of the Job

Besides being stressful, homicide investigations can affect detectives in other ways as well—mentally, emotionally, and physically. One detective told the story of a kid and his girlfriend who attempted to buy a little pot. They drove to a wooded area to make the buy, and the pot dealer shot the kid in the back of the head and did some "nasty things" to the girlfriend. When the detective got to the morgue, he saw that the kid looked much like his own middle son. There also were other similarities to the detective's personal life, and that had an emotional effect on him. The detective found it draining.

He also mentioned that some homicide detectives have "a lot of problems with baby deaths." He observed, "Those are sometimes difficult to work with. A baby dies at the negligence of a parent or a guardian. I had a friend who left homicide because he couldn't deal with the young lady who had taken a baby that she had just given birth to and put it into the back of a boat and it died from exposure."

Courtroom proceedings also can be emotional for some homicide detectives, as one homicide detective described:

> The time that I've gotten emotional about it happened in court when the finality of it … because these cases drag on for awhile, and you get to know the family members.… The son of a lady who was murdered, when he was testifying during the penalty phase and was able to [relate what his mother's loss meant to him] … and his wife, too. That's an emotional thing, and it was. I think both [my partner] and I were crying.

> And then I know we worked a case together … where a woman was shot and killed during a robbery, and she was a totally innocent victim. The first case was a mistrial. That was emotionally wrenching for us because we had to do it all over again and made it drag out for another year and a half.

Becoming emotional, however, is not always a bad thing; it can be a source of motivation, as a homicide detective expressed, "[T]he emotion though that's overwhelming, that keeps us going."

Another draining aspect of homicide investigations is the amount of time detectives spend in dealing with them. As one detective said, "It's draining, especially if you have a family." According to the detective:

> We always had a plan B. It was troubling to adapt when I left homicide because my wife and I would have to take two cars to every function we went to. We go down to my father-in-law's house, you got two cars. You take my son to baseball, you got two cars because I may have to leave.

> And that constant on-call status is tough. You are formally on call—we had four teams at the time—for seven days of the month, but you were informally on call 365 days a year. So if they need you, they called, and you went out. So that's the hard part of the whole thing, was the pressure it puts on your family.

Another detective described a similar family life and emphasized the importance of having an understanding spouse:

> I've been married to the same woman for 17 years. We have two kids.… I would say this and tell anybody that's looking to get into the homicide business: You better make sure she's on board. My wife knows the nature of the business. She knows the last-minute phone calls: "Hey, I can't make it. Something came up." The late-night call-outs. The biggest frustration for her … maybe not frustration but hassle: if I were on call. If I was up for a murder right now, I'd be up until we got one. Sometimes you'd go weeks without having one. That means if we go somewhere, we're taking two cars—if we *can* go somewhere. We can't go do some things just in case you get called out.… She's on board and she's supportive and she knows it's important to me. You better have her on board and do those things and take the kids to stuff, and she's been able to do that.

As much as he could, he tried to separate his professional life from his private life. He said, "I think I try to do a good job of turning it off.... [My job] is just like any other person in business with the stresses that I come home with. I've got things on my mind from work. It's not so much the emotional toll I think it's taking. It's more of this, this, and this to do tomorrow, and that type of thing." When asked whether his home was a haven for him, he said:

> Some days it is. I've got two school-aged kids. Yesterday I had a case where a woman basically starved her kid to death. It was pretty bad. Might have been the worst I've ever seen. I basically stopped ... I hadn't seen pictures of the baby, and I looked at the pictures and stopped what I was doing and went and got an arrest warrant for the mother. Dealing with that whole thing and then I walk in the door, and my wife is battling our son over his math homework. It's a relief in the fact that I think there's something totally different. This is still important. Whether or not he can multiply and divide fractions is still important, so ...

He laughed.

Another homicide detective had not been as fortunate with his family life as his other colleagues. He confessed that he had been married and divorced three times. He reflected on his bad luck:

> I don't think any one of [the divorces] had anything to do with my job as far as ... I don't know—maybe. Because you get called out at all hours of the night. You miss family functions that you should have been at ... or you'll have a decision to make: Do I go track down this witness tonight, or do I let my wife take my son to his karate school, or whatever? Go do this and let her do that, or should I do it because this is my night to do it? That could have some effect on my terrible history ... my marriages. I don't know.

Interestingly, investigating crimes did not affect the investigator's home life as much as the stress caused by the bureaucracy that did not let go at the end of the day: "Here again ... most of the stuff I take home has to do with bosses and things they want you to do that you think are ridiculous."

In addition to the emotional stress and the pressures on family life, the job of homicide detective also is physically demanding. According to one homicide detective:

> You're not eating, and then when you do eat, you're eating poorly. You're eating on the run. Lack of sleep has a tremendous effect on your health, and then working the hours that people get killed. It is usually dark. You're outside your normal work shift. It has a tremendous effect physically on you because of the demands that are made on you, especially as you get older. Some of these young guns that are out there can do that for quite awhile.... These guys are in their 60s and they're still humping homicides. They just slow down a bit, but they are still effective—just not as quick as they used to be.

The detective added:

> I try to stay in the best physical shape that I can. But, ya know, you can see the guys who came into homicide at 160 [pounds] and left at 220 [pounds]. And they've got the blood pressure problems. I've got a friend of mine right now who's got to go to a stomach band to get his blood pressure and cholesterol down. I don't know if that's necessarily a product of homicide, or if you were in robbery, you'd be doing the same thing.

Another detective also noted the physical demands and stress of the job:

> Well, you don't get the rest sometimes you need, that's for sure. And for a while, I was in pretty good shape. And that's my fault that I'm back out of shape. If you have a routine, for instance, where you go to the gym a certain time, that always gets interrupted in a homicide case.... Let's say you put in a thirteen-hour day, you don't feel like going to the gym afterwards. But you do feel like eating something. You sit and you eat and go to sleep. And you'll fall into that pattern. My weight through the years has gone up and down. I think that had a lot to do with it, other than being lazy as far as my gym regimen.

As for his eating habits, he remarked, "When you're in the middle of a hot case that's new, you don't have time [to eat]," but then he added, "We have pizza brought up to the office when we're really involved in something." He paused and then commented, "I don't think you can look around our squad and say any of us are in great physical condition. But I don't know how much of that is because we work homicide." His partner's immediate retort was: "A lot of it is because we're getting older...." To which, the other detective replied, "None of us eat right. Even if we can, we don't."

Sometimes homicide detectives lose sleep over specific aggravations. A detective related the following incident:

> I had a crime scene where as soon as I got there, my boss wanted me to go get some court order for cell phones because there were cell phones involved and everything. But I had eight witnesses who say it happened. I had a name of a guy and all I had to do was get a photo lineup and put it ... and now I'm on my way instead.... What good does it do to know where he is if I don't have a warrant for his arrest? I don't know, just things like that. I do go home and lose sleep over that.

He also volunteered: "But as far as seeing the dead body and all that ... it would have to be particularly gruesome for me to lose sleep over that part of it." A third homicide detective simply said, "I think I lose sleep like most people in business lose sleep; I know I have this, this, this, and this to do. This is anybody."

Regardless of the reason, sleep deprivation can adversely affect job performance. A homicide detective observed that:

> You know, working a case, fatigue can definitely affect you and affect your job performance. I know of a particular incident where we had worked almost twenty-four hours straight, and then we had to do a suspect interview. It wasn't good. It wasn't our best effort. There was fatigue. I know over the weekend, a guy in our squad ... he got called up for a murder at 2 a.m. They had worked it all day, found out who it was, got a warrant for his arrest, and went home. He walks in the door [at his home] at 1 a.m. He basically worked twenty-three hours straight, and the guy [suspect] turned himself in at the police station. So he had to turn around and go back. That's tough to do with your body.

Arrests Are Extremely Dangerous

In some departments, as mentioned previously, homicide detectives also arrest suspects, although in other departments that job is left to felony squads. One detective estimated that about one-third of the time, arrests are made out of state or out of the detective's jurisdiction. In most homicide cases, a warrant has been issued for the suspect's arrest. Warrantless arrests in homicide cases are rare, but when they occur, they usually are followed up with warrants. Arresting a homicide suspect does not differ significantly from the arrest of other felony suspects. As one detective put it, "When you arrest a felony suspect, they all should be considered extremely dangerous until some point in time where they are absolutely secured to the point [where] you know you're not going to get hurt." He "would not give one felon any more benefit over another one." His reason:

> Especially with the laws right now, that burglary suspect you are going to arrest, it could be his third strike — you don't know that. He could be doing life off that arrest. [The detective is referring to "three strikes and you're out laws," which in many states provide for an automatic life in prison sentence upon conviction of a third felony.] You have to treat them all — regardless of their age or what their warrant is for — with tremendous respect because they're all extremely dangerous. And as soon as you lose touch with that, the problems start to develop from there. When you read the cases of law enforcement officers that have been killed, why and the circumstances that they've been killed, somebody slipped up. Somebody got a little bit too complacent, and bad things happen. Those two [names a city] cops the guy shot. The guy is in the back seat of the car and he reaches up for the front seat and takes the deputy's gun off of him. How does that happen? How do you do that? Even as long as I've been doing this, complacency is nothing I've ever suffered from.

Another homicide detective explained why in his department homicide detectives generally do not make arrests: "Normally we send what we call the real police in to arrest them because when we want to interview them — if I'm the one that has to struggle with them or fight with them or cuff them — they're not going to want to talk to me." Not being the arresting officer also gives the homicide detective a psychological advantage when interviewing suspects:

> Once they [suspects] are in custody or jail, you get to interview them. So you're going to talk to them in a minute. And what that gives you is that arresting you is beneath me. I'm far more important than that. Now that you're in jail and in custody and these people have brought you to me, I'll speak with you because I have time. It's a psychological thing. You're not part of the rank and file. You got the white shirt on, which you should always have as a homicide detective. It gives you that advantage in the interview. And that's all interviews are, is taking every advantage you possibly can.

In addition, homicide detectives usually do not make arrests in one detective's department because it has a well-trained fugitive unit: "[W]e've got a fugitive unit that's unbelievable. They can find anybody anywhere. We ask them to go out and find the people and bring them to us. They know what to say to them. They know how to do everything right." In his nine years on the job, one homicide detective remembered making only one arrest; it was in the first homicide that he worked. In that case, the killer literally "fell into his lap": "A kid walked up to me at the crime scene because he was scared to death. He was involved in this robbery that went bad. But he just walked up to me and said I'm involved in this."

Regardless of who does it, arresting a homicide suspect starts an emotionally-challenging process for homicide detectives:

It starts a process of winner or loser. The fudge factor is gone, and it's time to show what you've got. And you just hope that everything you did is sufficient enough to get this guy convicted and put in custody. It starts a very emotional process because if you lose this thing, it's tough. I lost cases in raqueteering and organized crime when I was doing cases with the state attorney's office, and it's no big deal. It's just property and money. But when you lose these cases, there's a lot tied to them. Like when I used to make an arrest on the street for retail theft or something, you make the arrest, put the person in jail, and go home, and go, "Wow, It's over." When you make the homicide arrest, now the party has just started. That's what I've always tried to profess to the people who are new. In most investigations, the arrest is the finale. In homicide, it's part of the process. You don't just lock them up, send in the paper work, and look for something else to do. It's just part of the process.

Extracting Confessions and Other Evidence

For homicide detectives, a major part of the process is getting a suspect to confess to the crime. The hope is that the suspect can be turned into a defendant. A suspect becomes a defendant when formal charges are filed by the prosecutor. To formally file a charge or charges, the prosecutor must have probable cause that the suspect is guilty of the crime. Probable cause is based on tangible evidence. Evidence can take many forms, but nothing beats a confession. As one detective observed, "There is nothing more that a prosecutor likes to have than a suspect on tape admitting he killed the second party because they were a witness to the first murder. It's absolutely wonderful stuff." The detective related how easy it is sometimes to obtain a confession: "You're always surprised when a suspect confesses to a crime [for which] they know they're going to be in prison the rest of their lives. Why do people do that? It's not unusual at all that when you start interviewing people, they start confessing the things you would never, ever expect them to confess to. That's not an unusual thing." For example, in one case, confided the detective, the suspect was a lady who cut her husband's head off: "She was denying that right through the interview until she finally just gave it up and just started talking about it. That's quite a surprise. When she's describing how she cut her husband's head off, and the graphic detail that she got into."

Homicide detectives also have powerful techniques for extracting confessions from recalcitrant suspects:

> They confuse and disorient the suspect, they lie about physical evidence, about witnesses, about statements by other suspects; they pretend that they already have their case sealed and are only giving the suspect a chance to explain his side of the story; they pretend to understand, to sympathize, to excuse; they play on the suspect's fears, his biases, his loyalty to family and friends, his religion; they exhaust the suspect and wear him down; in some cases, they use violence, even torture.[3]

---

3. Samuel R. Gross (1996) "The Risks of Death: Why Erroneous Convictions Are Common in Capital Cases," *Buffalo Law Review* 44:469-500, p. 485; Barry Scheck, Peter Neufeld, and Jim Dwyer (2001) *Actual Innocence: When Justice Goes Wrong and How to Make It Right*. New York: Penguin Putnam, p. 116; David R. Dow (2005) *Executed on a Technicality: Lethal Injustice on America's Death Row*. Boston: Beacon Press, p. 26.

A detective described how he felt when he successfully manipulated a suspect into confessing: "You'll be interviewing with the suspect, and you don't know if it's true, but they bite. And they start talking, and you have to cover the emotion because you just did them. They don't know you did them, but you have to maintain that very stoic interview process. It's hard to do when you're giggling on the inside."

Thus, by using coercive and manipulative methods, homicide detectives often are successful in getting guilty suspects to confess. Sometimes, however, they get innocent people to confess, too. A study found that false confessions were the third most common cause of errors in capital cases behind only perjury by prosecution witnesses and eyewitness misidentification.[4]

Besides a signed confession, eyewitness identification of the suspect is powerful evidence. In noncapital cases, the crime victim is often able to identify the offender; in capital cases, that is not possible. Consequently, in capital cases, homicide detectives frequently must rely on evidence from other people, such as accomplices, jailhouse snitches, other disreputable characters, and even the defendant himself. Some offenders implicate innocent people to divert suspicion from themselves. Other people, who may or may not have had a role in the crime, perjure themselves for money or for other favors from criminal justice officials, such as having charges in another unrelated case dropped.

Winning and Losing

Homicide detectives frequently believe that the process produces winners and losers. Winning, for at least some homicide detectives, is defined as successfully completing the job—and it can be exhilarating. One homicide detective described it this way:

> [W]hen you work a case, and you get to the point when you've established probable cause to make an arrest and he can't beat it, there's no other feeling in the world; there's no other feeling like it. When you've got enough to arrest somebody for murder.... Also there's no better feeling in the world than when you hear "guilty" and you know that that person is going away, and it's because of all [your] efforts. There's no better feeling. That's kind of like the drug that keeps us coming back.... You're constantly seeking that feeling of knowing that you have probable cause to charge somebody and then when someone finally goes away for it.

Another homicide detective saw it very differently. He commented, "There's no elation to winning. Nobody is looking for accolades. You did the job you were assigned to do." However, for him, there is relief when it is over:

> A lot of relief. And that's a lot of pressure. And you just don't want people who commit murders walking the streets. And if they get out because of something you've screwed up, there's a lot of work there, a lot of burden. I would hate to lose a case on a technicality, and I've seen that already. So people walk from homicide—that's tough. If it's something you had no fault in, then that's not

---

4. Hugo Adam Bedau and Michael L. Radelet (1987) "Miscarriages of Justice in Potentially Capital Cases," *Stanford Law Review* 41:21-179.

your problem. That's how the system works. If it's something you screwed up, that's a tough nut. And if you screwed it up because of a lack of knowledge, something you were supposed to know, that's tough. It's a tough spot to be in, especially when there are people in the office with you, and they know that you lost a case because of something you screwed up. It's a hard one to get over.

Unfortunately, homicide detectives investigating potentially capital cases do screw up, with some regularity. When they are unable to solve a murder within a reasonable amount of time, homicide detectives sometimes cut corners and jump to conclusions. In particular jeopardy in such cases are people who are innocent of the crime being investigated but who have prior felony records. They often become the focus of criminal investigations, especially when police do not have other leads.

Law enforcement officers (or others who aid them) may even go so far as to lose, destroy, or manufacture evidence against a suspect. For example, in 1993, the West Virginia Supreme Court of Appeals ruled as invalid hundreds of blood tests that West Virginia prosecutors had used over a ten–year period to link defendants to crime scenes. In every case, the state police serologist had lied about, fabricated, or manipulated evidence to win convictions. There also was evidence that the serologist's supervisors may have ignored or concealed complaints of his misconduct. At least 134 prisoners may have been entitled to new trials because of the falsified testimony that put them in prison.[5]

An FBI investigation found that an Oklahoma City police crime laboratory chemist had misidentified or misinterpreted evidence or testified improperly in court in as many as 23 capital cases. Ten of those defendants have already been executed. Most controversial is the case of Malcolm Rent Johnson, who was executed for rape and murder on January 6, 2000. At Johnson's trial, the chemist testified that six samples of semen taken from the victim's bedroom were consistent with Johnson's blood type. However, when the evidence was reexamined after Johnson's execution, there was no semen present. State officials and the FBI scrutinized the chemist's work in about 1,200 cases. She was fired from her job in September 2001, after a hearing by an administrative panel into her alleged misconduct.[6]

A more recent case involved three fingerprint examiners in the Seminole County (Florida) Sheriff's Office. Because of their malfeasance, prosecutors must review more than 1,200 cases to insure that innocent people were not sent to prison. In many of those cases, print analysis was the sole piece of physical evidence against a suspect. In a case involving a death row inmate awaiting execution, the death row inmate was identified by fingerprints on a bloody knife, even though the fingerprints turned out to be inconclusive. In another case, a line of wood grain on the murder weapon—a wooden-handled knife— was mistaken for a fingerprint ridge. In other cases, fingerprint identifications made by one examiner were confirmed by other examiners even though they were wrong. The main culprit, who handled 870 of the cases under review, was an eleven-year department veteran with nearly twenty-five years of experience as a print examiner. Investigators do not believe the mistakes were intentional efforts to win convictions, but instead were due to the examiners' being tired, overworked, or under pressure to make positive

---

5. See *The Charlotte [NC] Observer*, November 12, 1993, p. 8A.

6. Deborah Hastings (2001) "Facts Disputed in Execution Case," *The Orlando Sentinel* (August 30), p. A3; Jim Yardley (2001) "Oklahoma Takes Close Look at Evidence in Capital Cases," *The Orlando Sentinel* (September 2), p. A5; Jim Yardley (2001) "Oklahoma Inquiry Focuses on Scientist Used by Prosecutors," *The New York Times* (May 2), p. A1; "Accusations Cost Chemist Job," *The Orlando Sentinel* (September 26), p. A13.

identifications.[7] Note that in all three of these examples the errors were discovered (although posthumously in Malcolm Johnson's case); how many such errors go undetected cannot be known.

Support for the Death Penalty

The police, both historically and as a group, have been loyal death penalty supporters in large part because many of them believe that capital punishment provides an added measure of security in their dangerous occupation (deterrence) and that it is the appropriate punishment for the most heinous crimes (retribution). Despite evidence to the contrary, most police officers cling to the belief that would-be killers often refrain from killing police officers because they fear being executed (general deterrence). At the very least, many police officers take comfort in knowing that an executed capital offender poses no threat to them — or anybody else, for that matter (incapacitation). Whether it is the appropriate punishment for heinous crimes because it pays the offender back for what he had done is debatable. Clearly, two-thirds of the world's countries and eighteen jurisdictions in the United States (seventeen states and the District of Columbia) are able to dispense justice and avoid calamity without resorting to capital punishment.

Nevertheless, according to a survey of more than one hundred police lieutenants and sergeants, nearly 90 percent of them favored the death penalty for persons convicted of first-degree murder.[8] More than 90 percent of those officers worked in law enforcement agencies in states with a death penalty.

Retribution was the primary reason the officers gave for supporing the death penalty; nearly 80 percent chose retribution. Deterrence was selected by nearly 60 percent of the officers. Death penalty support dropped to about 68 percent when the officers could choose the alternative of life imprisonment without the opportunity of parole. Another 10 percent of the officers were uncertain about the death penalty when given the alternative. White officers were 112 times more likely than nonwhite officers to favor the death penalty over life imprisonment without opportunity of parole.

When certain aggravating factors were added to a first-degree murder, officers' support for the death penalty increased slightly. For example, about 92 percent of the officers favored the death penalty for execution-style killings, and about 91 percent supported the death penalty for killers of police officers and multiple victims.

In contrast, death penalty support declined, sometimes dramatically, when first-degree murders were mitigated by various factors. For instance, officers' death penalty support

---

7. Rene Stutzman (2007) "Are Innocent Imprisoned? Fingerprint Errors Found," *The Orlando Sentinel* (May 4), p. A1; Rene Stutzman (2007) "State Finds 2 More Mistaken Print IDs," *The Orlando Sentinel* (May 8), p. A1; Rene Stutzman (2007) "Seminole Print-ID Scandal Widens," *The Orlando Sentinel* (May 11, 2007), p. A1; Rene Stutzman (2007) "Fingerprint Scandal Extends Grip," *The Orlando Sentinel* (May 24), p. B1. For more examples, see Barry Scheck, Peter Neufeld, and Jim Dwyer (2001) *Actual Innocence: When Justice Goes Wrong and How to Make It Right.* New York: Penguin Putnam, Chapter 5.

8. Gennaro F. Vito, Geetha Suresh, and William F. Walsh (2008) "Police Managers' Attitudes toward Capital Punishment," pp. 159-170 in R. M. Bohm (ed.) *The Death Penalty Today.* Boca Raton, FL: CRC Press.

decreased to about 59 percent when the offender was a juvenile, to about 56 percent when the offender was mentally ill, and to approximately 20 percent when the offender was mentally retarded. The U.S. Supreme Court has ruled that the death penalty cannot be imposed on killers who are juveniles, mentally ill, or mentally retarded.

About 88 percent of the officers favored the death penalty for the killers of female victims. Death penalty support also was somewhat attenuated when the killer was on drugs (86.4 percent), was under the influence of alcohol (85.3 percent), was sexually abused as a child (77.9 percent), and was not the triggerman in the homicide (62.4 percent). Death penalty support also decreased when officers were presented with evidence that the death penalty failed to deter homicides (82.7 percent), was more likely to be imposed on poor defendants (76 percent), was racially biased in its application (75 percent), was more costly than life in prison (69.9 percent), and that innocent persons had been executed (43.3 percent). The study's authors contend that police officers' beliefs and opinions about the death penalty are a product of police culture.

Because of the nature of their work, one might think that homicide detectives would be even more supportive of the death penalty than other police officers. According to one homicide detective, who described himself as a staunch proponent of the death penalty,

> If you thought you were right before you went there [to homicide], after you interview some of these clowns, you'll know you're right. When you can sit at an interview table and look a guy right in the eye and have him explain to you why he shot some guy in the head twice, and he's looking at you like, "What's the big deal?" Quite the social deviants out there. When you interview them one on one, you get a better understanding of why the death penalty is so necessary from my perspective.

He elaborated:

> I just don't believe — or I should say, I do believe that there should be a penalty for what you do, and I think the death penalty is quite appropriate for people who commit crimes heinous enough to get themselves sentenced to death. And believe me, those are rare. To get sentenced to death, you must have done something tremendously bad, and done it with such malice and forethought, and with so many aggravating circumstances, to get the death penalty is very difficult. So, if you got it, you deserve it.

The detective did not believe that the death penalty was a deterrent. "It's a pound of flesh," he said bluntly.

> There's absolutely nothing I've heard or read or studied that would indicate to me that someone did or did not commit a homicide because of the fear of the death penalty. If you're gonna do your wife, you're just going to take the chances. I think everybody has the same attitude when they get caught; that's pretty much foolproof. I never thought it was a deterrent. I thought it was a just reward.

When asked whether his work investigating homicides affected his opinion of the death penalty, another homicide detective replied hesitantly, "I don't know that it has a lot. I guess since I've never had a family member murdered ... I didn't have a strong opinion on it one way or the other. I guess I should correct that. Dealing with family members ... I think it might have [been affected]. I might lean more toward being in favor of it than I used to [be]." Still, he was troubled by what he saw as unfair disparities in who was charged with a capital crime and who was not: "Now that I'm into this, I see what the aggravators are. I have a tough time saying why is this a death penalty case and this is not, and all the aggravators that have to be present and aren't. That sometimes has confused me as to why certain ones are and others aren't."

When his partner was asked the same question, he stated, "It might be hard to believe, but I was never a big death penalty proponent—but not because of religious reasons. More so along the lines of it's unfairly distributed. Like [my partner] said, my opinion has always been, why are we placing more value on this human life as opposed to this?"

A 1995 survey of nearly four hundred police chiefs and county sheriffs found that, philosophically, a majority of them supported the death penalty, even though they did not believe it was an effective law enforcement tool.[9] About one-third of the law enforcement executives supported the death penalty and thought it worked well, nearly 60 percent supported the death penalty philosphically but did not think it was an effective law enforcement tool, and only 4 percent opposed the death penalty. Thus, more than 90 percent of law enforcement executives supported the death penalty, at least philosophically. That is slightly higher than the percentage reported for police lieutenants and sergeants in the previous study cited. However, unlike their subordinates, two-thirds of the executives did not believe that the death penalty significantly reduced the number of homicides or that it was an important law enforcement tool. To the contrary, two-thirds of the executives related that death penalty cases are difficult to close and consume a lot of police time. More than 80 percent of the executives did not believe that murderers think about possible punishments. As former Los Angeles Police Chief Willie Williams commented, "I am not convinced that capital punishment, in and of itself, is a deterrent to crime because most people do not think about the death penalty before they commit a violent or capital crime."

When the law enforcement executives were asked to select their primary choices from a list of possible ways to reduce violent crime, reducing drug abuse was their number one priority. Reducing drug abuse was selected by 31 percent of the executives. The next highest ranked choice for reducing violent crime was better economy and more jobs (selected by 17 percent of executives), followed by simplifying court rules (16 percent), longer prison sentences for criminals (15 percent), more police officers on the street (10 percent), reducing the number of guns (3 percent), and expanded use of the death penalty (1 percent). That's worth repeating: Only 1 percent of law enforcement executives selected expanded use of the death penalty as a primary choice for reducing violent crime.

When given the opportunity to respond to an open-ended question about areas that would have the greatest impact on reducing violent crime in their jurisdiction, the law enforcement executives most often cited sentencing reform, including truth-in-sentencing, elimination of parole and stiffer sentences (33 percent), followed by the development of family values and parenting skills (23 percent), education (15 percent), and more police (13 percent). The death penalty was cited by fewer than 2 percent of the executives and was ranked twenty-sixth among the solutions given.

The law enforcement executives also were asked about their main obstacles to success in protecting citizens and fashioning a safer society. The most frequently mentioned problem was again drug and alcohol abuse, selected by 87 percent of the executives as

---

9. Richard C. Dieter (1995) "On the Front Line: Law Enforcement Views on the Death Penalty," The Death Penalty Information Center at www.deathpenaltyinfo.org/front-line-law-enforcement-views-death-penalty (accessed 9/22/08).

either the "top two or three problems" or as a "major problem." Only 27 percent of the executives selected insufficient use of the death penalty as a major problem, while 63 percent of them considered insufficient use of the death penalty as a minor problem or no problem at all. When asked about the most cost-effective strategies for controlling crime, the death penalty ranked last. Only 29 percent of law enforcement executives considered the death penalty cost effective.

The law enforcement executives were more open to death penalty alternatives than were the police lieutenants and sergeants. When provided with the alternative of life imprisonment without opportunity of parole, combined with mandatory restitution to the victim's family, death penalty support among the executives dropped to around 50 percent. Fifty-two percent of the executives who supported the death penalty philosophically but did not believe it was an effective law enforcement tool preferred the alternative to the death penalty.

The police chiefs and sheriffs were wary of the political use of the death penalty. According to Ronald Hampton, President of the National Black Police Association in Washington, DC, "[The death penalty] is a political move, insensitive to the real needs of the people in this city." Eighty-five percent of the executives believed that politicians use their support for the death penalty in a symbolic way to show they are tough on crime. A majority of the executives believed that the time spent on capital punishment in Congress and state legislatures diverts the attention of our elected representatives from finding real solutions to the crime problem.

Conclusion

If the death penalty were abolished in the states that have retained it, murders would still be committed, and the police would still be expected to investigate the crimes and apprehend the perpetrators. Homicide detectives would still experience the stress of working long hours and the other physical demands of the job, the pressure to solve the crime, the frustration with police bureaucracy, and the difficulty of having to juggle their professional and personal lives. None of that would change. What would change is that the consequences of their mistakes would not be fatal—innocent people would not be executed—and the vast resources expended on capital punishment could be used for other police priorities, especially more effective methods of reducing violent crime.[10]

Detectives work closely with prosecutors to bring perpetrators to justice. In the next chapter, we'll look at the roles that prosecutors play in the process, as well as at how they affect, and are affected by, capital cases.

---

10. On the costs of capital punishment, see Robert M. Bohm (2012) *DEATHQUEST: An Introduction to the Theory & Practice of Capital Punishment in the United States*, Fourth Ed. Waltham, MA: Anderson/Elsevier, pp. 188–203.

Chapter 2

Prosecutors

Homicide detectives and prosecutors are partners in the fight against crime. They work together to protect local communities. As the prologue to the long-running television series *Law & Order* dramatizes, "In the criminal justice system, the people are represented by two separate yet equally important groups: the police, who investigate crime, and the district attorneys, who prosecute the offenders."

Prosecutors are especially important in the capital punishment process because they are the gatekeepers. They alone decide whether to charge a suspect with a capital crime. Prosecuting a defendant charged with a capital crime is a resource-intensive and time-consuming job. Prosecutors have the burden of proving beyond a reasonable doubt that the defendant did, in fact, commit the crime with which he is charged. If the defendant is found guilty, prosecutors also must convince twelve citizens that the defendant deserves to die.

Prosecutors must make sure that they get all the information from the police, that the defense gets all that information, and that the evidence has been processed. They must develop a trial strategy and prepare witnesses. Prosecutors are under constant pressure to achieve a good result for the victim's family and law enforcement. Because of pressures and expectations—and egos—prosecutors have been known to engage in unethical and illegal behavior, such as withholding exculpatory evidence (evidence tending to establish a criminal defendant's innocence), subordination of perjury, and use of improper evidence. Prosecutors also have been accused of refusing to release crime evidence for DNA analysis and racial discrimination. Like homicide detectives, prosecutors generally support the death penalty—how could they not?

This chapter looks at prosecutors and their role in the capital punishment process. Because most capital crimes violate state laws, they fall under the authority, or jurisdiction, of the state court system and its prosecutors. The prosecutor is a community's chief law enforcement official, whose primary responsibility is the protection of society. Depending on the state, the prosecutor may be referred to as the *district attorney, prosecuting attorney, county attorney, state's attorney, commonwealth's attorney,* or *solicitor.* In large cities, assistant district attorneys (ADAs) perform the day-to-day work of the prosecutor's office.

Gatekeepers of the Capital Punishment Process

Whatever they are called, prosecutors are the most powerful people in the capital punishment process. They are the gatekeepers and alone decide whether to charge a suspect with a capital crime. (Sometimes a committee of prosecutors makes the decision.) They sometimes try to minimize their awesome responsibility by saying that their role is only to give a judge or jury the opportunity to decide whether death is the appropriate punishment in a capital case. However, their role is much more pivotal: prosecutors decide whose life shall be placed in legal—and mortal—jeopardy. The only constitutional limits on prosecutorial decisions to seek the death penalty are that the decisions not be selective, vindictive, or otherwise motivated by bad faith.[1]

Ideally, prosecutors are supposed to charge an offender with a crime (capital or otherwise) and prosecute the case if, after full investigation, three—and only three— conditions are met: (1) they find that a crime has been committed, (2) a perpetrator can be identified, and (3) there is sufficient evidence to support a guilty verdict. In capital cases, prosecutors also must find at least one statutorily enumerated aggravating factor. On the other hand, prosecutors are not supposed to charge suspects with more criminal charges or for more serious crimes than can be reasonably supported by the evidence. They are not supposed to prosecute simply because an aroused public demands it. They are not supposed to be influenced by the personal or political advantages or disadvantages that might be involved in prosecuting or not prosecuting a case. Nor, for that matter, are they supposed to be swayed by their desire to enhance their records of successful convictions.

It would be naive, however, to believe that those factors do not have at least some influence on some prosecutors' decisions in capital or potentially capital cases, because all chief prosecutors in the United States are elected, except for those in Alaska, Connecticut, the District of Columbia, and New Jersey, where they are appointed. (None of those four jurisdictions has a death penalty statute.)

A Missouri death row inmate, who has since been executed, made this provocative observation about the influence of political factors on prosecutors' decisions to seek the death penalty:

> [Capital punishment is] grossly unfair.... There are a number of factors that come into play long before you reach the jury: the county you happen to be arrested in, and the political ambitions of the prosecutor—whether or not he's up for reelection any time soon, or whether he's just been reelected. If he's just coming into office, he probably won't be seeking the death penalty, because it's a lot more work and a lot more expensive for the county. However, if he's about to go out of office, and trying to secure reelection, nothing brings the headlines like notoriety. Like the death sentence.[2]

When asked about the decision to charge a suspect with a capital crime, one prosecutor (prosecutors interviewed for this chapter were chief assistant prosecutors or heads of their state attorney's homicide unit) explained that he was guided by the state's death penalty statute, which lists aggravating and mitigating factors, and by the victim's family:

> The capital sentencing statute sets forth what the aggravators are. It sets forth what the mitigators are. And we start there.... Sometimes it will be [the state attorney], myself, as the chief assistant, and our intake attorney—chief of intake

---

1. Cited in Wayne A. Logan (2006) "Victims, Survivors, and the Decisions to Seek and Impose the Death Penalty," pp. 161-177 in J. R. Acker and D. R. Karp (eds.) *Wounds That Do Not Bind: Victim-Based Perspectives on the Death Penalty*. Durham, NC: Carolina Academic Press, p. 170, n.7.

2. Stephen Trombley (1992) *The Execution Protocol: Inside America's Capital Punishment Industry*. New York: Crown Publishers, p. 239.

usually handles all the capital cases—and the trial attorney all have input on whether or not we think certain aggravators will apply in this case and what we think the mitigating circumstances are. We also consider what we'd think the family would like for us to do. And then we make the consideration whether we should do the death penalty.

He noted that the initial decision to seek the death penalty is tentative, because prosecutors do not always know at that point what all the aggravating and mitigating factors are:

[We arrive at the initial decision] with the understanding that we realize that there may be some aggravators that we don't know about. What we're more concerned about, and we have to guess about it sometimes, is what mitigation we may not know about—perhaps mental health issues … perhaps abuse as a child … those sorts of things. So, in fact, one of the things we try to do … we, meaning us and or the police … [is] to interview the defendant. We try to go ahead and sound them out about these things and find out as much as we can. A lot of times that is limited. So to some degree the initial decision is subject to change.

Another prosecutor described the decision to charge a suspect with a capital crime similarly:

Normally when a case comes in we're taking to the grand jury, there's a discussion of the facts with the state attorney; there's 15 aggravators that are outlined by the statute. So a lot of it's looking at what aggravators you have. If the defendant has a prior murder charge, we're always going to seek death. Depending on the brutality of the crime—the heinous, atrocious, and cruel [aggravating factor]— how strong that is. So a lot of it, it's the facts, when they come in versus the strength of the case. It makes it a tougher conviction if you're seeking death.

In addition to the decision to seek the death penalty, a prosecutor also might have to decide whether to offer or accept a plea bargain. A prosecutor related the dynamics of that process:

Well, the defense's job is obviously working on mitigation to get together what they think is mitigating about the case. One example was a defendant who had a long-term history of mental illness. Clearly, it was not something just sort of brought up prior to this case. He had mental health issues from his childhood back in Puerto Rico. And so, even though the facts of the case were heinous, we finally made a life offer in that case.

She provided another example: "I currently have a case that we're discussing plea negotiations on it. He has a prior murder but there's a self-defense issue. Since I've been head of the unit, we do notice of seeking less." Regarding the possibility of seeking a conviction on a lesser offense, she was quick to point out: "It's not used as a plea bargaining tool." She added, "I personally don't like to do that. I only seek death on cases where I really intend on going forward. That does not mean after tiers of discovery and looking at their mitigation and certain things of my case that there may not be an offer made. I just personally don't like that [to use the death penalty as leverage to obtain a plea bargain]." She then conceded that other prosecutors have been known to use the death penalty in that way: "I believe that there are … a jurisdiction nearby … is well known for that [using the death penalty as leverage in plea bargaining], according to the defense bar. I won't comment on that."

Another prosecutor denied using the death penalty as a plea-bargaining tool and explained why:

> Number one, we try to make a pretty valid decision whether or not we actually do think it's a death penalty case.... Number two, defense attorneys are fairly astute, and if you don't have a death penalty case, they're going to know it. And you're not going to bargain a whole lot if you don't have a death penalty case. I think it would be very unethical to have a case where you really don't have a death penalty case, and you threaten one. I don't think that would be an ethical way to go.

Another prosecutor explained his thinking about whether to offer a plea bargain:

> We look at whether or not we have a strong case. That's the single biggest factor. We look at, secondly, how strong the death penalty aspect of it is. How many aggravators do we have and what mitigation do we expect? And then we talk to the family of the victim, and we get their input, and we get the input of law enforcement as to how they feel about the case. And we rate all those things and decide whether it's a case we should [plea bargain]. These cases take amazing turns sometimes. I mean, one of the cases that I tried when I first came here ... the defendant had killed a 14-year-old girl and had disposed of her body. That had been 7 years since they had been looking for the body, and they couldn't find it. The family wanted to find the remains. So we offered a plea. Not only waived the death penalty but agreed to waive life and make it a second-degree murder in term of years. We would talk about that and see if he had any interest, and he didn't! So that was an interesting case because we tried it; we convicted him; [and] we got the death penalty. And then during the post-conviction phase, he took us to the body in exchange for us waiving the death penalty.

For this prosecutor, the wishes of the victim's family are given "a considerable amount" of weight in determining whether to plea bargain:

> I'm not sure how to describe it exactly. I suppose it could carry the day if it was a close call on the death penalty. On that case, I think it carried the day to a large extent. These folks, it's more than how they feel about the death penalty. It was an opportunity to give them some closure that anybody could sympathize with and understand that they need. So in that particular case, it was a huge factor.

When asked about honoring the wishes of the victim's family if they did not want to seek the death penalty, he replied:

> Well, we would take it into consideration but wouldn't necessarily do what they want depending on how horrible the murder was. The death penalty needs to be applied in a way that it's not arbitrary or capricious. So that means the family can't necessarily make the call because it gets arbitrary and capricious. We have to try and stay the course sometimes even though they may not want it.

Another prosecutor answered the question this way:

> There is some input [by the victim's family], but it's never the final decision. Obviously, most families don't understand that there's a statute that gives me 15 things [aggravators] to look at. And so in their case, they have a loved one die; of course, it's going to be the death penalty. When you have to explain these particular facts, we're not seeking the death penalty. You're occasionally going to have the family member that's anti-death penalty, and you explain to them we're

still going to seek it. I think that people don't know their feelings about the death penalty until someone in their family is murdered.

She also emphasized, "My client is the state" — not the victim or the victim's family.

Given the number of factors that a prosecutor might consider, the question arises as to how the decision to seek the death penalty or to plea bargain cannot help but be arbitrary or capricious. Recall that in its *Furman* decision, the U.S. Supreme Court ruled that arbitrary or capricious death sentencing violated the U.S. Constitution's Eighth and Fourteenth Amendments. A prosecutor responded, "It depends on if your definition of arbitrary or capricious is that anytime we don't have enough evidence to successfully process the case it's arbitrary or capricious."

The prosecutor was asked how determining the strength of the case was not arbitrary or capricious. It was pointed out that different prosecutors might have different ideas about how strong a case actually is; how strong the aggravators or mitigators are; or, for that matter, what the family's wishes are, especially if a family is divided on the issue. Some family members may want to pursue the death penalty, and other family members may not. Some family members may want to accept a plea bargain, and other family members may not. The same may be true about what the police wish to do. So, when dealing with all those factors, different prosecutors might make different decisions. Is that not arbitrary or capricious decision making? To which the prosecutor replied:

> Well, that's why [the state attorney] makes the final decision. He's the constant. He makes the call. He's been a prosecutor longer than I have, but I've prosecuted more capital cases than he has. While he's been state attorney, of course, he hasn't done that many cases. It's hard to run an office of that size and prosecute cases. So, while he's gotten away from death penalty cases, I've stayed involved. I'm still prosecuting a death penalty case right now. He relies not on my opinion but on my certain expertise about whether we can establish certain aggravators, and how we're going to lay those [out], and how strong they're going to be, and the mitigators, and I offer him my opinion as to whether or not it's a case that we ought to go forward on. And the attorney who's got the case gives us their insight as to the facts of the case, and we make our decision. And that decision is subject to change if the facts change; if what we think the facts are turn out not to be the facts. We like to think that's not arbitrary and capricious.

Prosecuting a Capital Crime

We know that "death is different." So, how does the prosecution of a defendant charged with a capital crime differ from the prosecution of a defendant charged with a noncapital felony? According to one prosecutor, "There's a higher standard of care, from our perspective. I certainly know when you talk to public defenders, you're going to find that they put their most experienced and most competent attorneys on those cases, and our office tries to do the same thing." Another prosecutor stated:

> Normally, the lawyers on the case are going to be better. If it's a court-appointed lawyer or the public defender, there are certain requirements they have to have before having a case. It's a lot more expensive, and it's a lot more time-consuming

because obviously [names a city] is a transient type community, and a lot of people have moved here. Normally, we're traveling out of state for depositions and also somewhat for the aggravating [evidence].

Once the decision has been made to charge a suspect with a capital crime, prosecutors must develop a trial strategy. Prosecutors have a decided advantage over most defense attorneys in capital cases because prosecutors generally have more resources available to them during the investigation and preparation for trial. If prosecutors are better prepared, have more credible witnesses, and have more interesting props or exhibits than the defense, then jurors may side with prosecutors because of their "showmanship" rather than because of the merits of their case.[3] Trial strategy ultimately depends on the circumstances of the case. A prosecutor explained:

> I think that you have to vary [trial strategy], obviously from case to case. Your strategy, if you've got a sympathetic victim and what some people refer to as an innocent victim, you may, shall we say, want to emphasize that. If you don't, then you may spend a lot of time trying to persuade the jury—even though the victim is not very sympathetic, nonetheless—it's a murder. You need to follow the law. So your strategies can be affected by those sorts of things. I think that sometimes your strategy is what order to present your testimony as opposed to deciding what evidence. For instance, in one of the cases we did, in fact, it was the one involving the little 14-year-old girl who had been buried, we decided we had a number of inmates who were going to testify that the defendant made admissions to. All of them were scalawags with terrible criminal histories, and we knew that the defense was going to have a lot of success impeaching their credibility. But he [the defendant] also made a mention to a preacher. So we felt like what we'd do is let the preacher clean it all up in the end. After they had all their fun about how could you possibly believe these people [the inmates], let them ask that question [about the preacher].

Some cases seem to try themselves because the evidence is so overwhelming. Basically, all a prosecutor has to do in such cases is simply call the investigating officers and, perhaps, forensic experts to the witness stand and ask them what they found. A prosecutor provided this example:

> Two defense attorneys decided that they were going to try [the case before] a jury on the issue of guilt. We had a videotaped confession, we had the victim's blood match [on the defendant's] clothing that he was arrested in by DNA. We had his shoe impressions match the bloody shoe impressions at the scene. There were two victims, but only one died. It was a husband and wife. The wife was available to identify him as the person who attacked [her husband] in the house. He was caught in their car at a bank the next morning trying to cash one of their checks he'd stolen.

With that type of evidence, the obvious question is, what was the defense? According to the prosecutor:

> They were trying some technical things. They were trying to knock out the burglary charges, and they thought that would help them with the applicability with one of the aggravating circumstances for the penalty phase. I personally thought that was the wrong approach. My thought was how do you ask a jury to believe anything you say after you get up and argue to them that a guy's not

---

3. Allison M. Cotton (2008) *Effigy: Images of Capital Defendants*. Lanham, MD: Lexington Books, pp. 150-151.

guilty with that kind of evidence. I've got to give them credit. It didn't work out all that badly. The jury recommendation was for death, but it was only 8-4. [In Florida, a jury's sentencing decision does not have to be unanimous as it does in most other death penalty states, because, in Florida, the jury only recommends a sentence to the judge, who may or may not override the jury's sentencing recommmendation. However, in Florida, as in all other death penalty states, the guilt-stage verdict must be unanimous.]

About the jury vote, the prosecutor concluded, "I think that's a function more of the jury than of the case. There were some folks who didn't have an open mind about the death penalty." He believed that the four jurors who did not vote for death slipped through the death qualification process during voir dire.

Another prosecutor had this say about her death penalty trial strategy:

You do the standard things you do in any murder case. You develop a theme and a theory of the case. It's your theme you want to develop, starting in jury selection. It's clearly in your opening statement. Your theme is going to be your persuasive story on how you're going to sell your case. Your theory, what happened, and ... are you going under first-degree murder or premeditation or felony or both. And you go through them and look at your witnesses and try to develop a way of putting them on. How it will develop your story the best. Strong evidence in the beginning and the end. The realization that you get ... there's a lot of just, management. If your witnesses are available, if you're flying people in, when can you get 'em in and on the stand.

Regarding the "story" to which she was referring, she quipped, "If you get jurors to cry in the opening, that's good." Thus, for this prosecutor, except for jury selection, the guilt phase of a capital trial is basically the same as any other murder trial. She observed that because of the inevitable state supreme court scrutiny during direct appeal, she has to be "aggressive but cautious" in capital trials. Asked what she meant by being "aggressive but cautious," she explained:

You are asking twelve people to convict someone that they then know you're going to come back and ask them to give the death penalty. I think there are a lot of people out there that are strong on the death penalty in theory. But when it comes down to personal vote, it's much tougher than some people think. I think there's some people that think they're soft on the death penalty until they see a case, that it's so brutal and heinous that it's different for them. I tried a case about a year ago, and my foreperson was a lawyer who was raised Catholic and had the whole being raised in a Catholic faith ... is going to be anti-death penalty. But you're a lawyer, so you have the law to follow. I don't think it was as difficult a decision as he thought it was going to be. But anytime you get a death penalty case, there's just a higher scrutiny on it for appeal.

When asked to further clarify what she meant by being "aggressive" in a capital trial, she said, "There has to be some passion in your case. There has to be a way of developing your case. That you get the jurors to feel what's so terrible about the case. On the other hand ... your evidence and what you're getting in, you need to make sure you're not pushing the boundaries." She provided some examples of "pushing the boundaries":

There's a lot of stuff, such as hearsay, statements made by people outside of court. Every criminal case there's probably some hearsay brought in, even though there might be some evidence against it. You need to be careful that you're not trying to bring in something [to which] the other side doesn't object, and then it's a problem for you later. There's something called William's Rule, which is prior bad acts of the defendant. Like in a domestic violence case, sometimes you can bring that in, but you have to be careful about it, because it's always going to be an appellate issue. So you have to ask yourself, how much do I really need to bring this in to prove my case? How much of it am I bringing in, because it's supposed to be there for a purpose to prove motive or ID? It's also going to prejudice the jury against the defendant if they hear about prior acts. Those type of things. You still have to be a strong advocate for your case and make sure your case is going to stand up on appeal.

In determining whether to try something that "pushes the boundaries," she stated, "I think that's where experience comes in. The case I just did, I had a younger lawyer sitting with me.... In part of doing it, you're also mentoring the other lawyer in the office saying, 'No, we're not going to do that because that could be an issue on appeal.' Where someone younger is thinking more on the conviction, and you can't think that way." So, before selecting any strategic argument in a capital trial, this prosecutor is always asking herself: Could this be an appellate issue?

Guilt Phase versus Penalty Phase

As noted, capital trials are unique because they are bifurcated with separate guilt and penalty stages. For prosecutors, the more difficult stage of the trial varies by case. One prosecutor commented:

> I'd say, on average, probably the guilt phase is the more difficult. There's more involved.... Many times your aggravators are proven during the guilt stage of the trial. So when you get to the penalty phase, you're not putting out a whole lot of evidence. Typically, it's almost required apparently, that the defense is going to put on some mental health expert to testify about [the defendant's] mental state at the time, child abuse, how many times they've fallen out of bed and hit their head. All those sorts of things to establish some mental health mitigation. Which means that you may be involved with one or two defense experts and one or two state experts that we are going to use to rebut that testimony. So, in that sense, it can get a little complicated. If you've got a case that's real simple on the guilt phase, then it may be that the penalty phase sometimes could be the more complicated portion.

Another prosecutor found the penalty stage in one of her capital trials more difficult than she had expected:

> In my hung jury case, I did not believe that the penalty phase was going to be difficult at all, because I was going under two aggravators: heinous, atrocious, and cruel and cold calculated premeditation. The facts [were established during the] guilt phase, except to recall a medical examiner, because she could elaborate more on the pain the victim would have undergone. So, in that particular case, [the defense attorneys] weren't [going to put on a lot of expert witnesses] ... if

they put an expert on, it was to say he didn't have mental health issues. So, I wasn't going to be calling in an expert and rebuttal. The judge was limiting me to one victim impact [statement]. So, I felt that the penalty phase really was just going to be argument.

She added, "I've had penalty phases where I felt the experts were really important and that took a lot of time, because the defense is not limited in how many experts they can use."

Victim-Impact Statements

The victim-impact statement to which the prosecutor referred above, typically describes the harm done to and the suffering of a victim and his or her family members. Family members present their victim-impact statements during the penalty phase of a capital trial. However, as the prosecutor pointed out, "because [a victim-impact statement is] not an aggravator, although we're allowed to present evidence of an impact statement, we're not allowed to argue it." A judge limiting a prosecutor to only one victim-impact statement is unusual. In fact, this was the first time this prosecutor had been limited to only one victim-impact statement. When asked how many victim-impact statements she usually put on, she replied: "Usually two or three. I had a case where I think a son, daughter-in-law, and granddaughter testified, and a victim advocate read a statement from two other family members. I did a case in which a local defense attorney's mother was killed. He did one alone [and one] with his wife." She believes she was limited to only one victim-impact statement in that particular case because "[i]t was his [the judge's] first death penalty case, and he was concerned that that would be an area for reversal." Asked whether the judge knew the law about the number of victim-impact statements that could be presented, she simply observed, "The law was argued to him, and he made his ruling."

Taking Care of Business

When asked what the most important aspect of prosecuting a defendant charged with a capital crime is, one prosecutor maintained, "Making sure that everything is covered. And you get all the information from the police, and you make sure the defense has all that information. Making sure that the evidence has been processed. You just have to be more meticulous." Another prosecutor said:

I think you have to become intimately familiar with all the facts. From that, you may learn additional facts that assist you. From that, you can figure out what your trial strategy is going to be and, of course, you can make your plans ... It's one thing to say, "I have a fact." The next question is, "How do I get that fact into evidence?" You have to plan those things.

He emphasized that knowing your witnesses is critical: "It's not enough to know what they say. You have to meet them, and talk to them, and have them tell you what they've got to say. You know, it's not just enough that they say, 'Oh I saw him do it' or 'He made an admission to me.' It's how they are going to be received. Are they going to be credible? Is the jury going to like them? Or are they going to dislike them?"

As for the most difficult aspect of prosecuting a defendant charged with a capital crime, one prosecutor simply stated, "The amount of time it takes." Another prosecutor was more specific:

> I would say that these cases tend to be complex. And you have to organize all of your evidence. You have to anticipate your legal issues and put the case together. And that process is the most difficult part. The size and the complexity of the evidence, I guess.... Maybe because mental health has now become a big part of that, that might on average be the most difficult part of putting a case together: the mental health evidence.

When asked about the worst aspect of prosecuting a defendant charged with a capital crime, one prosecutor cited the pressure of achieving a good result for the victim's family and law enforcement. Another prosecutor responded, "Watching some of the defendant's family members. Knowing their pain." When asked about the victim's family members, too, she amended her answer:

> I'd say both families. Watching the victim's family that, you know, when you get to the end of the case, they're not going to have the feeling they think they're going to have. It's not going to bring this person back to them. They may have a sense of justice, but death penalty cases aren't really over until [the offender is] executed, which is such a long time at this point. You watch the defendant's family. I've had some — a case last year — where I look at the family, and I think they tried to do a great job raising this person. And if anything, he was overindulged and spoiled, and you don't think that's going to make someone end up doing such a terrible thing like he did, which was to set a girl on fire. But when I watched the stepdad, who I think has done a phenomenal job in his pain, because he knows the inevitable is coming — there's no doubt that the guy was going to get convicted. And pretty much no doubt [it was going to be for] first-degree murder. Although he was so young, the facts were so heinous.... It's sad. The victim's family ... they all handle their grief differently, it comes down to, even if they hear the judge sentence the person to die, it doesn't give them the relief they're going to get.

Prosecutor Misconduct

Prosecutor misconduct is a major source of arbitrary and discriminatory application of the death penalty. It is also a principal cause of wrongful convictions. The most common forms of prosecutor misconduct are withholding exculpatory evidence, subordination of perjury, and use of improper evidence. Prosecutors also have been accused of refusing to release crime evidence for DNA analysis and racial discrimination.

Prosecutors know that legal procedure prohibits them from withholding exculpatory evidence from the defense. Exculpatory evidence, as noted, is evidence favorable to the accused that has an effect on guilt or punishment. Examples include physical evidence, evidentiary documents (such as a defendant's recorded statements to police, or reports of medical examinations or scientific tests), and lists of witnesses. A prosecutor's concealment or misrepresentation of evidence (typically referred to as a *Brady violation*; see *Brady v. Maryland*)[4] is grounds for an appellate court's reversal of a conviction or sentence.

Because suborning perjury is a criminal offense, it is difficult to believe that many prosecutors know in advance that their witnesses are lying under oath. But how can prosecutors ignore or not suspect the obvious motives of jailhouse snitches and the questionable incriminating evidence they provide?[5] It is also difficult to believe that most prosecutors are not privy to inmate informer argot about their deceptive practices: "'Don't go to the pen — send a friend.' Or: 'If you can't do the time, just drop a dime.' [Or:] 'Trouble? You better call 1–800–HETOLDME.'"[6] In one study, witness perjury was the foremost cause of wrongful convictions in capital cases.[7]

Sometimes prosecutors fail to dismiss capital charges against ostensibly innocent defendants. Prosecutors may be reluctant to dismiss charges even when the case is a weak one, especially if the public is clamoring for a conviction. Much of this has to do with ego. A sign seen in the Dallas County, Texas, prosecutor's office read: "Convicting the guilty is easy. It's the innocent that keep us working late."[8] The problem is that not only are some weak cases tried, but, as the quotation suggests, in some cases innocent defendants are convicted.

DNA analysis has proven to be an important tool in the successful investigation, prosecution, and exoneration of criminal defendants. Yet, despite relatively easy access to the technology, many local prosecutors refuse to release crime evidence for DNA analysis unless litigation is threatened or filed. They note that they have no legal obligation to cooperate because once a trial has ended, a convicted defendant has no absolute right to prove his or her innocence. They argue that the offender's interest in proving his or her innocence is outweighed by the state's interest in the finality of judgment.[9] Although refusing to release crime evidence for DNA analysis when possible innocence is at stake may not be prosecutor misconduct in a legal or technical sense, the belief that finality of sentence is more important than the preservation of innocent life is certainly debatable.

In some cases, following the exoneration of an innocent person who was wrongfully convicted and sentenced to death, prosecutors elect not to seek a death sentence when the actual perpetrator is found.[10]

Hopefully, most prosecutors follow the rules. But, of course, some do not. What happens to those prosecutors who get caught engaging in misconduct in capital cases? Not much. In a study of 381 murder convictions since 1963 that were reversed because of police or prosecutor misconduct, not one of the prosecutors who broke the law was

---

4. 373 U.S. 83 (1963).

5. Scheck et al., op. cit., Chap. 6.

6. Ibid., pp. 165-167.

7. Michael L. Radelet, Hugo Adam Bedau, and Constance E. Putnam (1992) *In Spite of Innocence: Erroneous Convictions in Capital Cases.* Boston: Northeastern University Press.

8. Patrick Lehner (1996) "Abolition Now!!!" www.abolition–now.com.

9. Scheck et al., op. cit., pp. xxi-xxii.

10. Stephen B. Bright (2004) "Why the United States Will Join the Rest of the World in Abandoning Capital Punishment," pp. 152-182 in H.A. Bedau and P.G. Cassell (eds.) *Debating the Death Penalty: Should America Have Capital Punishment? The Experts on Both Sides Make Their Best Case.* New York: Oxford, pp. 164-165.

convicted or disbarred. Most were not even disciplined. Current laws also protect prosecutors from civil suits even when they knowingly allowed perjured testimony or deliberately concealed evidence of innocence.[11]

When asked to respond to charges of prosecutor misconduct, one prosecutor stated, "Well all that I can say is that I think that prosecutors probably have a bad apple here and there and may intentionally do some of those bad things. But I know that I have never intentionally done any of those things, [even though] I've been accused of it in every capital case I've tried."

Given the amount of time and other resources devoted to capital cases—and the stakes involved—some prosecutors surely become emotionally invested in their cases. One prosecutor conceded, "I'm sure there's overzealousness out there." That may cause them to "push the boundaries," as another prosecutor mentioned earlier. Asked about "pushing the boundaries," one prosecutor volunteered:

> I mean if I have a case, and I was thoroughly convinced that the defendant had committed the murder ... I don't want them to walk, if I believe that, okay? But I would say this: As a younger attorney, sometimes it's harder to see the big picture, and to kind of divorce yourself from those emotional feelings and to sit back and evaluate it. The question sometimes is not whether or not it's actually exculpatory, it's "Is it likely to lead to exculpatory evidence?" perhaps.
>
> Then the other thing you've got to do is to make sure the record reflects that you've disclosed it, because you're going to find yourself litigating that four years down the road, and you're going to have no proof you've told the defense that. Not just disclose it, but formally disclose it. You may want to point it out. Not just give them the document, but point out that it indicates that there was another suspect.
>
> So, you know, it's with a certain amount of experience that most good prosecutors get to the point where they see the big picture. And I understand that. Hey, number one, I don't want to convict an innocent person and, number two, I've got nothing to gain by trying to hide it, because it's going to come out sooner or later anyway. So just tell them about it and do it formally.

The implication seemed to be that most accusations of withholding exculpatory evidence made against prosecutors, especially experienced ones, are more a product of miscalculation or just a bad call on the prosecutor's part about whether the evidence was actually exculpatory in the first place. In other words, most prosecutors accused of withholding exculpatory evidence do not intentionally try to mislead; rather, they honestly believe that the evidence is not exculpatory, and that is why they do not turn it over to the defense. In some cases, prosecutors may not know that they are in possession of exculpatory evidence. They simply miss it. As one prosecutor suggested, "You have a massive case of a thousand pages of discovery, and the police said something and you didn't get it."

Another prosecutor agreed that few prosecutors intentionally withhold exculpatory evidence and provided the following example of what he believed was an honest disagreement between a prosecutor and a judge:

> I can cite you a case that happened in [named a county], where the Chief Judge overturned a conviction in a real big murder case they had based on the fact that the prosecutors did not tell the defense of a witness who called their office during

---

11. Scheck et al., op. cit., pp. 226 and 233.

the course of a trial to tell them something about who they saw in the victim's vehicle. I can't recall exactly what it was. The prosecutor in that case took the position that it wasn't exculpatory in my opinion, and I didn't think I had to disclose it. And the judge disagreed with him. Well, the judge gave the defendant a new trial, and guess what? They retried the case, and the defense never even put that witness on the stand. That's how exculpatory it was.

The prosecutor contended that, in the end, little advantage is gained by intentionally withholding exculpatory evidence:

I'm sure there are prosecutors out there who honestly make mistakes. There may be some who think they can slip it by; maybe they do. But I can tell you the [state's] district attorney's association and the National District Attorney's Association all preach to everybody that this case is going to be gone over with a fine-tooth comb. If you think you are going to get away with exculpatory evidence, you are sadly mistaken. Disclose it, and disclose it formally so you can prove later you disclosed it. And that's what we preach.

Another prosecutor responded to accusations of withholding exculpatory evidence by simply saying, "I'll go back to where you have to be cautious. Discovery—I mean, my rule is 'When in doubt, give it out.' The scary part sometimes is making sure you've got everything from the police, even if you think it's not necessarily relevant. Make sure you've got it, and give it out."

Asked whether he used the testimony of "jailhouse snitches" and, if so, whether he offered them any incentives or favors to testify, one prosecutor commented:

The answer to the first part is easy: yes I have. I wouldn't term them "jailhouse snitches." I would call them "convicted felons who had information." And to answer your question … gosh, if we talk about capital cases, I'm pretty sure that I haven't ever offered them anything. If we talk about all the cases I've ever tried, and some of the cases where we had two robbers, I may have given one a sentence to a term of years and not sought as many years against him in exchange for his testimony. But in capital cases, no.

He then was asked how he got "convicted felons who had information" to testify, since he did not offer any incentives? He backtracked somewhat in his answer:

This is from my experience. In the course of the years, we mentioned [three cases that involved child victims]. In those cases, even convicted felons will testify against them [the child killers]. Those are the cases I'm thinking of. And you know what? They hoped it would help them, I'm sure. I know that they did. They can say later in front of a clemency board or in front of the court when asking for some sort of reduction, "I assisted the state." That was their hope, but we did not give them any reduction in sentence. And I don't know if I can think of any of them that got any in the end. They're still writing letters hoping that I'll help them.

You know—wait a minute, let me think. It's hard to remember every case. I know that in the [name] case, his sister had been convicted in federal court on a drug charge, and we promised to go over and testify at her sentencing hearing about her cooperation in order to see…. We didn't give her a reduction.

The prosecutor was reminded that he did, in fact, testify on the sister's behalf. He then provided the following rationalization and admission: "It wasn't me, if it makes any difference; it was my prosecutor [another prosecutor under his supervision]. We did give her that. We promised to make it known to the judge in her federal case that she had co-operated and testified against her own brother in our first-degree murder case." Another prosecutor readily admitted, "Most jailhouse snitches are going to be looking for a deal or something."

Prosecutors then were asked what made them confident that their convicted felons with information or jailhouse snitches would testify truthfully. One prosecutor's response seems a bit naive:

> I guess using the [aforementioned] case [of the sister testifying against her brother] as an example, I was impressed with the fact that she would testify against her own brother and thereby contribute to him being convicted of first-degree murder. I find that difficult to believe that if that were false, she wouldn't be able to do it. My experience has been that most folks in the criminal element are not going to voluntarily testify against a fellow felon, so to speak. They have to have some reason to do it. That reason could be that the crime committed was so horrible, like a child murder, and we've had those.
>
> In that particular case, she later recanted her testimony and claimed it was all a lie. But I was convinced that I couldn't understand anybody going against their own brother and making up a lie and saying, "He told me he committed a murder," and just lie about that. Other cases, sometimes we've done polygraphs to try and see. A lot of times, it's a comparison of the facts they provide with the other facts of the case. Checking whether or not they had the ability to know what they know, and checking whether or not they could have found it from another source, whether or not what they tell us is consistent with all the other evidence. And weighing all that along with whether or not we're giving him much.

Another prosecutor gave this example from one of her cases, "Two weeks prior to trial, a jailhouse snitch came forward with statements. He [the defendant] ended up pleading guilty and taking life imprisonment. Obviously, he did talk to the guy." She clearly believes that the defendant's pleading guilty is evidence of the informant's talking to the defendant and having incriminating evidence against him. However, even if that were the case, that did not guarantee that the informant would testify truthfully. The prosecutor then said, "With jailhouse snitches, obviously, you need to be cautious and make sure that their information supports it. You've got to have more than just that."

She admitted that she had not used any jailhouse snitches in a capital trial but said she wouldn't rule it out. When asked whether she offered incentives to any of her snitches, she hedged in her reply:

> Nope. The former detective who I had cases with, he came forward in the beginning, because there was a threat against me from the defendant. So, no, he hasn't been offered anything. One of them shows up in a lot of cases. He finished his time. He got a benefit from the last case he's involved with. It's a continuing favor to me, I guess. In that particular case, I have an interesting list of them [snitches]. One is probably going to get some assistance in his sentence. But I don't drop charges. I don't offer immunity. The best that's going to happen is a reduction of a sentence.

Apparently, at least to this prosecutor, a sentence reduction does not qualify as an incentive to testify. Asked if she would move a snitch to a different prison (another incentive to testify), she admitted that she had and was planning to do it again: "My codefendant who testified in this case, when he goes to prison, I'm going to request he's in a prison near his family." She added, "Most people that have been labeled as snitches normally are in protective custody anyway. There's certain prisons around the state that accommodate them."

At least for this prosecutor, then, there is ambiguity about what constitutes an incentive to testify. However, having established that she does, in fact, provide incentives to testify (though she may not admit to it), she described how the "incentive" to move a snitch to a different prison worked: "I can request that they [snitches] be put in one of the specific prisons." Prison inspectors, who, she explained, "investigate crimes in prison," have the authority to transfer inmates to other prisons. In her jurisdiction, the local prison inspectors were two former city police detectives. In fact, she was first told about her snitch's information by one of the prison inspectors, who got the information from another prison inspector, who got it from one of his own "professional" snitches, who happened to be her snitch's roommate. As for the incentive, she was having a conversation with one of the prison inspectors: "I said, 'You know, I have this kid that I would like to be put in a prison near his family.' His family has been very helpful in getting him to tell the truth and being very supportive of him even though he did something terribly wrong. I mean, this kid has been sitting in jail for three years now and won't be sentenced until he's testified." The prison inspector agreed to accommodate her.

As noted previously, prosecutors have been accused of refusing to release DNA evidence to post-conviction defense attorneys attempting to establish their clients' innocence. One prosecutor claimed that she could not refuse to release DNA evidence to a postconviction defense attorney, and, she noted, "We had a huge flurry of DNA postconviction work, but that's done by some other guys in my office." Asked whether they have denied giving DNA evidence to postconviction defense attorneys, she responded, "There has to be an evidentiary hearing … I think that they have contested cases that DNA is not going to prove what they say it's going to prove. I'm sure they've contested that."

Another prosecutor was more circumspect: "I'm sure that I have opposed that [giving DNA evidence to postconviction defense attorneys]." Asked why, he replied, "Because the prospective results of DNA testing would not establish innocence." But if that were the case, why would it matter? "Well," he explained,

> because there are finite resources to do DNA work and to litigate all those issues that come up. Someone wants to test and find out whose DNA is on an object. Is that going to make a difference in a case? If not, I oppose it. But you can argue it'll prove his innocence. And if the judge thinks it will, I think most of the judges are very willing to order it. If they think there's any possibility, most of the judges are going to do that. At least the ones I've been in front of. Sometimes, in my mind, it's just not going to do it; it's not going to establish innocence.

Even when the defense pays for the DNA testing, the prosecution incurs additional expenses. "If they're going to do that [test DNA]," the prosecutor said, "I'm going to have to invest the time and oppose their expert. I might have to get my own expert. I'm going to have to develop the context of the evidence and put forth witnesses to testify and salvage why it makes no difference. And we're going to do a lot of litigation and spend a lot of time on something that doesn't matter."

For him and other prosecutors, there has to be closure at some point. "Cases need to end at some point in time," he says. "Ya know? And I can understand, when there's a real issue, it can't end. But sometimes there's really no issue, even with DNA."

Racial Discrimination

One of the enduring claims about the death penalty in the United States is that it has been, and continues to be, employed in a racially discriminatory manner. Most discussions of racial discrimination and the death penalty have focused on the offender's race, and an impressive body of evidence shows that blacks are charged, convicted, sentenced to death, and executed in numbers far greater than their proportion of the population. Critics contend that the studies that have found racial discrimination simply show a racial disparity in the administration of the death penalty and not racial discrimination. They argue that the reason blacks are charged, convicted, sentenced to death, and executed disproportionately is that blacks commit capital crimes in disproportionately greater numbers.

The emphasis in recent years has been on a less obvious form of racial discrimination: victim-based racial discrimination. Whether the death penalty is imposed continues to depend on the victim's race. Evidence shows that since the restoration of the death penalty in 1976, nearly 80 percent of the more than 1,300 people executed have been convicted of killing a white victim, even though blacks and whites are murder victims in nearly equal numbers. Death penalty critics contend that the reason for this anomaly is that white life is valued over black life in American society.

Research shows that the primary source of victim-based racial discrimination in the administration of the death penalty is the discretionary behavior of prosecutors (and, to a lesser extent, juries). The prosecutors interviewed for this chapter were asked about the prosecutor's role, if any, in the racial disparity or discrimination, especially when it is victim-based. Not revisited here are their reasons for charging a suspect with a capital crime, which are relevant but were addressed at the beginning of this chapter. So, when asked about discrimination, one prosecutor was coy and said that she could comment only on her own cases: "My own cases don't fall that way.... My last four cases: black on black, white on white, white on white, West Indian on West Indian.... Those [last] two people were sometimes categorized as white, sometimes as black. So it's really hard for me to say that [there was discrimination]." When asked what happened in the black-on-black case, she replied, "It came back death."

When another prosecutor was asked whether he had any ideas about the evidence of victim-based racial discrimination, he responded, "Nope. I've done no empirical studies." He then was asked to describe his own sense about it, based on his own experience:

> I think I've seen a number of cases where we felt like we couldn't seek the death penalty even though it was a first-degree murder and the victim was black. I can offer explanations as to why we did it in those cases, and why we might do that in some of the cases that are white. In one of our lectures on the death penalty, one of my favorite state attorneys lectured, and he [explained] how to determine whether to seek the death penalty by the "vowel system."
>
> He assigned every vowel a description. So it was AEIOU right? *I* stood for *innocent victim*, all right? So if I have a victim like a 7-year-old child who's just completely innocent, and a defendant has murdered her, there's a component there that a jury is likely to want to give someone the death penalty for that. And, in fact, of course, it's been set forth in a statute that a child under 12, that is, in fact, an aggravating circumstance. If, on the other hand, the victim is a grown adult male, and that victim has a lengthy criminal history, and the

defense is going to make out — they may not be able to make out self-defense, but they're going to get to present evidence that he knew this guy's terrible reputation — that he was a thug, and he beat people up, and shot people. And he shot him in self-defense. It may all be a lie, but it's all coming in. It may not be a reason, but it'll come in. And the jury is going to see this as a horrible guy. How motivated are they going to be to impose the death penalty? Well, those kinds of issues come into play. Whether or not because of that empirical data arises, I don't know.

For this prosecutor, then, if the victim is unsympathetic, he may not be worth the state's expending resources on a capital trial. Asked whether that was accurate, he said, "Well it can make the difference if everything else is equal."

Picking Jurors

Prosecutors were queried about whether they routinely attempt to eliminate certain types of potential jurors during voir dire. One prosecutor remarked:

> You're looking for your standard state juror that can impose the death penalty. Obviously, you're going to lose the ones that impose death on everything. I look to eliminate the ones that maybe can be death qualified, but I get the feeling they're very soft on it, because I think they're going to hurt me in the guilt and penalty phase. My personal belief: one of the reasons I had a hung jury.

She was asked whether she would attempt to eliminate black jurors and women because they are less likely to impose the death penalty. "I'm looking to get a mixture," she said. "I think some of the old profiling and stereotypes have changed a lot.... Just the standard things: family all involved in the criminal justice system.... When I say involved in criminal justice, if you've got several family members that have prior arrests and bad feelings about law enforcement or something, they might be someone you're looking to get rid of."

When another prosecutor was asked whether he attempted to eliminate certain types of jurors, he answered quickly, "Yes, I do." When asked what type of potential juror he attempted to eliminate, he said, "I do not want somebody who I think is extremely liberal and opposed to the death penalty. Just like the defense doesn't want anybody who they think believes that the death penalty is something that ought to be imposed in every murder case." It was pointed out that death penalty opponents are excused for cause. To which he responded:

> If they say I would not impose the death penalty in any circumstance. Now they may say, I don't like the death penalty, and it should only be imposed on the most horrible of cases. Now, the jury selection is a situation where, if you looked at it brutally honestly, we get a fair jury because each side tries to eliminate jurors who they think won't be fair to their side, and they also try to get jurors who may be receptive to their side of the case. And that's what we try to do. The other kind of juror that I will try to eliminate is someone who I don't think has enough character or strength of will to really sit in judgment of someone and say, "You have committed this offense and you deserve the death penalty for it." I'm not saying I want someone who will always say that. But I want somebody who can say that if it's called for.

Asked whether there were any other types of people he would try to eliminate from a jury, he mentioned:

> I'd say we all look at our cases and we try to figure out how to learn things. A case involved a 14-year-old girl who was killed and the body was lost. In that case, the defense thought it would be best to have women in that case. They thought women would be less likely to impose death. We ended up with eleven women and one man. I tried to get more men because, at that time, I thought, generally speaking, men are more likely to be strong enough to say death.... We ended up with a 12-0 recommendation for death. That taught me something.

Interestingly, in his discussion of selecting jurors, this prosecutor never mentioned race.

Physical and Emotional Effects

One of the goals of this book was to discover how participation in the capital punishment process affects the participants physically and emotionally. That issue was posed to the prosecutors. One prosecutor had this to say:

> Well, the normal thing, of course, is that it's a lot of work and a lot of pressure. You've got a case where the family is looking to you to find some justice for them. Law enforcement is looking to you to do that. You're up against, usually, the best defense attorneys. You've got complex issues to deal with and a lot of facts to organize. Those happen in cases, and I think you'd expect that to be a part of it.
>
> And it affects you, and there's a certain amount of stress that goes with that. But the other side of it is, if you handle, let's say, the run-of-the-mill cases, there's a lot more, in my mind, gray areas. Should I convict this poor guy of burglary of a dwelling, which carries a mandatory minimum sentence? Or should I just charge, or perhaps take a plea to burglary of a structure, so that he doesn't score [receive a mandatory minimum sentence]? This kid who did this, and it's his first or second offense. He's got all this stuff going on in his life. Should I give him a break or not?
>
> When you're handling a death penalty case, you should be able to say in your mind, this guy doesn't deserve a right. This guy's done something horrible. And this guy does deserve the death penalty. And it becomes a little more black-and-white. You get a lot of positive feedback because you know you're doing something that truly matters to a lot of people. Not just family and not just law enforcement but the community as a whole, because you're taking a murderer off the streets. To some extent, you're making an example of them.
>
> There's a wonderful quote that I found by this fellow named Jeff Jacoby, up at the *Boston Globe*, who is an advocate of the death penalty. He said this: "When a vicious killer is sent to the electric chair or strapped on a gurney for a lethal injection, society is condemning his crime with a seriousness and intensity that no other punishment achieves. By contrast, a society that sentences killers to nothing worse than prison, no matter how depraved the killing or how innocent

the victim, is a society that really doesn't think murder is so terrible." What you see is this: people who commit armed robbery can get life in prison, and people who commit a second-degree murder can get life in prison and do. People who commit a crime like [a high-profile murderer] deserve something worse than what those people get. That's the argument. And I believe that.

Asked whether he ever second-guessed himself, he said, "Not in the cases that I've obtained the death penalty in." When queried whether he ever lost sleep, he asked, "Worrying about whether I've convicted an innocent person, and whether or not this person deserves the death penalty? Not over that." Since he has been a prosecutor, he estimates having handled about 30 first-degree murder cases.

He was asked how his capital cases affected him physically. He replied:

> I'm 58. I guess I've been fortunate in that it's not a day-to-day thing anymore.... I've done four first-degree murders since I've been over here [the prosecutor's office in which he currently works]. So, I haven't been under the gun day in, day out. There's been some relief. So perhaps that explains it. The other thing is, I try to get my mind off of it. I play tennis. I work out. I ride my bike. I like to do things that are an outlet other than worrying about cases.

When told that a public defender who did a lot of capital cases said he lost ten or fifteen pounds and some sleep during a capital case as a result of working out to increase his stamina, this prosecutor noted that he lost some sleep in that way, too. He added, "But I don't think it rises to the level of being a medical problem. I will lose weight in a medical trial, and I will lose weight in a weeklong trial. I won't lose ten or fifteen pounds. I'm only lucky enough to lose five pounds." When told another defense attorney believed that a capital case is the best weight loss program of which she knew, he responded:

> Well I think it is. There's stress and a lot of energy is burnt. And I wanted to go back to your question about losing sleep over cases. The reason I say [I do not] is because in all of my cases I've sought the death penalty and obtained the death penalty in, to me, they were pretty clear. Ya know? Is that because I became an advocate in the course of it all? I mean I don't know. I can certainly see that there were other cases that had come in the office, that, from the get go, I said, "I don't know if the death penalty is appropriate." If those had been my cases, I think it would have bothered me.

That brought up the question of whether he intentionally erred to the side of not seeking the death penalty in those middle-range cases, in which the evidence is not clear-cut or the aggravators are not clear-cut? In his reply, not all of his examples seemed to support his point:

> Well, I think so. I think it's a general rule. I have a case where the defendant's sister came and recanted. In that particular case, that was not a real strong case, and we offered him a plea to second-degree murder, just like I did [in another case]. Second-degree murder is a term of years. Now is it my fault [that he did not take the deal]? No, it's not my fault. That was the closest case on the facts that I can think of other than the dog scent case. That was a tough case. That was the one where the jury found him not guilty. And then this other case, the guy got the death penalty overturned eventually during post-conviction, but he's still serving his life sentence.

He then was asked directly: Do you think you reserve the death penalty for the "worst of the worst?" He claimed:

That is what we do. I mean if there's not at least one aggravating circumstance, don't even talk about it, other than to say there's not an aggravating circumstance. If there's one, you're probably not going to seek the death penalty on just one. Now, if it's heinous, atrocious, and cruel, and you have a really innocent victim ... you might give it a shot. I'm just saying I wouldn't rule that out. It's such an important thing. If you intentionally, tortuously kill somebody, I'm extremely offended by that. I can emotionally get the jurors to try and convict that person and give them the death penalty on that one aggravator. I feel that if they are that inhumane to another person and murder them, I don't have any sympathy for them. That's the bottom line.

Another prosecutor also was asked how handling capital cases affected her physically and emotionally. She said, "It's a very weighing thing to do. And you have to know a life is at stake. It's not like you get a death recommendation and walk out of the courtroom and go, 'Yee-hah!' Listening to a judge sentence someone to die: it's very sad. The bottom line is the victim is not coming back. And the victim' family is never going to have that feeling they think they're going to have."

She was asked whether she ever felt any empathy or sympathy for the defendants? She conceded, "In my first death penalty case, I did. The defendant had a true level of mental illness. The night before he did this, he was having a conversation with his jacket at the bar. I think he had a conversation with it around the time he was arrested." She then was queried whether he received the death penalty, even though he was insane. She answered, "Yes. There are a lot of people that are mentally ill that aren't insane. He broke into this young girl's house. He was staying in a halfway house right by her house. He broke in there and raped her every way imaginable and strangled her. So, I think that was kind of hard. Although he did kind of threaten to come back from the grave and kill me after he received the death penalty."

She provided another example of a defendant for which she had sympathy:

I had a guy a year ago that raises the whole question: is there truly a bad seed? Can people be born messed up? Or can your mom mess you up by the time you're three, because he started burning down his house at three? He spent a lot of his youth in the Connecticut system and had burned down a few of the places he'd been. Doesn't hate me. [Prosecutor's name] "I have nothing against you even though you're trying to kill me." Leaving the courtroom, "bye [prosecutor's name]." [The defendant] knows he can't be out in society. The day he was sentenced to die, he told the judge, at least maybe the victim got some justice.... That's the first time he's shown any remorse. He made the stupid mistake of testifying on his own behalf when trying to kill this woman five different ways. His parents were alcoholics and drug [addicts].... Even when they bring him home from these facilities, the house is really tense. I don't think he ever had a chance.

As noted above, she admitted that defendants had threatened her. Asked how she coped with that, she advised, "You just can't think about it. You practice certain safety measures, but you can't think about it. The reality is that defense attorneys are more in peril than a prosecutor.... [However,] I won't say there haven't been prosecutors killed.... There was a time I had [to be looking over my shoulder]. I was transported to and from work [because of a case]. But on a day-to-day basis, you don't live in fear."

She also was asked how handling a capital case affected her physically. To which she said, "Obviously you're really, really tired." She was asked about her eating habits during a capital trial. She said, "Well, I normally bring my own lunch during any trial." Asked if she ate junk food during a capital trial, she stated, "Nah. I work with another prosecutor. We basically try taking care of each other. You still make the efforts to try to eat healthy." What about exercise, she was queried. She replied, "You try to get some exercise in. Obviously, the last case I got sick in the middle of it, so that didn't really work. But you still try to get some in to get the stress level down."

She mentioned that she was married to another prosecutor. She was asked whether they "talked shop?" She noted, "We both prosecute murder cases. We've tried some together." Asked whether that was a good thing, she had this to say:

> You're with someone who truly understands what you're going through. I mean, bless his heart, he took me out to dinner even though he was in trial himself. That's kind of the standard thing to do for us. He has a son that we have part-time. So, you know, there are times where your life is devoted to the family and kids. My parents get more what we do than, I would say, his parents. That sometimes frustrates him. We can go over to my parents on Sunday night, and my dad's like, "Why'd they come? It looks like they need sleep." And my mom says, "Well, they need to eat anyway." Well, you've got someone who truly knows what you're going through. If one is in trial, the other takes care of the house and the food, so that takes care of eating more normal. If we're both busy, it's like, "Okay where are we ordering Chinese take out?" Still trying to eat healthy.

Death Penalty Opinions

The final question put to the prosecutors was whether their opinion of the death penalty had been affected by their work in prosecuting death penalty cases? One prosecutor responded, "Sure.... I think I've learned more and more about the death penalty. I've seen the law change through the years. I think that as a result of all that, I've become convinced that we have established about as good a system as you can for litigating these cases, and determining what the appropriate sentence is, and reviewing that, and determining the fact it was done appropriately." Asked whether he was a proponent of the death penalty before he went to law school, he said, "Never even thought about it. Came out of law school thinking I wanted to be a public defender. And I don't recall specifically what I thought about the death penalty at that point in my life, but I've got a feeling ... I don't really remember." After conceding that he was a death penalty proponent, he was asked when he first became one? He recalled:

> I think it was when I was spending some time as a prosecutor, and I learned that, in fact, the system did work and, in fact, unlike what my law professor had pretty much convinced me, there were not a whole lot of innocent people being [wrongly convicted]. That's what I thought coming out of law school. And I wanted to be an assistant public defender. And so, that is really what I wanted to do. I became an assistant state attorney because the opportunity arose to get in the criminal [justice] system. It's not what I wanted from the get go. My first opportunity was with the civil firm, and then the civil firm broke up.

And when they broke up, it was a great time for me to rethink what I was doing. I had met the chief assistant state attorney through litigation that our firm had with them, because we represented the county as the county attorney. And I met him, so I had a little bit of an in. So they hired me as an assistant state attorney. Somewhere in there I became a believer in the system. And at some point, after I started handling murders, I became convinced that there are times when the death penalty is appropriate.

Another prosecutor also was asked whether her prosecution of capital cases has affected her opinion of the death penalty? Her initial reply did not really answer the question: "I think the last few cases were not as tough on me as the first few cases were. I'm not sure if it's years of experience or how much … The first case I did, where I ended up being first chair … it came back life. The first one that went on death row, with the guy who had some mental illness, I think that was really hard." When pressed, she admitted that she was a death penalty proponent but added, "I think it should be used in only certain cases." Asked whether she had always been a death penalty proponent, she stated, "When I was in college, I don't know if I ever really thought about it. I don't think I thought about it until I was a prosecutor." She then was asked whether she had qualms about prosecuting capital cases at first? To which she replied, "What's good for me is that … we only seek death in the worst of the worst [cases]. I think that has made it easier." She also volunteered that she had no intention of viewing the execution of someone she had sent to death row.

Conclusion

Ray Marky, the Florida prosecutor who for years doggedly sought the execution of John Spenkelink, the second person executed during the modern death penalty era, and the first person executed despite vigorously pursuing all of his appeals, probably spoke for most prosecutors in capital cases when he told one of Spenkelink's appellate attorneys "that he didn't want us to think he was a bad guy, that he was just doing his job."[12] Immediately following Spenelink's execution, Marky realized how he likely would be remembered and how unfair it was: "I had to face the fact that somehow I'd come to epitomize the bloodthirsty prosecutor.… And I knew that wasn't me. I'd almost killed myself for the State of Florida. And I felt like, here I'm the goddamn black hat and all these people screwing with our system, they're gonna be the white hats."[13] Marky survived a heart attack later that year. He left the attorney general's office and took a less stressful job with a local prosecutor. One day he was given a death penalty case but instead of relentlessly pursuing it, as he would have done earlier in his career, he advised the victim's mother to accept a life sentence for her son's killer. He told her, "Ma'am, bury your son and get on with your life, or over the next dozen years, this defendant will destroy you, as well as your son."[14] He recalled, "I never would have said that fifteen years ago.… But now I will, because I'm not going to put someone through the nightmare."[15] He explained,

---

12. David Von Drehle (1995) *Among the Lowest of the Dead: Inside Death Row.* New York: Fawcett Crest, p. 94.
    13. Ibid., p. 106.
    14. Ibid., p. 379.
    15. Ibid.

"If we had deliberately set out to create a chaotic system, we couldn't have come up with anything worse. It's a merry-go-round, it's ridiculous; it's so clogged up only an arbitrary few ever get it."[16] By this time in his life, Marky had rejected a system that he had helped to create and worked so hard to uphold. Sizing up his long history with Florida's death penalty, he concluded, "I don't get any damn pleasure out of the death penalty and I never have.... And, frankly, if they abolished it tomorrow, I'd go get drunk in celebration."[17]

---

16. Ibid.
17. Ibid., pp. 379-80.

Chapter 3

Victims' Family Members

Imagine being notified by a homicide detective that a loved one has been brutally murdered. What could be worse?

That devastating experience is repeated thousands of times each year.

No one can blame homicide victims' surviving family members for seeking revenge in the guise of justice against their loved one's killer. In modern times, the task of obtaining vengeful justice for the grieving family falls to the prosecutor. Whether a prosecutor is able to provide that satisfaction to the grieving family by seeking the death penalty is debatable.

The public general believes that, at the least, the execution of their loved one's killer can provide the grieving family with "closure" to the ordeal, but that is a hollow promise for many victims' family members. Executions can provide legal finality to their devastating loss, but only for a few of them does it bring true closure. Having a loved one brutally murdered is a wound that never fully heals. The lives of surviving family members will be changed forever.

Ironically, for many victims' family members, the capital punishment process adds to their pain. So traumatic is their involvement with the criminal justice system that it has been referred to as "secondary victimization" and has been found to be, in many cases, more severe than the psychological trauma of the murder itself. Although a majority of victims' family members likely support capital punishment, a surprisingly large number of them do not. This chapter addresses the enduring victims of capital homicides: the victims' family members and their role in the capital punishment process. These co-victims generally are innocent and blameless. Yet, it is they who often suffer the most.

Revenge

Revenge is an age-old tradition. In primitive societies characterized by tribes and clans, it was customary and, in some cases, a sacred duty, for a murdered man's next of kin to seek revenge by killing the assailant or another member of his tribe or clan. If the next of kin refused to exercise his right and perform his duty, he would be held in contempt and ostracized by his family. This private revenge supposedly served the purpose of restraining wanton attacks and made men more careful in their ordinary relations. However, one unintended consequence of "blood revenge" was the creation of blood feuds between families that could span generations.[1]

---

1. See, for example, James R. Acker and Jeanna Marie Mastrocinque (2006) "Causing Death and Sustaining Life: The Law, Capital Punishment, and Criminal Homicide Victims' Survivors," pp. 141-

As nation-states emerged, the need to maintain social control among a diverse group of people became paramount. Thus, to maintain order, the nation-state monopolized the administration of punishment to individuals who transgressed against the state's rules. By allowing the state to seek revenge, victms' relatives were relieved of the need and duty to do so.[2]

Today, proponents of capital punishment argue that without it, victims' relatives are more likely to seek personal revenge. However, as Justice William Brennan observed in his *Furman* decision, "There is no evidence whatever that utilization of imprisonment rather than death encourages private blood feuds and other disorders."[3] During the hiatus in capital punishment in the United States between 1968 and 1977, there was no apparent increase in acts of personal revenge, nor do states without capital punishment have elevated levels of personal revenge. The 141 countries (as of 2012) that have abolished capital punishment in law or practice suffer no apparent problems either.[4] This seems proof that a need for revenge can be satisfied by an alternative punishment, such as life imprisonment.

Closure

Vindictiveness notwithstanding, victims' family members may support capital punishment for the closure it may bring to their loss. For most victims' family members, closure means "being released from their nightmare."[5] Franklin Zimring, a professor at the University of California Berkeley School of Law, maintains that in recent years, closure has replaced revenge as a primary purpose of capital punishment.[6] Zimring discovered that the term "closure" was first used by the print mass media in 1989 to describe a major objective of the death penalty.[7] This symbolic and linguistic shift in emphasis from revenge to closure, according to Professor Zimring, has been a "public relations godsend" for death penalty proponents that has transformed capital trials and executions—at least in the minds of the public—into politically palatable processes that serve the personal interests of homicide survivors.[8] He observed that the penalty stage of death penalty trials, for example, has become a "status competition" between the offender and those who were injured by the crime.[9] This shift in rhetoric has been especially important in retaining the support of people who distrust government, because for them it is much easier to support executions as a public service, such as garbage collection or street cleaning, than it is to contend with arguments that executions represent the excessive use of power by and for

---

160 in J. R. Acker and D. R. Karp (eds.) *Wounds That Do Not Bind: Victim-Based Perspectives on the Death Penalty.* Durham, NC: Carolina Academic Press.

    2. Ibid.

    3. *Furman v. Georgia* (408 U.S. 238, 1972) at 303.

    4. Amnesty International, "Abolitionist and Retentionist Countries" at www.amnesty.org/en/death-penalty/abolitionist-and-retentionist-countries (accessed August 27, 2012).

    5. Robert Jay Lifton and Greg Mitchell (2002) *Who Owns Death? Capital Punishment, the American Conscience, and the End of Executions.* New York: Perennial, p. 202.

    6. Franklin E. Zimring (2003) *The Contradictions of American Capital Punishment.* New York: Oxford University Press, pp. 57-63.

    7. Ibid., p. 58.

    8. Ibid., pp. 51-52.

    9. Ibid., p. 55.

the government.[10] As a public service, the death penalty is a private right and not a show of governmental power, which, for Professor Zimring, is consistent with the American tradition of community control of punishment and vigilante justice.[11]

Whether executions actually provide co-victims closure is a controversial issue. On one hand, a 2001 public opinion poll showed that 60 percent of Americans believed that the death penalty was fair because "it gives satisfaction and closure to the families of murder victims."[12] An Arkansas woman told a state prison board in 1997 that she did not want to watch her mother's killer be electrocuted, but she did want to be in the building "and watch the lights flicker. It would say, 'The end. It's closure.'"[13] A Texas mother awaiting the execution of her son's killer stated, "Most of my life it seems like I've been in the justice system. I can't go on with my life. I can't close that chapter until he's put to sleep. It's been twenty-two years."[14] Describing his decision to grant clemency to all Illinois death-row inmates following discussions with co-victims, Governor George Ryan said, "To a family they talked about closure.... They pleaded with me to allow the state to kill an inmate in its name to provide the families with closure."[15]

On the other hand, research on capital crime victims' families reveals that many co-victims, including some who support capital punishment, are offended by the idea that executions bring closure. For them, executions produce an outcome, but never closure.[16] As the daughter of a murder victim explained, "I get sick when death-penalty advocates self-righteously prescribe execution to treat the wounds we live with after homicide.... Those who hold out an event—execution—as the solution to pain have no understanding

---

10. Ibid., p. 62.

11. Ibid.

12. Cited in Franklin E. Zimring (2003) *The Contradictions of American Capital Punishment.* New York: Oxford University Press, p. 61.

13. Lifton and Mitchell, op. cit.

14. Ibid., p. 203.

15. Cited in Austin Sarat (2006) "Putting a Square Peg in a Round Hole; Victims, Retribution, and George Ryan's Clemency," pp. 203-232 in J. R. Acker and D. R. Karp (eds.) *Wounds That Do Not Bind: Victim-Based Perspectives on the Death Penalty.* Durham, NC: Carolina Academic Press, p. 220, n. 30.

16. On the meager research on co-victims, see James R. Acker and David R. Karp (2006) "Introduction," pp. 3-14 in J. R. Acker and D. R. Karp (eds.) *Wounds That Do Not Bind: Victim-Based Perspectives on the Death Penalty.* Durham, NC: Carolina Academic Press; Margaret Vandiver (2006) "The Death Penalty and the Families of Victims: An Overview of Research Issues," pp. 235-252 in J. R. Acker and D. R. Karp (eds.) *Wounds That Do Not Bind: Victim-Based Perspectives on the Death Penalty.* Durham, NC: Carolina Academic Press. On the issue of closure, see James R. Acker (2013) "The Myth of Closure and Capital Punishment," pp. 254-263 in R. M. Bohm and J. T. Walker (eds.) *Demystifying Crime and Criminal Justice, Second ed.* New York, NY: Oxford University Press; Roberta Roper (2006) "Finding Hope: One Family's Journey," pp. 111-125 in J. R. Acker and D. R. Karp (eds.) *Wounds That Do Not Bind: Victim-Based Perspectives on the Death Penalty.* Durham, NC: Carolina Academic Press; Stanley and Phyllis Rosenbluth (2006) "Accidental Death Is Fate, Murder Is Pure Evil," pp. 103-109 in J. R. Acker and D. R. Karp (eds.) *Wounds That Do Not Bind: Victim-Based Perspectives on the Death Penalty.* Durham, NC: Carolina Academic Press; Charisse Coleman (2006) "Matters of Life or Death," pp. 17-32 in J. R. Acker and D. R. Karp (eds.) *Wounds That Do Not Bind: Victim-Based Perspectives on the Death Penalty.* Durham, NC: Carolina Academic Press; Dan Levey (2006) "Feelings from the Heart," pp. 33-47 in J. R. Acker and D. R. Karp (eds.) *Wounds That Do Not Bind: Victim-Based Perspectives on the Death Penalty.* Durham, NC: Carolina Academic Press; Linda L. White (2006) "A Tiger by the Tail: The Mother of a Murder Victim Grapples with the Death Penalty," pp. 49-68 in J. R. Acker and D. R. Karp (eds.) *Wounds That Do Not Bind: Victim-Based Perspectives on the Death Penalty.* Durham, NC: Carolina Academic Press.

of healing. Healing is a process, not an event."[17] Similarly, the mother of a murder victim complained, "I don't know why the powers that be have come up with the word 'closure.' There is no closure, and there never, never will be."[18] Likewise, the father of a murder victim attending the execution of his child's killer, responded indignantly to a reporter's question about whether he was seeking closure: "Don't use that word with me.... I hate that word. I don't know who made that word up. There is no closure. So many people don't seem to understand that. There is no closure."[19] The parents of a murdered son and daughter-in-law believed they might be able to achieve acceptance or finality but not closure:

> Does anyone know or care to know that the favored term "closure" is so wrong and so offensive, even though it's most often used when talking about victims' families? There is no closure, nor can there ever be any. "Acceptance" or "finality" might be a better word, but that comes only after shock, fear, funerals, grieving, tears, heartbreak, police, trials, and then appeals, appeals, and appeals. It is only then that "acceptance" or "finality" begins to settle within us. However, all of the above events take place while crushed hearts are mourning the intentional death of a loved one.... You never fully heal after suffering the wounds that we have. But we've come to recognize the full weight of what those two murderers did, and this is the acceptance or finality.[20]

The father of a woman killed in the 1995 bombing of the Alfred P. Murrah Federal Building in Oklahoma City described his reaction to his loss, and why bomber Timothy McVeigh's execution six years later did not bring him closure:

> For many months after the bombing I could have killed Timothy McVeigh myself. Temporary insanity is real, and I have lived it. You can't think of enough adjectives to describe the rage, revenge, and hate I felt. But after time, I was able to examine my conscience, and I realized that if McVeigh was [sic] put to death, it wouldn't help me in the healing process. People talk about executions bringing closure. But how can there be closure when my little girl is never coming back? I finally realized that the death penalty is all about revenge and hate, and revenge and hate are why Julie Marie and 167 others are dead.[21]

A mother whose daughter was murdered described the "myth" and "empty promise" of closure and what homicide survivors really need — healing:

> While many people have swallowed the myth of closure, most of us know that there is no real closure — it is an empty promise. And there is nothing that the state can do to bring about what homicide survivors really need — healing — for healing is an inside job. It takes a long time, and it takes a lot of work on the part of the survivors. Certainly, the manner in which the state treats victims can either promote or inhibit the healing that is so badly needed, but the healing

---

17. Cited in Levey, ibid., p. 44.
18. Cited in Carroll Ann Ellis, Karin Ho, and Anne Seymour (2006) "The Impact of the Death Penalty on Crime Victims and Those Who Serve Them," pp. 431-444 in J. R. Acker and D. R. Karp (eds.) *Wounds That Do Not Bind: Victim-Based Perspectives on the Death Penalty.* Durham, NC: Carolina Academic Press, p. 436.
19. Lifton and Mitchell, op. cit., p. 204.
20. Stanley and Phyllis Rosenbluth, op. cit., p. 107.
21. Cited in Levey, op. cit., p. 38.

itself is a product of the active engagement with the grief process by the victims themselves.[22]

Research on co-victims emphasizes their immense suffering and loss, although the parents of the murdered son and daughter-in-law rejected the term "loss," just as they rejected the term "closure":

> And while talking about foolish words, too many doctors, lawyers, police department personnel, clergy, psychologists, and victim service people are quick to tell us they are sorry for our "loss." We did not "lose" our beautiful children. We have "lost" gloves, our way on a road trip, a bet, and our place in a novel; but our children were taken from us. They were murdered, not "lost." How wonderful if we could go to the Lost and Found department somewhere and find our children. How ideal that would be.[23]

Research on Co-Victims

Professor Margaret Vandiver of the University of Memphis Department of Criminology and Criminal Justice summarizes some of the results of the research on co-victims:

- The loss of a close relative to homicide is a shatteringly traumatic event. The pain, disruption, and trauma caused by homicide cannot be overstated.

- The trauma and difficulty of adjusting to loss due to homicide is such that survivors often experience post-traumatic stress disorder-like symptoms. Many survivors report losing their sense that there is any justice or safety in the world; many feel that life itself has lost all meaning.

- Survivors can expect to encounter difficulties in many other areas of their lives, including their marriages, relationships with children, friendships, and work.

- The experience of bereavement moves through several stages, including denial, anger, grief, and ultimately, resolution. These stages are necessarily distinct and do not always occur in the same sequence.

- The process of recovery takes years, if not decades. Expectations of quick grieving and recovery are unrealistic and damaging. Even after survivors resolve their grief, it is unlikely that their emotional lives will ever be the same as before the crime.

- Survivors often are not helped, and sometimes are further victimized, by the criminal justice system. Both formal and informal supports for homicide victims' survivors are dreadfully inadequate.

- The experience of isolation is very common — at the time they most need contact and support, families often feel the most isolated. The opposite situation of intrusion is often a problem as well, with unwelcome contacts from the criminal justice system, the media, and curiosity seekers.

---

22. White, op. cit., p. 65.
23. Stanley and Phyllis Rosenbluth, op. cit., p. 107.

- There seems to be much potential for advancing the process of healing through nonjudgmental, ongoing, emotionally involved listening, without suggestions as to how the survivors should feel or what they should do.[24]

Related to the last point, the sister of a murder victim explained how she and other murder victims' family members often are pulled in two opposing directions:

> Most often, we are expected to keep our sense of injury and rage whipped into a constant call for retribution (putting many families who do not seek the execution of their loved one's killer "in the wrong"), as if the only decent way to honor loss is to take another life, to create more brokenhearted families, more fatherless children … and to further assault communities already ravaged by violence, poverty, racism, and other problems. The pressure on victims' families to demand this dubious and macabre tribute to their loved ones can be tremendous, and not least of all from some of the victims' rights groups themselves.[25]

She continued:

> The other extreme, of course, is the pressure to eradicate any strong feelings as quickly as possible. Our cultural fixation with looking on the bright side, and sugaring up the bitter acid in all the lemons life sends our way, verges on hysterical, if not outright pathological. Grieving families are leaned on in ways small and large, subtle and overt, to hurry up and *get better*. We are often coerced — smoothly, and under the guise of concern — by friends, family, clergy, even support groups, to quickly turn the rage and devastation we feel into forgiveness. What would happen if we changed our message to families shattered by violence from: "Here, let us help you get over this," to: "We are here with you. We offer our presence for the duration of your pain and anger. We honor the strength and truth of those feelings. We are here to help to keep you from losing yourself in sorrow, and we will be here when you are able to step more fully into yourself as the weight of sorrow begins to lift."[26]

Opposing the Death Penalty

As the murder victim's sister alluded to above, some family members do not want their relative's killer executed. Among their reasons are:

- a general opposition to the death penalty;
- a belief that an execution would diminish or belittle the memory of their relative;

---

24. Margaret Vandiver (2003) "The Impact of the Death Penalty on the Families of Homicide Victims and of Condemned Prisoners," pp. 613-645 in J. R. Acker, R. M. Bohm, and C. S. Lanier (eds.) *America's Experiment with Capital Punishment: Reflections on the Past, Present and Future of the Ultimate Penal Sanction*. Durham, NC: Carolina Academic Press, pp. 616-617.

25. Coleman, op. cit., p. 20.

26. Ibid.

- a desire to avoid the prolonged contact with the criminal justice system that the death penalty requires;

- a desire to avoid the public attention an impending execution bestows on the condemned prisoner;

- a preference for the finality of a sentence of life imprisonment without the possibility of parole and the obscurity into which the defendant will quickly fall, over the continued uncertainty and publicity of the death penalty;

- a desire for the offender to have a long time to reflect on his or her deed, and perhaps to feel remorse for it;

- a hope that someday there can be some sort of mediation or reconciliation between the family and the offender;

- and if the offender is a relative, for obvious reasons.[27]

Another reason co-victims do not want their relative's murderer executed is that they do not want the murderer to "win." As the daughter of a murder victim explained, "If we let murderers turn us to murder, we give them too much power. They succeed in bringing us to their way of thinking and acting, and we become what we say we abhor."[28]

Revenge as Justice

Still, plenty of co-victims simply want revenge, often cloaked in the guise of justice. For example, an Ohio mother, who waited fifteen years for the murderer of her two daughters to die, admitted she would have "no problem injecting him myself. I could lie down and have a good night's sleep knowing that justice had been done."[29] The brother of a young black man, who had been beaten, stabbed, and strangled by a white racist attended the execution of his brother's killer in Alabama in 1997. He left the execution feeling that justice had not been done. He said, "I would rather have had [him] in a ring one-on-one for fifteen rounds … and whipped him the way he whipped my brother."[30] The father of a young man killed in Boston bemoaned the fact that Massachusetts did not have the death penalty. He stated, "I'd be the first one to pull the switch. I'm sorry. Some may disagree with me, that's perfectly your right. But I've lost a son I can't replace."[31] The widow of a doctor killed in New York in 1998, asserted, "If I have anything to say about it, I'll give him the lethal injection myself."[32] One of her sons believed that execution was too good for the killer and wanted him "tortured."[33]

---

27. Ibid., pp. 635-636.
28. Cited in Levey, op. cit., p. 44.
29. Lifton and Mitchell, op. cit., p. 199.
30. Ibid.
31. Ibid.
32. Ibid.
33. Ibid.

Grieving

Research has found that "grieving the loss of a loved one to homicide is one of the most difficult bereavement experiences."[34] As the widow of a murdered husband related, "You work hard the first year trying to recover, then the second arrives and you realize that with grieving there is no accomplishment; things will never change, nor will they ever again be the same. There is no reward. There's nothing at the end. Your loss is permanent."[35] When the victim is a child, the effect on parents has been described as "devastating," "a pain like no other," and "as an event that has incomprehensible, lasting changes on the family."[36] The same is often true for children when the victim is a parent. In a victim-impact statement, a father described the reaction of his young daughter who witnessed her mother's murder:

> My daughter was 22 months old the day she witnessed her mother's murder. Last month she celebrated her fourth birthday, the third one without her mother.... Beginning two days after her mother's burial and for the following week thereafter, Maureen's behavior became so erratic that it was virtually impossible to parent her. She would not eat, and although she had been weaned from her bottle more than four months before, she became reattached to it.... She would not sleep or nap until she was totally exhausted, and then she would constantly lie awake crying for her mother. She would cry hysterically for long periods of time, and no amount of holding or rocking soothed her. One of these jaunts lasted for four and a half hours.... It was 14 months after her mother's death until she would sleep again through the night. She would awaken from three to five times per night screaming, "No, no. Mommy, Mommy." From time to time, she still has nightmares with similar intensity, and to this day, she refuses to go to sleep without a light on.... For almost eight months after her mother's murder, Maureen would make stabbing motions to her chest while simultaneously saying, "Ug, ug, ug." ... Also for approximately eight months after witnessing her mother's murder, Maureen would poke at your eyes and attempt to choke you while you were holding her. When doing so, she would contort her face and make noises like a growling dog. Even now she refuses to wear constrictive clothing around her neck.... On every birthday and holiday, she notes her mother's absence. This last Christmas while visiting my mother-in-law in upstate New York, we were singing Christmas carols together when I noticed Maureen had become silent. Her shoulders were slumped. Her head hung down with her chin on her chest, and she sobbed, "I miss Mommy."[37]

---

34. Mark D. Reed and Brenda Sims Blackwell (2006) "Secondary Victimization Among Families of Homicide Victims: The Impact of the Justice Process on Co-Victims' Psychological Adjustment and Service Utilization," pp. 253-273 in J. R. Acker and D. R. Karp (eds.) *Wounds That Do Not Bind: Victim-Based Perspectives on the Death Penalty*. Durham, NC: Carolina Academic Press, p. 262.

35. Cited in Vandiver, op. cit., p. 624.

36. Shirley A. Murphy, Tom Braun, Linda Tillery, Kevin C. Cain, L. Clark Johnson, and Randal D. Beaton (1999) "PTSD Among Bereaved Parents Following the Violent Deaths of Their 12- to 28-Year Old Children: A Longitudinal Prospective Analysis." *Journal of Traumatic Stress* 12:273-291.

37. Vandiver (2003), op. cit., pp. 632-633.

Fear, Blame, Guilt, and Dashed Hopes

Whether the victim is a child, parent, or other close relative, homicide co-victims have been found to "experience greater horror, rage, desire for revenge, and fear than survivors experiencing bereavement when death results from other causes."[38] Regarding fear, one co-victim noted, "So if someone leaves and they don't come back at a certain time or I don't hear from them, then I worry myself sick.... I love them so much and I don't want to lose them and I'm always scared of that."[39] Some co-victims fear going out, even to church or the local store, and become reclusive.[40] This is particularly true when the murderer has not been caught. As the father of a murder victim explained:

> The cops say the fellow who shot [my son] was about twenty and sort of Scandinavian looking. I walk down the street and find myself hating every twenty-year-old I meet. If he's blond and tall, I want to strangle him — some guy who's probably totally innocent. Then, too, I get scared. Maybe the guy who killed [my son] will read about us in the papers. Maybe he'll come to where we live and shoot my other children. I wake up at night and am afraid for my family. We live in a constant fog of fear.[41]

Homicide co-victims also are more likely than survivors of other kinds of death to feel ashamed, vulnerable, powerless, and isolated if their loved one had been murdered in a stigmatizing circumstance, involving, for example, drug use or domestic violence.[42] Blame is sometimes directed at co-victims — or they blame themselves — for failing to control the behavior that led to the death.[43] Co-victims also may feel guilty that they survived or that they were unable to help their loved one, even though they were not present at the time.[44]

The consequences for the co-victims of the sudden, traumatic, and often violent death of a loved one can be even more complex and far reaching. Hope and dreams of a future life with the victim are dashed. A victim's death also precludes the possibility of resolving past disagreements or angry feelings that might have been resolved with the passage of time.

Intrapersonally, co-victims may experience a loss of personal control and independence; they may conclude the world is malevolent, meaningless, and incomprehensible; they may question their faith or religion; they may feel changed; they may become depressed; they may experience anxiety disorders (including panic and phobic reactions); they may be unable to work while attending legal proceedings, which might result in loss of income or employment. Years later, co-victims may experience flashbacks, have trouble sleeping, and, when able to fall asleep, awaken with panic symptoms and nightmares. Some co-victims have been diagnosed with post-traumatic stress disorder. Other co-victims abuse

---

38. Murphy et al., op. cit.
39. Cited in M. Regina Asaro (2001) "Working with Adult Homicide Survivors, Part I: Impact and Sequelae of Murder." *Perspectives in Psychiatric Care* 37:95-101.
40. Ibid.
41. Cited in Vandiver, op. cit., p. 619.
42. Reed and Blackwell, op. cit.; also see Carroll Ann Ellis, Karin Ho and Anne Seymour (2006) "The Impact of the Death Penalty on Crime Victims and Those Who Serve Them," pp. 431-444 in J. R. Acker and D. R. Karp (eds.) *Wounds That Do Not Bind: Victim-Based Perspectives on the Death Penalty.* Durham, NC: Carolina Academic Press, p. 433.
43. Ellis et al., ibid.
44. Asaro, op. cit.

or become dependent on drugs and alcohol. Interpersonally, family structures may be jeopardized because of the stress the murder puts on the family. This is especially true when the killer and the victim were related or in a relationship and family members take sides with one or the other. Family members also may feel isolated because of a loss of standing or other social support. Extrapersonally, co-victims can be impoverished because of loss of the victim's income or because of catastrophic medical bills incurred in an attempt to save the victim's life. Such changes in co-victims' financial status could result in the loss of their home or other possessions and a diminution of lifestyle.[45]

Surviving Siblings

One important, but relatively unstudied, subset of co-victims is the young siblings of murder victims. The bereaved siblings who have been studied have exhibited depression, post-traumatic stress disorder, and anxiety disorders. They have also evidenced symptoms of unresolved grief: "missing the dead sibling immensely; sadness and anger; trying not to think about the murder and avoiding reminders of the sibling; a sense of unreality; feeling the murder was just a bad dream; and finding the loss harder to deal with and get over than they had expected."[46]

Many surviving siblings find themselves experiencing contradictory thoughts. On one hand, they try not to think about the murder and to avoid reminders of it. On the other hand, they have intrusive memories about the murder, especially about the physical pain and fear their sibling might have experienced.[47] A fourteen-year-old boy who had refused to attend his brother's funeral commented that he felt "all jammed up like that," adding, "I try not to think about it [the murder]. It's only sunk in a little bit that he is dead. I like to think he's gone away to school."[48]

Avoiding reminders of the traumatic incident is difficult because there are so many triggering stimuli: holidays, birthdays, news stories, even the murder scene, which is oftentimes located nearby.[49] Because of the terrible memories the murder scene is likely to evoke, many families would like to move following the murder but are unable to do so because of long waiting lists for subsidized or affordable housing.[50]

Attempting not to think about their sibling's death precludes surviving siblings from talking to family and friends about it, prolonging the grief process. Some siblings cannot even allow themselves pleasant recollections of their dead sibling. One teenage sister gave away all of her necklaces because her murdered brother had worn them: "I don't like to touch things he wore. I'll just buy everything new."[51] An eighteen-year-old sibling remarked, "I'm not in a mourning phase because I can't accept it [the murder]."[52]

---

45. Ibid.; also see Murphy et al., op. cit.
46. Linda N. Freeman, David Shaffer, and Helen Smith (1996) "Neglected Victims of Homicide: The Needs of Young Siblings of Murder Victims." *American Journal of Orthopsychiatry* 66:337-345, p 340.
47. Ibid.
48. Ibid.
49. Ibid., p. 341
50. Ibid.
51. Ibid., pp. 340-341.
52. Ibid., p. 341.

Many siblings are so concerned about their parents' suffering that they are afraid to express their own grief and anxiety to them. A fourteen-year-old explained that her mother was "already too sad and worried," so "I just tell her, I'm O.K."[53] Some siblings report that their mothers are less attentive to them and monitor their activities less. One fourteen-year-old's mother was so depressed after his brother's murder she began to abuse alcohol. "I hang outside more … to keep away from how she acts," he said. "She worries a lot about me, but she don't bother me about going out."[54]

Many siblings of murder victims have problems with their peers. Schoolmates often are intrusive. They would talk about the murdered sibling "as if they knew him," even though they only knew about him from the media, or they would repeat news stories, with which the surviving sibling would disagree, about how the murdered sibling had been involved in crime.[55] Some surviving siblings would avoid peers who they suspected might have been involved in the homicide. As one teenager remarked, "You don't know. They might act nice to you, but they might have been one of them."[56] Other surviving siblings feel obligated to seek revenge and are encouraged to do so by their peers.[57] Until the killer is arrested, many siblings experience debilitating anxiety because they fear becoming another victim. Few murder victims' siblings receive the mental health care they need.[58]

Frustration with the Criminal Justice System

One common theme among murder victims' family members is frustration with the criminal justice system. So traumatic is the involvement of many co-victims with the criminal justice system that it has been referred to as "secondary victimization" and, as noted, has been found to be, in many cases, more severe than the psychological trauma of the murder itself.[59] Typical are the feelings of a wife whose husband was brutally murdered:

> How naïve I was to think that it would all be over after two appeals. There were years of appeals, requests for clemency, and struggles against appeals-court judges whose desire to abolish the death penalty overruled their responsibility as officers of the court to uphold the law.… *Why* did it take nineteen years to have that [death] sentence carried out? I have come to understand that the rights of those who do violence in this country are much greater than any survivor, and I hope people will understand that this serves to revictimize victims over and over again.[60]

A son whose father was murdered wondered "why it takes so long to carry out the sentence that was given to the wrongdoer.… It is a constant aggravation to think that, for years, our hard-earned tax dollars are used to support the offender who committed horrific acts against our loved ones. Moreover, the possibility that the offender might be granted a

---

53. Ibid.
54. Ibid.
55. Ibid.
56. Ibid.
57. Vandiver, op. cit., p. 618.
58. Freeman et al., op. cit., p. 342.
59. Ellis et al., op. cit.
60. Cited in Levey, op. cit., pp. 40-41.

stay of execution or clemency adds even more frustration to our grief."[61] A murder victim's husband had this to say about the appellate process: "Every time [his wife's parents] hear about another appeal, another delay, it throws them into a grave depression.... I think it happens to all of us. We're all thrown back to square one."[62] A mother whose daughter was murdered related how a families of homicide victims support group helped by preparing her for how she would be treated by the criminal justice system: "They knew that the criminal justice system is not really designed for the comfort of victims' family members; it is designed to deal with the perpetrators. Its personnel often do not understand how some of their procedures are demeaning and detrimental to us, and how often we feel that justice simply is not done."[63] Perhaps not surprisingly, research shows that the more satisfied co-victims are with the criminal justice system, the less likely they are to feel depressed or anxious.[64]

Death notification is one of the most traumatic events for co-victims because police officers are sometimes insensitive. In one case, a friend notified a woman that her son had been injured. She and her husband immediately got in their car and drove toward town, when they encountered a roadblock. The police told them, "You people get out of here ... get the hell out of here. We're dealing with a homicide." That is how they learned of their son's death.[65]

Oftentimes, co-victims learn about the perpetrator and the homicide by community word of mouth and not from investigating officers.[66] Co-victims frequently feel like they are a low priority to the police and in the criminal justice system. This is especially true if they are poor and black. As one mother reflected, "I guess because I am poor, they don't think they have to deal with me. I don't think they are really trying to find him [the perpetrator]."[67]

Several examples from Georgia in the 1980s show the racial dimension. In one case, the police informed a black father that his son had been murdered. That was the last time the man heard from any criminal justice officials. He learned on the street that a suspect had been arrested, but he was not told by anyone about any charges, court proceedings, or even a trial date.[68] In another case, a black man came home from church and found his murdered wife. The only contact he had with criminal justice officials was when he was briefly jailed as a suspect. He was not informed of the arrest, trial, or sentencing.[69] In a third case, police asked a black man to come to the police station to identify the possible murderer of his brother and girlfriend. When he got there, he was physically assaulted by the police and informed that he was a suspect in the murders. Later, he learned only through the media that arrests had been made. Neither he nor any of his family was notified about the arrest, the plea bargains, or the sentences imposed.[70]

This lack of information and poor communication contribute to feelings of powerlessness, mistrust, and anger on the part of co-victims.[71] When charges are filed

---

61. Shane Wagner (2006) "The Death Sentence: For Criminals or Victims?" pp. 69-83 in J. R. Acker and D. R. Karp (eds.) *Wounds That Do Not Bind: Victim-Based Perspectives on the Death Penalty.* Durham, NC: Carolina Academic Press, p. 77.

62. Vandiver, op. cit., p. 621.

63. White, op. cit., p. 53.

64. Reed and Blackwell, op. cit., p. 263.

65. Asaro, op. cit., p. 99.

66. Freeman et al., op. cit., p. 341.

67. Ibid.

68. Cited in Vandiver, op. cit., p. 620.

69. Ibid.

70. Ibid.

71. Freeman et al., op. cit., p. 341.

against an alleged killer, co-victims learn that the *state* is the victim, not their loved one. In most legal proceedings, the victim's name is rarely used.[72] Co-victims are frequently excluded from the courtroom, either on the pretext they may be called as witnesses or because of the fear that their emotional reactions might influence the jury.[73] If they are not excluded from the courtroom, having to sit and listen to a detailed description of the murder in detached medical and legal language can be extremely painful.[74] Also agonizing for many co-victims is sitting in the courtroom within a few feet of the defendant and not being able to express their feelings, either verbally or physically.[75]

When a defendant is found not guilty, co-victims may feel that justice has been denied them. They may feel the same way if the defendant is offered a plea bargain or is not sentenced to death.[76] The mother of a sixteen-year-old son who was murdered and whose killer plea-bargained to a lesser charge, had this to say: "He chased my son down and killed him, but they're letting him off, and there's nothing I can do about it."[77] On the other hand, some co-victims find relief in a plea bargain because it brings "judicial closure" to the case. Although judicial closure is not the emotional closure co-victims so desperately seek but rarely find, it has at least three advantages for co-victims. As a victim's advocate explained:

> To actually have the case legally finished means something huge. One, it means that there's a conviction. That means they're going to feel safe, that this person's not going to be out on the streets, [that] this person accepted guilt. The second thing that it means [is] they're not going to be harassed by the court, saying, "Oh we have an appeal coming up." They're not going to get those nagging letters that are going to drag them right back to the night their loved one was murdered. The third thing is, when a case is legally over, well, the media goes away. They're not going to open the paper on some random Tuesday morning, and, *wham*, it's not going to be in front of them all the time (emphasis in original).[78]

Reducing Secondary Victimization

A number of recommendations have been made to improve the experiences of co-victims with the criminal justice system and to reduce secondary victimization. Among them are:

- Police officers should be trained to be more sensitive when notifying co-victims of their loved one's death.

- A victim's advocate should be assigned to co-victims at the earliest opportunity. To that end, victim services should be established within law enforcement agencies or, better yet, should be independent of law enforcement agencies, prosecutors' offices, courts, and corrections agencies. Victim services should never be part of prosecutors' offices.

---

72. Asaro, op. cit.
73. Ibid.
74. Vandiver, op. cit., p. 621.
75. Ibid.
76. Asaro, op. cit.
77. Freeman et al., op. cit.
78. Elizabeth Beck, Sarah Brito, and Arlene Andrews (2007) *In the Shadow of Death: Restorative Justice and Death Row Families.* New York: Oxford University Press, p. 189.

- Co-victims should be informed about their legal rights.
- Co-victims should be advised about what to expect during the investigation.
- Co-victims should be asked if they have any concerns about their safety or security and, if they do, should have their concerns validated and be assisted with securing protective orders and the development of safety plans.
- Police officers should be trained about the importance of briefing co-victims about the progress of homicide investigations and the need for sensitivity when doing so.
- Effective protocols should be developed to guide the police in dealing with co-victims in open, unsolved cases.
- Police should be required to call co-victims (or at least a representative of the co-victims) when a suspect is arrested and told whether the suspect is in jail or out on bail.
- Co-victims should be informed of deliberations and included in case developments. To that end, protocols should be developed to specify the types of information about the case that can be shared with co-victims.
- Co-victims should be kept informed as the case progresses.
- Co-victims should receive court orientations and be accompanied to court by a victim advocate.[79]
- Co-victims should be provided mental health counseling, if needed.
- Co-victims should be provided financial support, if needed, for such things as sudden loss of income and funeral expenses.

One more controversial suggestion is to allow co-victims to veto a prosecutor's decision to seek a death sentence. An obvious problem arises when co-victims disagree about pursuing a death sentence. In that case, existing laws about family participation in estate and other similar decisions could be used, or the decision could be left to the prosecutor, or the decision could be to seek a sentence of life in prison without opportunity of parole.[80] Another controversial suggestion is to allow co-victims to recommend a sentence to the jury as part of a victim impact statement.[81] Such a practice is currently prohibited (*Payne v. Tennessee*),[82] but it may not matter, anyway. Research shows that co-victim testimony has little influence on sentencing outcomes.[83] A victim-impact statement "provides an opportunity for co-victims to tell the sentencing jury about how the crime affected them physically, emotionally, financially, and spiritually, and to reflect on the ultimate loss they have endured as a result of a heinous crime."[84]

---

79. Ibid., pp. 267-268; also see Ellis et al., op. cit., p. 439; Peter Loge (2006) "The Process of Healing and the Trial as Product: Incompatibility, Courts, and Murder Victim Family Members," pp. 411-429 in J. R. Acker and D. R. Karp (eds.) *Wounds That Do Not Bind: Victim-Based Perspectives on the Death Penalty.* Durham, NC: Carolina Academic Press.

80. Loge, ibid., pp. 423-424.

81. David R. Karp and Jarrett B. Warshaw (2006) "Their Day in Court: The Role of Murder Victims' Families in Capital Juror Decision Making," pp. 275-295 in J. R. Acker and D. R. Karp (eds.) *Wounds That Do Not Bind: Victim-Based Perspectives on the Death Penalty.* Durham, NC: Carolina Academic Press, p. 276.

82. 501 U.S. 808, 1991.

83. Ibid., p. 290; Theodore Eisenberg, Stephen P. Garvey, and Martin T. Wells (2006) "Victim Characteristics and Victim Impact Evidence in South Carolina Capital Cases," pp. 297-321 in J. R. Acker and D. R. Karp (eds.) *Wounds That Do Not Bind: Victim-Based Perspectives on the Death Penalty.* Durham, NC: Carolina Academic Press, p. 301-302.

84. Ellis et al., op. cit., p. 441.

Providing Psychological Relief

Some death penalty proponents argue that life imprisonment or a lesser punishment, rather than execution, may not provide the psychological relief deserved by victims' suffering survivors. For some families, anything less than an execution may be taken as a slight, "an indication that society does not value their relative or understand the magnitude of their loss."[85] For them, it is unfair that their loved one's killer will continue to experience many of the small joys of life, such as seeing the sun rise and set, celebrating birthdays, experiencing Christmases, and visiting with loved ones, while their loved one cannot.[86] The embittered parents of the murdered son and daughter-in-law expanded on this point:

> Imprisoned murderers can earn the equivalency of a high-school education or even a college degree. They can become accredited optometrists, podiatrists, or lawyers, and they can find "God" as well as become "model prisoners." But they are still murderers because they crossed that line between law-abiding, civilized citizens and murderers. They are evil. They cannot hide behind a degree, religious calling, or perfect behavior. Evil is evil is evil.... You cannot reverse a murderer's way of reasoning right from wrong.... Their way of approaching the world is already formed psychologically. You cannot reform them.... For us there were no appeals, no visitation rights except to gravesites, and no phone calls—all of which are comforts afforded to prisoners. We only have our precious memories. Whether the accused is sentenced to life without parole or death, our lives will never be the same. But inmates, unlike us, can attempt to shorten their sentences, see their family, and even call their loved ones on the phone.[87]

Death penalty opponents respond to these views in three ways. First, they acknowledge that an execution may indeed relieve feelings of profound loss but assume that, in many cases, the relief may be only temporary. The wife whose husband was brutally murdered did feel relieved following the execution of his killer, but it was not relief from feelings of profound loss nor was it closure:

> The sentence for the brutal, senseless murder of [my husband] has, after nineteen long years, finally been carried out. There is no elation, no joy, no feeling of revenge ... just a feeling of relief and the realization that the violence done to [my husband] will no longer threaten his wife and children. My strongest emotion, now and for the last nineteen years, has been deep, overwhelming grief.... This family will never be healed, but will always be healing.[88]

In the long run, death penalty opponents presume (there is no systematic research on the subject) that an execution may make the burden more difficult to bear because the desire for revenge appeases only the basest and most primitive characteristics of human beings. As one murder victim's family member put it: "Murder drives even the most loving and compassionate people to the edge of that fine line that separates our respect for life from our violent potentials."[89] The daughter of a murder victim does not think it is revenge

---

85. Vandiver, op. cit., p. 638.
86. Scott Turow (2003) *Ultimate Punishment: A Lawyer's Reflections on Dealing with the Death Penalty.* New York: Picador, pp. 52-53.
87. Stanley and Phyllis Rosenbluth, op. cit., pp. 106-107.
88. Cited in Levey, op. cit., p. 42.
89. Cited in Levey, op. cit., p. 36.

co-victims seek but relief from their pain, and that, in either case, they are likely to be disappointed: "I think people don't actually want vengeance. They would like to end their own pain. Sometimes they think it's a zero-sum game: if they can make someone else feel pain, theirs will go away. I just don't think it works that way."[90]

Regarding the long-term consequences of seeking revenge, the sister of a murder victim noted the dilemma she faced: "When [my brother] died and I emerged from the deepest levels of shock and sadness, it began to occur to me that I had an enormous decision to make. It further struck me that this decision might well be the only one I'd get to make about any of this, really.... *Who will I become, and who will I refuse to let myself be, now that my brother has been murdered in this way?*"[91] Her answer was defiant and hopeful: "*I will not let Hampton* [her brother's killer] *take me down, too.*"[92] She concluded, "It is one thing to survive tragedy. Most of us do, in whatever fashion, go on. But how to latch onto the audacity and means to thrive? How to resume cultivating faith, extending generosity, forgiving myself and others for our gravely flawed humanity? These are the ongoing challenges."[93]

It is instructive that only one-quarter of the approximately 1,100 people eligible to view Timothy McVeigh's execution were willing to do so. (U.S. Attorney General John Ashcroft approved closed-circuit television viewing for the survivors and relatives of victims of the Oklahoma City bombing.) Reasons for not viewing the execution included being opposed to capital punishment and not wanting to watch someone die. Many of those choosing not to watch believed that they had healed physically, psychologically, and spiritually; for them, viewing was an unnecessary diversion. They also feared that McVeigh's final statement might haunt them.[94] (Execution witnesses are examined in chapter 12.)

Still, being present at an execution, though clearly a difficult decision, may be considered a duty for some survivors, as it was for the parents of the murdered son and daughter-in-law (who witnessed the executions of both killers): "Asked if we chose to witness the executions, we faced great apprehension and much soul-searching. In the end we opted to be witnesses — not for any reason of revenge.... We opted to witness the execution because it was the final act we could perform for our children.... Each execution was gut-wrenching for us."[95] They had three reactions to what they witnessed: "(1) The process was too gentle — unlike the several bullets Sheppard fired into Richard's head. (2) It was now between 'him' and 'his' Maker. (3) Now, another mother will mourn her son's death, though it was her son's choice to commit murder and have her mourn."[96] In the end, their only consolation was that the executed killers would not be able to make another family suffer as they did: "We did not rejoice in nor mourn the deaths of the killers. They chose their destiny. We did not choose ours. We just found a deep relief in knowing that they could never commit this horrific crime against another family. And for that we felt some peace."[97]

How else do death penalty opponents respond to the contention that anything less than an execution may not provide the psychological relief deserved by victims' suffering survivors? They note that the families of many criminal homicide victims are likely to be

---

90. Ibid., pp. 44-45.
91. Coleman, op. cit., p. 27.
92. Ibid., p. 28.
93. Ibid.
94. "Some won't watch when McVeigh dies." *The Orlando Sentinel* (April 22, 2001), p. A3.
95. Stanley and Phyllis Rosenbluth, op. cit., p. 108.
96. Ibid.
97. Ibid.

disappointed and, in many cases, offended by the "justice" they receive. Very few of them will receive any of the presumed benefits of capital punishment because 98 percent to 99 percent of criminal homicide offenders are never executed. In the vast majority of criminal homicides, a death sentence is not even sought. Thus, many homicide victims' family members will feel that they and the homicide victim are unworthy and have been devalued by the justice system, because the killer of their loved one did not receive the maximum penalty allowed by law.[98]

Finally, death penalty opponents point out that even if an execution did make a loss easier to endure for the relatives of the victim, that advantage would have to be weighed against the painful effects of the execution on the relatives of the perpetrator. This attempt to balance the death penalty's effects on both families raises two key questions posed by Professor Vandiver: "Given that the crime cannot be undone, what can the criminal justice system offer to the victim's family? And what kind of sentence can be imposed on a defendant found guilty of first-degree murder that is commensurate to the crime, protects society, and yet does not destroy the defendant's family in turn?"[99] According to the mother whose daughter was murdered, "When we execute someone, we simply enlarge the circle of grief."[100] (The effects of the death penalty on the defendant's family are discussed in chapter 5.)

Conclusion

Many surviving family members of homicide victims suffer immensely and, unfortunately, will continue to suffer immensely whether or not the death penalty is the punishment for the crime. With or without capital punishment, most co-victims will still grieve, many of them will still seek revenge and call it justice, and nearly all of them will still experience the numerous emotional and physical hardships that accompany the death of a loved one to violent crime. Whether or not the death penalty is an option, most co-victims also will hunger for the elusive goal of closure, and some of them will still bristle at the contention that closure ever can be achieved.

What co-victims may not experience in the absence of capital punishment are some of the frustration with the criminal justice system, and the secondary victimization it causes. Of course, with or without capital punishment, death notification sometimes will still be made by insensitive police officers who will continue to ignore or clumsily address co-victims' needs. Co-victims will still be befuddled by the legal process; in some cases, will still be excluded from the courtroom, or, when they are not excluded, will still be tortured by the proceedings.

In the absence of capital punishment, however, co-victims will not be insulted when the death penalty is not sought for their loved one's killer. They would likely not have to experience a lengthy and agonizing appellate process or have to wait years—or decades— for the sentence to be imposed. They would also be less likely to be co-victims in the first place. As noted in the conclusion to chapter 1, with the abolition of capital punishment, the tens of millions of dollars squandered on the capital punishment process could be used for more effective methods of reducing violent crime.

---

98. Acker and Mastrocinque, op. cit., p. 149; Zimring, op. cit., pp. 55-57; White, op. cit., p. 64.

99. Vandiver, op. cit., p. 613.

100. White, op. cit., p. 66.

While the families of victims are dragged through the courts seeking justice — or sometimes revenge — defense attorneys are battling on the other side to preserve justice for their clients: the accused. The desired outcomes for these two factions are diametrically opposed, so that upon the conclusion of a capital case, not everyone will believe that justice was served. Regardless, defense attorneys are integral to the system, and it is to their work that we turn next.

Chapter 4

Defense Attorneys

For many victims' family members, the villain in the unfolding capital punishment drama—besides, of course, their loved one's killer—is the alleged killer's defense attorney. Victims' family members, among others, wonder how anyone could defend a brutal murderer. The answer is simple, if not fully appreciated.

The Sixth Amendment to the U.S. Constitution and several modern Supreme Court decisions guarantee the right to the "effective assistance" of counsel to people charged with crimes, including capital crimes. (The terms *counsel, attorney,* and *lawyer* are interchangeable.) The right to counsel extends not only to representation at trial but also to other critical stages in the criminal justice process "where substantial rights of the accused may be affected."[1] A defendant may waive the right to counsel and appear on his or her own behalf. However, given the technical nature of criminal cases and the stakes involved, anyone arrested for a crime, especially a capital crime, is well advised to secure the assistance of counsel at the earliest opportunity.

Indigent Defense Options

The vast majority of capital defendants are indigent. If a suspect cannot afford an attorney and is accused of either a felony or a misdemeanor carrying a sentence of imprisonment or death, the state is required to provide an attorney at its expense. Depending on the jurisdiction, indigent capital defendants may be assigned either a public defender, a court-appointed lawyer, or a contract lawyer. A *public defender* is paid a fixed salary by a jurisdiction, much like a prosecutor. A *court-appointed* lawyer is usually selected in one of two ways: In some jurisdictions, attorneys volunteer to represent indigent offenders and are appointed by judges on a rotating basis from a list or from lawyers present in the courtroom. In other jurisdictions, lawyers are appointed by a judge from a list of attorneys who are members of the county bar association. However, according to a defense attorney in private practice:

> It varies. There is a list of lawyers who are willing to take those cases and also, these days, qualified to take those cases. I think some cases are selected for reasons other than ... for example, if the case is going to be high-profile. I think there are a few judges that just kind of assume I would not back down from that kind of thing, because I've had some high profile cases. That's been the situation once or twice. It's kind of a mystery though, actually. I think, theoretically, they are

---

1. See, for example, *Gideon v. Wainwright*, 372 U.S. 335 (1963).

supposed to go through this list. But I don't know that any of us really knows how that happens. You just get a call from the judge's assistant that says, "We've got a murder case." They do or don't give you tidbits of information, and they ask if you're interested in taking it, and you say yes or no. Sometimes if you're lucky they'll give you a hint as to whether you've got the worst co-defendant … (laughs).

A *contract lawyer* is a private attorney who, individually or in conjunction with a law firm or bar association, bids for the right to represent a jurisdiction's indigent defendants. In certain situations, some jurisdictions employ a combination of indigent defense systems. For example, jurisdictions that regularly use public defenders sometimes contract out the defense of cases where there is a conflict of interest (for example, multiple-defendant cases) or cases that require special expertise (such as some death penalty cases). Many death penalty jurisdictions have special indigent defense systems for capital cases, especially at the appellate level.

Guilt or Innocence Does Not Matter

Lawyers sometimes are vilified for defending people who are unquestionably guilty of crimes. That lawyers sometimes succeed in getting guilty persons "off" by the skillful use of "legal technicalities" only makes matters worse. However, what some people fail to understand is that in the American system of justice, the role of defense lawyers is not to decide their clients' guilt or innocence. Rather, their task is to provide the best possible legal counsel and advocacy within the legal and ethical limits of the profession. Legal and ethical codes forbid lawyers, for example, to mislead the court by providing false information or by using perjured testimony (false testimony under oath). The American system of justice is based on the premise that a person is innocent until proven guilty. In the attempt to ensure, as far as possible, that innocent people are not found guilty of crimes, all persons charged with crimes are entitled to a rigorous defense. The constitutional right to counsel and our adversarial system of justice would be meaningless if lawyers refused to defend clients whom they knew to be guilty. Currently, this point is not fully appreciated by many trial judges:

> A generation ago, lawyers who represented death row inmates were admired by the courts even as they were often scorned by the public. They were viewed, by the courts and by a small segment of the population at large, as preserving the integrity of the system. These lawyers were willing to stand by the accused and the infamous in spite of minimal remuneration and frequent obloquy, and they were respected by the courts and by those who are faithful to the idea of the rule of law. But beginning around the mid-1980s, this attitude began to change. Death penalty lawyers came to be viewed as accomplices of murderers instead of defenders of the rule of law. They came to be regarded as something akin to mafia lawyers: people with sympathy for what their debased clients had done.[2]

---

2. Dow, David R. (2002) "How the Death Penalty Really Works," pp. 11-35 in D. R. Dow and M. Dow (eds.) *Machinery of Death: The Reality of America's Death Penalty Regime.* New York: Routledge.

In fact, defense attorneys in capital cases seldom ask their clients whether they are guilty or innocent. The issue is largely irrelevant to them. As one defense attorney explained:

> As a criminal defense lawyer, the issue that I am dealing with is "What can the state prove?" Certainly when you are reviewing discovery, there were questions and issues you had to discuss with your client that resulted in your client perhaps telling you what he or she had done. The attorney-client relationship, in a case where at some point you may find yourself making the recommendation that [your client accept] the life offer, if you start out interrogating the client like everyone else did, why should they trust you, and why should they listen to you? … If you're going to do death work for a long time, you have to be, on some level, nonjudgmental about the things that your clients have done. It's sort of, "good people do bad things," and I'd be naive in believing that I wasn't representing people who had, in fact, done the things that they were accused of.

She added:

> If you want a client to trust you and to take your advice and listen to you, when you're a criminal defense attorney, you're trying to help a client make a good decision about the resolution in their case. And give them legal advice and hope they take it. This is a person who obviously, at some point, made some bad decisions or they wouldn't be your client facing capital charges. To get them to a point where they can make a good decision about their future, I don't think that's consistent with, "Did you do it?" And then once the client says, "Yes I did," if I was a client, I would feel like, "Why do you want to have me if you just asked me if I did it and I told you that I did?"

Another defense attorney had a similar reply:

> My general approach to clients is not to ask that question [about guilt or innocence] until, well…. A general approach to a criminal case is about the evidence, not about what actually happened. It's really not a matter of guilt or innocence. It's guilty or not guilty, meaning is there enough evidence or is there not enough evidence. I frankly don't care whether or not the person is guilty, because it's not my job. My job is to guard the process and to vigorously uphold the process. And if everyone's done what they need to do and there's enough evidence, there will be a conviction; if not, there won't be. Now having said that, in a murder case, you're much more likely to have evidence that is very strong — ya know, caught the guy at the scene or five eyewitnesses and a confession — it's much more likely if it's obvious. In that situation then, yes, we talk about it at length. The defense may be in there as self-defense, or accidental, or the other dudes did it and I was just standing around, or whatever. Or there is likely to be at least mitigation in there.
>
> I think I've only had one murder trial where I went into the trial not knowing whether my client had actually shot the people or not. He denied it. I never pushed him over that denial … he did not testify, they did not have particularly great evidence. He was acquitted. He was ironically assassinated on Christmas Day the very next year on an obvious drug revenge thing, which leads me to believe that maybe he did it. I think that's the only time I've had a murder case where it wasn't just patently clear.

A public defender put the issue this way:

I think any defense attorney is going to talk to their client about "what did you do." Now whether that constitutes being guilty of something is … a person can kill another person and that may not be a crime. So to say, "Are you guilty?" I don't think that's something that any defense attorney is going to ask a client. Maybe, "What did you do?" or, "Tell me what you remember?" or, "Let's talk about this. Tell me what's going on."

Defense Strategy

Regardless of whether a defense attorney asks his or her client whether he is guilty, a client's confession to his defense attorney that he did, in fact, kill the victim or victims may affect trial strategy. According to a public defender:

As far as your strategy, it's going to affect certain things. You can't put on false testimony. You can't put on perjured testimony. You can't put the client on the stand if he's going to deny the act, if he told you he did the act, and you know he did it. So it can affect what happens, but the strategy is something that you're going to find is pretty fluid anyways. And it changes, you can have an overall goal. And the goal might just be, okay he did it, he shot the person. But it's a lesser crime, say, a heat-of-passion-type thing.

A defense attorney in private practice agreed: "The only way it would affect my trial strategy … [is] whether they testify or not. But as far as trying to get an acquittal, if they don't have enough evidence, it doesn't change it one bit." Another defense attorney in private practice had this to say about what she would do if her client confessed to her that he was guilty: "Only if they told the cops or they confessed to another person. Telling me they did it under attorney-client privilege obviously doesn't affect trial strategy at all. If they've confessed to law enforcement or some other individual, and that person is on the state witness list, and the confessions come in, that's going to affect your trial strategy."

As for overall trial strategy in capital cases, a public defender maintained that, besides the facts of the case, the client plays a major role:

I think the facts [determine trial strategy]. To some extent, the client is going to decide because the right to the defense is going to be theirs. You're telling, as a matter of law, this is what the law is. You know what the facts are. Let's see if we can put the law and the facts together and see what happened here. But to a certain extent, the client controls what the defense is going to be. And you'll get some different opinions on that. [Trial strategy is] very fluid. A lot's going to depend on what the state can prove. They have the burden. You may not get to put your defense on. If the state doesn't show up front, let's say, that it was a first-degree murder, than you go to the court at the end of the state's case and say, "I want you to rule, Judge, that he can only be convicted of a lesser crime because they haven't proved a greater crime." Your strategy might change in the middle of trial.

A defense attorney in private practice also mentioned the fluidity of trial strategy:

You decide it as a group. You decide it based on the facts and circumstances of the case: who the prosecutor is, who the judge is, who the victim is, who the victim's family is, who your client is, who your client's family is. There's no one thing that dictates a trial strategy. And it certainly changes over the months and the years that you are preparing. And it certainly changes when you find yourself in the middle of trial and something goes different than what you thought. And you have to make a decision then. Trial strategy is a very fluid thing.

Another defense attorney in private practice described what she considers when developing an overall trial strategy:

My process is figuring out what they have to prove ... the guilt or innocence, and build from there what the prosecution is. And kind of build from there and kind of look creatively at things. For example, [one client] severed his wife's head off and cut up a boy into pieces. He was charged with two counts of first-degree murder, and the state was asking for the death penalty. And [the client] was, this person that you meet, and immediately you think ... the nicest, cleanest, mildest, meekest, little sweetheart of a guy and fabulous family. And you're like "What the hell?" And ultimately he was found not guilty by reason of insanity, because we had the right experts involved.

She continued:

I don't know that lawyers always think to kind of look at what isn't obvious. I mean there are some things that ... the act itself was wacky and kind of pointed toward a mental health deal. But first meeting him ... it doesn't scream that out. It wasn't until you get confessionals and spend a lot of time with somebody that you realize that they are nuts. I guess the second tier is: you really have to get to know your client. Explanations and mitigations will develop the better you get to know your client and their family. If you really don't have a relationship with people, they're not going to tell you bad stuff about their family until they get to know you and trust you. It's an element of time more than anything else.

She also stressed that the prosecutor's evidence directs her trial strategy:

It definitely starts with what they can prove firmly, because the more your defense meshes with what you know the jury is going to believe is true, the more credible your defense is. That will go for guilt phase or mitigation. If you're trying to convince the jury of something that flies in the face of what you know they're going to be convinced of, that is going to cast doubt on everything else you say. For example, if there are four eyewitnesses in a videotape with your client there at the scene of the killing, your defense could be drugs, didn't mean to, his other buddy with the gun did it, he was just standing there. It should be a lot of things, but it shouldn't be he was off fishing with dad. You know the jury isn't going to believe that. Then when you get up in mitigation and say he was sexually abused as a child and did these wonderful things, they're going to be like, "Why should we believe you? You just showed us a crock of pooh." It has to make sense.

She explained that in most cases she has a good idea of how the prosecutor's case is going to unfold:

I'm going to say this, and I don't want it to come across as insulting. Once you do the depositions, and you talk with the lead detectives and witnesses, prosecutors who are, by all accounts, overworked—so I'm not blaming them for not being creative—[but] generally the prosecutor puts the detective and witnesses on the stand and says, what happened next, what happened next ... And you will have done the depositions, and you will have a relatively good idea of what they are going to do. You try to anticipate little tricks. Like I just got a notice of a new witness in one of my murder cases. She's a forensics person who deals with firearms and ballistics. I'm not sure what [the prosecutor is] up to, because there was no gun recovered (this is the third time we've tried this case, by the way), and he didn't call her the first time, and I'm pretty sure he's up to something. I don't know what it is. He doesn't have to tell me what he's up to. I'll take her deposition, and I can certainly talk to her about what she's talked to him about, and talk to her about what she did, and try to get at what the angle is. I've got a couple of ideas to explore as to what the angles are. You try to be firm, at least in your mind, as to why it is they call these people. And be ready for surprises, because trials always have surprises. And usually though, that's a good thing.

The Better Your Lawyer, the Better Your Chances

Experienced criminal trial lawyers maintain that no really capable defense lawyer should ever lose a capital case because, he or she should always be able to establish reasonable doubt. They point to Clarence Darrow, undoubtedly the most successful capital punishment defense attorney in American history, who, in more than one hundred capital trials, never had a client sentenced to death. One modern-day version of Darrow is Andrea Lyon, who not only is a death-qualified defense attorney but also a DePaul University College of Law professor and director of the school's Center for Justice in Capital Cases. Lyon has tried 132 murder cases and has taken 19 capital murder cases through the sentencing stage of a capital trial. She has not had a client sentenced to death. Ms. Lyon contended, "Who your lawyer is, is the single most important fact concerning whether you get the death penalty or not."[3] Research confirms Lyon's claim.[4]

Unfortunately, most capital defendants do not have attorneys as talented as Darrow or Lyon. Far from it. Most capital defendants are represented by defense attorneys who are inexperienced, untrained in life-or-death cases, unskilled, overworked, understaffed, unprepared, less resourceful, and less independent; who too often have been reprimanded, disciplined, or subsequently disbarred; and who frequently lose capital cases.[5] One notoriously incompetent Texas attorney, Ron Mock, had so many clients sentenced to death that people referred to a section of Texas's death row as the "Mock Wing."[6]

---

3. Mike Thomas, "New Casey lawyer: Hear her roar," *The Orlando Sentinel* (June 2, 2009), p. B1.
4. David R. Dow (2005) *Executed on a Technicality: Lethal Injustice on America's Death Row.* Boston: Beacon Press, p. 7.
5. See Talia Roitberg Harmon (2001) "Predictors of Miscarriages of Justice in Capital Cases," *Justice Quarterly* 18:949–968; Talia Roitberg Harmon and William S. Lofquist (2005) "Too Late for Luck: A Comparison of Post-*Furman* Exonerations and Executions of the Innocent," *Crime & Delinquency* 51:498–520; Marcia Coyle, Fred Strasser, and Marianne Lavelle (1990) "Fatal Defense: Trial and Error in the Nation's Death Belt," *The National Law Journal* 12 (No. 40, June 11):30–44; Barry Scheck, Peter Neufeld, and Jim Dwyer (2001) *Actual Innocence: When Justice Goes Wrong and How to Make It Right.* New York: Penguin Putnam, p. 336; *Bell v. Cone* (535 U.S. 685, 2002).
6. Stephen B. Bright (2004) "Why the United States Will Join the Rest of the World in Abandoning Capital Punishment," pp. 152-182 in H.A. Bedau and P.G. Cassell (eds.) *Debating the Death Penalty: Should America Have Capital Punishment? The Experts on Both Sides Make Their Best Case.* New York: Oxford, p. 160.

Some defendants have had defense attorneys who have fallen asleep during capital murder trials. One notable example was Houston, Texas attorney John Benn, who slept through most of his client George McFarland's trial. Remarkably, Benn's performance did "not offend the right to counsel guaranteed by the United States Constitution," the trial judge explained, because, "[t]he Constitution doesn't say the lawyer has to be awake."[7] Agreeing with the trial judge's assessment was the Texas Court of Criminal Appeals, which rejected McFarland's claim of ineffective assistance of counsel. Another Texas attorney who fell asleep during a capital trial was Joe Frank Cannon. Cannon continually dozed off while defending Calvin Burdine, and the Texas Court of Criminal Appeals again held that "a sleeping attorney was sufficient 'counsel' under the Constitution."[8]

A former public defender now in private practice believes that in some capital cases new, inexperienced defense attorneys do a better job than older, more experienced but jaded defense attorneys:

> I've seen lawyers in death penalty cases, who were not the most experienced, do an unbelievably good job because it's ninety-nine percent preparation. And fighting in the face of a losing battle throughout the entire thing, and doing it over everything there is to argue over — even though you know you're going to lose. And it's disheartening, and it's tiring. I've seen newer lawyers do better in my mind than some of the seasoned lawyers out there who I think, quite frankly, shouldn't be doing it anymore. They really don't have the heart left to do what it takes to really wage that war — the fight over somebody's life.... There is nothing worse ... I've had codefendant cases where I thought, "Oh shit." I felt bad that the codefendant's lawyer didn't do what needed to be done. And you know those outcomes are really affected, not just by the facts but also by who you have or how much time they are willing to put into digging stuff up. Lawyers might say, "There's really no mitigation, there's nothing there." F that. There's always something there. I've yet to have a case where you couldn't legitimately find something to talk about. Something to go to.

She provided the following example:

> In the case of [name of defendant], he killed the police officer. And he shot and almost killed the second police officer who ended up, not paralyzed, but physically handicapped for the rest of his life. I was appointed, and the first lawyer that I kind of got [as co-counsel] had [a] "there's nothing there kind of 'whatever' attitude." And then I got [name of lawyer], a local lawyer, fantastic lawyer involved in the case. There's all sorts of stuff, interesting cultural stuff. His [the defendant's] father was one of these functional crazy people. Immediately you say, "Hi" — normal, normal, normal. Well, after you talk to him for four or five hours, the guy's a lunatic. He would brag about his fabulous parenting job, because he used the rod. Spare the rod, spoil the child. And what a great job he did. So [the other lawyer] got him on the stand and just kind of let him unravel himself. The jury was just, mouth agape, at "Wow ... this guy's seriously telling us what a great father he is, and what a great upbringing this kid had." Some lawyers would have

---

7. Cited in Stephen B. Bright (2003) "The Politics of Capital Punishment: The Sacrifice of Fairness for Executions," pp. 127–146 in J. R. Acker, R. M. Bohm, and C. S. Lanier (eds.) *America's Experiment with Capital Punishment: Reflections on the Past, Present and Future of the Ultimate Penal Sanction*, 2nd Ed. Durham, NC: Carolina Academic Press, p. 136.

8. Ibid., pp. 136-137.

said, "Dad says he [the defendant] has a great upbringing, we have nothing to work with there." You had to look for it. His fourth-grade teacher, we found, who you're not going to believe this. She still had a card he [the defendant] had given her for Valentine's Day or something. From the fourth grade, she still had it. And we put her on the stand. She remembered him, and she talked about how sweet he was, and he did this and was really good at this and liked this girl. It was unbelievable. It brought the house down. If you don't take this person [the defendant] out of that moment where they did the worst thing possible you could do and reframe them as a total human being, you haven't done your job. It's a hard job. It's a really hard job.

In 1990, *The National Law Journal* published a study showing a general failure of the states to provide effective counsel to capital defendants. Not much has changed since then. At the beginning of the twenty-first century, only half of the then-thirty-eight states with death penalty statutes had adopted minimum guidelines or standards or created an agency to promulgate standards for the appointment of counsel at either the trial or appellate level, or both, in capital cases.[9] In none of those states, however, can the standards be considered particularly rigorous; they are truly minimum standards.

Money Is a Major Factor

Defense counsel in capital cases (including those in states with minimum standards) rarely has the resources necessary to mount an effective defense. In the 1990s, for example, attorneys in Alabama were being paid only $20 an hour for out-of-court time in capital cases, with a limit of $2,000 per case; Mississippi was limiting payment to $1,000 a case.[10] As late as 2004, Florida had a $3,500 cap on the payment for defense services in capital cases, meaning that state-funded lawyers in Florida capital cases were paid an estimated $3 an hour.[11] A paralegal working on a federal bankruptcy case was paid more per hour than a defense attorney in a capital case in Alabama, Georgia, Mississippi, and Virginia.[12] It is not unusual for attorneys in capital cases to be compensated at less than minimum wage, and states have been known to appoint attorneys in capital cases who submitted the lowest bids.[13]

A private attorney who has been court appointed in capital cases had this to say about compensation:

> The current hourly rate [in Florida], I want to say, is $120 [an hour] for first chair and $110 [an hour] for the co-chair. I believe that's correct. For a death

---

9. James R. Acker and Charles S. Lanier (1999) "Ready for the Defense? Legislative Provisions Governing the Appointment of Counsel in Capital Cases," *Criminal Law Bulletin* 35:429–477.

10. Stephen B. Bright (1997a) *Capital Punishment on the 25th Anniversary of Furman v. Georgia.* Atlanta, GA: Southern Center for Human Rights, p. 11.

11. Acker and Lanier, op. cit., pp. 448-489; Kenneth Williams (2005) "Ensuring the Capital Defendant's Right to Competent Counsel: It's Time for Some Standards," *The Wayne Law Review* 51:129-161 at http://web.lexis-nexis.com. (full address too long to reproduce here).

12. Bright (2004), op. cit., p. 168.

13. Stephen B. Bright (1997b) "Neither Equal Nor Just: The Rationing and Denial of Legal Services to the Poor When Life and Liberty Are at Stake," *Annual Survey of American Law* 1997:783–836.

penalty case, for what it's worth, it is a monumental pain in the butt. So much so that you have to hassle the county about the bill, and now you have to worry about the state paying the bill. And it is just monumentally painful. I've been saying for the last year that I won't take anymore [death penalty cases]. And I haven't. They've changed the contract in such a way that I won't take any until that gets resolved and goes through the court system. Because you couldn't possibly do a good job for what they're paying.

Florida recently changed its system. Attorneys are now paid by the state instead of by the county. The rates have also changed. As of May 24, 2007, Florida pays court-appointed counsel (both lead counsel and co-counsel) representing capital cases at the trial level a flat-rate maximum of $15,000. It pays a maximum of $100 an hour for capital cases that exceed statutory limitations or the flat fee.[14] Even so, the fee is just insufficient for many defense attorneys. According to the private attorney:

The hourly rate that you get paid, just for comparison sake, is less than a third of what I charge hourly for somebody divorcing and fighting over their Tupperware. So, in that sense, it is economically damaging to a law firm to take on those [death penalty] cases. Now, I will say that, years back, I took the cases knowing I was going to get the 90 bucks or $110 or $120. So I don't blame anyone for having made that questionable economic bargain. My beef is not with the hourly rate that I agreed to accept. My beef is the barrage of barricades that are put in front of you and the nitpicking and the ridiculous stuff you have to go through to get paid or get your people paid or to get the right experts involved or do the job itself. That's my complaint.

She then elaborated on the kinds of problems she has encountered:

For example, you have a complicated murder scene, and there's a question as to how the person died that is important to your case. And you don't have the knowledge or experience or education to even really know what the right questions to ask are. So you need your own forensics medical person. It happens a lot. And I would automatically pick up the phone and call [name of person]. He used to be a medical examiner here and is now in private practice. And he does forensic expert work. And I say, "Gosh, ya know, they're saying she died this way. But I've got these questions because of this." And he'd say, "Yeah I think … I need to take a look at that." So I make a motion saying I need help to get to the truth of the forensics team and the time of death and the way of death and the manner of death and all these things. He won't do it for the rate that the state wants to pay experts for because you just can't find medical people who take $135 an hour. Dream on, it's not going to happen. I need to hire this guy, he's here, he's local, I know him. This is the guy that I need. And the state objects across the board, and you've got to get a hearing now for everything. You have to go to the administrative judge, and she has to have a hearing in four weeks. And you get to there, and you've got to fight for why it is you need it. You've got to fight for why it is you couldn't get it cheaper. You've got [to tell her] how many

---

14. Justice Administration Commission at http://justiceadmin.org/4.%20Q%20&%20A%206-27-08.pdf (accessed October 24, 2008).

different people did you call [and why you could not] get them to do it for $130 an hour.

> Keep in mind that the litigation over the money stuff, I cannot charge for. I can't charge for the time I spent on the Internet or phone scanning [the region] for that brilliant forensics expert who's going to take $130 an hour. I can't charge for the time it takes me to write the motion up. I can't charge for the time I'm in the hearing arguing about it. You know, push comes to shove, the judges know you. And ultimately, I get what I need, but ohhh the time it takes to get there is just … aggravating. The other huge issue to me … let's take that example again. To later argue my guy would not have been convicted if I got the expert I needed. You have to have a record and have the appellate court be able to say, "Wow, she really needed this expert for all of these great reasons. She wasn't given the expert, and it really would have made a difference."

> Well, in order to do that, you either have to have, in your motion, all your reasons laid out, or at the hearing you have to have all of these good reasons. If I'm a Rockefeller or a prosecutor, I don't have to do that. I just hire whoever I want to hire, and I don't have to tell the other side all of my thought process in order to get money to do my job. So my practice is to attempt to get the judges to agree to let me do what we call, *ex parte*—without the prosecutor being involved in it, so they don't get to read those things. In this circuit, generally they allow that. Other circuits, they generally don't allow it unless you go through this rigamarole process…. It's those kind of things that make it hard to do the job the way you could do it if money wasn't a factor. Those are my aggravations.

About getting the necessary resources, she added:

> I consider myself to be much more tenacious [than most lawyers] about getting [what I need], finding ways to do cases. I think there are a lot of lawyers who … there's a chilling effect, with that whole factor. I think a lot of lawyers, understandably, don't go that extra eight miles to get the funding, because it's just such a pain. Ultimately, you do what you need to do. I generally have gotten what I needed.

Another private attorney who had accepted court appointments in capital cases had this to say about compensation:

> It was certainly less than what I made on private cases, but when you're representing indigent people, that's part of it. You accept a discounted rate. But yes, I felt, under the system, under the court appointments, I was paid fairly. I am no longer on the [appointment] list, now that they've gone to the $15,000 flat fee on the death case. Being a private practitioner, I can't afford to operate at a loss and put eight hundred hours into a case and only get paid $15,000 for it. I can't do that. Say you spend eight hundred hours at $15,000. [That is] $18.75 an hour. I bill out at more than $120 an hour. At $120 an hour, you can still cover your overhead. At $18.75 an hour, you can't cover overhead and can't succeed as a small business, being a sole-practitioner.

Not surprisingly, some jurisdictions that rely on court-appointed attorneys have trouble finding lawyers to represent indigent capital defendants. As one defense attorney related:

> There are circuits in the state where it is a critical problem. They are getting lawyers from other jurisdictions. I have a private case, murder case, in [names

a county] and every single time I go in front of the judge, he not kiddingly, but very kindly and jokingly, begs me to take an appointment. There are lawyers there that are handling eleven and twelve murder cases. I don't want to think about it. It makes my tummy hurt.

Some judges will not appoint capable defense attorneys to represent capital defendants even when they have the opportunity to do so. According to a Texas survey of trial judges, for about half the judges, a lawyer's reputation for moving cases quickly, regardless of the quality of the defense, was a factor in the decision to appoint a particular lawyer.[15] Some court-appointed attorneys may be less than zealous in their client's defense because they do not want to antagonize a judge and lose future business.[16] Some jurisdictions have attempted to provide more adequate resources in capital cases, but in none could the provision of those resources be considered generous. Most provide woefully inadequate resources. The Louisiana Supreme Court recently ruled that trial judges in death penalty cases could stop prosecutions of indigent defendants until the state provides the money to pay for an adequate defense.[17]

There Are No Substitutes For Training and Experience

Even if the necessary financial resources were provided, that would not compensate entirely for deficient training, knowledge, and experience. Defense attorneys, however, are not entirely to blame for this problem. Capital jurisprudence is a highly specialized area of the criminal law, and most attorneys have not received instruction in it. To help remedy that problem, some states, such as Florida, have created capital punishment defense agencies. The attorneys who work in the agencies handle only capital punishment cases and, thus, are able to develop expertise. This is no panacea, however: most of the agencies are understaffed and underfunded and, consequently, have only the resources to handle appeals. In some death penalty states, judges continue to appoint any lawyer licensed to practice law to represent a capital defendant, even if the lawyer's practice is limited mostly to real estate or divorce law.[18] Consequently, even when they are conscientious, appointed attorneys in capital cases may make numerous mistakes. A seasoned defense attorney described her first capital case:

> Oh God. It was so frightening. I had been out of the public defender's office for maybe two years. I had left the PD's office after being in felonies for nine months. In actuality, I had probably tried five felony cases at that point I took my first death penalty case. I took it as second chair, but the first chair was only marginally more experienced than I was. And she had some unbelievably high number of murder cases. So I really jumped in with both feet, without any of the training or experience I should have had. I think that the reality is, much of criminal

---

15. Cited in Bright (2004), op. cit., p. 168.

16. Ibid., pp. 168-169.

17. "Death Penalty Prosecutions May Be Halted if Funding is Inadequate," (2005) *ABA Journal* (April 15) at www.deathpenaltyinfo.org/article.php?scid=7&did=851.

18. Bright (2004), op. cit., p. 169.

defense is done by the newest lawyers out there. But our system is still better than other states where lawyers who are not even criminal defenders are poisoning cases. You have contract lawyers and wills lawyers and real estate lawyers having these things [death penalty cases] dropped in their laps. At the time I took the case, I didn't know how inadequately prepared I was. Ignorance is bliss. I had enthusiasm. By the time we got to trial, I was adequately prepared. But it certainly was a painful hurdle.

She noted that she tried her first capital case before the state instituted miniumum standards for defense counsel in capital cases, and that she never would have been given the case under the new standards. "Back then," she recalled, "the state association of criminal defense lawyers did a yearly death penalty seminar, and the people doing death penalty work were among the most devoted to the cause, sharing information." She remembered reaching out "to people who did that work." She got the seminar materials and educated herself. She described it as a "crash course," observing that there were "a lot of different aspects to it, legally, that you don't run into anywhere else. Aggravators and mitigators. People who've never touched a death penalty case would have no idea what those terms meant." Her client was sentenced to life imprisonment without opportunity of parole.

A former public defender now in private practice described her first capital case, in which she served as second chair:

> I had observed a number of capital cases. I had been mentored by some people in the public defender's office who had done capital work. I read a lot of material on it; talked to other lawyers who had tried capital cases. I had no idea if I was adequately prepared or not at the time that I did the case. Several years later, looking back, of course, I think that I should have had more experience, or I should have had more training. Like many things in life, you look back and think, "Oh, my God. They never should have let me do that." There's a trade off, when you try your first case. You don't know what to expect, you have no fears, you try things that you might not otherwise five or ten years later because you gain knowledge that makes you not do that [the things you tried before]. I was only responsible for a small number of witnesses and a small portion of the work. So, in that sense, the lead lawyer made good decisions, and he took on the bulk of the work, knowing that I didn't have the level of experience that I could.

She explained that she served as second chair in twelve to fifteen capital cases before she served as lead counsel in a capital case. Her extensive prior experience as second chair likely is atypical.

A long-time public defender offered the following description of his first capital case:

> I was assisting the trial attorneys. The jury found [his client] guilty, and I volunteered to do the closing argument to the jury [at the end of the penalty phase], which was, looking back, pretty stupid to volunteer to do that. It was. He got a life sentence. At the time, I felt prepared to do what I did. And that was solely the closing argument. That was all I did in that case.

He described his first experience as lead counsel in a capital case this way: "It was scary. You have no real idea how demanding it is, in all different areas. It's demanding in every conceivable way." He mentioned that he did not feel adequate as lead counsel in that case, which he tried alone without a second chair. In describing his inadequacies, he pointed to some of the many complicated subjects capital defense counsel need to know about to be effective:

> Every case that you do is going to have a different actual component to it. And with the evolution of scientific evidence and the categories that are out there, you need to have working knowledge of mental health because that's an important part of mitigation. And forensically, you need to have a working knowledge of DNA. Just basically ballistics and fingerprints and all that stuff. So there's a body of scientific knowledge out there I would have liked to have had more training in, specifically, in the fields that were germane to the particular case I was doing. And I had to get an expert to help me understand what was going on. And it's difficult to have not had prior exposure to DNA. And it's a horribly complex area … and to develop the … and it's not expertise, to develop a familiarity with it and to cross-examine the state's expert on a person's semen being found; things along those lines. I would liked to have had more training in those fields. I don't know if that's viable or if you can do that. Maybe the more diverse background you have, the better you are going to be. But that's a never-ending requirement, I think. No matter how much you get in all sorts of different areas, you still need to know more.

Beyond the Verdict

The penalty phase of the bifurcated trial is the primary difference between capital trials and those involving other felonies. Defense attorneys have differing opinions about which phase of the trial—the guilt phase or the penalty phase—is the more difficult one. One defense attorney simply stated that it depends on the case. Another defense attorney believed that both phases present unique and demanding challenges:

> In the preparation, the penalty phase is harder because there's a lot more time and work and emotional anguish. In the actual presentation, the guilt phase is more difficult emotionally because you're walking those fine lines and really trying to get an acquittal but not wanting to turn the jury off for what could be the most important part later. I hate making loser arguments. It's just not as fun arguing, "Don't convict somebody" when the case is so incredibly bad that there just isn't any other likely conclusion. It just isn't as fun to me. Whereas when you're putting on the penalty phase, at least by that time you've done all the work. At that point, you believe in it. You love these family members. It's cathartic for everyone. It's the "Oprah" portion of the trial which I personally enjoy. They're both hard in different ways.

A public defender considers the penalty phase the more difficult phase of the trial, without question. "By the time you get into the penalty phase, you're exhausted," he says. "You haven't gotten any sleep. All your nerves are on end. You're there, and you've got [your client's] life right there in your hands. It's emotionally, physically, and intellectually demanding."

Another reason defense attorneys consider the penalty phase the more difficult phase of the capital trial is because oftentimes there is indisputable evidence that their clients are guilty of the capital crimes with which they are charged. With an obviously guilty client, the guilt phase for many defense attorneys is merely a formality. However, an experienced defense attorney believes that viewing the guilt phase in that way is a mistake:

> Number one, if you prepare it [the guilt phase] well enough, there's always a chance that you're going to get an offer. If you can get a guy twenty to twenty-five years on a death penalty case, that's a victory. It may not feel like it to his mama, but it is. If you get creative, you might get a not-guilty-by-reason of insanity. It's not that frequent, but it can happen. The cases that go to trial, there are wild things that happen in trial that you can't foresee. If a jury senses that you are passionate about the case in an ethical, believable way, I think you're much more likely to carry that credibility over to the next stage. And sometimes it doesn't matter. You know, fuck it, make [the prosecutor] work for it. I may not win. It may be painful, but next time I'll get a better deal.

Conversely, some inexperienced defense attorneys naively believe that their clients will be acquitted in the guilt phase and therefore do not bother to prepare for the penalty phase. That, too, is a huge mistake. As one experienced defense attorney explained:

> The day you meet the client, you have to start working on the penalty phase. So you're working on two tracks at the very same time: one, the guilt/innocence phase and, two, the penalty phase in case there is a conviction for first-degree murder. And it's the only kind of case that you immediately start working on sentencing. And before your client is even indicted, and they've only been arrested, you're working on sentencing. You take a social history of the client, and in a capital case, I think you learn more about your client, their family, background, about mental health issues, family dynamics. You get to know far, far more about your clients than you would representing someone under a possession-of-cocaine charge, where you're going to deal with their addiction issues and guilt/innocence issues.

Another experienced defense attorney concurred:

> One of the areas that is the most different is the penalty phase. You go in assuming you're going to lose the guilt phase because typically the case is pretty bad. They [the prosecutors] have their ducks in a row. More often than not, you're going to lose the guilt phase, and you're going to have to deal with talking with the jury about whether they will recommend the death sentence. [In Florida, for example, the jury only recommends a sentence to the judge, who in capital cases has the ultimate authority in sentencing.] So all of the background and mental health information becomes critical, and you would never have to deal with that in a normal felony case. You would never have to go back and talk to school teachers or every single relative you can get your hands on. You would never have to get the down and dirty of the family history and the ghosts in the closet. You know, delve into the mental health issues so deeply. You have to do that from day one.

A long-time public defender similarly stated:

> You have to be able to demonstrate to the judge and jury the uniqueness of the person they are trying to execute. So, in addition to investigating the crime, you also investigate the life of the defendant. You find what you can about him or her. You try to get every piece of paper that has that person's name on it. You

talk to family members, friends, lawyers. You talk to the guards that have been guarding them, and you try to develop an extensive body of evidence you can present to defend the person.

Part of developing a mitigation case is overcoming misconceptions. As one defense attorney observed:

> Your client has misconceptions about what will or will not help them. And they're typically damaged in some way. They didn't get there coincidentally. They've either got drug issues or mental retardation issues or mental health issues. They've got something going on that got them in this position and so they're not going to be … even if they want to be, helpful … they're not usually affirmatively helpful. You got their families, who are going to be an integral part of whatever happens, and they're typically damaged, or they wouldn't have a damaged kid, and getting past their misconceptions about what's going to be helpful takes time. Ultimately you're going to have a jury that's going to have all sorts of misconceptions, and you have to keep them at the foremost throughout the process.

Defense attorneys who lack experience in capital cases are often stymied at the penalty phase. Many attorneys have experience pleading their client's innocence (the focus of the guilt phase), but only those lawyers who have tried several capital cases are experienced in making an affirmative case for their client's life in the penalty phase. As an experienced defense attorney related:

> Many defense attorneys fail to make the transition and do not adequately prepare or effectively present the defendant's penalty phase trial. For example, a defense attorney may structure a guilt trial strategy that is inconsistent with the penalty phase theory. This situation may negate any effective defense at the penalty proceeding since a consistent trial strategy increases the defendant's believability and credibility. Should a guilty verdict be rendered in the guilt phase, it is imperative that the jury believe the defendant's mitigating circumstances proffered in the penalty phase. Therefore, the defense attorney cannot plan the theory of the guilt phase trial independent of the penalty phase. She must develop and structure a defense theory that will include the penalty phase. Because the preparation required for structuring a bifurcated proceeding is categorically different from that required for a noncapital trial, defense counsel who may be very competent in complex noncapital criminal trials may, without training, be ineffective in capital trials.[19]

Another experienced defense attorney echoed the need to successfully integrate the guilt and penalty phases of the trial: "You have to do your best to integrate the story [about the defendant] with your defense in the guilt phase so that it doesn't look inconsistent. And so you start appealing to the humanity of the jury from the beginning in a way that you would never have to do if [the situation were whether your client] robbed the store or didn't rob the store." She added, "In one sense, I love that part. You get to go and be a part of the family. I just get emotional talking about it."

Other issues are also involved in coordinating the guilt and penalty phases of a bifurcated capital trial. According to a former public defender now in private practice:

---

19. Margot Garey (1985) "The Cost of Taking a Life: Dollars and Sense of the Death Penalty," *University of California, Davis Law Review* 18:1221–1273.

If you are arguing not guilty, then when you get to penalty phase, if the client is found guilty, you have the issue of, should they take the stand? Will that affect an appeal? Will the jury be looking for them to suddenly confess and accept responsibility now that they've been convicted? I think that there's certain strategy decisions. You have to make decisions about putting in mental health evidence or not. If there's some sort of issue that could affect or negate what the defense was by putting that on. I think, certainly, some theories are inconsistent between guilt and penalty phase. And you have to try to make the best decisions you can about those inconsistencies.

Whether it is the result of a lack of training, experience, or heart, many capital defendants receive what appears to be ineffective legal representation. Critics cynically argue that in practice the courts use the "mirror test" in determining whether a defense attorney is effective in a capital case: If the mirror fogs up because the attorney is breathing, then the attorney is effective. That may be why the Supreme Court has rarely granted relief on the grounds of ineffective assistance of counsel.[20]

Proponents of capital punishment argue that the reason the Supreme Court rarely grants relief in ineffective assistance of counsel claims is because most capital defendants have superior defense attorneys. Proponents argue that death penalty abolitionists do not show that ineffectiveness of counsel is widespread and that the evidence of ineffectiveness is mostly anecdotal and "grossly outdated."[21] A former public defender now in private practice believes that legal representation in capital cases has improved considerably during the past couple of decades:

There are a lot more seminars now focused on health issues, forensic issues; things that come up in the capital cases. I've now been to the NAACP's seminar in Virginia, I go to [regular seminars entitled] "Life over Death," "Life in the Balance," and "Making a Case for Life." I think that we prepare lawyers much better emotionally, legally, support system-wise.

You know, back when I was trying my first couple capital cases, the thought was we didn't want the same jury deciding guilt/innocence, since we do penalty phase. Because once they convicted our guy, we thought they'd want to kill our guy. In twenty-something years of doing capital work, I'll tell you my opinion has changed on that. I think most of the defense lawyers have changed their minds. One of the things involved resentencing. One of the things we learned was, in resentencing it's far more difficult to humanize your client. It's far more difficult to get a life sentence than if you tried the case and they heard all those horrible facts. Back then, you'd file the motion to have a second jury seated for penalty phase. I would never, ever do that now. God forbid someone gave that to me. I want the same jury who's kind of been through the emotional turmoil of the facts of the case [because] they have a better grasp of the appropriate sentence because they have more information. Back then, one lawyer did guilt/innocence; one lawyer did penalty phase. And again, you wanted the whole separateness, and the thought was, one lawyer who lost a case and got the guilt charge

---

20. Jonathan Alter (2000) "The Death Penalty on Trial," *Newsweek* (June 12), pp. 24–34; *Wiggins v. Smith* (539 U.S. 510, 2003); *Rompilla v. Beard* (545 U.S. 374, 2005).

21. Paul G. Cassell (2004) "In Defense of the Death Penalty," pp. 183-217 in H.A. Bedau and P.G. Cassell (eds.) *Debating the Death Penalty: Should America Have Capital Punishment? The Experts on Both Sides Make Their Best Case.* New York: Oxford, pp. 209-210.

didn't have any credibility left with the jury. Well, I totally disagree with that theory. No one teaches that theory anymore.

Now the whole theory is team defense. You do everything together and everything is as a team. The team is not just the two lawyers; hopefully, you have the investigator, the mental health experts, the forensic experts, and everybody else. It really is a group effort. You have this unified front, and a lot of things that we've learned about, no one knew about. You have much different mind-sets nowadays. Much different levels of preparation. We now have minimum standards for capital lawyers. Which is a great thing. We can use the Internet to communicate with other lawyers. Get other input and bounce ideas and have news flutters on the Internet that you can subscribe to that are devoted to capital cases that are much more focused. I think those are all great improvements.

Another former public defender turned private defense counsel expressed a similar view:

Now they have standards in place [in some states] that I think make a lot of sense. And that is you have to have been, if not involved in representing a murder case before, you have to sit through an entire trial. That alone would give a hint as to the variety of things you need to know about. And it [the standards] requires that you do one of the two seminars every year, which makes a lot of sense. It certainly would have gone a long way in preparing [for my first death penalty case].

Obstacles, Problems, and Challenges

Not all of the problems encountered in a capital defense are a defense attorney's fault. Some problems are inherent in the process. For a conscientious public defender, constant pressure and sleep deprivation are major problems:

It's just the pressure. [For example,] depending where the courthouse is, like in [names a city], you've got your morning commute. Work starts at eight-thirty. But before you get there at eight-thirty, you have to leave sometimes at six-thirty. So that is a couple hours. And at the end of the day, everyone else goes home to eat. And the defense and state attorney to some extent are preparing for what's coming tomorrow. They're going over their notes and their witnesses and stuff. So you're working until one or two in the morning. And if you get to sleep, you're going to wake ten or fifteen minutes later. You won't go back to sleep because your mind kicks into gear and then you take off again. And that goes on throughout the trial, and it gets worse and worse and worse. So that when you do get to the penalty phase, you're sleep deprived and emotionally deprived.

He added that because of the rigors of a capital case, "you'll lose ten to fifteen pounds easy." He noted that he had not met a defense attorney in a capital case who had not lost ten to fifteen pounds.

A former public defender now in private practice also cited pressure and sleep deprivation as problems, as well as becoming too emotionally involved:

Thinking of the police killing case, we did this out of county, and there was some pressure to get the case done more quickly because we took over a judge and another jury's courtroom and their personnel. And moved down for the duration. Our judge was living in his boat. And I think he was loving living in his boat because he was living in it for longer than he had to. And he was one of these people that had all of this energy and was perfectly happy working until eleven p.m. at night. I hit seven-thirty and my brain turns off. I found it very difficult to say things that made any sense at nine, ten, eleven o'clock at night. And there were a couple of times that we had to talk him into letting us break. It was so exhausting. Sometimes it's really hard to keep your mind going in a straight line. I would say my emotional connection to that client was a negative factor. I can't point to anything that I would have done differently or should have done that I ... ultimately some of the jurors thought ... felt how much I was emotionally invested and maybe voted life because of it. And saw him as human because I saw him as human. I probably got closer to that client and his family. I let my dislike of the prosecutor probably affect me more than I should have. There was one time in that trial that he made a smart comment to me at a sidebar, and I made a smart comment back to him that was smarter than his smart comment. And when we got up there, the judge made me apologize. [*Laughs*] The jury is listening to the whole thing and thought we both should have been on a playground. I've gotten much better about that kind of thing. It's hard. It's a battle. It's emotional. It's the heat of the moment. I think it's difficult for everybody to keep it professional every minute of a murder trial, on both sides. I like that prosecutor much more now than I used to.

Another problem is that some capital defendants refuse to cooperate at all or cooperate fully with their attorneys. For example, some defendants refuse to help their attorneys develop their life story to use as mitigation in the penalty phase. These defendants often want to protect their families from embarrassment by not revealing family secrets of child abuse and molestation. Sometimes defendants refuse to allow their attorneys to claim that their clients suffer from mental illness, even when the evidence strongly supports such a claim. Some defendants simply want to be sentenced to death, placing a considerable burden on their attorneys, who are required by law to zealously defend them.[22]

Defense attorneys have different ways of dealing with uncooperative defendants. A public defender explained how he handles mentally ill defendants who do not want their mental illness raised at trial or used in their defense:

A lot of people who are mentally ill don't like to air their laundry: abused as child, sexually abused as a child. They don't want to get that out there. All you can do is advise a client. You try to build a rapport or relationship with them. If they trust you, and they trust your advice, hopefully they see the need that you obtain that information. But a lot is going to depend on their motivation, too. If they are bipolar, depending on what stage they are in, sometimes they are up, sometimes they are down. Immediately after they are arrested, after a crime occurs, they are usually in a high emotional state. They don't want to talk to you. "Just execute me." The typical death penalty case takes years. It will take one, two, three years to get to trial, just to have been in the investigation that is going on and the litigation.

22. Scott E. Sundby (2005) *A Life and Death Decision: A Jury Weighs the Death Penalty*. New York: Palgrave Macmillan, p. 77.

So during that period of time, a position is taken early on. You try not to get them entrenched in it. You say, "Well, I'll talk about this," and you move through it as best you can. We're appointed by the public defender's office. We represent the people, and we advise them and save them money from hiring their own attorney. They say, "Look, I really, really want the death penalty. Do whatever you can to get the death penalty." It's the attorney's job to represent the client ... If that's what the client wants.

He gave an example:

For instance, you have a long-term criminal defendant. He's been in prisons all his life. He knows what [names a state] prisons are all about. He doesn't want to go back and spend the rest of his life, no air conditioning, and being out there and being harassed by guards and bigger inmates. If you're on death row, you have your own television set. You get to sleep soundly every night because you're in a one-man cell. No one messes with you. If you're going to die now, it's going to be by lethal injection. It's a consideration that if you have that client that knows the alternatives, and sees what's going on, it's in my position to say, "You can't do that." You try to persuade him from doing that. You try to point those things out. In the end, you are representing the client; this is what the client wants.

He continued:

The [U.S.] Supreme Court has said that the client is now in control. The client can tell you they don't want to put on mitigation. Now there's a distinction between being obligated ethically to research and investigate it, and to do as much as you can and develop as much information, and you can show it to the client so he can make an informed choice. Him saying, "Kill me. I don't care," doesn't relieve us of the obligation to go and look. Even without their cooperation, you contact their mother, you contact everybody. There are some attorneys who will present that to the court and proffer it to the court. In a [special] hearing [before a judge only], the jury doesn't hear it, but the judge needs to be aware of all the information, and [that] he [the defendant] doesn't want us to present it. By doing that, you're circumventing ... the client's desires are still getting in the record, and it's still there. It might be a run around the rules. Everybody has to decide what they want to do, and how they want to represent the client. You have to investigate it and hear what the client is saying. You have to develop the information that's there. Once you do it, it kind of depends on the defense, because he can waive it. He can waive all the mitigation you developed and say, "I do not want this put on." Ethically, do you represent him, or do you represent the client?

A defense attorney in private practice had this to say about dealing with uncooperative defendants:

You try to find a liaison — that is, a friend or family member that will talk to your client and try to get them to cooperate. You consult with mental health experts that you have on the team and see what suggestions they make.... Depending on your client's personal makeup, you may bring in their minister, who is maybe someone that can be a liaison. You can have a hearing with the judge, and they sometimes vent because they want the spirit of cooperation moving in the right direction. It depends on why they aren't cooperating; to what level they aren't cooperating. Sometimes you bring in another lawyer.

She noted that if all efforts fail, and the defendant remains uncooperative, you go ahead and try the case without the defendant's cooperation. However, she said that doing so presents some special difficulties:

> I think the biggest difficulty it represents is if your client is looking uncooperative to the jury, and if the jury sees that your client refuses to have any interaction with you, that hurts him in terms of the jury's outlook on their demeanor with you. Many times, juries come back and tell us that they noticed the interaction between the lawyer and client and whether it was forced or in some spirit of co-operation. Jurors come back and tell them that no one was sitting on the client's side of the courtroom. No family or friends showed up to be supportive in any way. All those things that are going on in the courtroom that we think go sort of unspoken, speaks clear and loud to the jury.

Another defense attorney in private practice has been fortunate not to have had any uncooperative clients in death penalty cases, but she knows colleagues who have. She described how she believes she would address the problem if she ever encountered it: "I know what I would do if my client told me not to do mitigation. I would put on every bit of mitigation I could. 'Look how crazy he is: he wants to die!' I would put him on the stand and show how crazy he was." As far as legally being able to do that, she had this to say:

> There will be three people they will have to answer to. They have to answer to me, and that, frankly, might be the most important consideration. I'm going to have to answer to the people who are reviewing my performance. If I were reviewing my performance, "What do you mean you can't talk him into it? You're a lawyer." Alternatively, you look at what the bar thinks. And you have to explain it to the bar that I didn't do what my crazy murder client wanted me to do. And I tried to manage to save his life by doing it? I'll take that risk. I'm willing to answer those questions. Can you imagine losing your license over anything more just? [*Laughs*]

When asked about the most important aspect of defending a person charged with a capital crime, the long-time public defender responded:

> Getting him [the defendant] away from the death penalty, because everyone charged with murder is potentially facing the death penalty. Right out of the box, you're representing a client charged with first-degree murder. You've got to move the death penalty off the table. But then you're talking about life without parole. Still a serious sanction, but at least you aren't dealing with the death penalty. To me that's the primary goal. Get that out of there. Then you're not qualifying the jury when you're picking the jury for guilt or innocence. So you gotta get away from the death penalty.

The time commitment was one of the most important aspects for a former public defender now in private practice:

> You can't do any of the things that need to get done without serious time com-mitment. That is just the bottom line. I guess that sounds easy, but it isn't. It's really difficult. There's a lot of other things that I think are vital. You've got to be well organized, which can be difficult when you're looking at tens of thousands of documents and photographs and evidence and maps and charts and one hundred witnesses.

In a case that I'm re-retrying … Oh, this is actually horrible. Two co-defendants. The first goes to trial, and we've got all the transcripts. And then we do redepositions. So we've got two and three transcripts of the depositions and two trials. And we tried it a second time. And it's just, ya know, figuring out how … to impeach a witness when you've got four different versions of one thing is mind-boggling. Organization, huge. Listening, huge.

Another former public defender now in private practice cited "credibility in front of the jury and believing in your case and believing you can represent your client." She also mentioned "believing that it's important to do everything possible in terms of preparation." She concluded, "I don't think there's any one factor; I think it's a whole combination of things."

For one of the former public defenders now in private practice, the most difficult aspect of defending a person charged with a capital crime is "standing next to them when they are sentenced to die. It's awful," she confided. For the other former public defender now in private practice, the most difficult aspect is "finding the time":

It's a lot of balls to keep in the air; in the criminal defense world, it's a very long period of time. You're talking a year to four years, very typically. It's a lot of things to keep straight and moving. It really takes a team effort. The emotional side, I don't really think about that a whole lot until we get to the trial itself, because I just don't want to go there. Even when we had the case that got moved — a guy who shot two police officers — I knew intellectually that was the kind of case that was much more likely than many others that I dealt with to actually get the death penalty. I knew, *duh*, that was going to be something that the jury was going to be extremely unhappy about. And there were a couple other aspects that were compounded. Intellectually, I knew that, but I didn't dwell on that part of it until I was in the thick of it. You kind of have to because you're talking to the jury everyday. You're talking to your client's worried family about it every day. And you kind of stop dealing with that reality then. During the trial, it's a huge looming fear, you know?

For the long-time public defender, the most difficult aspect of defending a person charged with a capital crime is "getting away from the death penalty. The state has too many advantages with it. They use it to leverage pleas."

Likewise, for the long-time public defender, the worst aspect of defending a person charged with a capital crime is the death penalty itself:

Just dealing with it and getting rid of it. That's where all the cost and focus is. That's the concern. With the death penalty, you're also dealing with all the problems that carried with it the litigation aspect of it. You're going to court, trying to get rid of it as a matter of law. And the courts are just turning their back on you; on all these issues we're talking about. You're not going to get any relief.

For one of the former public defenders now in private practice, the worst aspect of the trial is "the huge, looming fear" of losing, of the client being executed:

The fear that someone is sitting on death row with your name on him. I've never witnessed an execution. I have mixed feelings about it. Part of me thinks I really should because this is part of what I do. And part of me thinks I just can't take that additional layer of reality into consideration. That would make it that much harder to keep that barrier up. It's still the ultimate loss.

Doing God's Work

Defense work in capital cases can be mentally, emotionally, and physically taxing. According to the long-time public defender: "You get frustrated a lot. [Being sleep deprived, as he noted previously], that's part of it. You spend a lot of your off time thinking about it. You're always on the clock." As for the weight loss he discussed earlier, he explained:

> If you're experienced at it, if you've done it before, then you tend to get in better shape. You realize these things are marathons. You have to be in really good condition. So going into a trial, I will consciously go out and train. I will do whatever I can do to get my stamina up so when I get in there … otherwise you get wiped out. And you still get wiped out. And I can't speak for judges and prosecutors, but from a defense standpoint, it's very draining.

One of the former public defenders now in private practice shared this about the mental and emotional aspects of the job:

> It's exhausting. It's stressful. You're almost guaranteed to go to trial feeling like there was a lot more that you should have done. It's weighty. On the flip side, it's gratifying, it's stimulating and interesting. I know the public has a totally opposite view … I'm not a traditionally religious person, and I use this euphemistically, but I really feel I'm doing God's work. I think it's the way I'm made. I think it's the pinnacle of good I could do for society [*laughing*].

As for the physical part, she responded similarly to the long-time public defender:

> Fabulous diet plan, because I don't eat in trial. So it's a guaranteed five pounds off. It's stressful and tiring, but I've got to say it doesn't matter how … the concept of going into a murder or capital trial is more exhausting. Thinking about doing it is more exhausting than doing it. You go into automatic mode, physically. I wake up everyday refreshed enough, ready enough, alert enough, ready. I get home, and I think there's no way I can do it tomorrow. I can't do it another day. I can't do it another day. But lo and behold, I wake up refreshed, ready. I think your body just does what it needs to do.

The other former public defender now in private practice described the mental and emotional aspects of handling a capital case in these words:

> I think, mentally, it's much more of a challenge because you're dealing with issues that don't come up routinely. Emotionally, you've got the client and the client's family and the victim's family that you're dealing with, and your own feelings about the government killing one of its citizens. I think all of those things come into play. But if you do this for a long period of time, you obviously put those things in some sort of perspective that enables you to do your job.

Asked whether she went out and got drunk or went home and cried all night if her client was sentenced to death, she replied: "No. The first time I had a client sentenced to die, it's just such a bizarre experience to be a part of. And I got out of the courtroom and got on the elevator and most definitely shed a few tears. That's more about being part of a process that ends with this very conscious decision to kill someone. No, I've never gone on a binge or uncontrollably sobbed or anything like that." As for how handling a capital case affected her physically, she remarked with a laugh:

It's tiring and you miss going to the gym because you're in court all day long. There's certainly the physical effect that goes along with any long trial. And there's certainly other kinds of cases that you try that go on for two or three weeks, and you're spending eight hours in court all day, and you're coming back to the office to do other things. You're not sticking to your gym or run schedule.

Death Penalty Opinion

Defense attorneys were also asked whether their opinion of the death penalty had been affected by their defense work in capital cases. One of the former public defenders now in private practice stated that she had not become more or less opposed; she had just become more informed: "I was always against the death penalty. I certainly think I'm more educated about it and more informed about it, with regard to facts and statistics that surround it."

The other former public defender now in private practice was more effusive than her colleague. When asked whether her opinion of the death penalty had been affected by her defense work in capital cases, she responded:

> In, like, more, more, more, more convinced after doing capital cases that the death penalty is wrong? I don't know. I'm not sure it's possible that I could be more anti-death penalty than I was since I remember having my first opinion about the subject. Certainly that intellectual opinion has been made more real by seeing it in action. I can tell you that ... I don't know if I can put it into words. I have felt what seems like a lift, in a room [*crying*]. I swear, even the family of the victim, even the cop who is physically handicapped, testified emotionally, sat through the entire trial with his family, sat with the family of the deceased cop. There is some level, with me, for release or closure or something that I think people on the outside don't understand, the quality of closure that isn't ... now we get to go to the appeal process and eight years of fighting over that, or yes, or no, or maybe. I just think there's something appealing about knowing that it's done.

Asked whether she could clarify what she meant, she explained:

> There's something appealing about knowing that it's a life sentence. It's done in that moment for everybody in the room. It's a life sentence. You don't have to worry about it not being done. There's a closure that comes immediately that isn't, "Okay [*deep breath*], we have to get ready for everything after the trial." A life sentence gives immediacy to there being a closure. And you can just feel the room get less heavy. And even the victim's family. I'm not saying that I think in that particular case they were brought around to our way of thinking. I'm not saying if you put those folks on the jury they would have voted for life. I think a couple of them would have. And I think a couple of them got their own kind of closure by watching the penalty phase, and understanding in their own mind as to how this could happen, and how it came to be, this person, that place, doing that. By the end of the trial they were very cordial. I remember there were some really sweet interactions between the victim's family and my client's family.

And you're sitting there. It's a weird situation. There's the lovely, crying, sweet family of the man who murdered my son in cold blood. And we're going to sit here on a pew together for three or four weeks. It's hard.

Asked how common that is, that there is a sort of reconciliation or meeting of the minds, the metaphysical experience, she commented:

I don't know. I think the thing that seems to torture people is not understanding and not having a reason for things. Whether you like or dislike the explanation, I think sometimes that goes some way in … ya know, I wish there was a way that we could … and I know some lawyers do it. And I've never figured out a way to do it. I've been to seminars with lawyers who have contacted the victim's families and started that process earlier. I was too cowardly. I can't imagine doing that effectively in a way that wouldn't make things worse. I wish there were a way of giving them information ahead of time that right now they only get if they sit through a horrible murder trial and see horrible pictures and get a conviction. That's part of the process. If they're being nice … I know these are questions they have during the whole three years these cases are pending.

Finally, the long-time public defender offered this answer to the question about whether his death penalty opinion had been affected by his defense work in capital cases:

I'd have to say, yes. I've never been for [the death penalty], but I was never adamantly opposed to it as I am now. I can see a need for it. I can see certain situations [where] theoretically [it] might be a good thing. But the temptation to abuse it is such that it shouldn't be out there for anything. Theoretically, it's reserved for the worst of the worst. It's not. It's really not.

Conclusion

Defense attorneys clearly have been the weak link in the capital punishment process, although the situation may be changing in some states because of the implementation of minimum standards. Supreme Court Justice Ruth Bader Ginsburg has stated that her experience with death row inmates who have asked the Court for last–minute reprieves demonstrated that not one of them received really good legal help at trial. She also criticized the "meager" amount of money spent to defend poor people.[23]

Capital cases are a huge burden for defense attorneys. Since the vast majority of capital defendants are indigent, they must depend on indigent defense services. Defendants in jurisdictions with public defender systems probably receive at least adequate representation, but in those states that rely on court-appointed counsel, such as Texas, the quality of legal representation varies greatly. The paltry compensation provided for court-appointed counsel discourages experienced, well-qualifed attorneys from taking capital cases, and attracts inexperienced, hungry attorneys who are looking for work. For attorneys with successful practices, representing indigent capital defendants is largely a gift to their

---

23. Anne Gearan (2002) "Supreme Court Takes Up Claim of Poor Defense in Death Cases," *The Orlando Sentinel* (March 26), p. A11.

clients—a usually unappreciated gift of hundreds of hours of legal work that invariably takes a physical and emotional toll on the attorney.

Make no mistake: the quality of defense counsel matters. A Texas study by the governor's judicial council found that three-quarters of murderers with court-appointed attorneys were sentenced to death, while only about a third of those represented by private lawyers were so sentenced.[24] Another study that compared innocent capital defendants who were eventually exonerated and released from death row, and innocent capital defendants who were later executed, discovered that defendants with private lawyers at trial were nine times more likely to be exonerated and released from death row than defendants with court-appointed attorneys.[25] Few people likely consider it fair that a capital defendant's life depends substantially on whether he can afford to hire a private attorney.

While the defendant's life is, quite literally, in the hands of the defense attorney, his family often are at loose ends worrying about the fate of their loved one—even if that loved one is accused of, and quite possibly guilty of, a heinous crime. As with the families of victims, which we looked at in chapter 3, the families of defendants find their lives changed forever, and usually not in a good way. This is the subject we explore next.

---

24. Kurt Andersen (1983) "An Eye for an Eye," *Time* (January 24), p. 39; also see Talia Roitberg Harmon (2001) "Predictors of Miscarriages of Justice in Capital Cases," *Justice Quarterly* 18:949–968.

25. Talia Roitberg Harmon and William S. Lofquist (2005) "Too Late for Luck: A Comparison of Post-*Furman* Exonerations and Executions of the Innocent," *Crime & Delinquency* 51:498-520.

Chapter 5

Offenders' Families

Offenders' family members are the forgotten victims of capital punishment. Yet the effects of capital punishment on them can be as profound as they are for murder victims' families. Both sets of families have in common psychological and economic stress, anxiety, grief, depression, and other medical illnesses, as well as self-accusation, suicidal thoughts, social isolation, powerlessness, demoralization, and family disorganization.[1] However, as this chapter show, offenders' families differ in some important ways from victims' families who experience a loved one's death.[2]

As is the case with victims' family members, offenders' family members often feel victimized by the criminal justice system and the media. They feel as if they themselves are being punished. Only on rare occasions are offenders' family members assisted in navigating the capital punishment process, which elevates their already high stress levels. They are mostly voiceless in the process and often feel disoriented. They are unlikely to receive much help from their loved one's defense attorney, who is focused on trying to save the defendant's life.

A capital trial can devastate and traumatize an offender's family and cause major divisions within it. Few families are able to get through a capital trial unscathed. By the

---

1. John Ortiz Smykla (1987) "The Human Impact of Capital Punishment: Interviews with Families of Persons on Death Row." *Journal of Criminal Justice* 15:331–347; Michael L. Radelet, Margaret Vandiver, and Felix M. Barado (1983) "Families, Prisons, and Men with Death Sentences." *Journal of Family Issues* 4:593–612; Margaret Vandiver (2003) "The Impact of the Death Penalty on the Families of Homicide Victims and of Condemned Prisoners," pp. 613-645 in J. R. Acker, R. M. Bohm, and C. S. Lanier (eds.) *America's Experiment with Capital Punishment: Reflections on the Past, Present and Future of the Ultimate Penal Sanction.* Durham, NC: Carolina Academic Press; Margaret Vandiver (1989) "Coping with Death: Families of the Terminally Ill, Homicide Victims, and Condemned Prisoners," pp. 123–138 in M. L. Radelet (ed.) *Facing the Death Penalty: Essays on a Cruel and Unusual Punishment.* Philadelphia: Temple University Press; Joseph B. Ingle (1989) "Ministering to the Condemned: A Case Study," pp. 112–122 in M. L. Radelet (ed.) *Facing the Death Penalty: Essays on a Cruel and Unusual Punishment.* Philadelphia: Temple University Press; Elizabeth Beck, Sarah Brito, and Arlene Andrews (2007) *In the Shadow of Death: Restorative Justice and Death Row Families.* New York: Oxford University Press; also see David Kaczynski and Gary Wright (2006) "Building a Bridge," pp. 85-101 in J. R. Acker and D. R. Karp (eds.) *Wounds That Do Not Bind: Victim-Based Perspectives on the Death Penalty.* Durham, NC: Carolina Academic Press; Rachel King (2006) "The Impact of Capital Punishment on Families of Defendants and Murder Victims' Family Members." *Judicature* 89:292-296; Susan F. Sharp (2005) *Hidden Victims: The Effects of the Death Penalty on Families of the Accused.* Piscataway, NJ: Rutgers University Press; Sarah Eschholz, Mark D. Reed, Elizabeth Beck, and Pamela Blume Leonard (2003) "Offenders' Family Members' Responses to Capital Crimes: The Need for Restorative Justice Initiatives." *Homicide Studies* 7:154-181; Helen Prejean (1993) *Dead Man Walking: An Eyewitness Account of the Death Penalty in the United States.* New York: Random House; Joseph B. Ingle (1989) "Ministering to the Condemned: A Case Study," pp. 112–122 in M. L. Radelet (ed.) *Facing the Death Penalty: Essays on a Cruel and Unusual Punishment.* Philadelphia: Temple University Press.
2. Vandiver (2003), ibid., pp. 624-625; Beck et al., ibid., p. 9.

end of the trial, whether or not their loved one is found guilty, most capital defendants' family members have lost faith in the criminal justice system. Although offenders' family members may have supported capital punishment prior to their involvement with the process, few of them likely support capital punishment following their devastating ordeal. After a death sentence is issued, family members are left alone to deal with feelings of shame, fear, depression, trauma, suicide, stress-related health problems, and the constant threat that the state will soon execute someone they love.

Many family members consider their loved one's stay on death row a "living death." When a loved one has been sentenced to death, many family members experience an almost unbearable sense of helplessness or powerlessness to do anything about the sentence or the impending execution. The pain and suffering experienced by family members does not end with the execution or the funeral. For some of them, it never ends.

Offenders' Families Are Unique

Offenders' families agonize for years knowing that the state intends to kill their family member and by which method. They live in the "shadow of death." This causes family members to experience "anticipatory grief," a type of grief experienced only by families of death row inmates and, in some respects, families of terminally ill patients—although the families of terminally ill patients generally do not know the exact day and time their loved one will die. Added stress is caused by the hope that some court or governor will step in and save their family member.

Second, the family member's death will not be the result of a breakdown in the social order but, rather, a systematic function of government authority. The family member will not die by the hands of a vicious, depraved murderer but, rather, as a result of decisions made by ordinary citizens and respected and powerful members of society.

Third, the family member's capital murder conviction forever stigmatizes him as unworthy of living in a civilized society. The offender and, in many cases, his family are publicly disgraced and shamed. Few people will talk about him with pride. Family members sometimes are considered at least partially responsible for the murder. They often are blamed for making serious parenting mistakes.

Fourth, the family member's death is not mourned or regretted like the deaths of other people, except perhaps by his family and friends. Rarely do people express sympathy or show compassion for the family's loss. Instead, the family member's death is officially sanctioned, defended, eagerly awaited, and, in some cases, celebrated joyously.

Fifth, the siblings and children of condemned inmates often grow up with a feeling of familial dread and experience an increased probability of mental health problems and criminal behavior. They are likely to lose confidence in the criminal justice system and the U.S. government.

Finally, many offenders' families experience the double standard of the criminal justice system. According to Professor Vandiver:

> Family members of capital defendants frequently have been victims of violent crime themselves; indeed, it is not unusual for these families to have lost relatives

to homicide. Yet, because of class and racial inequities in sentencing, it is unlikely their relatives' deaths were punished with much severity. How ironic for these families that when a relative encounters the criminal justice system as a defendant rather than a victim, the system turns from leniency to severity.[3]

Parenting Is Important

Some accusations about offenders' families are fair, but some are not. For example, the belief that some family members are at least partially responsible for the murder because they made serious parenting mistakes is supported by research showing that death row inmates commonly experienced paternal abandonment; foster care and in-stitutionalization; family violence; physical, sexual, and emotional abuse; neglect; parental alcohol and drug abuse; poverty; and religious extremism.[4] Many death row inmates have been diagnosed with posttraumatic stress disorder, neuropathy, psychiatric illness such as clinical depression, substance abuse, mental retardation, and school behavior problems.[5]

Rarely, however, do parents and other family members deserve all the blame. Research shows that many capital defendants, despite the best efforts of their families, experience system or institutional failures. Schools, juvenile programs, medical and psychiatric services, child protective services, and other institutions routinely fail to recognize and address capital defendants' needs. In many cases, the systems and institutions fail to provide access to services even when capital defendants' needs are identified, leaving the defendants to fare for themselves during times when they need help the most.[6] Had services been available, or had they been better able to address child abuse, mental health issues, poverty, racism, juvenile delinquency, drug and alcohol abuse, and learning disabilities, there is no telling how many violent murders might have been prevented.[7] Families find it ironic that the government often fails to provide social service resources for their loved ones to stave off serious problems but manages to provide an abundance of legal resources when pursuing an execution.[8] In short, when a capital crime has been committed, there is plenty of blame to spread around.

Nevertheless, in many cases, offenders' families, especially parents, deserve at least some of the blame. Interpersonal violence is common in the families of death row or executed inmates. For example, many death row inmates' fathers subjected their sons to severe beatings, usually when the father was in a drunken stupor. Death row inmates were left outside as children, sometimes for days, following a beating. In one case, a father of a death row inmate set his son's pants on fire while the boy was wearing them. Several death row inmates' fathers fired guns at their feet as children, just to let them know who was boss in the household. Mothers stayed with violent, alcoholic, and abusive husbands for a variety of reasons. Among them, they were afraid of losing custody of their children

---

3. Vandiver (2003), ibid., p. 624, n. 18.
4. Beck et al., op. cit., p. 30-31.
5. Ibid.
6. Ibid., p. 199-200.
7. Ibid., p. 234.
8. Ibid., p. 200.

and, as a result, the opportunity to protect them; they were afraid their husbands would kill them and their children; or their religion prohibited divorce.[9]

Many mothers of death row inmates were incapable of adequately caring for their children. Many of them were mere children when they had children themselves; some mothers were as young as fourteen when they were married. Some mothers married young to escape their own abusive parents. Poverty, racism, and feelings of marginalization and exclusion were common. Few death row inmates' mothers had good support systems, and many of them neglected their children. Some of them were alcoholics or drug addicts. However, when Child Protective Services were called, mothers frequently were able to conceal their problems.[10]

Many death row inmates have severe psychiatric and neurological disorders. In some cases, their parents (or parent) recognized the problem and sought professional help. When they could not get help, they closely supervised their child. However, in many other cases, parents did not understand what was happening to their child. Although they recognized their child's abnormal behavior, they did not have any knowledge of mental illness, so they were unable to adequately address it. In some cases, because of religious beliefs, some parents attributed the problems to demons. Even if their child's problem had been accurately diagnosed, most parents of death row inmates could not afford to pay for mental health treatment or drugs.[11]

Punishing the Family

As is the case with victims' family members, offenders' family members often feel victimized by the criminal justice system and the media. They feel as if they themselves are being punished. Their punishment includes "intense negative media coverage, being ostracized in their churches and communities, verbal threats, and disrespectful treatment by members of the criminal justice system."[12] As the mother of a death row inmate explained, "There are no good days; there are days that are bearable and then the rest."[13] After her son's arrest, another death row inmate's mother described spending her time "pacing and crying, crying and pacing."[14]

Media coverage is devastating for many offenders' family members. One man reported that after his stepson's arrest, the family's nightmare began: "They showed right on TV where our house was. That's when the phone calls started. That's when people drove by and started honking their horns and making all kinds of obscene calls and shouts.... I have felt violated ever since then."[15] One mother described reading articles about her condemned son as "terrible. I would read and cry, just hurting. I can't explain when I read the paper what it did to me, and sometimes the newspaper would put a little more in it

---

9. Ibid., pp. 31 and 37.
10. Ibid., p. 38-39 and 41-43.
11. Ibid., p. 39.
12. Ibid., p. 55.
13. Ibid., p. 4.
14. Ibid.
15. Susan F. Sharp (2005) *Hidden Victims: The Effects of the Death Penalty on Families of the Accused.* New Brunswick, NJ: Rutgers University Press, p. 61.

than what actually happened."[16] Another mother confided, "What gets you is, you are driving down the road and all of a sudden you hear it on the radio, and you don't know it is going to be on the radio. It's like a knife being stuck in your chest and turned."[17] Family members were taken aback and hurt when a neighbor in an editorial for the local paper wrote, "Stick a needle in [their son's] arm and put him to sleep permanently."[18]

The worst part of media coverage for most offenders' family members is the incomplete and one-sided descriptions of their loved one and the portrayal of him as a "monster," villain," or "dirt." Family members would have liked people to know that their loved one was also, for example, a loving father, a decorated war veteran, or a local sports hero.[19] They want people to know that their loved one was more than the worst thing he did in his life. Family members also resent the media's suggesting that they are somehow complicit in their loved one's murderous behavior. The father of a death row inmate noted, "You [and your family] are viewed as guilty as soon as your son is arrested."[20]

One family faulted the media for ignoring their considerable effort to secure mental health care for their loved one, how the health system was inadequate, and how the hospital continually discharged their loved one before he was ready. No where was it mentioned that the hospital often discharged their loved one on the first day that health insurance no longer covered him. The media failed to note that the family did not have the resources to treat their loved one's illness or to protect him and his victims.[21] Family members also feared that negative media coverage about their loved one would influence prospective jurors. They did not believe that the jury selection process eliminates jurors who are biased by the media, especially when a change of venue is denied.[22]

Offenders' family members often become pariahs in their communities. The mother of a death row inmate recalled:

> Most people seemed [to] avoid us like we had the plague. Up until his arrest, we went out [every] weekend [to] eat with a couple, we did vacations together. Then nothing. About three years later, she called and asked me [to] stay with her; she had had surgery. Well, I went. During that time, I asked her why we didn't see them anymore. She said, "Your problems were [more] that we could take...."
> *Well*—hello! Wonder what she [thought] they were [for] us.[23]

Another mother recalled, "Most people just flat out said I had raised the devil himself. This came from friends, family, and complete strangers."[24]

The mother of a son who died on death row before he could be executed observed, "I think the public should show a little bit of compassion for the families of those who have a loved one on death row. After all, they did not commit any crime, and yet they are made to feel like they did. They are looked down at by the public as if they were scum, as if they were trash who had no right to live and were beneath them."[25]

---

16. Ibid., p. 58.
17. Ibid.
18. Ibid.
19. Ibid., p. 56.
20. Ibid.
21. Ibid., p. 57.
22. Ibid., p. 58
23. Sharp, op. cit., p. 31.
24. Ibid., p. 62.
25. Ibid., p. 165.

Two younger brothers of a death row inmate, one in the ninth grade and the other in the tenth grade at the time of their brother's arrest, were harassed at school. They were called names, their lockers were defaced, and threats were made against their lives. The situation deteriorated to the point that the principal suggested that it might be in the brothers' interests to be schooled at home.[26]

The mother of one death row inmate disclosed, "People that really know me have stood by me. It's the strangers who, when they find out that I'm [son's name] mother, act as if I have something catching. When it first happened, people would stand in groups and talk about [her son] killing this girl."[27]

Some death row inmates' family members have found human feces on their doorsteps or have received death threats following newspaper articles about their loved one. For one family, this behavior lasted for nineteen years between the time of arrest and the execution, because each year on the anniversary of the murder, the local newspaper published a picture of the victim's family at the victim's gravesite.[28]

In another situation, the sister of a death row inmate compared her family's experience to being drowned in the ocean by everyone around: "It was like they were pushing us under ... every time we come up they [the media and community] would push our heads back under."[29]

Some family members lose their jobs because of the publicity and community response to the murder.[30] Many family members are attacked. Most of the time they are verbal, but occasionally they escalate into something more: some family members have had their vehicles shot at.[31] A death row inmate's mother was afraid to leave her house: "You feel like someone is going to do something to you."[32] Leaving the house also was a burden for the brother of a death row inmate: "Oh, it's terrible. You feel ashamed, embarrassed, intimidated, scared."[33] Another mother reported, "I was scared, too, about being his mother. Like doomed. You feel like someone is going to do something to you."[34] After receiving several threatening phone calls, a single low-income mother who worked several jobs stayed awake nights in her living room: "I sat up because I was afraid to go to sleep, and I was watching over my family. I brought the kids into the living room—two were on the sofa and one was on the floor—and I would sit in the chair all night long."[35]

Religious Support

When it comes to providing support for offenders' families, religious leaders and religious communities are a mixed bag. Some are supportive and helpful, but others are

---

26. Ibid., p. 62.
27. Vandiver (2003), op. cit., p. 628.
28. Beck et al., op. cit., p. 59.
29. Ibid.
30. Ibid.
31. Ibid.
32. Ibid., p. 57.
33. Ibid., p. 52.
34. Ibid., p. 59.
35. Ibid.

not. In some cases, they turn their backs on the condemned inmate and his family. The mother of a death row inmate described her and her family's desire to start attending church again after her son's arrest. They were seeking emotional support and a spiritual connection. However, they found that the churches they attended were not receptive to them or their needs. She observed, "[They] kind of shunned us when they found out we were his family."[36] Another family, pillars of their church, who had given their time and money to it, were disappointed when "in their moment of pain, they did not feel like the church reached out to them and comforted them."[37] Some death row inmates' family members left their church because of its pro-death penalty stance.[38]

In some cases, religious leaders attempted to comfort the family and pray for them, but they ignored the inmate. As the mother of a death row inmate related, "It's not me that needs the prayers; it is my son, but they don't mention him."[39]

Destroying Families

A capital trial can devastate and traumatize an offender's family and cause major divisions within it. Few families are able to go through a capital trial unscathed.[40] A mother whose son was facing a capital trial felt abandoned by her extended family:

> I think most of my family just assumed he was guilty from the beginning. My mother was the only one that stood by him and has continued to stand by him. None of my family would come to the trial because they didn't want to be associated with him. Afraid of the repercussion … affecting jobs … clients, etc. Made me sick and to be honest, I have not had much use for them since. I have also quit attending any of the family functions. They do not offer to help me find a lawyer or help in any way to secure his freedom. It hurts me to even see them, so I don't.[41]

Another mother with a son on death row stated painfully:

> Most of my family thinks I should just write him off and forget him. Most of them do not even acknowledge that he is still alive.… One of my sisters thinks he should have been executed as soon as he was convicted. And she shares this with me every time his name is mentioned. Also, his sister thinks I should have nothing to do with him. She makes no effort to have anything to do with him.[42]

In cases of intrafamilial murder, in which some family members side with the victim while other family members side with the offender, a capital trial can be especially traumatic and polarizing.[43] As the mother of a death row inmate explained: "The family almost ceases.… Death would have been so easy.… This pain, there is no way to describe it. I

---

36. Ibid., p. 60.
37. Ibid.
38. Ibid.
39. Ibid., p. 59.
40. Ibid., p. 131.
41. Sharp, op. cit., p. 30.
42. Ibid., p. 62.
43. Beck et al., op. cit., p. 133.

don't know how to put it into words. The family dies. We went into hibernation, a stand still. Everything is going on but it isn't. Everything shuts down. Everything totally shuts down.... You just go through the motions, in a zombie like state."[44]

Losing Faith in the Criminal Justice System

Only on rare occasions are offenders' family members assisted in navigating the process, which elevates their already high stress levels. They are mostly voiceless and often feel disoriented. Ironically, before their loved one's arrest, many offenders' family members have positive impressions of the criminal justice system. Even after the arrest, many of them believe that justice will be done. Family members who believe that their loved one is guilty accept that he will be punished but hope that he will not receive a death sentence. Some family members assist the police in capturing their loved one, believing that their cooperation will help solve a heinous crime, prevent other crimes, and help their loved one avoid the death penalty.[45]

However, by the end of the criminal justice process, whether or not their loved one is found guilty, most capital defendants' family members have lost faith in the criminal justice system. As the father of a death row inmate and a successful businessman explained: "When you are brought up with a certain ideal and way of thinking about this country and then you find out that everything you have been taught is not true, that is when you get agitated and upset like I do. In this country you are guilty if you are arrested: period. And your family is, too ... you have to prove yourself [as a family member] innocent, and the press will not help you."[46] Another father expressed his disillusionment with the system: "I had always believed in the system. I thought it was fair. We were shocked at the way [the DA] lied in court. Now we know it can happen to anybody."[47] A mother pleaded with the district attorney that her son was innocent; the district attorney replied, "Lady, I don't care whether he did it or not, he is the one going down for it."[48]

Following her brother's execution, a sister stated, "[There is] nothing like knowing that your brother was put to death like a dog for something he did not do."[49] A father of a death row inmate related, "If every parent in this country knew how easy it was for a district attorney and judge to convict their child, the death penalty would not last 15 minutes."[50]

This sentiment is supported by available research. According to a study of the fully reviewed state death sentences imposed between 1973 and 1995, two-thirds were reversed at one of the appeal stages because of serious or prejudicial errors. The study found that in 82 percent of the reversals by state postconviction courts, the defendant deserved a sentence other than death when the errors were cured on retrial; and in 7 percent of the reversals, the defendant was found to be innocent of the capital crime. Eighty percent of

---

44. Vandiver (2003), op. cit., p. 626.
45. Beck et al., op. cit., p. 60.
46. Ibid., pp. 60-61.
47. Sharp, op. cit., p. 33.
48. Ibid. p. 76.
49. Beck et al., op. cit., p. 64.
50. Ibid., p. 61.

the reversals were due to ineffective assistance of counsel, prosecutor misconduct, unconstitutional jury instructions, or judge or jury bias.[51]

Dealing with Lawyers

Although some capital defendants have excellent lawyers, many do not. Many lawyers representing capital defendants are terribly incompetent or ineffective for a variety of reasons. The sister of a death row inmate was incredulous about the lawyer that the court provided her brother: "They had put this one attorney on his—on his case.... later on I found out that he had gotten a few DUIs and misdemeanor criminal things. But the main thing was that he did not know about trying a capital case. And it just amazed me, you know, that they put him on [her brother's] case and he didn't know a thing about the death penalty. It—shocked me."[52] Ironically, another sister of a death row inmate believed that the reason her brother was still alive was that his lawyer was so ineffective:

> They said that [her brother] could have represented himself better. And it turned out—it took five years—but it turned out to be a blessing because if you have an attorney that even does a halfway decent job, it is real hard—I mean if you lose it is real hard to get a new trial because they are going to say, "Well, you know, somebody had to lose and he did a halfway decent job." But in [her brother's case], you either want to have the very best attorney that money can buy or you want to have the very worst.[53]

Post-conviction attorneys can be incompetent and lazy, too. As a death row inmate's sister related:

> What this attorney did, he took the same appeal, changed the dates on it and sent it back in ... one that had already been denied.... I compared it to the other one and it was exact word for word. And that's when it really started getting frustrating because I knew he didn't know what he was doing.... [Her brother] got an agency to agree to fund the DNA testing, 'cause the attorney at the time kept saying he'd applied for the funding. They faxed him [the attorney] several forms, you know, to wire him the money. And that's when I was about to go crazy, you know. The—court said, you know—we don't have the money to fund DNA. So, [her brother] gets people to say—OK, we will give the money to fund this DNA test—and then his attorney didn't even take advantage of it.[54]

Oftentimes, family members suspect that mistakes are being made but are unfamiliar with standards of legal practice and feel powerless to do anything about the situation. When they do raise concerns to their loved one's attorney, they frequently are rebuked.[55] The mother of a death row inmate who was eventually executed blamed herself for her

---

51. James S. Liebman, Jeffrey Fagan, and Valerie West (2000) "A Broken System: Error Rates in Capital Cases, 1973–1995." The Justice Project, www.justice.policy.net/jpreport.html.

52. Sharp, op. cit., p. 70.

53. Ibid., p. 71.

54. Ibid., p. 70.

55. Beck et al., op. cit., p. 61.

son's poor representation: "You feel stupid, you blame yourself. I feel like my whole family was raped by the system. And we were, and we were left feeling so stupid."[56]

Sadly, many families spend their entire life savings on lawyers for their loved one and get little in return. For example, when one couple's son was charged with a capital murder, his parents spent all they had on what turned out to be incompetent private attorneys who were substance abusers, and who, the parents believed, exploited them:

> It took everything we had, and the attorneys would have taken more and we would have paid more, but our attorneys weren't good. We didn't know that until it was too late.... The one was on drugs. We didn't know that until well into the trial. He was overmedicated on Valium, and he was taking codeine for pain, and I don't [know] what all [else] he was taking—he just really had a pharmacy and the other one.... The lead counselor was drunk all the time. I mean, you could smell whiskey on his breath.... And see, we didn't know all those things. And of course, at this point in time, we paid—I don't know if we paid him $15,000 up front at that point in time or what, but it's not like we are going to get any of our money back. But I mean, I didn't have another $15,000 to $20,000 to go like shopping for another attorney.... They asked for more money in the middle of the trial, which is not really legal from what I understand. So I don't know how much they got out of the community and county, and yet we paid for the transcripts and we paid for the expert witness to fly down.... The doctor [the expert witness] never did see him [their son].... And you know the state has a bottomless pit to spend, and you know, not very many people—like O.J.—can outspend, but you almost have to outspend them to win.... We did the best we could with what resources we had. And now it's just—it's just been a nightmare and we just can't wake up from it.[57]

A particularly stressful event for some capital defendants' families is revealing the family's history to lawyers preparing a mitigation defense. As the brother of a death row inmate recounted:

> Family members are changing, and a great deal of pain is getting stirred up during the legal process: Dad's blaming himself, and Mom is blaming herself, and neither of them is saying it, but they were on the inside, and it is destroying them. Mom thinks they were too hard as parents, and Dad thinks they were too soft. From all of this, Dad was suicidal, and Mom was really suicidal. I was fearful. I was calling my mom and dad every day. I really did not think my dad would make it. I really thought he would have taken his own life.[58]

Sometimes family members make preparing a mitigation defense more difficult than it already is. Denial and shifting blame are common ways that defendants' families deal with the stressful situation. Family members may deny ever having any problems and, despite overwhelming evidence to the contrary, that their family member even committed a crime. They may also shift blame to a codefendant or the victim or believe that the crime was justified under the circumstances.[59] To cope with their misery, family members may shift blame to the media, the prosecutors, the judge, the defense attorneys, or, sometimes, other family members.[60]

---

56. Ibid., p. 62.
57. Sharp, op. cit., pp. 71-72.
58. Beck et al., op. cit., p. 54
59. Ibid., p. 131.
60. Ibid., p. 132.

Navigating the Legal Process

Capital defendants' family members also are troubled by issues involving "the admissibility and suppression of evidence, the handling of new evidence, coerced confessions, codefendants who received reduced sentences for information related to the crime, and plea bargains."[61] Arguably the most stressful of these issues for families is whether their loved one should accept a plea bargain. The choice involves a high-stakes gamble with their loved one's life. On one hand, if the defendant goes to trial, he may be acquitted, but he also may be found guilty and sentenced to death. On the other hand, if he accepts a plea bargain to avoid the death penalty, he is likely to spend the rest of his life in prison. The mother of a defendant who pled guilty explained the agonizing decision: "If it had not been a death penalty case, it would have been completely different. He would have gone to trial and had the opportunity to defend himself. Because it was a death case, we had no choice but to take the plea because the thoughts of losing him were so drastic."[62] She said she would second-guess herself about the decision for the rest of her life.

Another mother believes her son was innocent but "took the rap" to protect his family from retaliation:

> I believe my son to be innocent of shooting both of the victims and that his friend shot both—and he is paying the price for someone else's crime.... Also, my son feels he is protecting us from possible retaliation from his friend's brother.... Too many innocents are on death row who believed in the justice system and refused to accept a plea believing a trial by jury would set them free.[63]

The entire legal process is horrific for many capital offenders' family members. They describe the unfolding events as a nightmare and an experience they would "not wish on their worst enemy."[64] Nearly all family members are horrified by the possibility of the state killing their loved one, but many family members also are dumfounded that people actually want to kill their loved one. As the mother of a death row inmate observed, "I would look around the courtroom and think, 'You want to kill my child. This is my child.' It's just so awful. It is so awful that you cannot describe it."[65]

Going Through Hell

After a death sentence is issued, family members are left alone to deal with feelings of "shame, fear, depression, trauma, suicide, stress-related health problems, and the constant threat that the state will soon execute someone they love."[66] As the mother of a death row inmate described, "I have gained sixty lbs., take Prozac, see a shrink because I almost took my life. Doubled my smoking until I was hospitalized with lung disease. I stay in a state

---

61. Ibid., p. 54.
62. Ibid., p. 67.
63. Sharp, op. cit., p. 125.
64. Beck et al., op. cit., p. 126.
65. Ibid.
66. Ibid., p. 53.

of depression."[67] The uncertainty of the situation can create what has been called a "frozen sadness."[68] This suffering often spans years. The father of a death row inmate put it succinctly: "[W]e've been going through a — a fifteen year period of — of hell."[69] The younger brother of a defendant sentenced to death gave his perspective on this time dimension:

> I was eleven years old when I heard the judge pronounce the death sentence on my brother by electrocution until he was "dead, dead, dead." ... At that time, I didn't know when it would be carried out. I had an eleven-year-old imagination of electrocution. Those nightmares have haunted me for nineteen years now. I couldn't find anyone to express my feelings to. I was also condemned. My lifelong friends were told they couldn't play with me because I had a brother on death row.... I was always looked at as an outsider. My self-esteem dropped. My anger started growing. The fear that they could take away any person that I loved at any time increased.... I had no belief in anything.... I felt we were outcasts from God. It crushed all my self-esteem and faith. I was lost for a good many years.[70]

Many family members consider their loved one's stay on death row as a "living death." The daughter of a death row inmate expressed it this way: "It's like he's gone, never coming back, might as well forget it. I still feel he's not there. It's hard to feel your father is here when you can't see him every day or talk with him, or go sit in his house. Every day I think he's just waiting to be electrocuted. I feel he's beginning to die. A part of him has already died."[71] The sister of a female death row inmate stated, "Even though she's living, she's dead. Her clothes are packed in the closet. Could be thrown away like she's already dead."[72] Finally, the sister of a death row inmate asserted, "When you go through this, it's like his death for six or seven years now [the length of time he had been on death row], or the actual death itself."[73]

As noted previously, with a loved one on death row, some family members become social pariahs, but in other cases, family members voluntarily choose to socially isolate themselves, or worse. The daughter of a death row inmate remarked:

> After they transferred him to Holman [prison], I knew I lost him. I went into isolation. I stopped exercising. I'm out of shape real bad. I don't want to do anything. I don't want to go out of the house. I'm so depressed. I sit and cry. I lock myself in the house. I was trying to decide if I wanted to go on with my life or give up. I planned suicide. I wrote my note. I planned to take pills, do it the easy way. But God didn't want me to die. It wasn't my time.[74]

The sister of a death row inmate put it this way, "I'm alone. The whole family is alone. It's hell. It's like nobody cares or is concerned. Others enjoy life, and we go through this alone. After it happened, I went to the bridge to jump off. I can't swim, so that would have been it. Then I thought of my kids. They didn't need any more hurt, and that kept me going."[75] Another sister of a death row inmate stated, "I still feel like I'm going to have

---

67. Sharp, op. cit., p. 32.
68. Ibid., p. 53.
69. Ibid., p. 67.
70. Vandiver (2003), op. cit., p. 626.
71. Smykla, op. cit., p. 342.
72. Ibid.
73. Ibid.
74. Ibid., p. 343.
75. Ibid.

a breakdown. Even with my kids, anyone comes to talk with me and I just start all this crying. Really, I'm doing good sitting here talking about it. Last night I talked to my aunt and uncle about him, and when I got off the phone, I started throwing up."[76] Finally, the mother of a death row inmate had this to say: "During the first two weeks I started drinking too much. I stayed in the house. I wouldn't answer the door. I didn't do anything for a long time. Moving here helped. Nobody knows. It feels like other people don't understand what's happening or couldn't understand or don't want to understand or don't care. I don't know how other families feel or how they do. I don't know."[77]

Drinking is a common coping mechanism for the family members of death row inmates. As the daughter of a death row inmate reported, "I started drinking a lot after this happened. I drank real heavy and stopped exercising. I used liquor to escape. I used it to get drunk so I would have to think about nothing. I'd go to bars each night. I'd get so drunk I couldn't walk. I wouldn't talk with anyone. Then I got to where I didn't like the crowds, so I'd get a bottle, bring it home, and get drunk. This went on for four months."[78] The sister of a death row inmate related, "I used to drink only a little, but now that's changed. I'll have one or two shots in the afternoon and a couple cans of beer a day. I'll drink when the children aren't around, after they're in bed. When Texas executed that guy, I drank a six pack. Sometimes I'll sit up thinking until two or three in the morning. I'll go to Jiffy Mart and get a beer. It'll make me sleep."[79] The mother of a death row inmate said: "I started drinking too much then (when her son was sentenced). In the second and third year I started drinking real heavy. I put a little coke in it, and it sits here. I always fix the meals, but drinking keeps my mind from thinking too much, or else it intensifies my feelings and makes me drink more."[80]

When a loved one has been sentenced to death, many family members experience an almost unbearable sense of helplessness or powerlessness to do anything about the death sentence or the impending execution. The grandfather of a female death row inmate observed, "You know she's there, and there's nothing you can do. Your hands are tied. You try. You feel helpless. There's nothing you can do."[81] Likewise, the sister of the female death row inmate concluded, "There's nothing we could've done. Sure, if we had money she wouldn't be on death row. The lawyer wanted $5,000 and said he'd use his influence in the courthouse. We're poor people. There was nothing we could do."[82] The sister of a death row inmate noted, "Right now, what can I do? If the state says tomorrow he dies, what can I do? It's helpless and hopeless."[83] The girlfriend of a death row inmate resigned herself to what she believed was a political reality: "It's hopeless. I don't think he'd be cleared if he was given a new trial. You're from Alabama. You know the racial situation."[84] Finally, the sister of a death row inmate expressed the pain of her frustration: "It hurts you can't do anything. There's nothing you can do. It's like we're a million miles away and there's nothing we can do. Every day I wish I could do something, but I can't. It's

---

76. Ibid.
77. Ibid.
78. Ibid., p. 344.
79. Ibid.
80. Ibid.
81. Ibid.
82. Ibid.
83. Ibid.
84. Ibid.

very frustrating, extremely frustrating that we can't help him or make life easier for him while he's there."[85]

For most family members, their suffering reaches crisis level when a death warrant is signed. Their pain peaks just before the execution, but, for some families, the pain does not stop there. For them, the state has a cruel and agonizing surprise: a stay of execution.[86] Consider the experience of a death row inmate's cousin—the only family member to support him. The experience began on execution day when she arrived at the prison: "There was an officer at the gate, who asked what my business was here today. I said my name, and I just dissolved. His eyes filled with tears. When I had to go through that gate and tell the prison officials that I was there for my cousin's death, I fell apart. I just lost it."[87] She then recalled:

> We had started to say our goodbyes, and the lawyer came in and said, "We got a stay." I was like "we got to stay where?" She said, "No, a stay of execution." We could not believe it. The warden extended our visit because we were all so happy; even he [the warden] was happy, as this would have been his first execution. You go through the euphoria for about six weeks, and, then it's awful.[88]

Eventually reality hit, and she realized that once again she would have to experience the painful process of the state putting her cousin to death. Her sense of gloom was palpable: "[Y]ou say goodbye, you walk out of the room, and you think you will never see him again, and then you know tomorrow you get a stay, and you have to go back and say goodbye again. To say it one time is all you can do. Nobody can understand what it is like to do that." Her cousin received his second signed death warrant ten months later. Her reaction: "I was just as wrecked as the first time ... No one should have to go through a deathwatch twice." [89] She remembered the last few hours of her cousin's life:

> I still see the shift change during deathwatch. I still see the employees leaving with tears in their eyes saying goodbye to [her cousin]. I still see the corrections officer saying to me "I have been here nine years, and that man is my friend, and I am going to miss him." I asked someone on the death team if they would be going with [her cousin] all the way to the execution chamber, and he said to me, "if I had to go there, I would have to quit."[90]

The day of the execution, the condemned man's cousin became physically ill, and the warden suggested that she might want to leave the prison, to which she replied, "I don't care how bad I feel, I am staying here until the end because this is the last time I will see my family member because you are going to kill him."[91] A moment later, she added unapologetically, "So I was awful. But I had to be mad to go through it a second time."[92] In the end, she realized how ironic it was that the execution punished her and not her cousin: "You must be punished when you take a life, but by executing him, you didn't punish him, you punished me. [Her cousin] said he was tired of this place [prison] and that execution would set him free. I am punished. His daughter is punished. The people that loved him are punished. But not him."[93]

---

85. Ibid.
86. Beck et al. op. cit., p. 80.
87. Ibid.
88. Ibid.
89. Ibid.
90. Ibid., pp. 80-81.
91. Ibid., p. 81
92. Ibid.
93. Ibid., p. 89.

The sister of a death row inmate who received a stay of execution found it particularly cruel that prison guards had a betting pool on her brother's execution:

> [T]he guards have a pool going on whether he will be executed on his next execution date or not. When he told me that, I almost started crying; I said, "You mean they're betting on whether you're going to die?" because he said, "You know, one of the guards was mad because when all the stuff was in the media about them trying to get a stay of execution about the DNA. He lost a lot of money—the Supreme Court overruled it—and he lost a lot of money and he's been ticked off a lot ever since...." It just—it shocked me. It shocked me, it really did.[94]

Last-minute schedule changes, such as stays of execution, are common. In many cases, prison officials are insensitive to the stress and aggravation this causes family members. For example, one family expected a contact visit with their son at 3 p.m. the day before his execution. When they called the prison to confirm the visit, they were told the visit was scheduled for 2 p.m., and it was to be shorter than they originally expected. During the conversation, the death row inmate's father heard prison officials laughing in the background. Later, the father remarked, "This may have been a joke to them but not to me."[95] When the family got to the prison, they learned they had to visit their loved one behind glass. The father had to call the warden to get the contact visit, which was granted but cut short because of the time taken for the father to negotiate with the warden. The family's final visit with their loved one was scheduled on the day of the execution from 7 a.m. to 9 a.m. The family arrived at the prison early but was not escorted to the visitation room until well after 7. At 8:15, they were told the visit was over. The family vociferously protested the change in schedule and, in doing so, was unable to say goodbye to their loved one in the manner they had wanted. The father remembered:

> I didn't realize what happened at the time, but my wife informed me that she never got to say goodbye. They just took him out and left us standing there. We don't have a marker on the grave yet. She just can't put a marker there. But I think if we had closure [his voice trails off and the thought that it might be easier for his wife if she had been able to say goodbye is not spoken]. She lives with this every day.[96]

In some states, family members may witness the execution. The pain and agony they must experience watching their loved one being put to death and being helpless to do anything about it is unimaginable. They endure the misery to provide their loved one a last measure of support and love.[97] The agony of a wife who watched her husband being executed was reported in a church newspaper: "Darlene beat the glass and screamed in pain. Her two young adult sons tried to help as they patted her and said, 'Mama, don't cry. Mama, we are so sorry.' Finally, she collapsed and was taken to a hospital to be treated for shock and exhaustion."[98] A sister watched helplessly as her brother was executed: "He was aware and he was terrified. I was devastated—I wanted to go through the window to help him. And there was nothing that I could do—nothing. I had to watch him suffer. It was the worst moment of my life."[99]

---

94. Sharp, op. cit., p. 104.
95. Beck et al. op. cit., p. 81.
96. Ibid.
97. Vandiver (2003), op. cit., p. 628.
98. Sharp, op. cit., p. 87.
99. Ibid., p. 91.

During some executions, family members cannot help but know that outside the prison a bizarre ritual is taking place. In one area, death penalty opponents are holding a solemn, candlelit vigil, while nearby mostly drunken death penalty proponents are wildly celebrating the execution. The mother of a son who died on death row before he could be executed witnessed several of those post-execution celebrations. Her reaction:

> They laugh at the families whose loved one has just been exterminated.... They party, laugh and sing and cheer in front of a grieving family who loves their person no matter what he had done. I think the public should know that after they murder our loved one, we feel the same pain and rage as the family of a murder victim. I would tell them that there is no difference in a mother's pain at the loss of her son ... by the mother of a child who's been murdered on the street or the mother whose son has been executed. The pain is the same, and the public wants to exact the same pain on the perpetrator's family as the victim's family experienced.[100]

She added, "We are human beings, we feel, we cry, we laugh, and we feel the pain of losing our children, too, yet there is no sympathy for us. For we are hated as much as the one who did the crime."[101]

After the Execution

The pain and suffering experienced by family members does not end with the execution or the funeral. For some of them, it never ends. The mother of an executed son stated, "You'd think it would get better after time, but it doesn't."[102] Life after a family member's execution is particularly challenging for surviving children. They generally respond in several ways, including withdrawal, denial, anger, depression, involvement in criminal activity, dropping out of school, and drug use.[103]

Consider, for example, a daughter who was tormented by her father's execution. Before her parent's divorce and her father's execution, she was shy and well behaved. Following the execution, her personality and behavior changed radically. She began getting into street fights, hitting her mother, and cutting herself. She started having trouble sleeping because of constant nightmares, she became depressed, and she quit taking care of herself. She stated, "I don't care. I feel like the most important thing in my life was taken away from me. I don't care what happens to me—I really don't." [104] Near the first anniversary of her father's execution, she attempted suicide by cutting herself with a sharp object. She was rushed to a hospital and her life was saved, but her life has not gotten any better. She has been incarcerated in the local jail, and her family is worried about her boyfriend and other new friends.[105]

A sister described how the execution of her brother affected both her and her parents:

---

100. Ibid., p. 165.
101. Ibid.
102. Ibid., p. 28.
103. Beck et al., op. cit., p. 107.
104. Ibid.
105. Ibid.

It was never quite the same. It was like there was a piece missing, and there was just kind of a sadness that was over everybody. Mom was in her own little world. She was just sad—all the time. She was quiet. She didn't laugh as much as she used to. She'd get in her good moods, and then she'd get in a funk. When she was in a funk, she was sad all the time. She would sleep all the time. She would cry by herself. She would get mad at small things. And I know dad was always different.... They still took care of me the way they should have. But it was different. I hate saying this, but I remember just doing my own thing. They wanted to take care of me and make sure that I did the right thing, but I didn't really depend on them. I couldn't. They weren't really there, and I did not want to burden them.... I learned to close myself off and not talk about the problems I was having so that I wouldn't lay any more burdens on them.[106]

The children and siblings of death row and executed inmates have been called "the death penalty's dirty little secret" and "hidden victims" who "in many cases are primed to live out the self-fulfilling prophecy of society's belief about their families."[107]

Life following an execution is no easier for adult family members. Three years after her son's execution, a mother still could not mention his name. Another mother's life was still devastated two years after her son's execution. She was forgetful and often could not follow a conversation. She had gained a dangerous amount of weight, and her depression medicine did not alleviate her misery. Her daughter commented that when her brother was executed, "I lost my mother as well."[108]

For one family, what were once joyous holidays became macabre events. For them, "Thanksgiving marks the deathwatch and Christmas the execution" of their loved one.[109] Still another mother died in her sleep a year after her son's execution. Although a cause of death was never identified, her profound grief for her son over many years made her life unbearable. She probably died of a broken heart.[110] A sister whose brother was executed ten years earlier described how the execution was currently affecting her mother:

It is ... difficult for me to see my mother suffer like she does. She goes to the cemetery often and sits for hours. Sometimes she won't take off her pajamas nor answer her phone. My brother's room is still like it was when he left.... She lives in guilt every day and she is beating herself up for it. She feels totally responsible, and she is punishing herself. Her health is failing fast, and she is going to have a heart attack one of these days.[111]

A Different Kind of Grief

As noted at the onset of this chapter, the grief experienced by offenders' surviving family members is unlike the grief experienced by the surviving family members of almost any

---

106. Ibid., p. 108.
107. Ibid., p. 112.
108. Ibid., p. 87.
109. Ibid.
110. Ibid., p. 116.
111. Sharp, op. cit., p. 103.

other kind of death. The type of grief experienced by offenders' family members has been referred to as "anticipatory grief," "distorted grief," "disenfranchised grief," "chronic sorrow," and "nonfinite loss."[112] Regardless of what it is called, the grief associated with capital punishment and other traumatic losses can involve an all-consuming and continuous pain that changes the personality and life of the bereaved. It can be manifested in medical illnesses; radical changes in social relationships, including disruptions in social interactions; depression; and, to avoid a sense of loss, manic activity, sometimes with risky behaviors.[113]

For many offenders' family members, this type of grief begins with the crime and the arrest, but, for others it starts earlier with recognition of their family member's mental illness or alcohol and drug addiction.[114] The family of a death row inmate blamed themselves for their loved one's predicament and felt guilty about their failure to help him more and the damage it caused. The death row inmate's brother explained his and his family's grief:

> I felt like it was my fault that it happened, and I had that on me for a long time, and I couldn't shake it. I actually thought it was my fault. So much grief for what [my brother] had done. I mean we all felt like we had the gun in our hands that day. It was ridiculous because we did not, but it felt that way. Our blood killed their blood. It just really tore us up. I particularly felt very guilty because I wasn't more active in trying to get help [for him before the crime] .... We felt bad about, you know, like a double depression and double grief—that something terrible had happened to people in the community.[115]

Self-blame is common among family members. The mother of a death row inmate lamented, "It's all my fault. If I hadn't been working, I would've seen what was going on, and this wouldn't have happened."[116] The sister of a female death row inmate similarly observed, "It's all my fault. If I was with her, it wouldn't have happened. I'm guilty."[117] Another mother of a death row inmate reflected: "I worked twenty-six years. After work, I was a grouch. I wasn't the best mom. I know that. I worked every day. I hate to say it, but they grew up on their own. I looked at things wrong. I should have spent more time with the kids. I went over my whole life. It's all my fault. All that happened is my fault. Yes, I still feel that way."[118]

The grief continues through the trial and the seemingly endless appellate process that now averages nearly fifteen years between sentence and execution.[119] Some inmates have been on death row for decades awaiting their executions. Gary Alvord, for example, has been on Florida's death row since April 11, 1974.[120]

The shattering of their own hopes and dreams drives the grief experienced by many offenders' family members. They realize that they will not experience the joy of their loved one's getting married, having children, in some cases graduating from high school, or

---

112. Beck et al., op. cit., p. 117; also see Smykla, op. cit.
113. Ibid.
114. Ibid.
115. Ibid., 130.
116. Smykla, op. cit., p. 342.
117. Ibid.
118. Ibid., pp. 342-343.
119. "Capital Punishment, 2010—Statistical Tables," Table 8. U.S. Department of Justice, Bureau of Justice Statistics at http://bjs.ojp.usdoj.gov/content/pub/pdf/cp10st.pdf (accessed March 3, 2012).
120. Florida Department of Corrections, "Death Row Fact Sheet" at www.dc.state.fl.us/oth/deathrow/#Notables (accessed March 3, 2012).

perhaps even graduating from college. These family members become consumed with the "could/should/might have been" had life turned out differently. The mother of a death row inmate called the women of her online support community the "if only's," because they continually bemoaned that if only their sons had not been on death row, they could have seen them graduate from high school, or if only their sons had listened to their mothers and not their friends, they could have been grandmothers.[121]

The passing of social milestones punctuates their grief. For some family members, attending their friends and family's social milestones is heartbreaking. Some family members cannot bring themselves to attend these events. As the mother of a death row inmate explained, "It's just too hard. It makes me think about the time that we had together as families and the way my son played with their children. Now their son has a life, a future, and mine has a death sentence. I cannot look at [my friend's] children and not feel like a hole has swallowed me up."[122]

Life Without Parole — A Dream Come True

Almost without exception, offenders' family members would prefer their loved one to be sentenced to life imprisonment without the opportunity of parole (LWOP) rather than to death.[123] And for nearly all family members whose loved ones have been sentenced to death, a commutation to LWOP is a dream come true. Family members are able to relax again; they no longer have to live in the shadow of death. Their depression usually eases or vanishes; they are better able to cope with the trauma caused by having a loved one on death row; and they are able to form and maintain healthy relationships again.[124] The mother of a commuted death row inmate described the feeling as having a "big weight lifted off me."[125] Another mother whose son's death sentence was commuted was elated about finally being able to have a contact visit with her son: "I cried when I saw him and hugged him and smelled him. It is wonderful to have a physical connection with him."[126] Other parents of commuted death row inmates were proud that their sons were being productive in prison and trying to better themselves: one son was writing a book about his life so other African-American men would not make the mistakes that he did, while another son was sending letters to his mother's Sunday school classes telling students not to drink and take drugs lest they end up like him.[127]

Still, a sentence to LWOP instead of death, or the commutation of a death sentence to LWOP, does not eliminate all the concerns and troubles for family members. They now have to worry about their loved one's safety because he no longer is isolated on death row but instead is in the general prison population with other inmates.

Although family members can look forward to visiting their loved one for as long as they live, visitation presents potential problems and challenges. To visit, family members

---

121. Beck et al., op. cit., p. 118.
122. Ibid.
123. Ibid., p. 141.
124. Ibid., p. 143.
125. Ibid.
126. Ibid.
127. Ibid., pp. 144-145.

may have to miss work and other family responsibilities. In many cases, they must travel to prisons in rural areas not served by public transportation. They must comply with prison regulations about identification, dress, and receiving prior approval for visits, which may change frequently and without notice. Failure to comply with regulations can result in forfeiting the opportunity to visit even if they have traveled long distances. Some prisons do not allow contact visits, so family members may have to visit with their loved one through a wire or glass barrier.[128] Parents also realize that their imprisoned son probably will outlive them and worry about who will visit him, leave him money, or otherwise be there for him when they are gone. And although they are happy their loved one has escaped the death penalty, they wish society would recognize that their loved one's life still might be redeemable.[129]

Conclusion

With the commission of a crime—especially a capital crime—families of the victim and the offender are thrust into chaos, bombarded by a maelstrom of emotions ranging from, perhaps, revenge on the part of the victim's family to fear on the part of the offender's family. Friends and family members of the victim are looking for closure, while loved ones of the defendant are often seeking empathy—or at least compassion.

As noted in Chapter 3, the argument is often made that executions bring closure or other benefits to homicide victims' families. But the evidence regarding closure is mixed at best. Whether executions relieve the pain and suffering of homicide victims' families is debatable.

However, even if executions may provide relief, the infliction of pain and suffering on offenders' families to relieve the pain and suffering of victims' families is difficult to justify because the families of both the victim and the offender usually are innocent. More likely than not, the death penalty and executions cause immense pain and suffering to both victims' and offenders' families, as the testimonials in this chapter and chapter 3 attest.

Complex, painful emotions do not go away once the defense rests its case. Judges and juries play an important role in the process—roles that affect the defendant and his attorney, the prosecutor, and the families on both sides. In the next chapter, we will look at how judges fit into the capital punishment system, and how their participation in that system affects them. Then we will look at the role that jurors play, and how they are affected by their role in the system.

---

128. Vandiver (2003), op. cit., p. 627.
129. Beck et al., op. cit., p. 145.

Chapter 6

Trial Judges

While defense attorneys and prosecutors are preparing and presenting their cases, while the defendant ponders his fate, and while the families of both the accused and the victim wrestle with the after-effects associated with capital crimes, judges perform their critical role in the process.

Trial judges "manage" or "referee" capital trials to ensure that each capital defendant receives a fair trial. Their job is to defend the integrity of the process by requiring prosecutors, defense attorneys, and jurors (in jury trials) to follow established procedures. Capital trials are the only type of criminal trials in which the trial judge does not decide on a sentence, except in Alabama, Delaware, and Florida, where a jury's sentencing decision is only advisory, or in trials without juries. Following the jury's sentencing decision, trial judges announce in open court whether defendants will live or die.

Some defense attorneys feel more comfortable putting the life-or-death decision directly into the judge's hands by having their clients plead guilty or simply waive the right to a jury trial. They believe that undeniably guilty clients have a better chance of escaping the death penalty by admitting guilt and asking the judge to show mercy. They assume it may be more difficult psychologically for one judge to impose a death sentence than it would be for twelve jurors to do so.[1]

Capital trials differ from other criminal trials in several important ways, and trial judges must be knowledgeable about those differences. Perhaps the biggest difference, as noted previously, is that capital trials are bifurcated, with separate guilt and penalty phases. Judges disagree about which of the two trial phases is the more difficult. Some death penalty states require judges who preside over capital trials to receive instruction about the conduct of capital trials and be certified. Other death penalty states allow trial judges to learn the intricacies of capital trials "on the job."

For capital trial judges, the most difficult and worst part of the job is sentencing a defendant to death. Although trial judges take an oath to uphold the law, many of them are not strong proponents of the death penalty. Many of them could easily do without it. This chapter investigates the role of trial judges in the capital punishment process, and how that role affects them.

---

1. Robert Jay Lifton and Greg Mitchell (2002) *Who Owns Death? Capital Punishment, the American Conscience, and the End of Executions*. New York: Perennial, pp. 157-58.

Capital Trials Are Unique

In capital trials, as in other felony trials, judges are responsible for allowing the jury a fair chance to reach a verdict on the evidence presented. Judges must ensure that their behavior does not improperly affect the outcome of the case. They have ultimate control of the trial. They must manage the activities of both the prosecution and the defense and make decisions about whether evidence is omitted or excluded. In many jurisdictions, trial court judges are responsible for ordering adequate compensation for defense attorneys representing indigent defendants and for approving trial expenses such as the hiring of investigators, psychiatrists, and other experts.[2] Before juries retire to deliberate and reach a verdict, judges instruct them on the relevant law. This involves interpreting legal precedents and applying them to the unique circumstances of the case. Finally, as noted, judges ultimately pronounce whether a defendant will live or die.

Trial judges in capital cases must be knowledgeable about a variety of sometimes unique and complex issues, including:

- motion practice (some motions are unique to capital cases);
- current procedures in jury selection;
- substantive and procedural capital punishment case law;
- police investigative and interrogation methods;
- police investigating and reporting of exculpatory evidence;
- the risks of false confessions;
- the admissibility of forensic evidence in such areas as scientific trace materials, genetics, and DNA analysis;
- the application of new and different discovery rules;
- the risk of false testimony by in-custody informants ("jailhouse snitches") and accomplice witnesses;
- the dangers of tunnel vision or confirmatory bias (that is, where the police's belief that a particular suspect has committed a crime prevents them from objectively evaluating whether there might be others who are actually guilty, or where the judge routinely gives the testimony of police officers credence without subjecting it to the rigorous examination that the testimony of other witnesses may receive);
- the risks of wrongful convictions in capital cases.

Two Florida trial judges described what they believed made capital trials different from other felony trials. According to one trial judge, capital trials differ "in a lot of ways":

> First of all, the lawyers have to be certified to try a capital case—that is, the defense attorneys. The judges have to be certified in Florida before they can preside over a capital case. They have to take a five-day course that covers all issues unique to capital cases. And, of course, the jury selection is going to be quite different because jurors want to talk about if they're for or against the death

---

2. Governor's Commission on Capital Punishment (2002) State of Illinois at www.idoc.state.il.us/ccp/ccp/reports/commission_reports.html (Chapter 6).

penalty. [The capital trial is] bifurcated, meaning there are two separate phases: the guilt and the penalty phase. And the jury recommends a sentence, which is the only type of case where a jury can recommend the sentence, and ultimately the judge has to impose the death penalty. But the jury recommends life without parole or the death penalty. Those are just a few of the very significant differences between a capital case and a noncapital felony.

Another judge provided a longer list of differences:

The fact that you use a twelve-person jury in Florida instead of a six-person jury is one thing that's obvious. The fact that the trial is a bifurcated proceeding with a guilt phase and a penalty phase is another. The jury selection process is different. The pretrial discovery process is different. There are generally two lawyers that represent the defendant in a [capital] case instead of one—one of whom is called the "second chair" and is generally responsible for presenting mitigating evidence during the penalty phase of the trial. After the penalty phase is completed, in Florida, the trial judge has to determine what penalty to impose. And if the death penalty is imposed, the judge has to prepare a judge sentencing order justifying the imposition of the death penalty. The case then goes directly to the Supreme Court of Florida instead of the district court of appeal. [In a capital case] there's a one-year limitation after the case is final for the filing of a postconviction or relief claim on appeal, instead of two years. The postconviction claims have to be heard if they are legally sufficient and whether or not there is any basis for the claim. In noncapital cases, we can deny a postconviction claim if it's refuted by the record. But in capital cases we have to get an evidentiary hearing on it. I'm sure I've missed a few things.

Both judges noted that jury selection in capital cases is different. One judge clarified how: "Juries are death-qualified. And I use that in quotations—'Death qualified.'" He volunteered: "The data indicate that death-qualified juries are more prone to convict." Jury selection also differs in capital trials, observed the judge, "because [death penalty] cases are oftentimes notorious, and so it takes longer to select a jury in a capital case, simply because of the knowledge that the jury has in general about the case."

Florida capital trials differ in yet another way: they are trifurcated rather than bifurcated because Florida requires a *Spencer hearing* following the penalty stage, during which the judge hears mitigating evidence the jury does not hear. As a judge explained:

In fact, good defense lawyers will hold back a good statutory mitigating circumstance for the Spencer hearing. Because if the jury recommends the death sentence, you've still got that [the held-back mitigating circumstance] you can go back on to get the judge to justify hanging his hat on a life sentence. Of course, the Florida system is, in my way of thinking, really suspect after *Ring v. Arizona*[3] and the *Apprendi*[4] case. I just feel Justice Scalia [is] sitting in Washington waiting for the right case to come along from Florida to drop the shoe.

In Florida, a Spencer hearing must be scheduled in all capital trials. As the judge related, "Yeah, we have to schedule one. Sometimes nothing is offered, but we have to schedule one.... It's generally very short." The importance of the Spencer hearing in a capital trial varies greatly. The judge asserted:

---

3. 536 U.S. 584 (2002).
4. *Apprendi v. New Jersey*, 530 U.S. 466 (2000).

Well, it's a statutory mitigating circumstance, and the law requires us to at least give it some weight. A nonstatutory mitigating circumstance might not have any weight at all. For instance, if a person uses mitigation of being an alcoholic, that could be mitigating. But what if the person hasn't had a drink in twenty years? It has nothing to do with the case or with the crime or anything else. It might not be mitigating at all. On the other hand, if the person has no prior record and that's not submitted to the jury but is presented at the Spencer hearing as a statutory mitigating circumstance, that's a pretty important consideration.

Asked why having no prior record would not be raised at the penalty phase, he opined, "I think most defense attorneys would use lack of prior record with the jury. I mean, I'm sure they would."

Guilt Phase or Penalty Phase?

Judges disagree about which phase of the bifurcated (or trifurcated) trial is the more difficult: the guilt phase or the penalty phase. One judge maintained:

Oh, the penalty phase is much more difficult ... because the penalty phase is unique to capital cases. In a typical trial, if the jury finds the defendant not guilty, that's the end of the jury's work. They can go home, and the judge alone decides the sentence.

In the penalty phase, it's different for a lot of reasons. One, typically, you have a separate lawyer who is representing the defendant whose job it is to develop evidence for the penalty phase if the defendant is convicted. Number two, everything the defense lawyers do in the guilt phase is with an eye towards the penalty phase later on. They have to maintain credibility with the jury. Typically, capital cases have overwhelming evidence of guilt, and if the lawyer gets up during the guilt phase and says, "My client didn't do it, my client didn't do it," and then he is convicted, it's difficult in the penalty phase for that same lawyer to get up and say, "Well, he did it, but he shouldn't die." So the penalty phase offers unique problems for the defense lawyers. It's difficult because the defendants will typically present evidence of mental mitigation, like their childhood abuse, drug abuse, and mental health issues that they've had; maybe even mental re-tardation. So those are issues that you don't normally see in a noncapital trial, but they come up regularly in the penalty phase.

And, of course, it's harder because you have to guide the jury. The jury is the one that has to make the recommendation as a result of the penalty phase. And there are lots of evidentiary issues that are unique to penalty phase cases, things like getting in certain hearsay evidence, and a victim's family member can come in and make a victim impact statement in a capital case that they can't do in a regular case.

Another judge believed that the guilt stage is the more difficult stage:

That's when all the complicated evidentiary issues are raised. Forensics particularly.... You need to remember that most of the aggravating circumstances that are going to be presented come up during the guilt phase. The facts of the case present most of the aggravation. The things that are introduced by the prosecutor in the guilt phase are things like the fact the person has been convicted of a prior felony or a felony involving violence. So, generally, the state's presentation [at the penalty stage] is relatively easy and relatively quick. Sometimes they have nothing to add at all. It's the defense that comes in at that point and offers mitigation. And that's pretty easy. We give them all kinds of leeway. We don't really hold their feet to the fire like we do the state in the guilt phase. We just kind of let them go. Whatever they want to present to the jury, they get to present.

Training or Experience in Capital Jurisprudence

Many judges come to the bench without any practical experience with criminal law or procedure, especially capital punishment law and procedure. They learn the intricacies of their profession and the management of capital cases on the job. Both of the Florida judges interviewed for this chapter had at least some experience — and one of them had taken a now-required Handling Capital Cases course — before they presided over their first capital trials. According to one judge:

> As a lawyer, I practiced criminal defense, and, obviously, I was familiar with criminal trials. I tried a lot of cases. I tried only one murder case as a defense lawyer, and it was not a capital case. As I said earlier, in Florida you have to be certified as a capital judge to preside over a capital case. So I took that course. I also teach that course to other judges, so I had quite a bit of educational experience. But, truly, until you're there doing it for the first time, it doesn't really matter how much training you've had or preparation you've had. You just have to get in there and do it.

The judge believed that he was adequately prepared to preside at his first capital trial, but he did not think he was ready. "I think there is a difference," he explained. "You try to think of all the possibilities about what may happen during the course of the trial and how to respond to it. But things happen that are unforeseen and maybe even unforeseeable. And you just react to it, and you hope that you have enough experience and education to adapt as the circumstances warrant."

The other judge had more prior experience than the first judge, but he had not taken the now-required course:

> I was a prosecutor for two years, and I tried six or eight capital cases. But back in those days, rape was a capital case. I think I prosecuted three or four murder cases. I defended one capital case when I was practicing law. At the time that I became a judge, there wasn't a requirement for judges to take the current Handling Capital Cases course at the advanced judicial studies college. So that was, basically, my training.

Nevertheless, the judge felt adequately prepared to preside at his first capital trial. He recalled that, then as now, "I spend hours and hours and hours getting ready for these trials because I want to make sure that I understand what the evidentiary problems are going to be and that I understand how the play is going to unfold, if you will."

The Most Important Aspect of Being a Capital Trial Judge

The judges disagreed about what the most important aspect of being a capital trial judge is. One judge mentioned, "controlling the trial":

> I can tell you that the difference between presiding over a regular felony case and a capital felony case is that our responsibility is a lot different. I'm not there just to call balls and strikes in a capital trial. I have to be alert. I have to know what's going on because the dynamics of the capital trial are really different, and the conduct of the lawyers is going to be scrutinized all the way from Tallahassee to Washington, D.C. Sometimes five or six or seven times. And so I have a responsibility to pull on the reins, if necessary, and call the lawyers to the bench and tell them I'm not going to put up with this, or you're going to have to go on a different path, or something like that. I will interject myself in a capital trial more easily than I would in a regular trial.

The other judge cited making sure the defendant receives a fundamentally fair trial as the most important aspect of being capital trial judge:

> There are many important things, but the most important thing is to ensure that the defendant is receiving a fundamentally fair trial because everything that happens after that is based on the premise — the assumption — that the defendant got a fair trial the first time through. And if the defendant did not get — not a perfect trial but a fundamentally fair trial — then there are certain assumptions that you can't make on appeal or in postconviction relief. So you do your best to make sure the defendant received effective assistance of counsel, that he participated in the decision making during the trial, that he's aware of everything that's going on, and that he had an adequate opportunity to consult and meet with his attorney. All of those things are the very foundation for the appellate process that follows that can take ten, twelve, fifteen years.

The Most Difficult Aspect of Being a Capital Trial Judge

For one judge, the most difficult aspect of being a capital trial judge is "the decision. Once you decide that the death penalty is appropriate, it ain't any fun to walk into the courtroom and tell somebody you're going to put them to death." The other judge believed the most difficult aspect is "juggling all the balls":

> Keeping them all in the air at the same time. Making sure that the state has a legitimate opportunity to present its case and that the defendant receives a fair trial. To make sure that the jury is not overwhelmed by their job and their obligations. Keeping time management. Keeping the case going, because capital cases can take anywhere from two weeks to two months. Making sure that the jury is attuned; that they are focused. That they're not getting too emotional

with the case. And, of course, managing my regular docket while I still try the capital case. Often, you have media concerns, too. And so dealing with the media and handling them during a capital case is hard. And, of course, keeping your own emotions out of it because capital cases can become very emotional. Because judges are human, too.

The Worst Aspect of Being a Capital Trial Judge

Both judges believed that the worst aspect of being a capital trial judge was imposing the death sentence, but that was not all. One judge stated:

> Well, there's that [telling a defendant that he is sentenced to death], but the other thing is: a capital case just ruins your docket. They don't just give me one case and, when I finish it, say, "Here's another one." I have a caseload to deal with. And a capital case takes up an enormous amount of time, energy, and resources. They do it in the [state] supreme court, also. The [state] supreme court justices tell me that the capital cases are about five percent of their docket, but they take fifty percent of their time. That gives you an idea about it. When it comes back to me on postconviction relief, by that time, when I call the clerk to bring up the file, the clerk brings up the file in a shopping cart. They're very time-consuming, very resource-consuming.

Overriding a Jury's Decision

Only one of the two Florida judges had ever overridden any jury sentences in the capital cases over which they presided. He stated, "In Florida, the jury recommends. Here's the rule. The jury recommends life. The way we teach the capital course, when that happens, the only next question that comes out of the judges' mouth is to the clerk and that is, 'What is the credit for time served?' Impose a life sentence, and get done with it, because you're more than likely going to get reversed if you override a jury."

Nevertheless, a judge still has a statutory right to override, to which he added:

> You have that statutory right, but there has to be no basis for the jury's recommendation before you rule about it. On the other hand, if the jury comes back with the recommendation of death, then we have to independently re-evaluate the aggravating and mitigating circumstances and make an independent decision. And, yes, I have imposed the life sentence many times over the death sentence, over the jury.

He guessed that he had overridden the jury's death sentence three or four times. He explained why:

> I guess I just believed that the aggravating circumstances and the mitigating circumstances did not justify the death penalty. Juries aren't used to these cases, and they're not pretty cases. There's nothing pretty about them. You've got little

children who have been choked or strangled or shot or something. You've got blood and gore and problems with people looking at this stuff for the first time. And judges have to sit back and recollect these things a little bit differently. And also—this is an important point—there's a lot of mitigation that's offered in these cases that sounds like aggravation.

One of my colleagues had a capital case. He went home, and he's talking to his wife about it. He says, "Oh, there's a lot of mitigation in these cases. The defendant has a borderline IQ and was sexually abused as a child. His father is serving a life sentence. His mother is a prostitute. All this list of stuff. And he's, of course, a drug addict and an alcoholic." And my colleague's wife said, "That's not mitigation, that's aggravation. This is an opportunity to clean the shallow end of the gene pool." And I think juries think that way.

Judicial Misconduct

In a recent study of Missouri death penalty clemency petitions, the following allegations of judicial misconduct or error were found:

- not permitting the defense to present evidence of an alternative theory of the case;
- not permitting the defense to present certain mitigating evidence;
- denying the right of defense experts to offer evidence;
- failing to order a psychiatric examination prior to trial;
- prejudging the case;
- incorrectly finding fact;
- refusing to give certain jury instructions;
- failing to admonish the prosecutor for an improper closing argument;
- allowing a highly prejudicial photograph during the penalty phase;
- failing to permit withdrawal of a guilty plea;
- not having jurisdiction[5]

Although the judges did not believe that they personally had engaged in any misconduct or that their capital trial performances had been affected by any extralegal factors such as divorce, illness, lack of sleep, or political considerations, they understood how such problems could affect other capital trial judges. One of the judges stated:

I could see where political pressures could come to bear on a capital case. Number one, we are elected representatives, so every six years we have to run or at least stand to run.... Let's say a police officer was brutally murdered, and that case came to trial, and the jury made, let's say, a close recommendation between life and death, or even a life recommendation. And the judge might think, politically, his career might be in jeopardy if he or she didn't impose the

---

5. Cathleen Burnett (2002) *Justice Denied: Clemency Appeals in Death Penalty Cases.* Boston: Northeastern University Press, p. 103.

death penalty in light of the victim. Didn't happen to me, but there have been several cases in the Florida Supreme Court where they have reversed a judge and imposed death, even though the jury recommended life. And in one case, the supreme court reversed the same judge three times because he overrode the jury's recommendation twice. And the victim was a police officer, and the judge was up for re-election at the time. So those are real political pressures that exist.

The other judge answered similarly that he hadn't had any problems:

No. But let me tell you that probably isn't universally true. I would think that political considerations come into mind when judges preside over these cases, especially in certain parts of the state. And, you know, a judge that does not impose the death penalty in [one region of the state] may very well [face political] opposition [as a judge because he or she is perceived as] a judge that's soft on crime, or whatever. This never bothered me. I just rule the way I want to rule, and I've never gotten any opposition. And now I'm not going to ever run again, so I don't really have any political pressure at all. In fact, I have, you know, none.

[However,] I don't see how it can't help but play a role in some cases. Now, it may play a role, but the decision may be correct anyway. And I think that since we've been teaching this capital punishment course, judges around the state have taken their responsibility more seriously. The number of reversals for death penalty cases has dropped remarkably since we've started teaching this course. If you think you have a political problem presiding over one of these cases, go try automobile accident [cases] or mortgage foreclosure [cases] for awhile, and let someone else handle these [death penalty] cases.

The judge cited an example of questionable behavior on the part of another judge:

We had a judge in [named a city], who's retired and is dead now, and he got reversed I don't know how many times. In his opinion, if someone was dead, why impose the death penalty? He was one of those guys you just couldn't teach. And so the Supreme Court just kept reversing his cases.... I can't think of anybody right now on the bench, and I know most of them, that I think [would] use the death penalty as a political tool to get reelected. If that's the concern, I just don't think that happens.

An incumbent might not use the death penalty as a political tool; however, the political opposition might use it that way. For example, a Cleveland, Ohio trial judge was denigrated as "soft on crime" because of his views on crime and punishment, including the death penalty. His reaction:

The issue of crime and punishment is easily exploited. I can't remember the last person in public office who said what I've said. They don't want to get labeled soft on crime. But I'm not going to be manipulated by anyone calling me soft on crime. The fact is no one wants to stand up for the rights of defendants until they're in a jam themselves. No one wants to speak on behalf of the poor and disadvantaged unless they know someone who's poor and disadvantaged. I think that's an indictment of our society. I mean, how tough is tough enough? We have 2 million people incarcerated in this country. That is more than any other country, including China. In the case of capital punishment, I'm not talking about releasing these people. What we're talking about is not having the state engage in institutionalized violence. It sends the wrong message. It's not restorative justice, it's vengeance. It's not a deterrent. So what is it? It's retribution.[6]

Reversals and Exonerations

Between the two Florida judges, only one of them has had a death sentence overturned on appeal. Neither one has had a capital conviction overturned. The judge with the single blemish on his record believes the reversal would not have occurred today:

> It's an interesting situation.... It involved a man who bludgeoned his wife to death with a hammer while she was sleeping. And there was ample evidence of premeditation. Substantial premeditation. Cool, calculated premeditation. But the supreme court said, "Well, it was just a domestic situation. We can't have the death penalty on that." Since that time there's been a lot of focus on domestic violence. I doubt it would have been reversed today.

Neither of the judges has had a defendant he sentenced to death exonerated. One of the judges, nevertheless, made an interesting observation about the effects of exonerations in general:

> I know that Florida leads the country in exonerations overall. I don't know what the figure is on death penalty exonerations, whether we lead the country. But I bet we're in the top three. And I think that's had a very big impact on jurors; the idea of DNA and people being exonerated well after the fact. I think this gives jurors a great pause before they recommend the death penalty nowadays because they may be afraid that ten or twelve or fifteen years from now that person will be exonerated as a result of new evidence or new scientific break-throughs. I think that creates more of an uphill battle for prosecutors than they ever had to deal with.

Judging Themselves

The judges rated their own performances in their capital trials. One judge mused:

> I think I did pretty well. There are things I could have done better. There are things I would probably do different. The way I handled the jury. Time management. Reining in the attorneys on certain things. Anticipating problems that might occur. That's really the issue for judges: sort of thinking ahead of the lawyers and thinking around corners and preventing things from happening before they ever do, rather than reacting to them. But I thought, overall, I did a pretty good job.

The other judge evaluated his performance this way:

---

6. Daniel Gaul, Cleveland Judge, *Cleveland Free Times*, 11/22/2000, cited in "Death Penalty Quotes," (January 2006), available online at http://people.freenet.de/dpinfo/quotes.htm (accessed June 1, 2009).

Oh, I think whenever we do a capital trial, I'm way more prepared than I am in a normal trial docket. For instance, I've got a trial starting on Monday [it was Friday], and I've never even looked at the files. I'm not going to, because I don't know which cases are going to go to trial. So, I could spend a whole weekend reading files, and then on Monday morning they all enter pleas, and I've wasted a day. Generally, on a typical felony case, I can come up to speed during the jury selection.

Emotional and Physical Effects

An informal survey of seven Florida trial judges who have sentenced defendants to death reveals how various aspects of capital cases affect them personally.[7] As noted previously, Florida trial judges differ from their colleagues in most other death penalty states in two significant ways. First, Florida trial judges may override a jury's sentencing recommendation. Alabama and Delaware are the only other states that give its trial judges that power. Second, Florida trial judges must satisfy two minimum standards before they are allowed to preside in a capital case. They must have presided "a minimum of 6 months in a felony criminal division or in a division that includes felony criminal cases," and they must have "successfully [attended] the Handling Capital Cases course offered through the Florida College of Advanced Judicial Studies." By meeting the two standards, a judge is "qualified" to preside over a capital case for three calendar years, after which the judge must attend a capital case refresher course during each following three-year period to remain qualified. Upon request of the chief judge of the judicial circuit court, the chief justice of Florida's Supreme Court may waive the requirements in exceptional circumstances.[8]

The management of a capital trial with all that it entails might seem like an emotionally charged and stressful responsibility, particularly in the state of Florida, where the trial judge has the ultimate sentencing responsibility. However, results from the informal survey of the seven Florida trial judges, and an interview with one Florida trial judge by this book's author, suggest otherwise. Another Florida trial judge interviewed by the book's author was the exception. He found that capital trials affected him mentally or emotionally:

It's the most difficult. It's the most emotionally taxing trial that there is. There's just so many things to think about, so many land mines you have to avoid. And, of course, understanding the irrevocability of your decision. Ultimately, you want to get it right. A lot of pressure. A lot of stress on all of the participants, whether it's the police, the prosecutors, the defense, the witnesses, the jury, myself, my staff. There is a lot of tension that you undergo in a capital case that you don't see in a regular case.

Regarding the physical demands of a capital trial, he said:

---

7. Henry Leyte-Vidal and Scott J. Silverman (2006) "Living with the Death Penalty," *Judicature* 89:270-273.

8. Florida Rule of Judicial Administration 2.215(b)(10) at http://74.125.45.104/search?q= cache:K8H7CRMft7UJ:www.floridasupremecourt.org/decisions/2008/sc07596.pdf+Florida+Rule+of+ Judicial+Administration+2.215+(10)&hl=en&ct=clnk&cd=1&gl=us.

It wears you down. In fact, most long trials tend to wear me down anyway, just like it does the lawyers. But, obviously, a capital case even more so: the length, the media attention that you've got to control; picking a jury, and usually a larger jury. The panel that you pick from is larger because of the length of the trial and the media attention and because people have strong opinions about the death penalty. If I would typically bring in thirty people to pick a jury from, I would have to bring in a hundred people or more to pick, because I've got to pick twelve jurors, of course, instead of six. And a lengthy trial; many people can't sit that long. And then the jury has to understand that they may be sequestered after the guilt phase or even during the guilt phase. It's very taxing physically over the course of a trial. I find that I don't really get sick, but I am definitely worn down by the end of the trial.

The other judge was more stoic:

I don't know I could do this job if I let it affect me mentally or emotionally. Quite frankly, sometimes the decisions that you have to make in these cases are not nearly as tough as they are in child custody cases, or dependency cases, or things like that. Our job ... not everybody could do this job or would want to do this job. If I would let this stuff get to me, I would be a basket case.

He did not have any secrets or things that he did to prevent the capital trial from "getting to him." He simply stated, "I just decide the case and move on." It was mentioned to him that a public defender said that he loses ten to fifteen pounds during a death penalty trial; that he will go work out just to get in shape because of the amount of stamina it requires. The judge observed, "That's true with the lawyers. The only thing I've noticed, as I get older, you're just getting older. Yesterday afternoon I took twenty-five pleas. Ten years ago that wouldn't have been a big deal to me, but I went home and was tired." He volunteered that he slept well at night.

Pronouncing Death

As noted previously, both the most difficult and the worst aspect of being a capital trial judge is imposing the death sentence. Each of the surveyed Florida judges remembered with great clarity the day he or she sentenced a defendant to death. One judge recalled the suspense prior to pronouncement of sentence:

I knew that the victim's family, who wanted death, would be in the courtroom, along with the defendant and his family. No one, except for me, knew for sure what I was going to do. The hardest part is reading the order and knowing the end. Everybody is hanging onto every word you say. It was a shame. It took a full ten to fifteen minutes before they knew for certain the outcome of the case, which I already knew.[9]

After noting the length of time it took to reach the outcome, the judge added that he put a yellow sticker on one of the pages to remind him to "slow down."

Several judges thought it important to look the defendant in the eye when pronouncing sentence. As one judge explained, "When I was sentencing the defendant, I looked into

---

9. Leyte-Vidal and Silverman, op. cit., p. 272.

his eyes. I felt that if I was sentencing him to death that was something I needed to do. Otherwise, I couldn't do it."[10] Another judge related, "I make eye contact with the defendant. If I was imposing the death penalty and I didn't have the backbone to look at the defendant while reading it, then I had no business passing the sentence."[11] A third judge expressed a similar sentiment and the difficulty he had:

> I read the full order to the defendant. I found it difficult to do, and it should be. Judges shouldn't be so disconnected, signing a paper and walking off. While I was reading the order, you could hear a pin drop. All eyes and cameras were on me, and my eyes were on the defendant. I intentionally looked at him, because it's my job. I said, "I sentence you to death for the murder of [victim (s)]."[12]

While reading the sentencing order, a judge who had developed a rapport with the defendant during a lengthy trial apparently found some comfort in the defendant's reaction: "The defendant looked up at me and from his eyes was saying, 'I know you have to do this.'"[13]

For some judges, pronouncing sentence is an emotional experience; other judges are able to effectively suppress their emotions; and still other judges claim they experience no emotions at all. One of the judges who found the experience emotional had this to say:

> At the moment I began to read the order, the courtroom was silent. The defense attorneys sat with their client. I was looking at the defendant and thinking, "Hey buddy, I'm reading an Order and if it's affirmed, somebody's going to put deadly stuff in your veins and take your life." My voice quivered and trembled. Anyone who doesn't experience that has either no emotions or is wired differently than most people.[14]

Another judge did not know how emotional the experience was for him until after the trial, when a corrections officer told him what he'd seen: "As I was reading the order my voice was constant. However, my leg was shaking during the entire time. I didn't realize it during the two hours it took me to read the order."[15]

One of the judges explained that remaining detached is a necessary part of the job: "If you can make it through x years in the criminal division, you have to disassociate yourself from the crimes. If you get caught up in the emotions, you are no good to either the system or yourself. I am not cold. I have to be detached from it emotionally. You have to be detached."[16] Another judge felt much the same way:

> Worrying about crying or any such thing is not even a factor. I have been in this business so long, I am padded from the emotions. It's something that is a part of my job. So when I do it, I do so dispassionately. I am not jaded. [Imposing the death penalty] was just not as difficult as I thought it would be … it was deserved. That made it a lot easier.[17]

---

10. Ibid.
11. Ibid.
12. Ibid.
13. Ibid.
14. Ibid.
15. Ibid.
16. Ibid.
17. Ibid., pp. 272-273.

Another judge echoed the same point:

> I don't sweat over the decision once the jury makes its recommendation. It is
> not pleasant, but it is something you have to do. When I took the job, I said I
> would do it if necessary, so I do it. Once I come to the appropriate conclusion,
> I just do it. A trembling or quivering in my voice is not an issue.[18]

Once sentencing is completed, judges react differently. Some judges just move on to
the next case, while other judges recompose themselves. According to one judge, "I only
relive the experience of the case once the defendant's motion for post conviction is filed
and I hear it. Once I address the motion, I go on to something else."[19] After one case,
another judge just returned to his chambers and then went to lunch. Following another
case, this same judge moved on to the next pending case without taking a recess. He
stated, "It was business as usual because that is the business we are in."[20]

Other judges find the experience more taxing. One judge related, "[Imposing the death
penalty] is emotionally draining. Afterwards, I came back to chambers, closed the door,
and took a few moments to reflect."[21] Ditto another judge: "After I imposed the death
penalty, I was emotionally drained. I didn't have any counseling or night mares [sic]."[22]
Still another judge recalled, "It was both physically and emotionally draining. I felt weary
inside."[23]

Some judges were relieved the trial was over: "It was a long trial and a high profile
case. [During the reading] I wanted to appear 'judicial.' The presence of the media was
just an added pressure." Afterward, the judge went back to his chambers and telephoned
his wife. "I stayed around for a while and then went home."[24] Another judge simply stated,
"When it was over, I breathed a heavy sigh of relief."[25]

None of the judges felt the need to talk with a mental health professional about his or
her decision to sentence a defendant to death. Each judge was convinced that the defendant
he or she sentenced to death deserved the penalty. As one judge put it: "If it is the penalty
that I need to impose, I take no pleasure in it. However, once I am satisfied with my
decision, it doesn't bother me. I am doing what I am supposed to do."[26]

Death Penalty Opinion

The judges reflected on the effects their capital trial experiences had on their death
penalty opinions. One judge confessed:

> I wouldn't say as much as by my capital trial experience as much as my teaching.
> I've been teaching a capital course here in Florida and now nationally for about

---

18. Ibid., p. 273.
19. Ibid.
20. Ibid.
21. Ibid.
22. Ibid.
23. Ibid.
24. Ibid.
25. Ibid.
26. Ibid.

five years. And I've learned a lot about the death penalty in different jurisdictions as a result of my teaching. But I still equivocate quite often about the death penalty. There are lots of pros and cons about it. And I do think there are circumstances where a defendant in a case who commits a particular type of crime has legally forfeited his right to live in society. I go back and forth over it—not the religious or moral issues, or the legal, for that matter, because I have no problem applying it—but certainly the economic factor. In Florida, there are a lot of small jurisdictions that simply cannot afford to try a death penalty case. When you think there should be uniformity and predictability throughout the state, there are certain counties that choose not to seek the death penalty because it would bankrupt the city or the county. Well, that should lead people to question the legitimacy of our death penalty scheme. Because where a person lives may define where they spend the rest of their lives or whether they're going to die as a result of their crime. And I don't think that's very equitable.

When another judge was asked whether his death penalty opinion had changed because of his capital trial experience, he asserted, "No. I have my understanding of how it works, of course, because I've dealt with it so much. My basic opinions of the death penalty haven't changed." In response to the question of whether he supported the death penalty (it was assumed that he did), he offered this surprising retort:

No. Quite frankly, I think we can do without it very well.... I don't think it enhances the criminal justice system in any way. It costs way too much money. It takes way too much time and effort and energy. We don't execute very many people, so it's not very effective. You know, we just have to go through the motions for it as long as the legislature and the people think that the death penalty is important. And I think the people think the death penalty is important, because I don't think they understand it.

He then explained how he could administer the death penalty, given his opinion about it: "I took an oath, raised my right hand, and said I'd be a circuit judge. So I do my job. I'm not morally against the death penalty. I just don't think it works, and I don't think there's a system that can be devised that will work."

A California trial judge went further in expressing his antipathy toward the death penalty: "Human error, inequities, biases and personal ideologies create the problems that have caused my rejection of the death penalty. Because these frailties will not magically vanish, capital punishment cannot be implemented with any sense of balance or fairness, thus it must be abolished."[27] A Washington state trial judge drew a similar conclusion:

Gross numbers of executions are being carried out in some states or regions of the country. An alarming number of convictions have been found to be wrong, and the death penalty is unfairly inflicted upon the poor, minorities and the under-represented. [The] death penalty as a response to any criminal behavior no longer has validity and should be repealed, because it is impossible to administer with justice and fairness.[28]

---

27. Donald A. McCartin, former Orange County Superior Court Judge and former death penalty supporter who sent 9 convicts to death row, *Orange County Register*, 6/24/2005, cited in ibid.

28. David A. Nichols, Washington State Superior Court Judge, *Seattle Times*, 11/8/2003, cited in ibid.

Some death penalty commentators have suggested that many death penalty proponents only want a death penalty "on the books," or support it only in theory, but really do not care very much whether it is imposed, or want it imposed rarely, only in the most heinous of cases. One judge agreed with that interpretation, noting:

> They haven't had an execution in New England for years. I think the last execution in New Hampshire was in 1939 or something. Yeah, but they still have the death penalty on the books; they just never use it. You go to a state like Georgia, where you think the death penalty is a popular thing—they very seldom have death cases in Georgia. I happen to know some of the judges in Chatham County, where Savannah is. They said their prosecutors never seek the death penalty. It's just too much trouble.

The evidence on this point is persuasive. Most death-sentenced and executed inmates come from an extremely small number of jurisdictions. Since 1976, when the U.S. Supreme Court reinstated the death penalty, more than 1,300 people have been executed. Five death penalty states (Texas, Virginia, Oklahoma, Missouri, and Florida) account for nearly two-thirds of those executions. Texas, alone, has executed 37 percent of the total.[29] In those five executing states, moreover, death sentences are concentrated within only a few counties. In short, the vast majority of death penalty jurisdictions are reluctant to execute.

A judge offered his prediction about the death penalty's future:

> I think the death penalty is here and is going to stay with us for a long time.... I think if the death penalty ever goes away, either in Florida or elsewhere, I don't think it will be based on moral or religious principles. I think it will be based on either the advent of new DNA technology—somebody who is executed and is later exonerated—or it will be based on economic factors: the fact that it's too expensive now to try a death penalty case.... It'll likely be an economic-based decision by the voters.

Conclusion

As noted previously, Supreme Court Justice William Brennan observed in his *Furman* opinion that "death is different," and death is certainly different for capital trial court judges. Not only is a capital trial structurally different from other felony trials (capital trials are either bifurcated or, as in Florida, trifurcated), but capital trials also require a specialized jurisprudence with unique procedures such as the death qualification of jurors. In some states, such as Florida, judges now must receive special training before they may conduct a capital trial. In other states, judges are left to fend for themselves and learn to manage capital proceedings by trial and error.

Some capital trial court judges readily admit that their jobs are stressful, emotionally taxing, and physically demanding. Some of them are undoubtedly influenced by extra-legal factors, especially political considerations. Some judges find capital cases less onerous than other types of cases, such as child custody or dependency cases. Particularly troubling

---

29. Calculated from data at the Death Penalty Information Center at www.deathpenaltyinfo.org (accessed March 4, 2012).

for many capital trial judges is imposing the death sentence. But some present a stoic image and consider a capital trial as just part of their job. Once the trial is over, they simply move on to the next case. There's no telling whether this characterization accurately reflects the judges' true feelings or is bravado concealing deeper psychological problems.

Many capital trial court judges are not strong death penalty proponents; many could easily do without it. Their opposition generally is not for religious or philosophical reasons but rather for practical ones: they do not believe that the death penalty deters crime—capital or otherwise. In addition, they believe it is too costly, continues to be imposed in an arbitrary way and for political gain, and wrecks havoc with their court dockets. If they had not sworn to uphold the law, they probably would impose fewer death sentences than they already do. (The annual number of death sentences in the United States has dropped steadily from a high of 328 in 1994 to a low of 104 in 2010.)[30]

Whether or how deeply judges are affected by capital crimes remains a question, but, either way, they must shepherd each case through the system, dealing with defense attorneys, prosecutors, and jurors. As with others involved in capital trials, jurors play complex roles and often endure lasting effects of their involvement. We examine these effects in the next chapter.

---

30. Death Penalty Information Center, "Sentencing" at www.deathpenaltyinfo.org (accessed March 4, 2012).

Chapter 7

Jurors

Trial judges, prosecutors, defense attorneys, and jurors are the four major participants in capital trials. Jurors arguably have the greatest responsibility in capital trials because they alone decide whether a defendant lives or dies (except in Alabama, Delaware, and Florida, where a judge decides).

In the 2002 case of *Ring v. Arizona*,[1] the U.S. Supreme Court ruled that the Sixth Amendment right to a jury trial requires that juries—not judges—determine whether death is the appropriate penalty in a capital case. That means that a jury (in a jury trial) must find capital aggravating factors beyond a reasonable doubt.

Whether jurors are up to the responsibility of deciding whether capital defendants should live or die is debatable. Ideally, jurors should be open-minded and assume that the defendant is innocent until proven guilty. However, jurors are human beings and, as such, invariably have attitudes and biases that may affect their judgments. In addition, jurors in capital trials are death qualified; any person who could not impose the death penalty regardless of the circumstances is not allowed to serve on a jury in a capital trial.

Not surprisingly, many jurors find their life-and-death responsibility an emotionally draining and stressful experience. As this chapter shows, the rules and process of jury selection—as well as the structure and procedures of the trial—make the burden of sentencing a defendant to death (or life imprisonment without opportunity of parole) easier to bear. They enable jurors to "morally disengage" from the realities of their decision. Nevertheless, most jurors would refuse to serve in another capital trial, try to get out of it, or serve reluctantly. Only about one-third of jurors would welcome the opportunity to serve again. Most do not change their death penalty opinions as a result of their jury experience. This chapter explores the role of jurors in the capital punishment process.

The Wisdom of Capital Jury Trials

Critics of the capital jury system consider it absurd that jurors are given the responsibility of determining who should live and who should die. As one critic observed:

> [H]ow do people judge other people's actions when they do not live in their head? The overwhelming task of having to sit and listen to a set of facts as they are told by people who did not witness the event, about people whom they have never met before, and about circumstances that most people have never experienced, is given to ordinary citizens; our system requires it. Without any

---

1. 536 U.S. 584.

expertise, experience, general knowledge of, or predilection towards the events or people that they are being asked to judge, jurors are charged with the responsibility of rendering a "reasonable" verdict. It is not so much the fact that this task is nearly impossible to accomplish (putting aside personal views and experiences to judge the very same in others), but rather the fact that most people put faith and confidence in this process is what offers a subject for scrutiny.[2]

Perhaps people would have less confidence in the process if they knew that jurors frequently are found to be "sleeping, daydreaming, grooming themselves, or doodling in notebooks" instead of paying attention to the proceedings.[3] Perhaps the process would be challenged more if people knew that jurors are expected only to make a good-faith effort at deciding a case correctly and that despite this, they fail too often (no one knows how often) to make the correct decision.[4]

Dr. William Bowers, principal investigator of The Capital Jury Project[5] and the preeminent authority on the subject, has a cynical view of capital juries. As Bowers related in an interview:

> It dawned on me ... that juries had become a kind of sacred cow. They allow the judges and the lawmakers to report that the public, indeed, plays a central role in the death penalty. It gives the average citizen the sense that it's "the people," not the state, that is ordering executions. The illusion that *people* are "doing it" keeps public support high. Basically, without a jury system, we could not have a death penalty. (emphasis in original)[6]

Open-Minded and Unbiased — or Predisposed and Prejudiced?

Ideally, jurors should be open-minded and presume that the defendant is innocent until proven guilty. However, jurors are human beings and, as such, invariably have attitudes and biases that may affect their judgments. As noted previously, the process of *voir dire* is supposed to eliminate any potential jurors whose attitudes and biases may render them incapable of fairly judging the defendant, but sometimes biases are unconscious or hidden. Jurors might not be aware they have them, or they may conceal them. As one prosecutor observed about potential jurors: "Some people were probably thinking about

---

2. Allison M. Cotton (2008) *Effigy: Images of Capital Defendants*. Lanham, MD: Lexington Books, p. xiv.

3. See, for example, ibid., p. 150.

4. Ibid., p. xiv.

5. The Capital Jury Project (CJP) "is a continuing program of research on the decision-making of capital jurors that was initiated in 1991 by a consortium of university-based researchers with support from the National Science Foundation (NSF). The Project has been administered nationally by Dr. William Bowers.... The findings of the CJP are based on three- to four-hour, in-depth, interviews with persons who have served as jurors in capital trials. Phase I of the Project has completed over 1,200 interviews from jurors in 353 capital trials in 14 states." "Capital Jury Project" at www.albany.edu/scj/CPRIjuryproj.htm (accessed May 1, 2009).

6. Robert Jay Lifton and Greg Mitchell (2002) *Who Owns Death? Capital Punishment, the American Conscience, and the End of Executions*. New York: Perennial, p. 152.

their attitudes and opinions for the first time as they filled out the [juror] questionnaire ... so it's important to use this [*voir dire*] process to dig a little deeper."[7] Sometimes jurors are seated despite their biases. For example, in one capital trial, a juror was seated after telling the court during *voir dire* that she did not believe psychologists or psychiatrists and would not consider their testimony. In this particular trial, most of the defense's case rested on the testimony of psychologists and psychiatrists that the defendant was brain damaged and that the brain damage affected his judgment and behavior.[8] Because of her bias, did the juror simply ignore most of the defense's case?

Many potential jurors are biased from the onset of a capital case because of exposure to the media's typical one-sided coverage. The media provide potential jurors with a "framework for understanding" a capital crime.[9] The media tend to focus on the most dramatic and heinous aspects of the crime. Rarely are the offender and his or her crime put in historical or social context. The offender's personal history and background—factors that might humanize the offender and mitigate the crime—generally are ignored. Thus, potential jurors are exposed to portrayals of capital offenders as animals or monsters, as something less than human, something to fear and despise. Not surprisingly, then, research shows that the more a potential juror is exposed to negative media information about a capital offender, the more likely he or she is willing to convict the offender *prior to the death penalty trial*.[10] The irony is that most murderers are not like the media portrayals of them. As law professor David Dow, who has represented more than thirty death row inmates, relates, "What is arresting about nearly all murderers is how ordinary they are, how unremarkable they appear."[11]

One remedy for the influence of pretrial publicity is a change of venue, but judges are reluctant to grant one, even when prejudicial publicity has been extensive, community awareness of the crime is very high, and there is significant prejudgment of the case in the communities where the trial is to be held.[12] Judges are reluctant to grant change of venue motions because a change of venue is expensive when the trial is not held in the jurisdiction where most trial participants live. This is particularly true in capital cases, which typically are more complex and lengthy than other types of cases. The political risk of changing venues in capital cases is also a reason why elected judges are reluctant to grant them. When a highly publicized capital crime has been committed, judges, for political reasons, generally are more responsive to community sentiment to hold the trial in the jurisdiction where the crime was committed than they are to the constitutional rights of defendants.[13]

Another solution to the influence of pretrial publicity is the elimination of potential jurors affected by it during *voir dire*. However, as noted previously, biased jurors are hard to detect. This is especially true of *automatic death penalty* (ADP) jurors: those who would automatically vote for the death penalty following a guilty verdict in a capital case. Evidence from the Capital Jury Project, which interviewed more than one thousand jurors who participated in capital trials, suggests that an average of 14 percent to 30 percent of capital

---

7. Ibid., p. 141.
8. Cotton, op. cit., p. 166.
9. Craig Haney (2005) *Death By Design: Capital Punishment As A Social Psychological System.* New York: Oxford University Press.
10. Ibid., p. 62.
11. David R. Dow (2005) *Executed on a Technicality: Lethal Injustice on America's Death Row.* Boston: Beacon Press, p. 183.
12. Ibid.
13. Ibid., pp. 97-98 and 113.

jurors — between about two and four persons on a twelve-person jury — are ADPs.[14] Research reveals that potential jurors (ADPs and others) often claim that they can be impartial, even when they know they have been exposed to negative pretrial publicity that has prejudiced their opinion of the defendant.[15] Research also indicates that the biasing effects of pretrial publicity are not reduced by judicial instructions to ignore it.[16]

According to research, *voir dire* and death qualification are independent sources of bias in capital cases (especially when jurors are questioned in a group rather than individually after being sequestered). These processes have been found to "'condition' jurors to a particular point of view or set of expectations."[17] For example, potential jurors can be prejudiced by the responses of other potential jurors during *voir dire* and, in an effort to be seated or excused, may structure their answers to questions based on the reactions of judges and trial attorneys to the other potential jurors' responses to the same questions.[18]

Prolonged discussion of penalty at the very start of the trial during *voir dire* and death qualification, a unique aspect of capital trials, has been found to predispose potential jurors to believe (1) that the defendant is guilty and that he will be convicted and sentenced to death, (2) that judges and attorneys share their guilt-prone views, and (3) that the judge in the case favors the death penalty. These beliefs, in turn, divert jurors' attention from the presumption of innocence. The discussion of penalty at the onset of the trial also desensitizes potential jurors to the prospect of imposing the death penalty. In addition, death penalty opponents are excluded from participating in capital trials, so many potential jurors believe that the law disfavors death penalty opponents. Finally, because they are required to publicly affirm their commitment to capital punishment during *voir dire*, potential jurors are more likely to believe that the death penalty is the appropriate punishment when confronted with a hypothetical capital case. They also are more likely to vote to impose it.[19]

Another source of bias is the capital trial itself. Capital trials are unique among criminal trials because only in capital trials are juries required to make the sentencing decision. To do so, "normal, law-abiding persons" who become jurors in capital cases must overcome a deep-seated inhibition to sentence someone to death; they must be able to morally disengage from the realities of their decision. The trial structure and sequencing of evidence; the formal, legalistic atmosphere of the trial; and various legal doctrines allow them to do that.[20]

Moral Disengagement

Moral disengagement is facilitated by the dehumanization of the capital defendant. As noted previously, this starts with typical media portrayals of the capital offender as a

---

14. Ibid., p. 287, n. 53.

15. Ibid., p. 63.

16. Ibid.

17. Haney, op. cit., p. 117; also see William J. Bowers and Wanda D. Foglia (2003) "Still Singularly Agonizing: Law's Failure to Purge Arbitrariness from Capital Sentencing," *Criminal Law Bulletin* 39:51-86.

18. Haney, ibid.

19. Ibid., pp. 120-132.

20. Ibid., pp. 141-143; also see Robert Weisberg (1983) "Deregulating Death," pp. 305-395 in P. B. Kurland, G. Casper, and D. J. Hutchinson (eds.) *The Supreme Court Review, 1983*. Chicago: University of Chicago Press.

monster or an animal. The trial is structured so that the first opportunity to humanize the capital defendant comes at the end of the trial: during the penalty phase, when mitigation evidence can be presented. Even then, court rules give the prosecution the opportunity to present its evidence of aggravation first. During the guilt phase, the jury hears only the prosecution's description of the crime's brutal details. Moreover, the prosecution's typical theory of the crime — that the defendant is an inherently evil person entirely responsible for his or her crime — usually coincides with jurors' stereotypical beliefs about crimes and punishment. Not surprisingly, then, before jurors are exposed to any mitigating evidence, they become frightened of the defendant (assuming that they were not already), which provokes punitive and vengeful feelings and a concern about the defendant's future dangerousness, whether or not that issue is explicitly raised at trial. As one juror revealed, "Um, he scared me.... I mean, I looked at him and he was trying to intimidate us. He'd pick one person and just stare at them almost the whole trial."[21]

Another juror had a similar experience: "He had a cold look to him, you know he'd glance over at us and whatever he was looking at it looked like that he could look right through it. It was frightening to look at him. He had this tattoo-like thing on his face with a cross and a blade or something like that. I assumed that it was something demonistic."[22]

Oftentimes the defendant unwittingly jeopardizes his own chances during the trial. Many jurors pay more attention to a defendant's appearance, demeanor, and reactions than to the evidence presented. For example, when jurors see a clean-cut defendant in a suit and tie at the defense table, they may conclude that the defendant is trying to deceive them following the prosecution's presentation of photos showing the defendant as a totally different person being booked into jail with long hair, scruffy beard, and tattoos everywhere.[23] Also, a defendant frequently does a disservice to himself in the eyes of jurors by failing to show signs of remorse and repentance during the trial. When a prosecutor, for instance, shows photos of the victims' bodies, and the defendant fails to show any emotion, jurors may decide there is little hope for redemption. A few tears shed by a defendant may mean the difference between a life sentence and a death sentence.[24]

Another way defendants could humanize themselves in jurors' eyes is by testifying on their own behalf during the guilt and/or penalty phase of the capital trial. Defendants have a constitutional right both to testify on their own behalf or to remain silent. Furthermore, trial court judges are obligated to instruct jurors that a defendant's choice not to testify is not to be held against him. Such instructions, however, often fall on deaf ears. Data from The Capital Jury Project show that many capital defendants are damned if they do testify and damned if they do not.[25] Many jurors expect or want defendants to testify, and they interpret the defendant's refusal to do so as an obvious admission of guilt, an indication he has something to hide, or, at the least, a sign that he is not sorry or does not feel remorse. Some jurors find it difficult to understand why defendants do not use the opportunity to proclaim their innocence, express sorrow, show remorse, or

21. Michael E. Antonio (2006) "Jurors' Emotional Reactions to Serving On a Capital Trial," *Judicature* 89: 282–88, p. 286.

22. Leigh B. Bienen (1993) "Helping Jurors Out: Post-Verdict Debriefing for Jurors in Emotionally Disturbing Trials," *Indiana Law Journal* 68: 1333–1355, p. 1340, n. 27 (accessed online).

23. Scott E. Sundby (2005) *A Life and Death Decision: A Jury Weighs the Death Penalty.* New York: Palgrave Macmillan, p. 31.

24. Ibid., pp. 32-33.

25. Michael E. Antonio and Nicole E. Arone (2005) "Damned If They Do; Damned If They Don't: Jurors' Reaction to Defendants' Testimony or Silence During a Capital Trial," *Judicature* 89:1-10.

beg for mercy. Testifying sometimes gives defendants the opportunity to provide a different explanation for ambiguous evidence or to counter a prosecutor's argument.

Commenting about a defendant's failure to testify, one juror surmised:

> [Whether or not the defendant testified] came into play more than you would think, I think actually a great deal because he ... just never really gave a darn. You know, even a couple of the folks said ... that they weren't really for [the death penalty, but] they said he just showed no remorse, doesn't care, he's not sitting up begging for his life or anything. And I think that if he would've taken the stand and begged ... people would've maybe changed.[26]

Another female juror had a similar reaction:

> If he had just turned around to the jury and said, "I didn't mean to do it." Or, "I'm sorry I did it.... It was dumb to do it." Or something, you know—just something, you would have had compassion for this person. But they sit there, and they say absolutely nothing! I don't care if they get torn up on the stand by the prosecuting attorney! At least say a few words to the stands when it's a capital offense! I mean, there are twelve people that are going to decide the rest of your life. For God's sake, say a few words to them! I mean, that's how I feel about it.[27]

Some jurors do not understand that there are legitimate strategic reasons for defendants not to testify on their own behalf. For example, by not testifying, defendants avoid helping prosecutors make their case. Prosecutors have the burden of proving guilt beyond a reasonable doubt, which is made easier by defendants who implicate themselves. By testifying, defendants leave themselves open to questioning about their prior criminal records, something that defense attorneys frequently want to avoid. Many defendants make poor witnesses and do not help themselves by testifying, especially if they are psychologically or emotionally unfit for the task. Data from The Capital Jury Project reveal that only a small minority of jurors found that a defendant's testimony left them with a favorable impression. The vast majority of jurors reacted negatively to a defendant's testimony. They believed that the defendant was lying and were unsettled by the defendant's lack of emotion, especially his failure to show sorrow or remorse. Or, when he did show emotion, they believed it was fabricated or insincere. Some jurors found defendants to be arrogant or smug. In short, a defendant's testimony can backfire. As one juror described it: "He read his little statement they had given him. He just didn't sound like that was anything at all he wanted to say. He was apologizing to the family and saying he was sorry, but he didn't even do a good job of it. Acting isn't his strong suit."[28]

A female juror felt similarly:

> He came up to this podium very nicely dressed with a long, legal pad and a Bible in his hand. He stood up there, and he read a statement that was obviously prepared by his lawyer. He said how sorry he was for this family and the other people that had survived, for the trauma that they had to go through. And I mean it was just—that was really the wrong thing for his attorney to do. Bad move. They could have told that young man, "You know, you are up there pleading for your life. Now go to it." I mean, "Really express yourself!" I guess it could have maybe been looked over by his attorney, but he certainly should have said

---

26. Bienen, op. cit., p. 1344; also see Antonio and Arone, op. cit.
27. Benjamin Fleury-Steiner (2004) *Jurors' Stories of Death: How America's Death Penalty Invests in Inequality.* Ann Arbor, MI: The University of Michigan Press, p. 61.
28. Ibid., p. 63.

it in his own words. He came across as insincere. He was very insincere—no remorse whatsoever.[29]

All of this helps explain why many capital jurors believe that the defendant should be sentenced to death, *before the penalty phase of the trial begins*. To effectively deal with this structural barrier, defense attorneys must be able to make a strong case for mitigation during the penalty phase and overcome what many jurors believe is commonsense. However, as noted in chapter 4, many defense attorneys in capital cases lack the training, professional experience, time, and resources to do the job properly. The "emotionally distant and decontextualized legal language by which the process proceeds" makes efforts at humanizing the capital defendant even more difficult.[30]

Being Manipulated

A few interviewed jurors bemoaned the lack of hard facts or evidence about the crime and the defendant brought out at the trial. One juror grumbled that the defense attorney and the prosecutor "turned the courtroom into a theater instead of a place for facts in defense of a person's life or the prosecuting of it. They didn't allow us to be smart enough to know anything.... Both attorneys tried to manipulate the jury into seeing what they wanted them to see, instead of presenting the facts as they were."[31] Another juror stated, "I was extremely upset that the justice system failed. I felt it failed by not bringing out all of the factors that influenced (the defendant's) commission of the crime. It still bothers me to this day. He needs to be in an institution where he can get help."[32]

When facts about defendants' lives were brought up, it weighed heavily on the minds of some jurors:

[I] think about the fact that it was ... a child basically who did it.... I guess that the biggest thing is that ... his mother never came to the trial at all and that really just ticked me off. His father is every kind of pervert you could think of ... [a] beater, abuser, molester, homosexual, you name it. His father and mother ... should have been on trial, not him. That's kind of my impression. Because they're as much to blame for his situation as he is.[33]

Another frustrated juror observed:

During the first part of this case, when they couldn't bring up his mental stability, so much of it was left for us to really (decide). It wasn't clear-cut. He was guilty, but there was nothing clear-cut. Each and every one of us felt they wanted to do the right thing, give every part the right amount of weight, and make a good decision, something you could go home and sleep with. It was emotionally draining.[34]

Also working against the capital defendant and contributing to moral disengagement is legal doctrine that forbids detailed discussion during the penalty phase of prison

---

29. Ibid., pp 95-96.
30. Haney, op. cit., p. 146.
31. Ibid., p. 288.
32. Ibid.
33. Bienen, op. cit., p. 1346.
34. Antonio, op. cit., p. 288.

conditions or future prospects should the defendant be sentenced to life imprisonment without opportunity of parole.[35] If jurors were made aware of some of the realities of LWOP and the death penalty, they might feel more comfortable sentencing convicted capital defendants to life. Realities such as:

- modern maximum security prisons have high levels of security;
- prison life is harsh, make no mistake about it;
- evidence shows that the death penalty is no greater deterrent than LWOP;
- defendants sentenced to LWOP only rarely engage in violent acts in prison, almost never escape or are released in error, and sometimes are rehabilitated and make positive contributions while in prison;
- LWOP is nearly always less expensive than the death penalty.

Furthermore, legal doctrine prohibits telling jurors details of the execution the defendant may face if sentenced to death and how that execution may affect his family and friends. This, too, contributes to moral disengagement. It also creates asymmetry because there is no prohibition on exposing jurors to the violence and gore of capital crimes or to the effects on the victims' surviving family and friends.[36] In addition, prosecutors are allowed to introduce evidence about a defendant's prior criminal convictions during the penalty phase to show that the defendant poses a future danger and that the current crime is not an isolated event. Such evidence generally is not allowed during the guilt phase unless it has a direct bearing on the current crime.[37]

Knowledge of the execution process, incidentally, may not matter anyway. Research shows that most jurors are skeptical about an execution ever being carried out after a death sentence is imposed.[38] This skepticism is justified in states such as California, for example, where only 13 of more than 700 defendants sentenced to death between 1977 and 2011 have been executed.[39]

Confusion and Misapprehension

Moral disengagement also may be the product of jurors' misunderstanding or confusion about their sentencing responsibilities. A considerable amount of research shows that jurors frequently misapprehend judges' capital-sentencing instructions, particularly those that apply to mitigation. Especially troublesome is evidence from The Capital Jury Project indicating that nearly 75 percent of jurors "acknowledge that sentencing instructions did not guide their decision-making on punishment but served instead as an after-the-fact façade for a decision made prior to hearing the instructions."[40] Many jurors inappropriately

---

35. Ibid., p. 154.
36. Ibid.
37. Sundby, op. cit., p. 17.
38. Haney, op. cit., p. 157.
39. Death Penalty Information Center at www.deathpenaltyinfo.org/number-executions-state-and-region-1976 and www.deathpenaltyinfo.org/death-sentences-united-states-1977-2008 (accessed March 6, 2012).
40. William J.Bowers and Benjamin D. Steiner (1999) "Death by Default: An Empirical Demonstration of False and Forced Choices in Capital Sentencing," *Texas Law Review* 77:605–717; William J. Bowers and Benjamin D. Steiner (1998) "Choosing Life or Death: Sentencing Dynamics in Capital Cases," pp. 309–349 in J. R. Acker, R. M. Bohm, and C. S. Lanier (eds.) *America's Experiment*

make their sentencing decisions before the sentencing phase of the trial begins, and oftentimes those decisions are pro-death.[41]

Rather than correcting those misapprehensions, established legal doctrine presumes that jurors understand and follow judges' instructions, even when they do not. And when jurors ask questions, legal doctrine presumes that they understand the judge's answers, however unhelpful they may be. Many judges refuse to clarify instructions even when jurors make it clear that they are confused and need help. At most, many judges simply repeat the original instructions. Long-standing legal doctrine also prohibits jurors from researching on their own the meanings of key terms that confuse them.[42]

In an attempt to overcome this latter problem, some courts or legislatures have provided juries with definitions of confusing terms. However, in many cases, this has not helped. For example, the Virginia Supreme Court has provided the following definition for the term "depravity" in the phrase "depravity of mind": "a degree of moral turpitude and psychical debasement surpassing that inherent in the definition of ordinary malice and premeditation."[43]

One of the issues about which jurors often seek clarification is the meaning of the phrase "life without parole." Data from The Capital Jury Project reveal that jurors frequently have mistaken views about LWOP and, consequently, vote for death even though they would vote for life if they were assured that the defendant would never be released from prison. As a North Carolina juror related, "We all had decided if we were absolutely sure that he would never have gotten out of prison we wouldn't have given him the death penalty. But we were not sure of that."[44] Many jurors do not believe that LWOP actually means that a defendant will be imprisoned for life. In fact, many capital jurors believe murderers will be back on the streets far too soon, typically in about fifteen years or less.[45] For example, a female juror was certain defendants not sentenced to death would get out of prison:

> We were discussing how our prisons are so overcrowded now. It's already a fact that there are people being released that would normally have been in prison a lot longer. I mean, if it gets worse, who knows what's going to happen in the next ten, fifteen, or twenty-five years in our prisons? My boyfriend's mother works at the Department of Corrections, and, I mean, just knowing what you hear — you know, street talk. Everybody knows that you can commit a murder these days and be out in no time. It really alarms me.[46]

A male juror complained that a fellow juror who was a "life holdout" did not understand that "life does not really mean life":

---

with Capital Punishment: Reflections on the Past, Present and Future of the Ultimate Penal Sanction. Durham, NC: Carolina Academic Press, p. 328; William J. Bowers (1995) "The Capital Jury Project: Rationale, Design, and Preview of Early Findings." *Indiana Law Journal* 70:1043–1102.

41. William J. Bowers, Marla Sandys, and Benjamin D. Steiner (1998) "Foreclosed Impartiality in Capital Sentencing: Jurors' Predispositions, Guilt–Trial Experience, and Premature Decision Making." *Cornell Law Review* 83:1476–1556; Bowers and Foglia, op. cit.

42. Haney, op. cit., pp. 183-184; also see Sundby, op. cit., p. 50.

43. Sundby, ibid., pp. 10-11.

44. Lifton and Mitchell, op. cit., p. 156.

45. Bowers and Steiner (1999), op. cit.; also see Theodore Eisenberg and Martin T. Wells (1993–1994) "Deadly Confusion: Juror Instructions in Capital Cases," *Cornell Law Review* 79:1–17; Haney, op. cit., p. 85; Anthony Paduano and Clive A. Stanford Smith (1987) "Deathly Errors: Jurors Misperceptions Concerning Parole in the Imposition of the Death Penalty," *Columbia Human Rights Law Review* 18:211-257; Bowers and Foglia, op. cit.

46. Fleury-Steiner, op. cit., pp. 39-40.

One of the jurors held out—this guy from [another country]. He was a very in-telligent man, but I don't think he appreciated a lot of the unsaid things about the American criminal justice system [*laughs*], such as life does not mean life. And frankly, if there had been a complaint at that time, there probably would have been a mistrial. I felt like the jury badgered him to the point to where he changed his vote. He thought that life means life, your whole life. It's probably not one of the things that you discuss or are supposed to discuss legally. But this guy really thought that you could sentence someone to life and he would be never released into society. And that was a problem.[47]

Judges in many jurisdictions are legally barred from clarifying that issue for jurors.[48] In jurisdictions that do permit judicial clarification, the response a judge provides can determine whether a jury returns a sentence of life or death. If a judge responds in un-ambiguous language that a defendant sentenced to LWOP will spend the rest of his natural life in prison, a jury is often likely to sentence a defendant to LWOP—frequently in a matter of minutes. On the other hand, if the judge refuses to answer the question or explains ambiguously that a governor has the power to commute sentences, the jury is usually quick to sentence a defendant to death.[49] Most jurors are reluctant to take risks with dangerous offenders. As one female juror explained:

I think the single most important factor was probably to make sure that he didn't get back out on the street.... I couldn't help but think what if he got out and murdered some other poor little girl. I would feel I was responsible for turning him back loose when I could possibly help do something about it, and I felt that this was my duty as a citizen to stand up and do the right thing, to not be afraid to make a decision right or wrong. One way or the other, to do the best I know how to do and I think that's a citizen's responsibility.[50]

Another female juror voiced similar concerns about the defendant, combining several common themes:

The bottom line was we all felt he wasn't remorseful. He would do it again. He was a scary person that we didn't want to be around. We had an obligation to society to be sure he wouldn't be out on the streets again. And we didn't feel that life in prison was long enough. There was a strong possibility with good conduct he might be out rather quickly. If he had acted more remorseful in any way, that certainly would have been something we would have talked more about.... He was probably his own worst enemy. If only he had looked during the trial like he did during jury selection. At that time, he looked like a nice kid. I mean, during the trial he certainly convinced the whole jury that he was someone we would not want to meet alone in a dark alley.[51]

The cumbersome and intimidating procedures in the way that the court handles jurors' questions also are a disincentive for jurors to seek clarification. For example, in one case, during deliberations a juror requested a witness's testimony to be reread to the jury. Before the judge granted the request, he first consulted with the prosecutor and defense attorney and then reconvened the court with all participants present, including the defendant, the

---

47. Ibid., p. 117.
48. See, for example, *Simmons v. South Carolina* (512 U.S. 154, 1994); *Ramdass v. Angelone* (530 U.S. 156, 2000); *Weeks v. Angelone* (528 U.S. 225, 2000).
49. Sundby, op. cit., pp. 147-148.
50. Ibid., p. 1344.
51. Ibid., p. 99.

lawyers, jurors, and court personnel. This process is typical, as judges guard against possible reversal on appeal by ensuring the defendant and attorneys are present whenever the jury is in the courtroom.[52] Such a time-consuming procedure discourages jurors from asking questions — assuming, of course, jurors even know they are confused and need help.

The misapprehension of jury instructions causes at least two significant and related problems. The first is that jurors may simply ignore the parts of the sentencing instructions they do not understand. For example, they may ignore mitigating evidence if they do not understand what mitigation means. Second, lacking guidance and left on their own, jurors are likely to resort to stereotypes and impermissible factors that, in turn, lead to arbitrary and discriminatory decision making — the very outcomes the sentencing instructions are supposed to help eliminate.[53]

A recent study showed that jurors regarded the exact same mitigating and aggravating evidence very differently, depending on whether the defendant was white or black (less so for aggravating evidence). Specifically, testimony that the defendant was abused as a child, had untreated psychological problems, and was a drug abuser was found to be significantly more mitigating for white defendants than for black defendants.[54] Furthermore, in some cases with black defendants, some jurors "inappropriately converted some of the mitigating factors [for example, that the defendant was abused as a child and had untreated psychological problems] into aggravating factors (by indicating that their presence in the case inclined them toward a death rather than life sentence)."[55]

Many jurors also underestimate their sentencing responsibilities, seeming to believe that they are only to follow a prescribed formula in determining a sentence in capital cases. For them, it is "the law" or "legal instructions" that ultimately determines whether a capital defendant lives or dies. For some jurors, "the law" or "legal instructions" "authorizes" them to impose the death penalty and, at the same time, relieves them of any personal responsibility in making the decision.[56] Other jurors cope by shifting responsibility to the "state." As one female juror confided, "I guess thinking over and over, rehashing that all I was doing was my job as a juror. I wasn't the one that was putting the guy to death, the state was."[57] Still other jurors assume that the sentence they impose is only preliminary and nonbinding, because it will be reviewed and corrected, if necessary, by an appellate court.[58] In *Caldwell v. Mississippi* (1985),[59] the Supreme Court opined that for jurors to believe that "the responsibility for any ultimate determination of death will rest with others" is an "intolerable danger." Such thinking on the part of capital jurors may lead to arbitrarily imposed death sentences.

---

52. Ibid., p. 66.

53. Haney, op. cit., pp. 187-188; also see Cotton, op. cit., pp. 153-154.

54. Ibid., p. 206; also see William J. Bowers, Benjamin D. Steiner, and Marla Sandys (2001) "Death Sentencing in Black and White: An Empirical Analysis of the Role of Jurors' Race and Jury Racial Composition," *University of Pennsylvania Journal of Constitutional Law* 3:171-274.

55. Haney, ibid.; Bowers et al., ibid.

56. Haney, ibid., pp. 179-180; Sundby, op. cit.; Bowers and Foglia, op. cit.; Weisberg, op. cit.

57. Fleury-Steiner, op. cit., p. 89.

58. James R. Acker and Charles S. Lanier (1998) "Death Penalty Legislation: Past, Present, and Future," pp. 77–115 in J. R. Acker, R. M. Bohm, and C. S. Lanier (eds.) *America's Experiment with Capital Punishment: Reflections on the Past, Present and Future of the Ultimate Penal Sanction.* Durham, NC: Carolina Academic Press; Bowers and Steiner (1998), op. cit., pp. 320-321; Joseph L. Hoffmann (1995) "Where's the Buck? — Juror Misperception of Sentencing Responsibility in Death Penalty Cases," *Indiana Law Journal* 70:1137–1160.

59. 472 U.S. 320.

The Effects of Jury Deliberations

The dynamics of jury deliberations also play a major role in capital case sentencing decisions. The law in most death penalty jurisdictions requires a jury to decide unanimously whether a capital defendant lives or dies. If it does not reach a unanimous decision, the result is a hung jury—following which the judge declares a mistrial, and the prosecutor must decide whether to retry the case.

Judges want to avoid hung juries if at all possible. In fact, they have jury instructions, variously referred to as "shotgun charges," "hammer charges," "third-degree charges," "dynamite charges," and "nitroglycerine charges," intended to encourage jurors to continue deliberating and reach a unanimous verdict.[60] Many jurors consider a hung jury as a failure on their part. The most heinous cases and the least heinous cases rarely present problems. In the former, juries almost always return death sentences and in the latter, they almost always return life sentences, regardless of the individual characteristics of jurors.[61] It is usually only the "middle-range" cases, those that are less clear-cut, that present problems.

When jurors begin deliberations, one of the first things they do is take a vote to determine where the jury stands on sentence. In most cases, jurors are not unanimous on the initial ballot. This is not surprising, because jurors, although death qualified, still bring unique perspectives, experiences, and beliefs to jury deliberations, often resulting in different reactions to the same evidence. Consequently, it is always possible that another jury, with a different group of jurors, would decide the case differently.[62]

Research shows that the initial vote often foretells the final vote. For example, as part of the Capital Jury Project, a study of South Carolina capital jurors discovered that if eight or more jurors voted for death on the first ballot, the jury invariably returned a death sentence. On the other hand, if fewer than eight jurors voted for death on the first ballot, the jury was almost guaranteed to choose a life sentence. In this study, a life sentence was easier to obtain than a death sentence. The study also found that a juror's first vote was influenced by the juror's race, religion, and how strongly the juror believed that death was the appropriate sentence in the case. Black jurors were more likely than white jurors to vote for life on the first ballot, but not on the final one. In the end, all jurors generally voted with the initial majority, and, because black jurors rarely comprised a majority of jurors, majority rule usually meant white rule. In addition, jurors who identified themselves as Southern Baptists, almost all of whom are white, usually voted for death on the first ballot, as did jurors who felt strongly that death was the appropriate sentence in the case.[63]

In another study using data from The Capital Jury Project, the influence of race in jury decision making was found to be strongest in black defendant-white victim cases.[64] The racial composition of the jury made a difference. For example, on the first ballot in black defendant-white victim cases, two of every three white jurors believed that the punishment should be death, while two of every three black jurors believed that the punishment should be life imprisonment. On the final vote, the jury was three times more likely to

---

60. Sundby, op. cit., p. 154.

61. Theodore Eisenberg, Stephen P. Garvey, and Martin T. Wells (2001) "Forecasting Life and Death: Juror Race, Religion, and Attitude Toward the Death Penalty," *Journal of Legal Studies* 30:277-311.

62. Sundby, op. cit., pp. 133-134.

63. Eisenberg et al., op. cit., pp. 303-304 and 277.

64. Bowers et al., 2001, op. cit.

impose a death sentence if there were five or more white males on the jury than if there were four or fewer white males on the jury. However, if there was at least one black male on the jury, the jury was twice as likely to impose a life sentence, compared to juries that had no black members. Additional black male jurors only slightly reduced the chances of a death sentence. The study revealed that white and black jurors in black defendant-white victim cases saw the same defendants, the same evidence, and the same arguments in the same cases very differently. As one juror commented, "What most distressed me was the assumption, so unexamined as to be chilling, on the part of the white jurors, that they belonged to a world, if not to a species, wholly distinct from the blacks of Trenton's underclass whom they were empowered to judge."[65]

In the study, white jurors were more likely than black jurors to see black defendants as likely to pose a future danger to society and to return to the streets if not sentenced to death. Black jurors, on the other hand, were more likely than white jurors to see black defendants as remorseful and deserving of mercy. Black jurors were also more likely to wonder whether the black defendant was the actual killer or whether the murder met the criteria to warrant the death penalty in the first place. On each of these issues, men of each race took a more extreme position than women; still, black females were closer in position to black males, and white females were closer in position to white males. These findings were independent of socioeconomic status. One reason why the presence of at least one black male juror significantly increases the likelihood a life sentence in black defendant-white victim cases is that the black juror is sometimes able to help white jurors better understand and appreciate the defendant's life history and how it mitigates the crime.[66]

Reaching Unanimity

Research confirms that the way a jury ultimately reaches unanimity on the sentence involves a complex social-psychological process. Classic psychological research shows that people have a desire to conform and fear being wrong.[67] People tend to trust a confident majority, even when it is wrong, because they do not trust their own judgment. However, if just one other person joins a person in his or her judgment, the power of the majority to alter a person's correct position is significantly reduced. If that one other person defects to the majority's incorrect position, the other person's ability to resist the majority declines dramatically. This dynamic is especially likely to occur when people must announce their positions publicly, and there are only two options from which to choose, as occurs in death penalty cases.

The study of South Carolina jurors found that the more serious the crime, the less willing a juror was to switch his or her initial vote from death to life; conversely, the less serious the crime, the more willing a juror was to switch from death to life.[68] The more strongly a juror supported the death penalty, the less likely he or she would abandon his or her first vote, while the less strongly a juror supported the death penalty, the more likely he or she would abandon his or her initial vote.[69] Ironically, most people, when

---

65. Ibid., pp. 1341-1342.
66. Sundby, op. cit., p. 151.
67. Sundby, op. cit., pp. 81-84, citing the research of Solomon Asch and others.
68. Eisenberg et al., op. cit., p. 304.
69. Ibid., pp. 303-304.

asked whether they could resist the majority's influence and give the correct response, respond *yes*. Yet, research shows that is not true in many cases.

The ability to resist a majority's position that is believed to be wrong is further complicated by mental and physical fatigue, stress, depression, insomnia, nightmares, a sense of isolation, and other maladies as jury deliberations are drawn out.[70] For instance, during the penalty phase, a female juror found the isolation from her support network troubling:

> The penalty phase was very hard, emotionally difficult. I think part of the reason it was so difficult is you couldn't talk to anybody you know, you couldn't talk to your husband, wife, anybody about the case and it was very hard ... it was just hard because you thought about it for 24 hours and you know because ... it went for so many months ... once a decision was made I was okay. It was just during the process that was very hard.[71]

Other jurors, in an attempt to get holdouts to change positions, may try to make them feel guilty by demanding that they switch focus from the defendant to the victim and the victim's family.[72] Some holdout jurors are subject to personal attacks, both physical and mental. Black jurors have complained of being ostracized, deceived, and intimidated by white jurors.[73] When a holdout juror succumbs to the pressure and changes position to conform to the majority, the juror sometimes describes the process as being "brainwashed."

Life holdouts typically differ from death holdouts on their reasons for changing positions. To change positions, life holdouts generally have to be convinced by the majority that a death sentence is the only appropriate sentence and to holdout for life violates the law and his or her oath as a juror. If they view their position as a product of an honest understandable difference of opinion, life holdouts will rarely change position.[74] Death holdouts, on the other hand, are likely to change their positions to avoid a hung jury. They do not want to make the taxpayer finance another trial and do want to guarantee that the defendant will at least spend the rest of his life in prison. They rarely concede that a life sentence is a just outcome and often view their fellow jurors as "gutless" or "wimps."[75]

Some jurors express regret and guilt that the wrong sentence was imposed. A juror who believed a death sentence was warranted, even though a life sentence was imposed, lamented, "I don't know that I have ever in my life felt something so strongly and not been able to follow through on it. That the death penalty was called for and that's what we should've given and we didn't."[76] A second juror felt much the same: "[The] horror of the crime stays with me. I feel a just punishment wasn't given."[77] Jurors who believed that a life sentence should have been imposed instead of a death sentence expressed regret and, oftentimes, guilt, including guilt about being persuaded by other jurors to change their votes. A female juror commented, "[I]t's a very heavy burden to decide the death penalty. I have doubts about whether that was the right or best solution. The best

---

70. Sundby, op. cit., pp. 87 and 168-169.
71. Antonio, op. cit., p. 284.
72. Ibid., p. 88.
73. Bowers et al., 2001, op. cit., p. 261.
74. Sundby, op. cit., p. 156.
75. Ibid., pp. 156-157.
76. Ibid.
77. Ibid.

answer, the best punishment."[78] Another juror explained, "[P]art of the group recommended an execution that I don't believe was appropriate. I questioned whether I stand up for what I believe. I feel almost like I was brainwashed (by the others). I believed their projection of me that I was not a valuable juror."[79] Finally, a third juror had this to say: "I was right, but didn't stick with my decision. I changed my vote when I didn't believe in what I was doing."[80]

Sometimes jurors vote a certain way for idiosyncratic reasons. For example, a female juror questioned whether the death penalty might be in the defendant's best interests, saying:

> For me as a former probation officer for six years, I had seen several youth authorities. I had been to the state prison. I knew about what happens to sort of pretty, young boys and how they are used and abused. I really feared that was what was going to happen to David. So I really wasn't sure whether we would not be doing him a favor to give him the death penalty.[81]

Sometimes jurors vote a certain way for the wrong reason. According to one disgusted juror:

> Yeah, the one thing I think that really bothered me the most [was] when it got right down to the nitty gritty of the whole thing. When the judge was going to sequester everybody ... all of a sudden all of those who were holding out changed their minds because they didn't want to be sequestered. And that has bugged me since the time it ... happened.... I told my husband about it ... I said, "[M]y God ... can you just imagine if it was you or I on trial like that and because they were going to hold the jury over, they decided to change their mind and you['re] guilty?" That's scary. That's what scared the pants off of me right there.[82]

Making Mistakes

If a juror later realizes that he or she voted wrongly for death instead of life, there is little he or she can do to correct the mistake except petition the governor for clemency, an option that seldom succeeds.[83] Courts have an aversion to second guessing jury decisions and allowing jurors to cast doubt on a verdict that has been rendered. Short of some external influence, such as an attempt to bribe a juror, courts do not allow participants in a legal proceeding to challenge a verdict.[84] As the preceding discussion reveals, structural and social-psychological factors create corrupting biases in the way the death penalty is administered. These biases affect all capital defendants to varying degrees, but they adversely affect black capital defendants even more, particularly when their victims are white.

Given what is known about capital jurors, it should not be surprising that they sometimes get it wrong. That is, they wrongly convict capital defendants who are actually

---

78. Ibid.
79. Ibid.
80. Ibid.
81. Fleury-Steiner, op. cit., pp. 76-77.
82. Bienen, op. cit., p. 1341.
83. Ibid., p. 102.
84. Ibid., pp. 100-101.

innocent. Since 1973, 140 people in 26 states have been released from death row because of evidence of their innocence (as of March 6, 2012): 71 of them were black, 55 were white, 12 were Latino, and 2 were of another race.[85] The 140 people represent about one death row inmate released for every nine that have been executed. However, the 140 exonerated death row inmates are only those whose innocence has been discovered; no one knows how many innocent people remain on death rows.

Death penalty proponents argue that these data demonstrate that super due process works because it has dramatically reduced, if not eliminated altogether, wrongful executions. None of the 140 people released from death row was executed. While that may be true, many of them spent years on death row despite their innocence and probably would have been executed if not for sheer luck. Death penalty proponents maintain that, among the more than 7,500 defendants sentenced to death under modern death penalty statutes, there is no incontrovertible evidence that a single innocent person has been executed. The key word here, of course, is *incontrovertible*. Although there may not be definitive proof that an innocent person has been executed under modern death penalty statutes, there is substantial evidence that at least two-dozen people have been executed in error since 1976 and the implementation of super due process.[86] In addition to all the structural and social-psychological factors described above, another explanation of how these miscarriages of justice occur is simpler: human beings make mistakes. Even conscientious jurors are fallible.

The Toll on Jurors

Thanks to The Capital Jury Project, information about the effects of jury service on jurors is available.[87] Because they were actual jurors in capital cases, they were all death qualified, so none of them was opposed to the death penalty under all circumstances. About sixty percent of the jurors found the experience of jury service emotionally upsetting; the other forty percent did not. In a study using only 67 of the capital jurors who provided detailed information, about one-quarter of them reported that they enjoyed serving, describing their experience as "exciting," "a learning experience," "educational," and "very rewarding."[88] For many of them, it helped clarify their feelings about the death penalty. As one male juror explained, "I felt like I was part of it, it wasn't like watching TV or reading about it, I was actually involved in it ... I finally had to admit how I felt about it and was surprised that I could impose it with no guilt. It was personally enlightening for me and helped me to resolve some of the philosophical questions I had had about the death penalty."[89]

Other jurors who found the experience to be a positive one enjoyed the collegiality and solidarity they established with their fellow jurors.[90] As one juror recalled, "It was

---

85. Death Penalty Information Center, "Innocence" at www.deathpenaltyinfo.org/innocence-and-death-penalty (accessed March 6, 2012).

86. See Robert M. Bohm (2012) *Deathquest: An Introduction to the Theory & Practice of Capital Punishment in the United States*, 4th Ed. Waltham, MA: Anderson, Chapter 7.

87. Thanks to William J. Bowers for generously providing me with some of the data from The Capital Jury Project.

88. Michael E. Antonio (2006) "Jurors' Emotional Reactions To Serving On A Capital Trial," *Judicature* 89:282-288.

89. Ibid., p. 284.

90. Bienen, op. cit., p. 1342.

a really good group of people.... [W]hen it was over, we all walked out to the parking lot together and we stood there in a circle for quite a while just talking.... [T]he foreman of the jury said 'just remember: eleven other people decided this with you.' "[91] Another juror commented, "We lived together so intimately and in such an emotional atmosphere for 4 1/2 weeks ... Then it's over in a flurry of video cameras and press coverage. Suddenly you're separated from the only people who understand what [you've] been through."[92]

Such jurors were the exception, however. Nearly three-quarters of the jurors in the aforementioned smaller study, and more than 60 percent of all jurors, as noted, found the experience troubling, "emotionally upsetting" or "emotionally draining." The most stressful part for most of the jurors was making the life-or-death decision. Many of the jurors cried during deliberations. One male juror articulated how difficult the decision was:

> While I felt I had a duty to do it, under any circumstances whatsoever when you're responsible for the taking of the life of another individual it's a very serious thing and that's emotionally upsetting, it's hard to do, you wrestle with it a lot. As to whether or not that's really the thing you ought to do. Because once you've taken that individual's life, there's absolutely no chance for any change whatsoever. That person's eternal fate is sealed at that time and you wrestle with that—that's an emotional thing—and you think—am I really doing the right thing? It's a hard decision to make, but it's a decision somebody's got to ... the most serious issues in my opinion are life and death decisions and they're hard.[93]

Another male juror agonized over the decision: "I had emotional indigestion for a while. I kept recycling this thing in my mind over and over. I wondered what I could have done to [have] kept this from happening. What could society have done to prevent this? I couldn't do anything. I finally had to accept our decision."[94]

One juror found the task more difficult than he originally thought:

> I remember going into that [penalty] phase of the trial praying an awful lot for guidance, [to] tell me what to do, because I remember not feeling sure if I could do it. I remember in jury selection they asked my opinions on the death penalty, and I said, if you asked me that any other time, I would have told you how adamantly and strongly I believe in it, but sitting across the room [and] looking somebody straight in the face and knowing that it's gonna be my decision, you know, it's not quite so easy.... [95]

The realization of what he had just been a part did not hit a male juror until his drive home from the courthouse. He recalled:

> I mean they release you ... we went through the circus and everything ... you go down to the garage to the car, you jump in your car and drive home ... and I was on (the) freeway ... and it just hit me ... what the importance of what we had just done. I was kinda like in a fog 'cause I don't remember much driving from the garage at (the) Courthouse ... but just these realizations. I just suddenly

91. Ibid.
92. Ibid., p. 1342, n. 31.
93. Antonio, op. cit., p. 284.
94. Ibid., p. 285.
95. Bienen, op. cit., p. 1340, n. 25.

realized the importance of what had happened. My vote with 11 other people … that some man is going to die. It didn't really hit that much until then.[96]

Another juror had second thoughts:

> [W]e were split on the decision of punishment. There were a few of us [who] wanted the death sentence, and there were those who wouldn't go along with the death sentence … because they didn't feel it was their right to take someone's life … which I, … in a way go along with … thought, here I am sitting here saying that this kid should have his life snuffed out. [I]t starts weighing on your mind.[97]

Two female jurors, who served on juries that returned life sentences, expressed concern about how the jury's decision would affect the victim's family members. One confided, "I lost it after the trial, I started crying. It was emotionally exhausting. I felt like I let the (victim's family) down."[98] The other female juror expressed a similar sentiment: "[I] really broke down afterwards. I felt bad for the family. I didn't know it'd be so hard."[99]

Other jurors were afraid that the defendant or victim's family members would retaliate against them. As one juror noted:

> After the trial was over, there was a lot of fear in the jury about the family — like they would be out there waiting when we got out if we sentenced him to death. So we asked the sheriff's department to bring the security people in when we gave down the sentence and keep the people in the courtroom until we were all out of the building. You never know. You don't know the family.[100]

Another juror was concerned about feeling uncomfortable if she encountered the defendant's family members or friends:

> I was — I was looking over my shoulder because you know a lot of the family/friends, and, as a matter of fact, that very next day (I saw them in) the Costco's … oh, God (Interviewer: Do you think they recognized you right away?) Well, I was like worried. I hope they don't recognize me 'cuz what would you say? What would you do? How would you respond? You think of those things. Yeah — a little paranoia.[101]

About the victim's family, a juror stated, "I had dreams her parents were chasing me in Safeway for not convicting him of the death sentence … I would always imagine I would run into them at the store. I never did. (Interviewer: Were they angry at you? So they were chasing you, is that it?) Yeah, her parents were angry at me…."[102]

Religion sometimes plays a role during deliberations: "[W]e had jury members that were crying…. I remember before we even started on that day holding hands around the room and praying and asking God to give us wisdom on what to do."[103] A female juror described her secret meeting with a "life holdout" while they were sequestered for the night in a hotel:

---

96. Ibid.
97. Bienen, op. cit., pp. 1344-1345.
98. Antonio, op. cit., p. 285.
99. Ibid.
100. Ibid.
101. Ibid.
102. Ibid.
103. Bienen, op. cit., p. 1345.

[The resister] was really upset. She came down to my room one night.... We were trying to seek answers and to do the right thing. We got together and studied and read from the Bible to get some kind of help there. We went to the Scriptures, and we had a meeting of the minds there. I told her after we had another ballot that I had changed mine from life to death. She said, "I am so confused right now, I don't know what to do." I told her that it helped me a lot to pray about this every night and to just ask God for guidance. I said, "Ask God, because I know that it's bigger than that. God will forgive us if he knows what we did was out of good intentions."[104]

Jurors can relieve themselves of the psychological burden and responsibility of their decisions by praying and seeking divine intervention. They can rationalize that God is making the decision to sentence the defendant to death.[105]

Some jurors got physically ill. For one female juror, the burden of serving was too much. She recalled, "I couldn't sleep and I got physically sick, you know vomiting. (Interviewer: How long did that last after? I mean days, months, weeks?) Days, but I still, I mean it's better now, but for a while, a few years it really did disturb me just thinking about [it] and anytime I'd hear his name or even see the building where the restaurant was located [the crime scene]...."[106] Another female juror reacted in a similar way: "[I] took it to heart and I really wanted to do the right thing. I put too much into it and got sick. I never want to be on another one [jury]—too much stress. I take it all too serious and when it's over, I let it all out. I tried so hard to be fair and do the right thing."[107]

Most of the jurors, especially those who served on juries that returned death sentences, experienced lingering mental and emotional effects days, weeks, months, and years after the trial ended. Some jurors called it "postjury blues." Several jurors described changes in their relationships and lifestyles and the inability to forget what they had heard or seen during the trial.

A few female jurors reported threats to their marriages. Said one: "I had a very difficult time, my husband, we almost separated over it." Asked how her spouse felt when she was called to jury duty, she replied, "He wanted me to get out of it. I was so depressed. I felt out of control. I would thrash in my sleep. I had to move out of my bedroom. I was so helpless. I finally just lost it and I stopped talking."[108]

Another female juror found the lingering effects of the trial emotionally draining, recalling:

For a long time I would think about both of them [presumably the victims], they would be the last thing I thought about before I went to sleep and the first thing I thought of when I got up. I don't know if it's like that on other trials, but for capital murders it's very profound. You do get very involved with them and their families. It's like a forced intimacy. Just because [the] trial is over they don't disappear out of your head right away.[109]

Thirty-six percent of all jurors also had trouble sleeping. Some of them had nightmares about acts of reprisal by the defendant. This was especially true of female jurors in capital cases that ended with the defendant receiving a life sentence. Nightmares about crime scene

---

104. Fleury-Steiner, op. cit., p. 113.
105. Lifton and Mitchell, op. cit., p. 143.
106. Fleury-Steiner, op. cit., p. 286
107. Ibid.
108. Ibid., p. 286.
109. Ibid.

photographs or photographs that showed the victim's body also were prevalent. For example, one female juror recounted how the jury was shown the murder weapon during the trial—a small rock covered with the victim's blood—and how she could not get the image out of her head: "[J]ust driving down the road last summer, we went on vacation afterwards up in New England, and I'd see a rock in a field and I would burst into tears … it has been kind of a nightmare thing."[110] Similarly, a male juror was disturbed by the gruesome photographs of victims' bodies he viewed during the trial: "Yes, during the trial I would wake up and well, I would have dreams of the pictures and all that you would see and I would wake up in the middle of the night seeing that."[111] According to one juror, "Um, I kept seeing reoccurrences of the crime [while I was sleeping] … and during the day too. I would think back to the trial. I probably did that for a few months afterwards."[112] Another juror stated, "[I] had trouble sleeping a couple days … afterwards, not during. Just wanted to forget, but it's hard to do. Next day trying to forget about (it)—you go to work and someone says, 'you fried the S-O-B.' Want to get it out of your mind, but it's kind of hard to do that."[113]

Several jurors had difficulties at work:

> After the trial, uh, the first day that I went back to work, somebody came up and said, "Hi, how ya' doing?" and I just cut loose crying and I cried for an hour solid, and my boss was in the office that day, just on a routine visit, and that poor man didn't know what to do! [He] kept saying, "She's gotta get some help!" He thought I was having a nervous breakdown, but I mean, it was just, it had to come out somewhere, I guess … I thought about it all the time, ya know.[114]

At work, another juror felt that he had to keep defending his sentencing decision.[115] Still, another juror recounted, "I was a little upset or worried about a co-worker who was black that I liked. I thought he might think I was a racist."[116]

Jurors' experiences affected their views of serving on another capital jury in the future. About one quarter of all jurors either would refuse to serve in another capital trial (10.6 percent) or would try to get out of it (15.7 percent). Another 40 percent would serve reluctantly. Only about one third of the jurors would welcome the opportunity to serve again. Remarks included: "I told the judge, 'if you get another case like this, don't call me.'" "Never want to be on another one—too much stress…." "I don't want to do it again. It was a very gory murder…." And "It was an experience I will never forget and I'll never do again. They even call me again, I'll check into a mental ward first."[117]

Some of the jurors thought that the court should provide counseling to jurors at the end of the trial. A few jurors admitted to having received counseling from a minister, a spouse, or a psychiatrist. One juror discussed what he perceived as the court's lack of concern for jurors, saying:

> I also think it sucks that they do not offer counseling to the jury for all this bullshit, you know. But if it was offered, I definitely would of taken them up on it. In fact this (the juror interview) has been therapeutic to go through and work through some of this. This really gives me better closure to it. That's another

---

110. Ibid., p. 285.
111. Ibid., p. 284.
112. Ibid.
113. Ibid.
114. Ibid., p. 286.
115. Ibid.
116. Ibid.
117. Ibid., p. 287.

thing the system is lacking in. It's like okay, thank you, goodbye. You know. I've just given you 4 months of my life and now you're just kicking me out.[118]

Counseling or debriefing of jurors by trained mental health professionals has been ordered by judges following criminal trials in a few exceptionally disturbing or stressful cases, but it is not common.[119] Perhaps it should be provided more frequently or even routinely following capital trials. Capital jurors deserve more than a simple thank you for their service.

Death Penalty Opinion

The last issue addressed here is whether the experience of serving on a capital jury had any influence on a juror's opinion about the death penalty. Remember that all of the jurors questioned in The Capital Jury Project were death qualified. Nearly 80 percent of the jurors reported that their personal feelings about the death penalty had not changed. About 9 percent of the jurors admitted being more opposed to the death penalty, and approximately 12 percent stated that they were more in favor of the death penalty as a result of their jury service. Thus, although many jurors find their jury service in capital cases emotionally taxing and stressful, and few would welcome the opportunity to serve again, most did not change their opinions about the death penalty as a result of their experience.

Conclusion

Most capital trial jurors find their jury experience emotionally upsetting, mentally and physically exhausting, or worse. Especially stressful for them is making the life-or-death decision. These problems do not stop with the end of the trial, either: many jurors experience postjury blues. Based on their capital jury experience, many jurors would either not serve again, try to get out of serving, or serve reluctantly.

Research shows that many jurors are not up to the task. They are biased, make premature decisions, and are easily manipulated. They too often make mistakes. Given what is known about capital trial jurors, the wisdom of allowing ordinary citizens to determine whether other human beings—even those who have committed heinous crimes—should live or die is questionable.

Although the work of jurors may be over once their decision is read, the capital punishment process is far from finished when the judge strikes his or her gavel. The appeals process extends the case, often for months or years. Postconviction counsel then enter the fray, and it is these participants and the appeals process that we turn next.

---

118. Ibid., p. 288.
119. Bienen, op. cit.

Chapter 8

Postconviction Counsel

The gavel is struck; court is adjourned. But the capital case is far from over. With a conviction and death sentence, the appeals process begins, as does the work of postconviction counsel. The role of postconviction counsel is to represent death row inmates by reviewing the work of prosecutors, defense attorneys, trial judges, and jurors to ensure that the trials and the death sentences were fair. A win for postconviction counsel is any sentence other than the death penalty.

The Postconviction Process and Legal Representation

The U.S. Supreme Court has held that capital defendants have a constitutional right to counsel at trial and, if a state provides it, at the automatic appellate review or direct appeal.[1] If a defendant is indigent, as most capital defendants are, then the state is obligated to provide "the effective assistance of counsel" at both stages.[2] Beyond the direct appeal, however, the Court has ruled that the Constitution does not provide a right to counsel at any of the discretionary appellate stages.[3] That means that neither death penalty states nor the federal government are obligated to provide counsel to indigent death row inmates at either state or federal capital postconviction (*collateral*) proceedings. Its reason, as explained by former Supreme Court Chief Justice William Rehnquist, is that counsel is unnecessary to meaningfully access the discretionary review process.[4] By the time a case reaches the discretionary appeal stages, notes Justice Rehnquist, a sufficient record has been established to inform an appellate court whether to grant or deny review.[5] That record is comprised of a transcript or other record of the trial proceedings, briefs from the direct appeal setting forth claims of error, frequently an opinion by the state supreme court disposing of the case on direct appeal, and, perhaps, submissions from the death row inmate himself. According to Justice Rehnquist, no formal presentation by counsel

---

1. Defendants have a Sixth Amendment right to counsel at trial (*Gideon v. Wainwright*, 372 U.S. 335, 1963) and a Fourteenth Amendment right to counsel at an automatic appellate review (*Douglas v. California*, 372 U.S. 353, 1963).
2. *Evitts v. Lucey*, 469 U.S. 387 (1985); *Cuyler v. Sullivan*, 446 U.S. 335 (1980); *McMann v. Richardson*, 397 U.S. 759 (1970).
3. *Coleman v. Thompson*, 501 U.S. 722 (1991); *Murray v. Giarratano*, 492 U.S. 1 (1989); *Pennsylvania v. Finley*, 481 U.S. 551 (1987); *Ross v. Moffitt* 417 U.S. 600 (1974).
4. *Ross v. Moffitt*, ibid., p. 615.
5. See ibid.

is needed, although he concedes that "a skilled lawyer, particularly one trained in the somewhat arcane art of preparing petitions for discretionary review," might be helpful. He concludes by emphasizing that states should not be discouraged by the Court's position from passing legislation making counsel available to convicted defendants at all stages of judicial review.[6]

The Importance of Postconviction Counsel

Justice Rehnquist's reasoning arguably underestimates the importance of postconviction counsel, particularly in capital cases. Competent postconviction counsel can assist an appellant in at least three important ways. First, counsel can help an appellant investigate, discover, present, and preserve all relevant claims of constitutional error, including those errors that could not have been raised on direct appeal.[7] Second, counsel can assist an appellant raise postconviction claims that, with a few narrow exceptions, must be raised and considered on their merits during state postconviction proceedings to be eligible to be heard during any subsequent federal *habeas* proceeding.[8] Third, counsel can assist an appellant raise claims properly at the federal level so that the appellant does not lose the opportunity for federal *habeas corpus* review.[9]

State and federal appellate courts generally will not consider claims that are not filed in a timely manner, and, frequently, death row inmates are not aware of the time limits. Competent counsel can make sure that claims are filed on time. Losing the right to file a claim because a time limit has expired can be disastrous for a death row inmate. A study of the fully reviewed state death sentences imposed between 1973 and 1995 found that two–thirds of them were reversed at one of the appeal stages because of serious or prejudicial errors.[10] The study found that in 82 percent of the reversals by state postconviction courts, the defendant deserved a sentence other than death when the errors were cured on retrial, and in seven percent of the reversals, the defendant was found to be innocent of the capital crime. In addition, 40 percent of the 599 first federal *habeas* petitions filed between 1973 and 1995 were granted. The number of reversals in death penalty appeals has been decreasing dramatically in recent years, not because of greater fairness in the system or fewer constitutional errors but because death row inmates are simply less likely to prevail. Nearly all constitutional errors today are subject to harm analysis and "proving that an error was harmful is difficult or impossible."[11]

The irony is that "it is easier in our system to convict someone who did not commit a crime than to have that conviction set aside once we have evidence of the person's

---

6. Ibid., p. 618.

7. Celestine Richards McConville (2003) "The Right to Effective Assistance of Capital Postconviction Counsel: Constitutional Implications of Statutory Grants of Capital Counsel," *Wisconsin Law Review* 31:31-113.

8. Ibid., p. 33.

9. Ibid.

10. James S. Liebman, Jeffrey Fagan, and Valerie West (2000) "A Broken System: Error Rates in Capital Cases, 1973–1995." The Justice Project, www.justice.policy.net/jpreport.html.

11. David R. Dow (2005) *Executed on a Technicality: Lethal Injustice on America's Death Row.* Boston: Beacon Press, pp. xxii-xxiii and 44.

innocence."[12] Without competent postconviction counsel, in short, the chances of an unjustly convicted or innocent death row inmate being executed increase greatly.

Recognizing the problem, Congress enacted legislation to provide indigents with competent postconviction counsel at the federal level and to encourage death penalty states to provide it at the state level. In the Anti-Drug Abuse Act of 1988, Congress created a mandatory statutory right to counsel for indigent death row inmates seeking federal *habeas corpus* review.[13] Before 1988, indigent death row inmates pursuing federal *habeas corpus* relief only had a discretionary right to counsel based on a federal magistrate or federal courts' conclusion that the interests of justice required the appointment of counsel.[14] To encourage lawyers to take postconviction cases and to enhance their competency, the 1988 legislation created (1) maximum hourly rates for in-court and out-of-court time that could be increased periodically by the Judicial Conference (as of January 1, 2010, the maximum rate was $178 per hour for federal postconviction work in capital cases)[15]; (2) reimbursement caps, which could be exceeded with court approval, for "investigative, expert, or other services" as long as they are "reasonably necessary"; and (3) competency requirements, specifying that at least one of a federal *habeas* defendant's appointed attorneys "must have been admitted to practice in the court of appeals for not less than five years, and must have had not less than three years experience in the handling of appeals in that court in felony cases."[16] A problem with the competency requirements, however, is they do not require any special competence in capital litigation.[17] Furthermore, a court does not have to follow the competency requirements, as long as the appointed attorney's "background, knowledge, or experience would otherwise enable him or her to properly represent the defendant, with due consideration to the seriousness of the possible penalty and to the unique and complex nature of the litigation."[18]

In the Antiterrorism and Effective Death Penalty Act of 1996, the Court granted streamlined federal *habeas corpus* proceedings to states that mandated and properly compensated competent state postconviction counsel.[19] One of the primary incentives received by the "opt-in" states is a shortened statute of limitations. Instead of the usual one year to file their federal *habeas* petitions, death row inmates under the new rules have just six months.[20] In addition, the new rules change the start of the limitations period from completion of the Supreme Court's *certiorari* review, if it is sought, to the affirmation by the state supreme court of the conviction and sentence on direct review.[21] These rule changes could disadvantage death row inmates in at least three ways. First, death row inmates could lose as many as 90 days of their six-month window just preparing a direct appeal *certiorari* petition.[22] Second, they could lose more time, and perhaps all of it, preparing the state postconviction relief application and preparing and pursuing the post-

---

12. Ibid., p. 133.
13. McConville, op. cit., pp. 34-35.
14. p. 46.
15. United States Courts at www.uscourts.gov/FederalCourts/AppointmentOfCounsel.aspx (accessed March 8, 2012).
16. McConville, op. cit., pp. 47-48.
17. Ibid., p. 48, n. 98.
18. Ibid. p. 48.
19. Ibid., p. 35.
20. Ibid., p. 57.
21. Ibid.
22. Ibid., pp. 57-58.

conviction decision *certiorari* review.[23] Third, because the legislation does not specify "when the entry of [the] order [appointing state conviction counsel] must occur or which court must enter it," the death row inmate's window could slam shut before he could obtain postconviction counsel.[24] Moreover, unlike the Anti-Drug Abuse Act of 1988, Congress failed to provide any guidance to states as to the amount of compensation post-conviction counsel should receive or to the content of competency requirements, leaving both decisions to the states' discretion.[25] It did, however, prohibit death row inmates from challenging in federal *habeas corpus* proceedings the competence of state or federal post-conviction counsel.[26]

In addition to the two pieces of federal legislation, some states on their own initiative also have provided postconviction counsel for their death row inmates. According to a recent survey, 30 of the then-36 death penalty states and the federal government provided a mandatory right to postconviction counsel, four states (Alabama, Delaware, Kentucky, and Nebraska) provided a discretionary right to counsel, and two states (Georgia and New Hampshire) provided no right to postconviction counsel.[27] Twenty-six death penalty states had competency standards or a basic competency requirement; however, only 14 death penalty states required both experience and training or knowledge of death penalty or *habeas* jurisprudence.[28] Only one state, Florida, required the monitoring of postconviction counsel's performance.[29] Thus, all indigent death row inmates pursuing federal *habeas corpus* review and many indigent death row inmates pursuing state postconviction review receive the assistance of statutorily granted counsel.[30]

Unfortunately for death row inmates, the provision of a statutory right to counsel does not entitle them to the constitutional right to the "effective assistance of counsel."[31] That means indigent appellants who receive postconviction counsel have no legal recourse when their postconviction lawyers make egregious errors.

Counsel Options for Indigent Death Row Inmates Pursuing Federal Habeas Corpus *Review*

The federal courts originally had three options in meeting the statutory requirement to provide postconviction counsel for indigent death row inmates pursuing federal *habeas corpus* review.[32] First, they can appoint attorneys from the private bar. Those attorneys submit vouchers for payment to the Administrative Office of the United States Courts, which allocate funds according to provisions in the Criminal Justice Act of 1994.[33] Although the act does not prescribe any limitation on the amount that can be paid for services, in *In re Berger* (1991), the Court limited appointed counsel representing death row inmates before the Supreme Court to $5,000 in fees.[34] A second option is to appoint attorneys

---

23. Ibid., p. 58.
24. Ibid.
25. Ibid., p. 61.
26. Ibid.
27. Ibid., p. 64.
28. Ibid., p. 65.
29. Ibid., p. 66.
30. Ibid., p. 67.
31. *Wainwright v. Torna*, 455 U.S. 586 (1982).
32. See Roscoe C. Howard, Jr. (1996) "The Defunding of the Post Conviction Defense Organizations as a Denial of the Right to Counsel," *West Virginia Law Review* 98:863-921.
33. 18 U.S.C. S 3006A, 1994.
34. 498 U.S. 233.

employed by federal public defender organizations, which are funded through grants made available by the Judicial Conference of the United States.[35] A problem with these first two options is that neither one guarantees the appointment of attorneys with expertise in capital jurisprudence.[36]

The third and best option (for death row inmates) was the appointment of attorneys employed by Postconviction Defender Organizations (PCDOs), which were originally called Death Penalty Resource Centers. Congress created those agencies in 1988.[37] They dealt only with capital cases and related postconviction issues and employed full-time, salaried attorneys, investigators, and support staff.[38] In the mid-1990s, they operated in 20 of the then-38 death penalty states.[39] The Judicial Conference funded PCDOs through grants that were contingent upon the receipt of state funding for any state court work PCDOs did. In fiscal year 1994, the 20 PCDOs received nearly $20 million for their work on capital cases.[40]

Because of the success of PCDO attorneys in getting convictions and death sentences overturned, the agencies came under fire from death penalty proponents, who won the day. On January 6, 1996, President Clinton signed into law HR–1358 (Pub. L. No. 104–91, 110 Stat. 7). The law provided a budget of approximately $262 million for the Federal Judiciary's Defender Services but stipulated that none of the money was to be spent on PCDOs after April 1, 1996—to allow for an orderly end to the program.[41] After the 1996 fiscal year ended on September 30, no further federal funding of the PCDOs was to be provided.[42]

With the demise of PCDOs, the federal courts are left with only the first two options of providing attorneys for capital defendants pursuing federal *habeas corpus* relief. The debate in Congress suggested that the abolition of PCDOs would save the government about $20 million annually,[43] but the Chief Judge of the U.S. Court of Appeals for the Eighth Circuit, Richard Arnold, disagreed. He predicted "that elimination of the PCDOs will significantly increase delays in handling an ever-increasing death penalty caseload by creating an insufficient pool of qualified and experienced attorneys to handle the petitions."[44] It has been estimated that attorneys in capital cases spend an average of 700 to more than 1,000 hours on federal postconviction proceedings.[45] The 1986 American Bar Association survey found that lawyers spent an average of 1,037 hours on federal postconviction litigation.[46]

Counsel Options for Indigent Death Row Inmates Pursuing State Postconviction Proceedings

In June of 1985, Florida was the first state to create a PCDO—the Office of Capital Collateral Representative (CCR). However, from the beginning, the agency was woefully understaffed. According to Mike Mello, one of the original CCR lawyers:

---

35. 18 U.S.C. S 3006A(g)(2)(A), 1994; 28 U.S.C. S 605, 1994.
36. Howard, op. cit.
37. Ibid., p. 904.
38. Ibid.
39. Ibid.
40. Ibid.
41. Ibid., p. 914.
42. Ibid.
43. Ibid., p. 915.
44. Ibid.
45. Robert L. Spangenberg and Elizabeth R. Walsh (1989) "Capital Punishment of Life Imprisonment? Some Cost Considerations," *Loyola of Los Angeles Law Review* 23:45-58.
46. Raymond Paternoster (1991) *Capital Punishment in America*. New York: Lexington, p. 205.

[W]e were being hyped as this grand experiment. In reality, it was a place with four roll-out beds in the office because there was never a chance to leave. I don't know the words to describe just how hard the work really was—in terms of hours or complexity. We worked one hundred hours a week, never less, often more. That spring of 1986, I literally lived in the office. Our personal lives disintegrated into nonexistence. You might think about going to a movie, or hanging out for an evening with friends ... but then you'd compare that to rereading a trial transcript that might turn up another issue to save a life. And you'd stay at work. I thought it was never going to end. I thought I would end first.[47]

Despite Mello's complaints, former Florida Supreme Court Chief Justice Gerald Kogan was impressed with the work of the CCR lawyers:

We are fortunate in the State of Florida, although there are those who will not agree with me on this issue, that we do have a very competent group of attorneys. We call them the Capital Collateral Representative Office, who represents condemned prisoners after they have been sentenced to death and after they've been incarcerated and after the public defender or the private counsel who has represented them has long since been disassociated with the case. And they do a magnificent job to raise all of the possible issues that can be raised before us. So, at least, the condemned, for the most part, have had, hopefully, the best legal representation that is possible.[48]

Probably because of its success, the CCR was dissolved by the Florida legislature in 1997, and replaced with three (now two) Capital Collateral Regional Counsels (CCRCs) whose primary responsibility is representing Florida indigent death row inmates in post-conviction proceedings. In 1998, the Florida legislature created a registry of qualified attorneys to handle the overflow of cases from the CCRCs. Currently, there are two registries. The first registry includes the names of 140 private attorneys who are eligible to be appointed by circuit court judges presiding over a case to represent Florida indigent death row inmates in the state collateral appeals process.[49] The second registry includes the names of 88 private attorneys who are eligible to be appointed by U.S. District Court judges presiding over a case to represent Florida indigent death row inmates in the federal collateral appeals process.[50] Some of the attorneys are on both lists. At present, Florida has nearly 400 death row inmates.[51]

The Role of a Postconviction Attorney

A Florida postconviction attorney (PCA) summarized his role in a capital case as making sure that the trial and the sentence are fair. He added: "Make sure there is sufficient

---

47. Ibid., p. 271.

48. "Speech Given by Former Florida Chief Justice Gerald Kogan," The Death Penalty Information Center at www.deathpenaltyinfo.org/speech-given-former-florida-chief-justice-gerald-kogan (accessed July 8, 2009).

49. Commission on Capital Cases, "Registry Attorney" at www.floridacapitalcases.state.fl.us/c-registry-attorney.cfm (accessed August 30, 2009).

50. Commission on Capital Cases, "Federal Registry" at www.floridacapitalcases.state.fl.us/c-federal-registry.cfm (accessed August 30, 2009).

51. Florida Department of Corrections, "Death Row Roster" at www.dc.state.fl.us/activeinmates/deathrowroster.asp (accessed March 8, 2012).

evidence of guilt and that the defendant received due process and a fair trial. [Make sure] the state wasn't allowed to introduce improper or unreliable evidence. For the penalty phase, along the same line, make sure death is justified in this particular case and that the defendant had a whole opportunity to be heard, for example." Role breadth depends on assignment and trial experience is critical, as another Florida PCA stressed:

> Depending on the purpose for which I am appointed, my role can be limited, for example, dealing only with a mental retardation issue. If the appointment is for the initial direct appeal to the Florida Supreme Court, the role is significantly larger. Virtually every detail of the case must be examined. It is important to have trial experience in a capital case. Oftentimes, lawyers are appointed to represent a capital defendant on appeal that have never tried a capital case. The penalty phase of a capital trial is unlike anything in the criminal justice system. Often, the state will be presenting penalty phase evidence during the guilt portion of the trial.

Ironically, another PCA mentioned that trial attorneys in capital cases "almost never" handle appeals. He stated, "We kind of specialize. I don't do trial work. I only do appeals. Most trial attorneys don't want to do appeals."

According to one of the Florida PCAs, the major difference between the appeal of a client charged with a capital crime and a client charged with a noncapital felony is "in the appeal of the penalty and sentencing phase issues. The guilt phase portion of the appeal is similar to a noncapital appeal." Another PCA commented, "I guess [the capital appeal is] more stressful.... It's more time-consuming, a more serious case. You want to dot every *i* and cross every *t*."

As for the differences between the various levels of appeal and postconviction review, one PCA observed, "The direct appeal involves a comprehensive review of essentially all legal issues from the guilt and penalty phase of the trial. Postconviction appeals to the [Florida] state supreme court are more defined and narrow and focus only on the failure of trial counsel to appropriately represent the defendant at trial." Another PCA provided more detail:

> The direct appeal goes directly to the Florida Supreme Court in a death penalty case. [Unlike appeals in non-death penalty cases that first go to the intermediate court of appeals.] [If the trial court decision is affirmed by the state supreme court] it's pretty much common practice to file a petition for a *writ of certiorari* in the U.S. Supreme Court. And then once that process is over, conviction is final at that point. Postconviction counsel, they're appointed to review the trial attorney's [performance] for ineffective assistance of counsel, to investigate and make sure they didn't make any mistakes. Part two would be maybe to introduce newly discovered evidence or something of that nature. There's a reinvestigation of the facts. Did any witnesses [recant] when the trial was over? Things like that. If that's denied, then it's the 3.851 motion, that's what it's called. That would be an appeal directly to the Florida Supreme Court. That same collateral attorney would do the proceedings in the federal trial court, which would be a petition for a *writ of habeas corpus....* [O]nce you get in the federal court ... you're kind of looking through the same arguments you've made in the state court, but only through a federal lens, meaning is the state of Florida violating [the] federal constitution? It's a slightly different angle, where something might be allowed by the Florida Supreme Court but the federal court will step in and say that violates federal law.

The PCAs generally felt adequately prepared to represent their first capital clients on appeal. One said, "I have attended numerous seminars put on by the Capital Collateral

Commission and the Public Defenders Association. These seminars always include a block of instruction on postconviction and direct appeal issues. It is interesting to see how slowly the direct appeal issues change over the years." Another PCA pointed out the minimum requirements that an attorney must have before he or she is allowed to handle capital appeals. They include a certain number of hours of continuing education on capital punishment and prior experience with first-degree murder or serious felony appeals. As for how adequately prepared he was to handle his first capital appeal, he stated, "Yes I did [feel prepared]. But it's definitely challenging. The whole new thing there is the penalty phase; it's either going to be life or death. It's a whole new ballpark. I just put more time into it and made myself more ready."

Selection and Compensation

One of the Florida PCAs has served as both a private attorney and a court-appointed attorney, while the other Florida PCA served as a court-appointed attorney with contracts with Florida's Capital Collateral Commission. The selection and appointment of post-conviction counsel in Florida are governed by statute, which provides in part:

> The executive director of the Commission on Capital Cases shall compile and maintain a statewide registry of attorneys in private practice who have certified that they meet the minimum requirements of s. 27.704(2), who are available for appointment by the court under this section to represent persons convicted and sentenced to death in this state in postconviction collateral proceedings, and who have attended within the last year a continuing legal education program of at least 10 hours' duration devoted specifically to the defense of capital cases, if available.... [T]he executive director shall provide to the Chief Justice of the Supreme Court, the chief judge and state attorney in each judicial circuit, and the Attorney General a current copy of its registry of attorneys who are available for appointment as counsel in postconviction capital collateral proceedings.[52]

As one of the PCAs remarked about court appointed postconviction attorneys in Florida: "There's not that many of us." Another Florida PCA noted that he was one of only three attorneys in one of the judicial circuits qualified to handle capital appeals.

Once the state postconviction proceedings are over, the PCA almost always files a writ of *habeas corpus* in federal court. At the same time, the PCA applies to the federal court to be appointed as the appellant's attorney. If qualified, the federal court will make the appointment.

Compensation can be a touchy subject for PCAs because, among other concerns, conscientious PCAs generally turn down other cases that may interfere with their representing a capital client. Florida law currently provides a flat fee of $2,000 for representation on capital appeals in the state appellate courts, which one of the PCAs called "ludicrous." Another PCA stated that he invested, on average, 600 to 700 hours on an initial direct appeal, which amounts to between $2.85 and $3.33 per hour. However, Florida law also provides a way for PCAs to get paid more:

---

52. The 2009 Florida Statutes, Title V, Chapter 27, Section 710 at www.leg.state.fl.us/STATUTES/index.cfm?App_mode=Display_Statute&Search_String=&URL=Ch0027/SEC710.HTM&Title=-%3E2009-%3ECh0027-%3ESection%20710#0027.710 (accessed August 28, 2009).

If the chief judge or designee finds that counsel has proved by competent and substantial evidence that the case required extraordinary and unusual efforts, the chief judge or designee shall order the compensation to be paid to the attorney at a percentage above the flat fee rate, depending on the extent of the unusual and extraordinary effort required. The percentage shall be only the rate necessary to ensure that the fees paid are not confiscatory under common law. The percentage may not exceed 200 percent of the established flat fee [or $4,000], absent a specific finding that 200 percent of the flat fee in the case would be confiscatory. If the chief judge or designee determines that 200 percent of the flat fee would be confiscatory, he or she shall order the amount of compensation using an hourly rate not to exceed ... $100 per hour for a capital case. However, the compensation calculated by using the hourly rate shall be only that amount necessary to ensure that the total fees paid are not confiscatory.[53]

Apparently, Florida chief judges or their designees recognize the "ludicrous" rates the legislature has provided. Both Florida PCAs report being successful in getting paid by the hourly rate, but it has not been easy. As one of the PCAs put it: "The compensation was fair [he had received between $40,000 and $100,000 for his capital appellate work, and the lower amount was for the limited issue of addressing mental retardation], [but] "the agony of dealing with the state to get paid was not fair." The other PCA expressed a similar frustration:

I've been lucky not to have that [being paid only the flat fee] yet. I tell you, though, I've got to be really creative with my arguments to get around that.... [Then] I have to cross my fingers and hope that at the end of the case I'm going to be compensated properly. It's almost like rolling the dice. Because the Florida legislature has dramatically cut court-appointed attorney's fees to an unconstitutional level. Let me just say one other thing: if I was court appointed at a federal court on a misdemeanor charge, it would be $110 an hour [more than the $100 an hour Florida pays for a capital appeal].

The state of Florida also pays a maximum of $1,000 to represent a death row inmate applying for clemency.

One of the Florida PCAs described the bureaucratic process of getting paid: "Because you get paid [by the state], it's a bureaucratic entity of non-lawyers telling you what you can and cannot bill. They are just horrible ... the encounter. The law means nothing to them. They do whatever they want. They don't feel like paying you, they won't pay you." The "they" he is referring to is the Justice Administrative Commission. As he noted, the Commission "is run by non-lawyers [who] sit there and nitpick a lawyer's itemized bill or nitpick anything they can, do anything humanly possible to get out of paying a bill. It's absolutely horrible. Not only are we not paid well, we have to waste so much additional time trying to get paid, it really dilutes it well below our hourly rate."

If getting paid and paid fairly for postconviction work in Florida are so frustrating and agonizing, then why do attorneys accept court appointments? According to one PCA:

When the court-appointed system changed, and the new flat fee cap came out, a lot of attorneys dropped off the court appointed list because they couldn't financially do it. They would ask several times, please stay on. If you are an appellate

---

53. The 2009 Florida Statutes, Title V, Chapter 27, Section 5304 at www.leg.state.fl.us/STATUTES/index.cfm?App_mode=Display_Statute&Search_String=&URL=Ch0027/SEC5304.HTM&Title=-%3E2009-%3ECh0027-%3ESection%205304#0027.5304 (accessed August 28, 2009).

attorney, that's all I do, so I just stayed on. Firstly, I love doing appeals so that's part of it. I don't want to say that somebody has to do it, but when our system changed, it was like that for a while.

Michael Mello, who worked as an attorney with Florida's Capital Collateral Commission during the 1980s and, thus, was not court appointed, reflected on what motivated him to represent condemned prisoners:

> There are few other paying jobs that would permit me to spend all of my working time and energy fighting the system of government-sponsored homicide. I believe this system is an unambiguous disgrace to civilized humanity.... My experience supports [the conclusion] that the death penalty can never be administered in a fair and evenhanded way. A clear sense of the system's basic unfairness is an important motivating factor for my work. A second motivation is the belief that effective advocacy can reveal latent injustices and therefore force the system to work as it should, even in the most apparently hopeless and seemingly clear-cut cases.... [Third,] post-trial investigation almost always discloses important factual information not discovered by trial attorneys, who often work with extremely limited resources.... [Finally,] the cases document that the "modern" death penalty is just as unfair as ever, that the new procedures are merely cosmetic, and that fundamental flaws in the system still exist.[54]

Focus of Appeals

According to one of the Florida PCAs, the primary grounds for the appeals in his cases—ranked from most frequent to least frequent—were the "death sentence was not supported by the aggravators the jury found in the penalty phase and the sentencing judge relied upon in imposing sentence; [the judge's] failure to suppress physical evidence; [the judge's] failure to suppress defendant's statements; [and the prosecutor's] failure to disclose evidence favorable to the defense." He also expressed concern that Florida courts "have completely ignored" recent U.S. Supreme Court decisions dealing with capital punishment:

> I do not understand how the Florida courts can find the Florida sentencing statutes constitutional when Florida law does not require that aggravators be proven beyond a reasonable doubt, allows only a bare majority of jurors to find that an aggravator has been proved by a greater weight of the evidence, and allows the trial judge to instruct the jury that its "verdicts" in the penalty phase are only advisory and that the trial court makes the final sentencing determination.

Another PCA cited two "automatic" grounds for appeal in his capital cases:

> Well, there are two things that the Florida Supreme Court reviews automatically. Those are the biggest two. One is sufficiency of the evidence. Two is whether the sentence of death is proportionate. Basically the Florida Supreme Court looks at other death sentences, based on fact patterns ... it's a comparison between other death penalties. That is the biggest one that I pursue.

---

54. Michael Mello (1989) "Another Attorney for Life." Pp. 81-91 in M. L. Radelet (ed.) *Facing the Death Penalty: Essays on a Cruel and Unusual Punishment.* Philadelphia: Temple University Press, pp. 82-83.

Regarding proportionality review, the PCA related his concerns:

> In 2006, the ABA [American Bar Association] conducted a huge critical analysis of Florida's death penalty scheme. One of their main points of critique, where the Florida Supreme Court drastically failed, and I agree, their proportionality analysis is not extensive enough because they're not comparing it to enough cases. Right now, the Florida Supreme Court is comparing the case to other death penalty cases. Now there is no comparison to cases such as where death was sought by the state but the jury returned a life recommendation. There's no comparison to cases where the state attorney didn't even ask for the death penalty. To make true proportionality as to what was relayed in that report, you need a database to clock this information. The review is so primitive that it doesn't have constitutional muster. It's just not a valid comparison.

Without a database, complained the PCA, the Florida Supreme Court compares cases based on their own previous published opinions: "They try to find similar fact patterns or mental health history or history of substance abuse. Basically, it's kind of like looking up the aggravating and mitigating circumstances."

As for other grounds of appeal, the PCA stated:

> Just to be clear, I always raise the proportionality to the constitutionality about it. For other things, I've used the trial of the guilt phase, there's often a motion to suppress maybe. Maybe a statement wasn't read right. A suspect was in custody and Miranda wasn't read right or something. They like to record conversations. One thing that is common are the jailhouse informants. You've got the guy's cellmate coming in and telling us he did this, that and another. Those are just so unreliable. That's often the focus of the motion to suppress, things like that.

Ineffective assistance of counsel is another basis for appeal, but the PCA does not make the claim very often: "I do raise that on occasion on direct appeal. Normally, direct appeal is now the avenue for that.... [I]neffective assistance of counsel must be apparent on the face of the record. That's very hard to show because [the appellate judges] think that the trial attorney might have some hidden strategy or reason for doing what he did .... It's very rare of them to review that on direct appeal. Very rare."

That said, he added: "I see a lot of mistakes. Yes. That's when there are two attorneys as well. I see a lot of stuff that should have been objected to. A lot of times, they don't make an objection properly or timely. But they still have the right constitutional arguments. And it kills me."

Another PCA had this to say about the defense attorneys whose work he reviewed on appeal: "My impression is that the majority do not really understand the penalty phase issues, and the state runs all over them at trial."

One of the PCAs offered his opinion as to why trial counsel make so many mistakes: "Because with the new court appointed attorney system, a lot of qualified guys dropped off the list. There's a lot of newer guys and inexperienced guys ... they're just not as good because the rates are so low."

The PCAs expressed concerns about prosecutorial [mis]behavior during capital trials. While conceding that "capital case prosecutors are generally better trial attorneys [than their defense counterparts] and have good organizational skills in terms of handling physical evidence and moving it into evidence," one PCA said this about prosecutor misconduct: "I can't say they engaged in illegal or unethical activities, but they damn sure dance right next to the flame. Overzealousness in opening and closing statements are typical problem areas when the prosecutor comments on evidence that was not heard by the jury or interjects opinion as to what the evidence has been or will be."

Another PCA also mentioned closing arguments when asked whether he confronted prosecutor misconduct very often: "Oh yes. Usually in closing arguments. They might make a comment about him not talking to the police or not coming up with a story that fits trial or something like that. Just inflammatory and degrading remarks on the defendant's character. Repeatedly calling him a liar and adding some other ammunition into that." About prosecutors suborning perjury, he said, "Almost impossible to prove, but I think it happens fairly regularly." As for prosecutors withholding exculpatory evidence, he remarked: "That would be a *Brady* violation. Hard to prove, but that does happen. You can't prove whether it's intentional or not half the time. For *Brady*, it doesn't really matter. There's a question of, 'Can you find it?'"

On Being a Capital Case Postconviction Attorney

According to former CCR attorney Mello: "My goals [were] to ensure the inmate knows that all hope is not lost—that the battle continues and that he will not be abandoned—but also that the outlook is grim and that he should be preparing himself to die."[55] Of course, PCAs want to win, and winning ultimately means preventing the execution. However, for most PCAs, winning ultimately means to win time.[56] By delaying an execution, favorable new evidence may be found, death penalty laws may change, a new governor more inclined to grant clemency may be elected, and so forth.

For another Florida PCA, the most important aspect of representing a death row inmate on appeal is "understanding and knowing the current state of the law on the issues on appeal, especially penalty phase and sentencing issues." A third Florida PCA stated:

> Most important ... is increasing [the compensation] and fixing the court appointed attorney system. It is absolutely horrible. It really needs to be challenged. It's really a Sixth Amendment right-to-counsel violation; [also,] court-appointed attorneys aren't paid so well by the statutory cap. [Another issue is] you don't want to feel rushed. That's part of it. That's an overriding kind of concept. But the most important thing on a capital case, it's just to dissect and analyze the entire trial. They'll do the record on appeal with a fine-tooth comb. That's what I do. I have a great attention to detail. I'm a good appellate attorney. I'm an excellent legal researcher. The two go hand in hand. Go through it carefully.

The most difficult aspect of representing a death row inmate on appeal, according to one of the PCAs, is: "Knowing the uphill battle you face in trying to get a conviction set aside or a death sentence commuted to life." As for another PCA:

> I would probably have to say worrying about being adequately compensated at the end.... I don't say that to be sounding greedy. What I said before on that, I turn down a lot of cases to take a capital case. When I'm not being paid properly,

---

55. Ibid., p. 86.
56. Ibid., p. 85.

it's like a double-whammy. [Another difficult aspect is] just knowing that the ultimate penalty is at stake, this last chance or last resort.

For one of the PCAs, the worst aspect of representing a death row inmate on appeal, not surprisingly, is getting paid and paid fairly. Another PCA cited: "The constant feeling that you are beating your head against a wall."

One of the PCAs said that he was affected mentally, emotionally, and physically by his postconviction work; the other PCA stated, "Appeals do not bother me." The "affected" PCA maintained that his postconviction work was "very stressful, whether I think the guy did it or not. I know that his life is in my hands and that's a lot of pressure. There's no question about it.... It's stressful." He confided that he has lost sleep and had bad dreams about his cases.

Death Penalty Opinion

With their in-depth participation in the capital punishment process, one might wonder whether their death penalty opinions had been affected by their capital postconviction work. One of the PCAs put it this way:

> Hard to say ... Prior to the criminal defense practice of law, I was a deputy sheriff for about ten years. I worked the road the entire time and was shot at twice. I had a pretty conservative attitude about criminal justice and fully supported the death penalty. I am still fairly conservative about most things, but the death penalty makes absolutely no sense to me at the ripe old age of fifty-eight. A life sentence after a conviction for first-degree murder serves the needs of the community and protects the public from the defendant. The money the state spends to obtain and sustain a death sentence is a tremendous burden on the taxpayers and on the justice system. The death penalty is not a deterrent to murder. The death penalty only serves to provide the revenge a segment of the community needs to experience when there is a murder.

Another PCA answered the question this way:

> That's a good question. Even through law school, I've always been in favor of the death penalty. I think it's a good thing. But through the ... defense appellate work and capital defense work in general, there is an unacceptable risk that an innocent person is getting killed. So that's the problem. Do I have a problem if this person did it, and I knew he did it? Then yes, he should get the death penalty, and I'm all in favor of it. But knowing the state of justice in Florida and the court-appointed attorney system and the overworked public defenders and the low-paid court appointed attorneys, it's unacceptable if an innocent man is convicted. There's no question about it. In that sense, it has changed my view and yes, I am not in favor of the death penalty. It is too unreliable.

He then was asked whether the reliability of the process could be improved to a sufficient degree that he would not be troubled by it anymore? He replied: "Probably not because there are some other circumstances that are at play that have nothing to do with the state of Florida and have nothing to do with any statutory scheme. That is, witnesses lie or witnesses are wrong. Witnesses have agendas that cannot be uncovered. In that sense, there's always going to be some unreliability."

Conclusion

PCAs have an important role in the capital punishment process. They make sure the trial and sentence are fair. Despite the significance of their role, court-appointed PCAs complain about compensation. In Florida, for example, they argue that the flat fee provided ($2,000) is woefully inadequate and, for some of them, even when they can get the hourly rate ($100 per hour) for "extraordinary and unusual efforts," the amount is inadequate for the time and effort expended. Perhaps more troublesome for court-appointed PCAs is getting paid by the state. The bureaucratic process has been described as frustrating, agonizing, and a roll of the dice. Consequently, many experienced attorneys have taken their names off the list of qualified PCAs, leaving court-appointed postconviction defense work to less qualified and less experienced attorneys.

Another concern expressed by at least some PCAs is that by performing their role they also help to legitimate the capital punishment process. CCR attorney Mello stated, "I am a participant who advocates for the condemned, but a participant nonetheless." He then asked, "Was I serving to legitimate the system by helping to provide sanitized executions, executions with the aura of legalism and therefore the appearance of fairness?"[57] Because Mello believed that capital punishment could never be administered in a fair and evenhanded way, he was troubled by this realization. If the death penalty was abolished, of course, PCAs would not be faced with the dilemma.

In many ways, postconviction attorneys and appellate court judges work in tandem. The role of appellate court judges in capital cases is to provide additional layers of scrutiny to the work of the lower courts and their participants. Appellate court judges are the subject of the next chapter.

---

57. Ibid., p. 87.

Chapter 9

Appellate Court Judges

Appeals are rare in noncapital criminal cases. In the first place, about 95 percent of all criminal cases are resolved with a plea bargain, which precludes a trial and appeals. Even in the small percentage of cases that are decided by trial, appeals are unlikely because, in most cases, there are no legitimate bases for appeals and, in all cases, there is no constitutional right to an appellate attorney. However, because death is different, a capital defendant's trial outcome is likely to be reviewed by some combination of state supreme court justices, state intermediate appellate court justices, federal district court judges, federal appellate court judges, and justices of the U.S. Supreme Court.

The role of appellate court judges in capital cases is to provide additional layers of scrutiny to the work of the lower courts and their participants. Appellate court judges review cases to ensure that all of the lower court rulings are consistent with the law and that there is sufficient evidence to warrant the death penalty. They must deal with an extensive case record and a complex trail of precedent that changes frequently. They also try to move the cases to final resolution as expeditiously as possible. If necessary, appellate court judges can stop an execution to review a case.

Automatic or Direct Appeal

The first and only appeal required by most death penalty states is the automatic or direct appeal, which occurs regardless of the defendant's wishes. Direct appeals are unique to capital cases. In noncapital cases, an appeal is not automatic and, in most death penalty states, it is first made in an intermediate court of appeals and not in the state supreme court. When the state supreme court agrees to hear an appeal from an intermediate court of appeals in a noncapital case, the intermediate court of appeals has already reviewed the trial record, so the issues presented to the state supreme court are more limited than in an appeal of a capital case. In a noncapital case, the state supreme court generally will be asked only to resolve issues of law and, in many cases, will not need to review the trial record. In the direct appeal of a capital case, in contrast, the state supreme court will carefully review the trial record, scrutinizing particularly the sufficiency of the evidence and the rulings of the court. As one former state supreme court justice stated, "I think the greatest concern that we had was if the evidence warranted conviction for the offense, whether the standard for capital punishment had been met." Another former state supreme court justice commented, "It's my view that the role of an appellate court judge is to attempt to apply precedent and, where there is no precedent, then to try to bring the best reason ... to [the] particular issues that you're confronting." He added that his opinion about capital punishment is irrelevant.

Small Part of the Caseload — Inordinately Large Amount of Time and Resources

Not much has been written about or by appellate judges in capital cases at either the state or the federal level. A notable exception is Associate Justice Brent Dickson, who analyzed how capital punishment affected the Indiana Supreme Court.[1] The judge related that from 1977, when the Indiana legislature passed its new death penalty law, through 2004, the state's trial courts imposed the death penalty on 90 defendants. The cases "produced 148 Indiana Supreme Court majority opinions, 45 reversals of the sentence with the defendant no longer eligible for the death penalty, but [now to serve] a sentence other than death ... and 16 executions." In the 16 cases that resulted in executions, "there were 33 state trial court proceedings (including trial, retrial, and postconviction hearings), 44 state supreme court majority opinions and substantive orders, and 25 federal court opinions."

Since 1990, when the Indiana legislature added a special rule to the death penalty statute "regarding the appointment, qualifications, and compensation of trial and appellate counsel in capital cases," and until November 15, 2005, Indiana prosecutors had sought the death penalty for 174 defendants, of whom four were acquitted or had the charges dropped before trial, and 30 were sentenced to death. Of the 30, three have been executed, nine sentences have been reversed — with the defendant now serving a sentence other than death — and 18 defendants' cases at the time were under review in the appellate courts or the defendants were awaiting new trials.

From 1995 through 2004, capital cases accounted for less than one percent of the Indiana Supreme Court's caseload but more than seven percent of its written opinions. Thus, each opinion in a capital case "represented a substantially disproportionate investment of judicial time and effort." The reason, according to Judge Dickson, was threefold. First, because of the finality of the sentence, the reviewing court tried to be more thorough and comprehensive. So, for example, the court was likely to consider more claims on the merits and be disinclined to apply procedural forfeiture — such as losing the right to raise a claim because a motion was not filed in a timely manner. Second, capital appeals generally presented a greater number of issues than noncapital cases, "often including issues on which there [was] no basis under existing law, but wherein counsel [was] requesting a reexamination of precedent or seeking to preserve an issue for federal review or in anticipation of possible future modification of the law." Third, particular attention in the research and writing of capital case opinions was required because of relatively frequent U.S. Supreme Court decisions that altered criminal procedure and capital punishment jurisprudence.

In response to those differences between capital and noncapital cases the Indiana Supreme Court promulgated special rules for capital cases. For example, Indiana Supreme Court rules allow longer appellate briefs in capital cases than in other felony cases. Appellants in Indiana capital cases are permitted to submit briefs up to 100 pages long, whereas in noncapital cases appellant briefs are limited to 50 pages. Another accommodation

---

1. Brent E. Dickson, "Effects of Capital Punishment on the Justice System: Reflections of a State Supreme Court Justice," *Judicature* 89:278-281.

was allowing appellants in capital cases to submit longer trial transcripts. It is not unusual for the trial transcript in the direct appeal of a capital case to be 3,000 to 5,000 pages, or more. The record on subsequent collateral review in capital cases frequently is twice as large. (In the infamous Ted Bundy case, the Florida Supreme Court justices were "faced with the combined records of two trials comprising some twenty-eight thousand pages.... [T]he files filled an entire room.... [It] was the largest and most complicated criminal case in the court's history.")[2]

The Indiana Supreme Court pays particular attention to mitigation issues. Not only do mitigation issues require a detailed examination of the trial record, but they also generally involve special scrutiny of expert testimony on oftentimes complex medical and social science factors. These rules and practices increased the amount of time and effort it takes Indiana Supreme Court justices and support staff to research, analyze, and write their opinions in capital cases.

Additional time and effort were expended on collateral proceedings, which capital defendants take every opportunity to use. Once a death sentence was affirmed on direct appeal the Indiana Rules of Procedure for Postconviction Remedies allowed a defendant to seek postconviction relief by filing a petition asserting claims not resolved on direct appeal. The petitions generally necessitated a full evidentiary hearing in the trial court, including extensive prehearing discovery. At the least, a petition claiming ineffective assistance of trial and/or appellate counsel was filed in nearly every capital case.

If the trial court denied postconviction relief, the defendant might again appeal to the Indiana Supreme Court, which required it to render a second opinion. If the Indiana Supreme Court affirmed the denial of postconviction relief, a defendant might request to file a second or successive petition for postconviction relief. Those petitions were routinely authorized in Indiana as long as the defendant's request established a reasonable possibility that the petitioner was entitled to relief.

Additional judicial time and resources were required once a capital defendant had exhausted all of his appeals and the date of his execution drew near. Frequently, last minute requests were made to consider allegedly new or previously overlooked issues. Judges made every effort to expeditiously decide the requests. Additionally, each impending execution required about 160 hours of additional time by the Indiana Supreme Court's staff attorney for a variety of legal and administrative functions regarding the execution. When the execution was imminent, usually following a denial of executive clemency, the justices put themselves and their staff "on call" to address any last-minute filings. State police were in charge of providing special security for the judges during this period.

Capital punishment impacted the time and resources of Indiana Supreme Court justices in other ways. For instance, because of their concern with the quality of legal representation in capital cases, Indiana Supreme Court justices worked hard for the creation of Indiana Criminal Rule 24. The rule prescribes special procedures for capital cases, requires the appointment of two trial attorneys to represent each indigent capital defendant, specifies minimum qualifications and compensation for both lead counsel and co-counsel, and addresses the workload limits of appointed counsel.

Indiana Supreme Court justices also had been concerned with the public perception of its efforts in capital cases. That is one reason they were so thoughtful and careful in

---

2. David Von Drehle (1995) *Among the Lowest of the Dead*. New York: Fawcett Crest, pp. 298-99.

drafting opinions and orders. The justices understood that highly visible capital cases were often the basis by which the public formed its opinions about the court's operation, efficiency, fairness, and reliability. They also realized that the way the public perceived their handling of capital cases contributed to the public's trust and confidence in the judiciary generally. Consequently, the Indiana Supreme Court employed information officers, who were assigned to assist the media in understanding the complexities of capital cases and the court's role in them. The justices fully recognized that their jobs might depend on the success of court information officers because unpopular death penalty decisions can play a major role in judicial retention elections. Chief Justice Rose Bird and Justices Cruz Reynoso and Joseph Grodin of the California Supreme Court, Tennessee Supreme Court Justice Penny White, Mississippi Supreme Court Justice James Robertson, Justice Charles Campbell of the Texas Court of Criminal Appeals, and Washington Supreme Court Justice Robert Utter, all lost retention elections in large part because of unpopular decisions in capital cases.[3]

Proceed With the Execution

Another appellate court judge who has written about the death penalty is Gerald Kogan, who, during 40 years as a prosecutor, a defense attorney, a trial judge, and an appellate court judge and chief justice of the Florida Supreme Court, was involved in the disposition of more than 1,200 capital cases. Justice Kogan has been an outspoken critic of the capital punishment process. Following is a description of his role in an electrocution execution as chief justice of the Florida Supreme Court.[4]

As the time of execution approached, Justice Kogan was on the phone with the governor's counsel. If a stay of execution had been granted, he would inform the governor's counsel that the prisoner should not be executed, and the governor's counsel would relay that information to the warden of Florida State Prison. If the execution had commenced, the warden would order the execution team to "stand down." If no stay had been granted, then Justice Kogan would inform the governor's counsel of that fact and tell him that all state law requirements had been met and the execution could proceed. The governor's counsel would relay that information to the warden, who then would begin the execution. Justice Kogan remained on the phone with the governor's counsel, who provided the justice with a play-by-play of the execution.

After the warden gave the prisoner an opportunity to make a final statement, the justice was told that the warden was placing the hood over the face and head of the inmate. The next statement the justice heard was: "Mr. Chief Justice, the electricity has been turned on." Justice Kogan remarked, "That is a very, very troubling moment for me." He thought: "I just hope to God that this person is in truth and in fact guilty of the crime for which [he has] been convicted and I hope that this person meets all the criteria that the State

---

3. Robert M. Bohm (2012): *An Introduction to the Theory and Practice of Capital Punishment in the United States*, 4th ed. Waltham, MA: Anderson, pp. 323-24.

4. Information on Justice Gerald Kogan is from "Speech Given by Former Florida Chief Justice Gerald Kogan," The Death Penalty Information Center at www.deathpenaltyinfo.org/speech-given-former-florida-chief-justice-gerald-kogan (accessed July 8, 2009).

has set out in the State law for the purpose of execution." The next thing he heard was: "Mr. Chief Justice, the electricity has been turned off and the doctor is examining the prisoner." The next few moments seemed like an eternity to the justice, but, finally, the governor's counsel informed him that the doctor had pronounced the prisoner dead and gave him the official time of death.

That was a very sobering moment for Justice Kogan because he knew that he could have stopped the execution. The justice considered it an "awful responsibility" that forty-five years ago he never imagined that he would have to make. He thought: "God, help us all if we have made a mistake," and he knew mistakes had been made. He stated:

> [T]here is no question in my mind, and I can tell you this having seen the dynamics of our criminal justice system over the many years that I have been associated with it … that convinces me that we certainly have, in the past, executed those people who either didn't fit the criteria for execution in the State of Florida or who, in fact, were, factually, not guilty of the crime for which they have been executed.

He then explained how such mistakes could be made:

> [T]he State makes deals with more culpable defendants in a capital case [and] offers them light/life sentences in exchange for their testimony against another participant or, in some cases, in fact, gives them immunity from prosecution so that they can secure their testimony. The use of jailhouse confessions, like people who say, "I was in the cell with so-and-so and they confessed to me." Or using those particular confessions, the validity of which there has been great doubt. And yet, you see the uneven application of the death penalty where, in many instances, those that are the most culpable escape death and those that are the least culpable are victims of the death penalty. These things begin to weigh very heavily upon you. And under our system, this is the system we have. And that is, we are human beings administering an imperfect system.

Justice Kogan does not categorically oppose the death penalty and can think of exceptional cases in which it might be justified:

> Now there are certain cases where you can probably justify the death penalty and I discuss this with many friends of mine. And I say to them, "What would you do in situations if Adolf Hitler were on trial for murder, for genocide?" or "What would you do in the case of Adolf Eichmann?" and many others that we could name. And even my friends who are the staunchest opponents of the death penalty say that, yes, there can be those cases where the conduct of the individual is so egregious that Society does have the right to terminate their existence. But that isn't what we are talking about here. We are generally talking about persons who have committed one homicide in their lifetime, not people who have killed hundreds of thousands or millions of people as an act of genocide.

Dealing with the Death Penalty

Two former state supreme court justices were asked about their experiences with the death penalty. First they were asked to name the most important aspect of being an appellate court judge in a capital case. One of them said, "Well you certainly want to ensure that all of the rulings are consistent with the law, and also you want to ensure that there is sufficient evidence to warrant the imposition." He continued:

> And then, of course, the delay in getting these cases heard and resolved has been a source of constant comment and agitation. I know that [the governor], when I was chief justice, it was an issue that he harped on. And yet … there were folks on death row [for whom] all the opinions and all the appeals had taken place. Everything was right for a [death] warrant to be issued, but no [death] warrant was issued…. [W]e told the [state supreme] court how important it was to get these cases resolved expeditiously. And we've also, hopefully, emphasized how important it is for the U.S. Supreme Court to get the appeal done promptly. Now there's some things in that process that we don't have control over; for example, the federal *habeas corpus* procedures…. So there are a lot of things that the state doesn't have control over. If it's going to be imposed, the agony of waiting on everybody is not a positive aspect of the proceeding.

The other judge had this to say about the most important aspect of a capital case:

> I think that you certainly have to pay attention to the details of what's in the record and to try to understand what the issues [are] that are being presented … you have to have as full and [as] complete [an understanding] as possible…. The one thing that does differ in capital cases is that there has been a great deal of development of the law at the U.S. Supreme Court (USSC) level. And it's necessary to come to those cases with a deepened understanding of how the issues have developed, both at the state supreme court and at the USSC. And you have to stay current in the development of the law because the USSC has changed the law over the years. It is very necessary to read the USSC cases on a current basis.

The justices were also asked to cite the most difficult aspect of being an appellate court judge in a capital case. One judge answered: "I think that it's the fact that you are dealing with an extensive record and a complex trail of precedent that you have to really stay on top of and how the law is developed in that area. That is difficult because the laws change so much." The other judge related: "Just making sure that you have carefully reviewed the proceedings below and carefully reviewed the rulings made by the court. That there is sufficient evidence to warrant the imposition of the death penalty."

The worst aspect of being an appellate court judge in capital cases was the next issue addressed. One of the judges mused: "You know, no death penalty case is easy, because you're not supposed to impose the death penalty unless it's the most heinous and aggravated circumstance. And so, you know, the facts of a case are certainly not pleasant to read, but, nonetheless, I've never experienced any negative emotional response to our responsibility of reviewing a death case." The other judge commented: "[I]t was certainly not the type of case that I would have preferred to [have] been involved in. I have much more experience as a lawyer in civil areas. But [death penalty cases] were a significant part of the time that you are reviewing cases at the court. You know it's a matter that you try to become an expert in."

Regarding the mental, emotional, and physical effects of reviewing death penalty cases, one of the justices related, "I was often very concerned about the extreme violence that you see in those cases. I [learned] that cocaine was a violence producer because so many of the cases that I saw had some measured drug involvement. To a degree cocaine was implicated." As for the physical effects, he stated:

Many times ... you're reading a long record, it's physically demanding, and, as I say, the review of capital cases requires you to read long records and long briefs, and that is an exhausting experience in many instances. But, you know, I don't feel like ... the fact that it was a capital case was or caused it to be physically exhausting. I think it was the fact that you had to pay close attention to the details that were in both the record and the briefs. And so that was exhausting. And you did it, obviously, because it's a capital case, but you also do it in a number of other types of cases where you do have occasion to look at long records.

The other judge had this to say:

I have been blessed.... I really have. I struggle with these issues, but it is very rare that they cause me to lose sleep. But, I've got to struggle with them, and I come to a point of peace that this is what I ought to do. I look back over 34 years of judging, and I'm sure that there are a lot of folks that disagree with me. But I don't know of any decision that I would have made differently.... I have had to decide some [tough cases] where the public was outraged at the decision, but I felt like I had to follow the law. And those cases were ultimately affirmed. You just get over it. So, no I've never had any physical [problems].

Finally, the judges were asked whether their death penalty opinions had been affected by their experiences as an appellate court judge. One judge responded:

Not really, no. Because that question sort of implies that I ... could make a decision as an appellate judge as to whether there should be or shouldn't be the death penalty, and that's not the way that I perceive [my] role on the court, because the precedent in Florida had found the death penalty to be constitutional. And so, since the death penalty was constitutional, it was a question of the application of the death penalty statute to particular facts, and the review of how the courts did that.

The other judge asserted:

Well, in some respects it has. Primarily, I have questioned whether or not it is an appropriate expenditure of funds for the enormous amount of money that goes into the carrying out of the death penalty. Because we not only have the reviews of the death penalty by the [state] supreme court, but then we have post-conviction motions in the trial court. And then those get reviewed by the [state] supreme court and then those cases go to the Supreme Court of the United States and then they come back.

I don't have [the information] right at my fingertips ... but there is information available as to the cost of appellate review of capital cases. Most of [that information indicates that] you can keep someone in prison without the possibility of parole for a lot less than the money you spend on appeals in a capital case. I [also] understand that there is a political aspect of the imposition of the death penalty. While I was a trial judge, I actually imposed the death penalty in a case. But it took from 1982—I think it was when I did that—until 1999 for the guy to have been electrocuted.

Asked about the moral or philosophical aspects of capital punishment, he replied:

When I was considered to be a circuit judge back in 1970, I had to confront the issue of whether or not I could, as a part of my jurisdiction, impose the death penalty. I struggled with that. But after much prayer and consultation and confirmation, I determined that I could if I felt the evidence was sufficient to meet the law.... I struggled with it, but I came to the conclusion that I could do it and I did do it. No judge, I think, would say, "I really enjoyed doing it."

Federal Courts of Appeal

Among the rare accounts of a federal appellate court in action in a capital case is former U.S. Attorney General Ramsey Clark's description of John Spenkelink's final appeal.[5] Spenkelink was the second person executed under post-*Furman* statutes, the first person executed under Florida's new post-*Furman* statute, and the first person executed against his will under post-*Furman* statutes.

According to Clark, he and his associates obtained a stay of execution for Spenkelink from federal district court judge Elbert Tuttle of Atlanta on the grounds that Spenkelink's trial attorney had been ineffective. Two days later, Clark received a phone call at seven-thirty in the evening from the clerk of the U.S. Court of Appeals for the Fifth Circuit, in New Orleans. The clerk informed Clark that he was setting up a conference call between Spenkelink's attorneys, the Florida attorney general, and three judges of the appellate court: Judges James P. Coleman, Alvin B. Rubin, and Peter T. Fay, the last of whom turned out to be unavailable. The purpose of the call was for the appellate judges to rule on the state of Florida's request to set aside Judge Tuttle's stay. Clark described the conference call as a nightmare:

> We were told at the beginning not to record what was said. The court did not have our papers. We had not seen the State's papers.... There was loose, unstudied, uninformed discussion about whether Judge Tuttle had jurisdiction, whether he entered a final order, whether the Court of Appeals had the power to review his order.... We asked for time to file affidavits and a response to the State's motion. The merits of our petition for a writ of habeas corpus had been barely even discussed ... the call was over shortly after 8 p.m.[6]

Then, at ten minutes before midnight, the clerk of the appeals court called Clark from New Orleans with a page-and-a-half order to read. Clark related that the order cited four cases that had not been mentioned previously and were irrelevant to the issue at hand. The order stated, "We are convinced, for reasons which will hereafter be stated in formal opinion, that the aforesaid stay should be vacated." The order also specified that "the motions of Spenkelink for time in which to file supporting affidavits, etc., is denied.... This order vacating execution granted by Judge Tuttle shall become fully and formally effective at the hour of 9:30 o'clock Eastern daylight savings time, Friday, May 25, 1979.... Judge Rubin reserves the right to dissent for reasons to be assigned."[7]

Clark maintained that the appellate justices acted without jurisdiction:

> Judge Coleman based jurisdiction on an appellate rule even though no appeal had been taken, so the case was not even properly before his court. He ignored

---

5. Cited in William J. Bowers, with Glenn L. Pierce and John F. McDevitt (1984) *Legal Homicide: Death as Punishment in America, 1864–1982*. Boston: Northeastern University Press, pp. 368-370.

6. Ibid., p. 368.

7. Ibid., pp. 368-369.

the habeas corpus statute, which denies the Court of Appeals jurisdiction over original petitions for habeas corpus. He considered a stay order a "final order" in violation of a statute that required a certificate of probable cause—a stay order that was clearly made in order to preserve jurisdiction.[8]

Clark concluded by posing several provocative questions:

> Why did Coleman proceed after years of careful, painstaking litigation to compel exhausted lawyers and the court to discuss a life-and-death case late at night over the phone, without exchanging papers, without giving time for review or study, without allowing time for supporting affidavits? Why did he not wait until Judge Fay could hear the argument? Why did he cite four irrelevant cases never mentioned in the papers or the discussion in an order written at home and dictated over the phone to a clerk? How could he decide the matter without having facts to judge whether there had been effective assistance of counsel? Since Judge Fay did not hear argument and should not have voted, and because Judge Rubin ultimately dissented, how could he decide to vacate Judge Tuttle's order? And why had he not given his reasons? Judges deciding death cases ought to give reasons.[9]

One possible answer to Clark's questions about what clearly was a "rush to judgment" and likely an atypical proceeding is the desire of Judges Coleman and Fay to have Spenkelink executed before his death warrant then in force, expired. His death warrant was set to expire at noon on May 25, 1979. The proceeding also shows the degree to which the personal and/or systemic agendas of the appellate judges affected their judgment.

For some appellate judges, participating in the capital punishment process is no easy task. One example is the late Robert S. Vance of the U.S. Court of Appeals for the Eleventh Circuit, which hears cases from Florida, Georgia, and Alabama, and has been referred to as the "death court" for the many death sentences it has confirmed.[10] Judge Vance once told one of his law clerks that "he did not believe in capital punishment" and that if he were a legislator, he would vote against it; if he were the governor, he would commute death sentences; and if he were on the U.S. Supreme Court he might hold the death penalty unconstitutional.[11] His son divulged that the judge found death penalty cases "to be almost unbearable."[12] Nevertheless, during his tenure on the bench, Judge Vance confirmed many death sentences because he was convinced that the defendants had received fair trials, and "he knew that it was not his role to change that system to suit his personal preferences."[13] In 1989, a package bomb killed Judge Vance, but his wife pleaded with the prosecutor not to charge the suspect, Walter Moody, Jr., with a capital crime. The judge ignored her request, and Moody was convicted and sentenced to death in Alabama.[14] As of April 1, 2012, Moody remained on Alabama's death row awaiting his execution—more than twenty years after the crime.[15]

---

8. Ibid., p. 369.

9. Ibid.

10. Robert Jay Lifton and Greg Mitchell (2002) *Who Owns Death? Capital Punishment, the American Conscience, and the End of Executions*. New York: Perennial, p. 159.

11. Ibid., pp. 159-60.

12. Ibid., p. 160.

13. Ibid.

14. Ibid.

15. The Criminal Justice Project (2012) *Death Row U.S.A.*, NAACP Legal Defense and Educational Fund, Inc. (Spring).

The U.S. Supreme Court

Another glimpse into the minds of appellate judges in capital cases can be had from examining the candid public statements about capital punishment from recent U.S. Supreme Court justices. What is fascinating about this evidence is how many justices have voted to uphold capital punishment even though they were personally opposed to it. However, before examining the remarks of those justices, first consider the statements about capital punishment by justices who are or were adamantly opposed to the penalty, have voted against it at every opportunity, and are or have been frustrated with the intransigence of their court brethren on the subject.

First and foremost was Justice Thurgood Marshall, who voted to overturn every death sentence that came before the Court. Justice Marshall believed capital punishment is a cruel and unusual punishment in violation of the Eighth and Fourteenth Amendments because the penalty is excessive, and the American public would reject it if it were fully informed about its purposes and liabilities.[16] He argued the death penalty was excessive because it was "unnecessary to promote the goal of deterrence or to further any legitimate notion of retribution."[17]

Also in this category is Justice William Brennan, Justice Marshall's "comrade in arms" on the issue of capital punishment. Justice Brennan's consistent opposition to capital punishment was based on the moral principles that "the State, even as it punishes, must treat its citizens in a manner consistent with their intrinsic worth as human beings, [and] a punishment must not be so severe as to be degrading to human dignity."[18] These moral principles, in turn, "require us to hold that the law has progressed to the point where we should declare that the punishment of death, like punishments on the rack, the screw, and the wheel, is no longer morally tolerable in our civilized society."[19] For Justice Brennan "our civilization and the law [have] progressed to this point and that therefore the punishment of death, for whatever crime and under all circumstances, is 'cruel and unusual' in violation of the Eighth and Fourteenth Amendments of the Constitution."[20]

Another justice in this category is Arthur Goldberg, who personally considered the death penalty an abomination, and who in the early 1960s maintained that it was applied arbitrarily, haphazardly, capriciously, and in a discriminatory way against disadvantaged minorities.[21]

Next are the justices who have upheld the death penalty even though they personally opposed it, or justices who have upheld the death penalty but have had an epiphany and now oppose it. Among the justices in this category were Justice Warren Burger and Justice Harry Blackmun, who, over the course of their Court tenures, consistently voted to uphold the constitutionality of capital punishment. In their *Furman* opinions, both justices

---

16. *Gregg v. Georgia*, 428 U.S. 153 (1976), pp. 231-232.
17. Ibid., p. 241.
18. Ibid., p. 229.
19. Ibid.
20. Ibid.
21. Michael Meltsner (1973) *Cruel and Unusual Punishment: The Supreme Court and Capital Punishment.* New York: Random House, p. 32; Stuart Banner (2002) *The Death Penalty: An American History.* Cambridge: Harvard University Press, p. 248.

revealed that, had they been legislators, they would have voted to either abolish the death penalty or severely restrict its use.[22] Late in his career, Justice Blackmun issued his famous *mea culpa*:

> From this day forward, I no longer shall tinker with the machinery of death. For more than twenty years I have endeavored—indeed, I have struggled—along with a majority of this Court, to develop procedural and substantive rules that would lend more than the mere appearance of fairness to the death penalty endeavor. Rather than continue to coddle the Court's delusion that the desired level of fairness has been achieved and the need for regulation eviscerated, I feel morally and intellectually obligated simply to concede that the death penalty experiment has failed. It is virtually self-evident to me now that no combination of procedural rules or substantive regulations ever can save the death penalty from its inherent constitutional deficiencies. The basic question—does the system accurately and consistently determine which defendants "deserve" to die?—cannot be answered in the affirmative. It is not simply that this Court has allowed vague aggravating circumstances to be employed ... relevant mitigating evidence to be disregarded ... and vital judicial review to be blocked.... The problem is that the inevitability of factual, legal, and moral error gives us a system that we know must wrongly kill some defendants, a system that fails to deliver the fair, consistent, and reliable sentences of death required by the Constitution.[23]

Justice Lewis Powell, who had dissented in *Furman* and had regularly supported the death penalty in cases decided by the Supreme Court, told his biographer four years after he had retired from the Court: "I have come to think that capital punishment should be abolished ... [because] it serves no useful purpose.[24]

Justice John Paul Stevens had voted to uphold the death penalty for 30 years but now believes it violates the Eighth Amendment ban on cruel and unusual punishment:

> I have relied on my own experience in reaching the conclusion that the imposition of the death penalty represents the pointless and needless extinction of life with only marginal contributions to any discernible social or public purposes. A penalty with such negligible returns to the state (is) patently excessive and cruel and unusual punishment violative of the Eighth Amendment.[25]

Finally, there are those justices who have not explicitly stated their opposition to capital punishment but have publicly remarked on its serious deficiencies. Both Justice Sandra Day O'Connor and Justice Ruth Bader Ginsburg have expressed concerns about the quality of legal representation in capital cases. In arguing that lawyers in capital cases should be required to meet minimum standards and be better compensated, Justice O'Connor stated in a speech to a women's law group in Minneapolis that "if statistics are any indication, the system may well be allowing some innocent defendants to be executed."[26] Justice Ginsburg, speaking at the University of the District of Columbia, acknowledged that she

---

22. Meltsner, ibid., p. 305.

23. *Callin v. Collins*, 510 U.S. 1141 (1994), pp. 1145-1146.

24. Cited in Michael L. Radelet and Marian J. Borg (2000) "The Changing Nature of Death Penalty Debates." *Annual Review of Sociology* 26:43–61.

25. Mark Sherman (2008) "Stevens Declares Opposition to Death Penalty," USAToday, April 16 at www.usatoday.com/news/washington/2008-04-16-1705347481_x.htm (accessed 9/7/08.

26. Thomas Healy (2001) "Swing Justice O'Connor Expresses Qualms about Death Penalty," *The Orlando Sentinel* (July 4), p. A4.

supported a proposed moratorium on the death penalty in Maryland. She observed that her experience with death row inmates who have asked the Court for last-minute reprieves demonstrated that not one of them received really good legal help at trial. She also criticized the "meager" amount of money spent to defend poor people.[27]

Conclusion

The primary job of the appellate courts is to ensure that capital defendants receive a fair trial, and the appellate courts have been busy. Former Florida State Supreme Court chief justice Gerald Kogan reported that capital cases made up about three percent of the Florida Supreme Court's caseload; yet, they consumed almost fifty percent of the justices' time.[28] This level of scrutiny by the appellate courts is for good reason. From 1973 through 2005, at least 28.5 percent, and as many as 68 percent, of all convictions or sentences in death penalty cases nationwide were overturned on appeal.[29]

Until the mid-1990s, it was possible for death row inmates to employ the dual system of collateral review numerous times. Now, however, because of Supreme Court decisions, the passage of the federal Antiterrorism and Effective Death Penalty Act of 1996, and similar measures by state legislatures, access to both the federal and state appellate courts has been made more difficult. Proponents of these types of decisions and legislation believe that most appeals are frivolous and are simply delaying tactics, and they hope that the new rules will greatly reduce the long delays in executions and the high costs associated with the entire capital punishment process.

The charge that many appeals are frivolous and delaying tactics is problematic on two counts. First, a postconviction attorney has a professional obligation to assert at every level of the proceedings what otherwise might be deemed a frivolous claim if that claim "might conceivably persuade even one judge in an appeals court or in the Supreme Court."[30] Second, according to the study of the fully reviewed state death sentences imposed between 1973 and 1995 described in Chapter 8, two-thirds were reversed at one of the appeal stages because of serious or prejudicial errors.[31] The study found that in 82 percent of the reversals by state postconviction courts the defendant deserved a sentence other than death when the errors were cured on retrial, and in seven percent of the reversals the defendant was found to be innocent of the capital crime. Eighty percent of the reversals were due to ineffective assistance of counsel, prosecutor misconduct, unconstitutional jury instructions, and judge/jury bias.

---

27. Anne Gearan (2002) "Supreme Court Takes Up Claim of Poor Defense in Death Cases," *The Orlando Sentinel* (March 26), p. A11.

28. "Speech Given by Former Florida Chief Justice Gerald Kogan," op. cit.

29. The lower figure is from Sourcebook of Criminal Justice Statistics Online, Table 6.0002.2005 at www.albany.edu/sourcebook/pdf/t600022005.pdf (accessed August 22, 2009). The higher figure is from Liebman, James S., Jeffrey Fagan, and Valerie West (2000) "A Broken System: Error Rates in Capital Cases, 1973–1995" at www2.law.columbia.edu/instructionalservices/liebman/ (accessed August 22, 2009).

30. Monroe H. Freedman (2003) "The Professional Obligation To Raise Frivolous Issues in Death Penalty Cases." *Hofstra Law Review* 31:1167-1180.

31. James S. Liebman, Jeffrey Fagan, and Valerie West (2000) "A Broken System: Error Rates in Capital Cases, 1973–1995" at www2.law.columbia.edu/instructionalservices/liebman/ (accessed August 22, 2009).

As noted in Chapter 8, the number of death penalty appeal reversals has been decreasing dramatically in recent years, not because of greater fairness in the system or fewer constitutional errors, but rather because legal procedure has reduced access to the appellate courts, especially the federal courts, and, when access is granted, death row inmates are simply less likely to prevail. Nearly all constitutional errors today are subject to harm analysis and "proving that an error was harmful is difficult or impossible."[32]

Despite the reduced number of reversals, the appeals process persists. While PCAs and appellate court judges review and ensure the fairness of trials, death row inmates remain incarcerated. The families of the victim and the condemned often wait and wonder about when the process will end—about whether and when the death sentence finally will be imposed. In the meantime, prison wardens guard their inmates while the capital punishment process grinds on. Like the others involved in the process, prison wardens do not go unscathed by their experiences with the death penalty, as we examine in the next chapter.

---

32. David R. Dow, (2005) *Executed on a Technicality: Lethal Injustice on America's Death Row.* Boston: Beacon Press, pp. xxii-xxiii and 44.

Chapter 10

Prison Wardens

In prisons with execution chambers, prison wardens are responsible for supervising and carrying out state-mandated executions. Most of them do it with an outward stoicism that belies, for some of them, profound inner turmoil.

In fact, a remarkable number of prison wardens who have overseen executions were already, or have become, death penalty opponents. Their reasons vary but generally include:

- the exorbitant costs of capital punishment;
- the irrevocability of the punishment;
- the pressure that last-minute appeals put on governors and courts that are forced to substitute hastiness for considered judgment;
- the inhumanity of longs stays on death row;
- the lost contributions that prison inmates could make;
- the arbitrary and discriminatory way in which the death penalty is imposed;
- the absence of evidence of a marginal deterrent effect; and
- the hypocrisy of killing people to teach people that killing is wrong.

Prison wardens who oppose the death penalty participate in executions because it's their job. But some admit that executions make them feel dirty, like they are simply pawns of the system.

Unlike defense attorneys, prosecutors, trial judges, jurors, postconviction attorneys, and appellate judges, prison wardens on death row get to know and observe death row inmates for many years. In some cases, they have become friends with death row inmates, which makes executions especially emotionally excruciating. As Donald Cabana, warden of prisons in Florida, Missouri, and Mississippi, put it, "There is part of the warden that dies with his prisoner."

The End of the Sewer Pipe

Bill Armontrout was warden of Missouri State Penitentiary in Jefferson City, Missouri, from 1984 until 1989, when he was promoted to deputy director of the Division of Adult Institutions in the Missouri Department of Corrections. As warden, he was responsible for implementing Missouri's change in execution methods from cyanide gas to lethal injection. He also was responsible for carrying out Missouri's first execution by lethal injection in 1989, the first following the state's reinstatement of the death penalty in 1975.

In an interview published in the *Wall Street Journal* shortly after becoming warden, Armontrout described his new role as executioner: "I look at the criminal justice system as a sewer pipe and I'm just at the end of it. The police did their job, the courts did their job, now I have to do my job."[1] As for the difference between executions by lethal injection and lethal gas, Armontrout related, "Oh, there's no comparison.... I would say lethal injection is so much more humane. There is no gasping, no jerking with lethal injection. It's just going to sleep. Closing your eyes and going to sleep. With gas, there's gasping. Their eyes bulge out, they try to hold their breath. It is much more painful than lethal injection."[2]

Armontrout and his executive assistant, Mark Schreiber, created the Missouri Protocol, a detailed set of procedures that governs the job of carrying out executions in Missouri. According to Schreiber, the protocol is key to the state's execution process because it provides participants with a sense of collective responsibility. As Schreiber described: "We all work together.... It's a collective thing. Everyone is properly trained. They know what they're supposed to do, and take care of business."[3] Since its creation, the Missouri Protocol has been revised many times in an effort to reduce problems through trial and error.

One of the issues a warden must address is what to do with prison staff who are opposed to the death penalty or otherwise do not want to participate in an execution. Armontrout explained his policy:

> [W]e make it where if a person—say I put you on a security post or whatever, and you don't believe in the death penalty—all you have to do is tell me *personally* that you don't want to be involved with it. No questions asked, and you'll be dropped. Because people do have feelings, you have to understand. And I've had a number of staff, once they've been assigned, ask not be assigned. And that's just between me and them. That's their belief, and I honor that. (emphasis in original)[4]

The most difficult aspect of an execution for Armontrout was a stay of execution:

> It is very tough. The longer it drags out, the tougher it is. I noticed something with this last one.... The United States Supreme Court turned this one down at five minutes till nine that evening. So, at nine o'clock that evening, we knew that we were going to be going a little after midnight. The staff were tired. We got tired just from the tension. I was very tired after that was over that evening, because I knew from nine o'clock onward, a three-hour period, I knew what we were going to do. There wasn't any wondering about it. We knew that there was no more appeals, nothing else, that this guy was going, you see.[5]

He continued: "Standing down is very difficult mentally. Because you're so prepped for this thing, you see. I've found that when we go ahead and do the chore that we have to do, that you're not as depressed as you are when you stand down. That standing down just tears you up. You're so keyed to it. You're so tired."[6]

Armontrout described how the actual killing affected him personally:

> I look at it this way. I've made peace with myself on this thing by knowing that the fellow that's being executed has had every chance of appeal. He's had his trials; the number of appeals the guy has had—the United States Supreme Court

---

1. Cited at www.allthingswilliam.com/crime.html (accessed August 4, 2009).
2. Stephen Trombley (1992) *The Execution Protocol: Inside America's Capital Punishment Industry.* New York: Crown Publishers, p. 115.
3. Ibid., p. 119.
4. Ibid., p. 110.
5. Ibid., p. 113.
6. Ibid., p. 259.

three times, Eighth Circuit three times, the local court of appeals three or four times. When you know that the case has been scrutinized that closely, then it makes you feel much easier. I believe in the laws of our country. I've been around the world several times. We *may* not have the most perfect criminal justice system in the world, but it's the best *I've* seen. It affords the person an ample opportunity to prove his innocence.... So I'm at peace with myself because I know that this guy's case has been looked at a number of times. And I do personally believe in the death penalty. It may not be a deterrent for the next person, but it is for that person. (emphasis in original)[7]

It's My Job

Another prison official tasked with creating his state's execution protocol was Peter Matos, a former prison guard and warden who became Connecticut's deputy commissioner of corrections in 1995.[8] Creating the execution protocol and assembling and training the execution team were part of his duties, although in hindsight a considerable amount of his time and psychological capital was expended for little return. Connecticut abolished its death penalty on April 25, 2012. Prior to that Connecticut had executed only one person since 1960. That person, Michael Ross, was executed on May 13, 2005, for the murders of four women. Ross was a "volunteer"; he did not pursue any appeals.[9]

Matos's efforts and his reactions to his assignment provide valuable insights into the psychological effects of preparing and participating in executions. Matos had stated that he had an open mind about the death penalty and would carry out the law if required. When pressed about his death penalty opinion, he responded:

> Well, I don't know, I'm, I'm—this is my job. People say, "Well, if I had a job like that, I'd leave it." Well, yeah, well—this is the profession I have chosen. If we have to carry out an execution, I would hope that it's something that's been carried out by the letter of the law. Yeah, I may feel uncomfortable with it. But I'm obviously going to carry it out.... Unfortunately, that's my job.[10]

He admitted in a *Hartford Courant* interview that "there was *no* humane way of killing someone" (emphasis in original).[11] He favored lethal injection only because it gave execution team members "some peace of mind."[12] From the outset, he was concerned about the psychological effects of executions on his staff. He commented, "A lot of people always say, 'Oh, I have no problem, I can handle it.' Well I don't really know if people can handle it until after it happens.... Even if they're not in the room, they [may be] in the building and they know that someone's being executed down the hall. We probably have to work with some depression and psychological effects on staff after the fact."[13]

---

7. Ibid.

8. Robert Jay Lifton and Greg Mitchell (2002) *Who Owns Death? Capital Punishment, the American Conscience, and the End of Executions.* New York: Perennial, p. 74.

9. The Criminal Justice Project (2009) *Death Row U.S.A.*, NAACP Legal Defense and Educational Fund, Inc. (Winter).

10. Lifton and Mitchell, op. cit., p. 77.

11. Ibid., p. 75.

12. Ibid., p. 76

13. Ibid., p. 75

Matos's wife was not happy about his new assignment. He had not told her about it, and she learned what he was doing from a friend at work. When she confronted her husband, he said, "I'm not running a guillotine or anything, honey. I'm only setting up the process."[14] When the public learned what he was doing, he received a lot of mail. Much of it was supportive of his efforts, but some of it was morbid and disturbing. He received letters laced with gallows humor and packages with unnerving gifts. He noted that some people "think I'm Saddam Hussein's little brother."[15]

When it came time for Matos to assemble the execution team, a large number of the volunteers claimed that they had no misgivings about participating in executions. These were not the type of people he wanted. "I don't really think they understand, and I think those are definitely the people I would *not* have as part of the team.... I want somebody who's going to be concerned about what they're going to do," he explained. "I don't want [them] to have [such] a negative reaction that it's going to destroy their personal lives, but I want to make sure they understand the consequences of what we're doing." (emphasis in original)[16]

Matos seems like a decent man, so how was he able to participate in executions? He readily admitted that he was "uncomfortable" with the idea of executing another human being and would not include as a team member someone who was not at least apprehensive about it, but he avoided the ethical questions about capital punishment by maintaining that executions were part of his job, the profession he had chosen.

It Always Bothers You

Jim Willett worked in corrections for 30 years and was warden of the Walls Unit (also known as the Texas State Penitentiary at Huntsville, or the Huntsville Unit) in Huntsville, Texas, from 1998 until his retirement in 2001. The Walls Unit is a maximum-security prison where the state's death house is located and, since 1924, has been the site of all Texas executions. During his three years as warden, Willett oversaw 89 executions.[17] About those executions, Willett pondered:

> The executions seem to effect [sic] all of us differently. Some get quiet and reflective after, others less so, but I have no doubt that it's disturbing for all of us. It always bothers you. It does me. [For example,] when we had six executions in ten days, my wife told me I was short with her and the kids. [Also,] I can't be certain I didn't help execute an innocent person. There may have been people who said "I did it" to protect somebody else. I do worry about my staff. I can see it in their eyes sometimes, particularly when we do a lot of executions in a short period of time. So far this year we've done thirty-three, and I'm guessing we'll get some place close to fifty by the end of 2000. That'll be a record. I'll be retiring next year and to tell you the truth this is something I won't miss a bit.

---

14. Ibid., p. 76.
15. Ibid.
16. Ibid.
17. From "Witness to an Execution" (Transcript), Radio Documentary by Sound Portraits at http://soundportraits.org/on-air/witness_to_an_execution/transcript.php, Copyright © 2000 Sound Portraits Productions. All Rights Reserved (accessed June 4, 2009); Patrick Beach (2002) "Jim Willett," *Esquire*, Vol. 137, Issue 3 (March 1).

The best part of leaving the job is not having to watch anybody die. There are times when I'm standing there, watching those fluids start to flow, and wonder whether what we're doing here is right. It's something I'll be thinking about for the rest of my life.[18]

An Empty and Futile Act

Warden Willett is not the only prison warden to have doubts about capital punishment. Another is Jeanne Woodford, former director of the California Department of Corrections and Rehabilitation from 2004 until 2006 and the former warden and first female warden of San Quentin State Prison from 1999 until 2004. Woodford worked in corrections for three decades and presided over four executions. She stated recently, "To say that I have regrets about my involvement in the death penalty is to let myself off the hook too easily. To take a life in order to prove how much we value another life does not strengthen our society. It is a public policy that devalues our very being and detracts crucial resources from programs that could truly make our communities safe."[19]

Woodford related that she was not soft on crime. Her main concern was keeping the public safe, especially her children and grandchildren. She realized that some people were dangerous and must be removed from society forever, but she believed that capital punishment was not the answer. Woodford would replace capital punishment with life imprisonment without the opportunity of parole.

She cited the example of Robert Lee Massie, over whose execution she presided in 2001. Massie was first sentenced to death in 1965 for the murder of a mother with two children. When the U.S. Supreme Court temporarily abolished the death penalty in 1972, his death sentence was commuted to life imprisonment with opportunity of parole. Massie was paroled in 1978. A few months later, he murdered a sixty-one-year-old liquor storeowner, for which he was convicted again and sentenced to death. Obviously, had Massie been executed for his first murder, he could not have killed his second victim. If anyone deserved to be executed, there was no better candidate than Massie.

Yet, of Woodford's four executions, Massie's stood out to her as the strongest example of "how empty and futile the act of execution is." She remembered the night of the execution clearly. It was March 27, 2001. She was the last person to talk with Massie before he was executed. After she spoke with him, she had the witnesses brought in, looked at the clock to make certain it was after midnight, and received signals from two of her staff who were on the phone with the state supreme court and the U.S. Attorney General's Office to make sure that the execution was not going to be stopped. It was not. She then gave the order to proceed with the lethal injection. Massie was dead a few minutes later.

Woodford recounted that she did her job even though she did not believe it was the right thing to do. For her, executing Massie did not make the world any safer than permanently imprisoning him.

---

18. "Witness to an Execution," ibid.

19. Jeanne Woodford (2008) "Death Row Realism," *Los Angeles Times* (October 2) at www.latimes.com/news/opinion/opinionla/la-oe-woodford2-2008oct02,0,6875731.story (accessed October 15, 2008).

To those people who ask why the state should pay to keep people like Massie locked up for life, Woodford answered, "It's cheaper—much, much cheaper than execution." She wishes the public knew how much capital punishment costs. She explained that California spends an additional $117 million each year pursuing the execution of its death row inmates. Just housing an inmate on death row costs California an extra $90,000 per prisoner per year more than what it would cost to house the prisoner with the general prison population. A statewide bipartisan commission recently concluded that California must spend an extra $100 million each year to fix the many problems with capital punishment in the state. If the California legislature follows the commission's recommendations, Woodford estimated that California's capital punishment system would cost more than $200 million a year more than a system in which the maximum punishment is life imprisonment without opportunity of parole.

Abolishing capital punishment, argued Woodford, would free up money that could be used, for example, to investigate unsolved homicides, modernize crime labs, and expand effective violence-prevention programs. The money also could be used to intervene in the lives of at-risk children and to invest in their education. Such spending priorities might stop the production of people such as Robert Lee Massie, who was abused and neglected as a child in the state's foster care system.

Is the World Any Better Off?

Lewis E. Lawes, longtime warden of New York's Sing Sing prison (1920-1941) and a president of the American Prison Association (1923), has been called the most famous and accomplished prison warden in American penology. Lawes was born in 1883, and grew up a half mile from the New York State Reformatory at Elmira, where his father worked as a guard. When he took the warden's position at age 37, he was the youngest warden of Sing Sing to date. Sing Sing had a reputation of breaking wardens. There had been ten wardens in the twelve years before Warden Lawes; some of the previous wardens lasted only a couple of months.[20]

In the early 1920s, Warden Lawes conducted an informal survey of other prison wardens to ascertain their positions on the death penalty. Of the 47 wardens that responded to the survey, 23 were in favor of the death penalty, 17 were opposed, and 7 were evenly divided for and against.[21] In a letter to Warden Lawes, Thomas J. Tynan, warden of Colorado State Penitentiary (1911-1915) explained his position:

> I am unalterably opposed to capital punishment, have always been and probably will always be, as I do not believe there is any deterrent in capital punishment....
> I realize that society often is exasperated over some hideous crime that is committed, yet the infliction of the death penalty is no deterrent, and very few, if any, of the men I have known who were executed, ever gave any thought to the penalty when the crime was committed. On the other hand some of the best men I have ever come in contact with behind the prison walls were men who had been sent to the Penitentiary under the death penalty and whose sentences have been commuted to life imprisonment, so it is better by far to give the offender

---

20. John Jay Rouse, "Firm But Fair: The Life of Sing Sing Warden Lewis E. Lawes" at www. correctionhistory.org/html/chronicl/state/lawes/lewiselawesnotes1.htm (accessed March 9, 2009).

21. Lewis E. Lawes (1969, orig. 1924) *Man's Judgement of Death: An Analysis of the Operation and Effect of Capital Punishment Based on Facts, not on Sentiment.* Montclair, NJ: Patterson Smith, p. 59.

a chance to reclaim himself, repent of his crime and possibly save his soul, than it is to inflict the death penalty upon him. Capital punishment never lessens crime nor will it ever do so.... [22]

Other early twentieth-century prison wardens expressed similar views, including Harry L. Hurlburt (Michigan State Prison), Charles E. Linscott (Rhode Island State Prison), Lester D. Eaton (Maine State Prison), G. T. Jameson (South Dakota Penitentiary), Mordecai S. Plummer (New Castle County Workhouse, Wilmington, Delaware), and Charles B. Galbreath (Wisconsin State Prison).[23]

R. F. Coleman, warden of Texas's Huntsville Prison, resigned on January 1, 1924, when he learned that in two weeks Texas intended to execute condemned inmates by electrocution rather than by hanging, which it had used sparingly. Coleman told reporters: "A warden can't be a warden and killer, too.... The penitentiary is a place to reform a man, not to kill him."[24]

As for Warden Lawes's views on the death penalty, he wrote:

> My own conviction against capital punishment is based upon personal experience of twenty years, upon contact with hundreds of murderers whom I have known and with whom I have talked in very solemn moments, upon close observation of what we choose to call "legal execution." I have seen many men die in the electric chair. Under our laws the court sentences the murderer to die "during the week beginning ..." The actual day and the hour within the week is my responsibility to fix. I alone determine the exact moment when that life shall be extinguished. I always wonder afterward whether the world is any better off; whether what has been done in the name of the law is consistent with the spirit of religion, consistent with the right progress of civilization.[25]

The Cross that Every Warden Must Bear

Clinton T. Duffy, another prison warden who opposed capital punishment, was born in 1898, and grew up in San Quentin Village just outside the prison's east gate.[26] His father was a San Quentin guard for 30 years. Duffy's wife, Gladys, also grew up in San Quentin Village; her father was Captain of the Yard. In 1929, Duffy began a seven-year-stint as the warden's secretary, followed by five years as secretary and historian of the Board of Prison Directors and one of the secretaries for the Board of Prison Terms and Paroles. He then served eleven and a half years as San Quentin's warden. At the end of his term as warden, he had become the longest serving warden in San Quentin's history, which dates back to 1852. He retired five years later after serving as a member of the Adult Authority Board, the successor to the Board of Prison Directors.

About the death penalty, Duffy wrote:

---

22. Ibid., pp. 139-140.
23. Ibid., p. 140 and 142.
24. Lifton and Mitchell, op. cit., p. 101.
25. Lawes, op. cit., p. 60.
26. William J. Duffy, Jr., "Warden Clinton Terry Duffy" (a biography) at http://freepages.history. rootsweb.ancestry.com/~sanquentin/sqsp/wardens/ctduffy.htm (accessed March 8, 2009).

Death is death, no matter how it occurs, and execution by the state is as deliberate as premeditated murder and far more nerve-wracking for all concerned. I hated the death penalty in my youth and, after thirty-two years of correctional experience, I abhor it even more today.... I watched sixty men die by hanging in the eight years that I served as secretary to the warden of San Quentin. In my eleven and one half years as warden, I supervised the executions of eighty-eight men and two women.... Each of the 150 executions I watched was a separate and distinct ordeal, unsavory, nauseating, and infuriating. I faced them all with dread and I look back on them with revulsion. My final execution as warden in 1951 was the last I shall ever see.[27]

Duffy believed that other participants in the death penalty process were just as averse to it as he was and that they dealt with their role by rationalizing and compartmentalizing their level of responsibility:

The cop on the beat says, "All I did was arrest the man." The district attorney says, "All I did was present the evidence." The jury says, "All we did was review the evidence and come to our conclusion." The judge says, "All I did was follow the jury's conclusion and pass sentence in accordance with the law." The officers escorting the man to prison say, "All we did was take him where the judge ordered he must go." The guards say, "All we did was make sure he didn't escape." The higher-court judge says, "All I did was look for errors when I reviewed the case." The executioner says, "All I did was throw the switch when the warden told me to." The warden says, "All I did was see that the sentence was properly carried out after the governor told me there was no reason to do otherwise." And the governor says, "All I did was adhere to the laws passed by the people of my state."[28]

Another indication of aversion to the death penalty for Duffy was the lack of pride and satisfaction it provided the participants. As Duffy remarked, "I've heard many an official proudly declare after performing a brave and unselfish act, 'I was glad to do it; it was only my job.' I've never heard anyone say, 'I was glad to take part in this execution; it was only my job.'"[29] He added:

If the death penalty were right and proper, it would be carried out in public places and anyone would be free to watch it. If it were a source of pride instead of shame, the participants would be heroes and the condemned the villains they were meant to be. Instead, it's the other way around.... I never knew an executioner who admitted his profession to the outside world, either while he was active or after he retired.... Outside of the condemned man himself, I think the executioner takes the worst beating of all when someone has to die in the gas chamber.[30]

Duffy opposed the death penalty for a variety of reasons. "I hated the death penalty on principle before I went to work at San Quentin, and I hated it more when I had to watch it in operation," he wrote. "But principle and personal distaste, which first inspired my hatred, have long since been superseded by far more compelling reasons."[31] None of his reasons is original; all of them had been articulated before him, and most of them

27. Clinton T. Duffy with Al Hirshberg (1962) *88 Men and 2 Women* (London: Victor Gollancz), p. 17-18.
28. Ibid., pp. 19-20.
29. Ibid., p. 20.
30. Ibid. and p. 250.
31. Ibid., p. 252.

continue to be argued today. What is unique about his observations is that they come from a long-serving warden of one of the toughest maximum-security prisons in the United States.

Duffy hated the death penalty "because it is so terribly final." He observed, "Once it is carried out there is no turning back, no reconsidering, no righting what might be a tragic wrong."[32] He hated the death penalty "because it puts such pressure on governors and courts that they are forced to substitute hastiness for considered judgment, and hastiness should never be a factor when human life is at stake."[33] He was referring to last-minute appeals. As for governors, Duffy wrote, "To commute or not to commute is a question that has been plaguing governors for more than a century, and they should be relieved of this power of life or death so distasteful to most of them."[34]

Duffy hated the death penalty "because of its inhumanity": "Doomed men rot in a private hell while their cases are being appealed, and they continue to rot after a death date is set. They live in the company of misery, not only their own but their neighbors."[35] Duffy believed, "One night on death row is too long, and the length of time spent by the Chessmans and Phyles and Adamsons and De la Rois and Smiths and Allens constitutes cruelty that defies imagination. It has always been a source of wonder to me that they didn't all go stark, raving mad."[36] The Chessman to whom Duffy referred was Caryl Chessman, the so-called "Red Light Bandit," who, in 1948, was convicted on 17 counts, including robbery, kidnapping, sexual abuses, and attempted rape. He was sentenced to death and spent 12 years on death row before his execution. At the time, Chessman's 12 years on death row was an unusually long stay. In 2010, the average time between death sentence and execution for all death row inmates was nearly 15 years.[37] Gary E. Alvord has been on Florida's death row since April 11, 1974. One can only wonder what Duffy might have said about Alvord.

Duffy also hated the death penalty "because it is a brutal spectacle." He noted, "There is nothing good about an execution, and no one is satisfied when it is over. Even those who say that justice has been served leave the death house white and shaking and determined never to return."[38] Duffy participated in executions by hanging and lethal gas. He might have felt differently about an execution's brutality had lethal injection been the mode of execution employed. However, some witnesses to lethal injection executions share Duffy's feelings. Consider, for example, Florida's lethal injection execution of Angel Nieves Diaz on December 13, 2006:

> Mr. Diaz took 34 minutes to die and was seen to be struggling for breath, moving, attempting to speak, and grimacing in pain for the first 24 minutes of the procedure. At his autopsy the medical examiner discovered 11- and 12-inch blisters on his right and left arms, respectively. The problem was that when the execution technician inserted the IV, he pushed the needle through the vein into the surrounding soft tissue. Because the mistake delayed the absorption of the lethal chemicals, Mr. Diaz was administered a second dose.... According to several other ... medical doctors, the blisters on the arms of Mr. Diaz were classic

---

32. Ibid.
33. Ibid., p. 253.
34. Ibid., p. 254.
35. Ibid.
36. Ibid.
37. U.S. Department of Justice, Bureau of Justice Statistics, "Capital Punishment, 2010—Statistical Tables," Table 8 at http://bjs.ojp.usdoj.gov/content/pub/pdf/cp10st.pdf (accessed April 24, 2012).
38. Duffy, op. cit., p. 254.

signs of sodium thiopental entering muscle/flesh, as opposed to the bloodstream, meaning that little or no anesthetic was delivered to his central nervous system before the suffocating drug and the caustic potassium chloride were introduced into his bloodstream.... These same doctors came to a general consensus that the inmate probably died in agony.[39]

Another reason Duffy hated the death penalty was "because it is so horribly unfair." He explained:

A Nixon and a Murphy die after a drunken brawl, while a Bender lives after a deliberately planned murder. A Regan dies and a Fellows lives because a phone call [staying his execution] was made seconds too late; yet both are equally guilty. Three men die for one murder while one man lives after killing five. A Chessman dies for a non-fatal kidnapping while Brown lives after committing an almost identical crime.[40]

He elaborated on the arbitrariness of the penalty with an argument that is as true today as it was more than four decades ago:

A man does not die for the crime he commits. He dies because he committed it in the wrong state, or in the wrong county of that state, or at the wrong time, or because he faced a tough judge or jury goaded by a determined district attorney, or because he couldn't afford adequate counsel. There is no rhyme or reason or consistency to the imposition of the death penalty, for human factors are involved, and the thoughts and actions and conclusions of human beings are variable and unpredictable.[41]

Duffy made another argument about the arbitrary application of the death penalty; an argument (except for the part about rape, which no longer is a capital crime) that continues to be made:

A man dies because of his sex or the color of his skin. Women are rarely executed for crimes comparable to those that lead men to the gallows or the gas chamber or the electric chair; yet their victims are quite as dead, their acts often quite as atrocious. Negroes are more likely to die than white men and for less serious crimes. Rape is a capital offense in most southern states and if committed on a white woman by a Negro almost surely means execution. On the other hand, a white man who murders a Negro may get off scot free.[42]

Duffy also lamented that the death penalty "is a terrible waste of human energy." He remarked:

A Warren or a Chessman or a Greig or a James have [sic] something to contribute to others, even if it must be only to other convicts. Chessman was the best teacher of illiterates I ever saw. Warren had much to offer and, in fact, did many things for his fellow death-row prisoners before he died. James and Greig were more than a cut above the average convict in intelligence. But even the uneducated, the untalented, the untrained can be taught to help others. There is a place for everyone somewhere, in or out of prison; no one is completely bad, completely useless. A Bluebeard Watson can develop into a hospital orderly with the touch

---

39. Gavin Lee (2008) "A Painless Cocktail? The Lethal Injection Controversy," pp. 93-110 in R. M. Bohm (ed.) *The Death Penalty Today*. Boca Raton, FL: CRC Press, pp. 103 and 107.
40. Duffy, op. cit., pp. 254-255.
41. Ibid., p. 255.
42. Ibid.

of a butterfly; a Bill Hightower can write gags and philosophy which give pleasure to thousands of fellow inmates.[43]

Duffy hated the death penalty "because it does not allow for extenuating situations, for mental aberrations or psychological disturbances." Duffy explained:

> I submit that no one who commits a murder is quite sane at the moment of the commission, that even a murder in cold blood has been planned and carried out by a person driven temporarily mad by circumstances beyond his control. I think it is a mistake to judge a man responsible for his actions because he was responsible before and after his crime. It is only his condition *during* the crime that counts, yet rarely is temporary insanity accepted by the jury as a valid defense.[44]

Duffy hated the death penalty "because it makes a mockery of our moral code." According to the warden:

> It is wrong for all to kill as it is for one; yet when the state kills, it's legal and when an individual kills it's not. In effect, the death penalty permits the state to say, "Do as I say, not as I do," and sets a horrible example for others so inclined to follow. Worse, perhaps, it lends logic to the rationalizing of convicts who, almost to a man, present the argument, "If it's all right for you to kill, why shouldn't it be all right for me?" The answer, of course, is that it isn't all right for anyone, but this is more than the criminal mind can grasp.[45]

Duffy hated the death penalty "because it almost always hits the little man, who is not only poor in material possessions but in background, education, and mental capacity as well.... Individuals of better than average ability, like Chessman, are few and far between."[46] This remains true today.

Finally, Duffy hated the death penalty "because it is not the deterrent to crime that its advocates claim." He recounted, "Time after time I have asked men about to die, 'Before you killed, did you stop to think of the consequences?' Invariably the answer was, 'No.' I have asked the same question of thousands of killers who did not get the death penalty but could have, and not one replied that he thought of the punishment when he committed the crime."[47] He further observed:

> Men kill in anger or frustration or jealousy or hatred or fear or cold blood. They planned murders or committed them by accident or what seemed to them necessity. They killed on the spur of the moment because they happened to have weapons in their hands. They killed for money, for love, for revenge, for sex, for satisfaction. They killed to cover up evidence of other crimes. They killed because they were drunk or "hopped up" or mentally ill. But they never expected to get killed themselves. If they thought of anything, it was that they wouldn't be caught. The possibility of execution never entered their minds.... If a man is bent on murder or finds himself in a situation where murder seems the only solution, he will murder, regardless of the penalty. Killing the killer definitely doesn't deter others from killing.[48]

---

43. Ibid., pp. 255-256.
44. Ibid., p. 256.
45. Ibid.
46. Ibid., pp. 256-257.
47. Ibid., p. 22.
48. Ibid., pp. 22-23.

After more than four decades, there is still no evidence that shows that the death penalty has a greater marginal deterrent effect than an alternative penalty such as life imprisonment without opportunity of parole.

What alternative to the death penalty did Duffy support? He did not explicitly say, but it probably was a sentence of imprisonment *with* opportunity of parole. Like his predecessor as warden, Big Jim Holohan, Duffy opposed sentences of life imprisonment without opportunity of parole (LWOP). He wrote:

> When he was warden of San Quentin, Big Jim Holohan used to say, "Rob a man of hope and you rob him of everything." This was one reason why he (Holohan) favored capital punishment. He thought a person was better off dead than having to face a lifetime in confinement, and he was violently opposed to a sentence of life without possibility of parole. To him this was more cruel, more inhuman, more savage than the death penalty.[49]

In the concluding chapter of his fascinating memoir, *88 Men and 2 Women*, Duffy reflected on the 90 people he gave the orders to execute at San Quentin State Prison: "I had accepted this duty because I had to accept it. It was the cross that every warden must bear in a capital punishment state. He knows this goes with the job; if he can't take it he's in the wrong business."[50] Duffy did his duty, but he hated every aspect of it.

Doing the Warden's Duty

Wayne Patterson was a lifelong death penalty opponent. He worked in the Colorado correctional system for more than 40 years and served as warden of the Colorado State Penitentiary in Canon City from 1965 until 1972. He attributed his death penalty opposition to his mother: "I was against it for no particular reason, I guess, other than moral feelings.... I guess it had to do with my mother's religion. My mother taught that only the Divine was the entity that decided life or death."[51]

Despite his opposition, Warden Patterson is known for presiding over the last execution in the United States for a decade. On June 2, 1967, he pulled the lever to initiate the execution of Luis Jose Monge by lethal gas. Executions did not resume in the United States until 1977, when Gary Gilmore was executed by a Utah firing squad. Monge's execution was the only one that Patterson conducted. About that execution, he employed a familiar rationalization: "If you want to be the warden, you do the warden's duty."[52]

Doing the warden's duty, as has been documented here, is rarely easy. Patterson wrote that his predecessor, Harry Tinsley (1955-65), who notched eight executions, "advocated for abolition and would get sick every time he had to kill someone.... Harry Tinsley died

---

49. Ibid., p. 175.
50. Ibid., p. 252.
51. Terje Langeland, "The Executioner's Song: Job's Not all It's Cracked Up to Be," *Colorado Springs Independent* (July 6, 2009) at www.csindy.com/gyrobase/Content?oid=oid%3A6093 (accessed July 6, 2009).
52. Ibid.

a thousand deaths each time." According to Patterson, following an execution, Warden Tinsley "went to bed ill."[53]

Patterson diminished his execution responsibilities by sharing them with the pro-death penalty citizens of Colorado. He remarked, "As far as I was concerned, every person that voted for it in Colorado at that [1966] referendum [favoring executions] had his hand on the lever, same as I did."[54] One difficulty for wardens, according to Patterson, is "You become acquainted with them [the death row inmates].... Now, your gonna kill them? It isn't very pleasant."[55] Like so many other wardens, Patterson was all too familiar with the arbitrary nature of capital punishment. He observed:

> I know, personally, of so many people that are so depraved, they would stomp you out like an ant on the floor if they got the chance.... But those weren't the ones who got executed.... They were either too smart to get caught, or rich enough to hire good lawyers. Monge was a guilt-ridden man who was nearly suicidal before he was executed.... Those were the [kind of] guys who were executed—not the people I thought belonged in the chamber.[56]

Also, like some many other wardens, Patterson did not believe that the death penalty was a general deterrent. He noted, "I've had murders in the shadow of the gas chamber.... They don't think about it [the death penalty]."[57] He is convinced that the switch to the more "humane" lethal injection method is also indicative of people's unease about the death penalty. However, he considers that rationale a "sham." States Patterson: "No execution is any more humane than any other.... You're dead when it's over."[58]

Patterson believed that Colorado, like so many other death penalty states, "likes to have the law on the books, but they don't want to use it.... There was thirty years between executions—what does that tell you?"[59] That pattern has held in Colorado during the modern death penalty era. As of August 15, 2012, Colorado had executed only one other person since it executed Monge in 1967.

Would My God Forgive Me?

Another prison warden who opposes the death penalty is Donald A. Cabana, who has served as warden of several different prisons in Florida, Missouri, and Mississippi. He did not always oppose the death penalty, however. In his memoir, *Death at Midnight: The Confessions of an Executioner*, Cabana explained his conversion:

> I spent most of my career as a prison administrator convinced of the need for capital punishment. I had always been something of a bureaucratic utopian, fully committed to the notion that if the government deemed capital punishment necessary then it must be so. I had forgotten to search beyond the law and political

---

53. Ibid.
54. Lifton and Mitchell, op. cit., p. 78.
55. Langeland, op. cit.
56. Ibid.
57. Ibid.
58. Ibid.
59. Ibid.

rhetoric and examine the morality of it all. Not until I was confronted with supervising and carrying out the ultimate retribution did I begin to question the
process in earnest. The execution of Edward Earl Johnson served as a milestone,
an event at which to pause and wonder. But it was the execution of Connie Ray
Evans that became, for me, a personal moment of truth.[60]

Just before Evans's execution, Cabana recalled, "Contemplating the difficulty of watching
a man die, especially when strapped in a chair while his lungs are filled with poison gas,
I shook my head. What the hell was I doing here? How had my career come to this? It all
seemed so unreal, yet I knew that reality was only moments away."[61]

Evans's execution on July 8, 1987, was not Cabana's first. For that one, Missouri's Bill
Armontrout came to Mississippi to help his friend and, as Armontrout put it, "do a com-
plimentary one for him."[62] Nevertheless, for Cabana, Evan's execution had a greater
personal meaning for him than any other:

> In the course of almost four years, during my many visits as warden to death
> row, we [Evans and Cabana] had developed something of a relationship. Getting
> to know him had been a rewarding experience, and our communication with
> each other was something I believed we both genuinely looked forward to. Now
> it was all rapidly coming to an end, as the time arrived for me to give the order
> that would put him to death.[63]

Before taking the final walk, Evans, Cabana, and the chaplain prayed. When they
finished, Evans asked Cabana "if the warden would be embarrassed if an inmate hugged
him." Cabana, "searching fruitlessly for comforting words," silently embraced Evans "for
a long moment."[64] As officers strapped Evans into the chair, Cabana remembers silently
praying "for a quick and painless death for my prisoner, and a process free of mechanical
failure or human error for me."[65] Both mechanical failure and human error during
executions had occurred in the past. Cabana then related, "Suddenly aware of feeling
exhausted from the emotional roller coaster I had been on, I knew I would feel relieved
when it was all over."[66]

Cabana then walked into the chamber to read the death warrant and ask Evans if he
had any last words. Cabana described what happened next:

> Positioning myself directly in front of my prisoner, fumbling with the death warrant
> in shaking hands, I slowly began to read the document. In a quivering, staccato
> voice, I read for what seemed an eternity. Gazing into Connie's eyes, I stumbled
> through the closing chapter of this bizarre ritual, asking him if he wished to make
> a final public statement. His eyes welled with tears now, and I was struck by his
> childlike appearance. This was not the same cold-blooded murderer who had arrived
> on death row six years before. His tears were not just those of a young man fearful
> of what lay beyond death's door; I was convinced they were also tears of genuine
> sorrow and pain for the tragic hurt and sadness he had caused so many people.[67]

---

60. Donald A. Cabana (1996) *Death at Midnight: The Confession of an Executioner*. Boston: Northeastern University Press, p xi.
61. Ibid., p. 4.
62. Lifton and Mitchell, op. cit., p. 80.
63. Cabana, op. cit., p. 6.
64. Ibid., p. 9.
65. Ibid., p. 10.
66. Ibid., p. 12.
67. Ibid., p. 14.

Cabana continued: "How insane the whole process seemed! I knew this man, I believed his life was worth saving. I had argued so forcefully to the governor. Even though he [the governor] was privately sympathetic, legally and politically there were no grounds that would allow him to justify commuting Connie's death sentence."[68] Cabana had not forgotten the victims of Evans' crime—a widowed wife and children left fatherless—but he "questioned how an execution would end the lifelong pain and suffering endured by the victim's family."[69] He thought to himself, "Killing Connie Ray Evans would not bring his victim back from the grave."[70] Cabana added quickly, "I was not feeling sorry for him, or pitying him. Evans had committed a terrible crime, for which he needed to spend the rest of his natural life in prison."[71]

Evans asked to whisper his final words to Cabana privately, and Cabana leaned down to hear them. Evans thanked Cabana for being his friend. Evans then said, "From one Christian to another, I love you."[72] Cabana was speechless and related being in shock, "shaken to my very soul." Since the execution of Edward Earl Johnson less than two months earlier, Cabana "had slept with troubled dreams, fitfully trying to make sense of the whole thing."[73] Looking at Evans, Cabana wondered to himself whether he would ever sleep peacefully again.

Cabana stepped out of the chamber and ordered it sealed, "realizing that some of my self remained inside."[74] He then explained, "There is part of the warden that dies with his prisoner. Nobody else can suffer the intimacy of impending death, or experience the pitiable helplessness involved, in the same way as the warden and his condemned prisoner. Both are victims, unwilling captives of a human tragedy that is presented on a stage shrouded by mystery."[75]

Following the execution, Cabana offered a now familiar rationalization:

> There was a certain philosophy I had developed regarding the entire issue of capital punishment. My personal feelings were not germane to any part of the process. I had a job to do; I did not look forward to carrying out an execution; I tried to handle the situation as just another part of the job. I had often witnessed the cold, unfeeling violence of inmates, and over time my senses became numbed by it. I presumptuously concluded that I was both prepared and well suited for playing the role of executioner.[76]

Cabana realized he was wrong:

> Nothing, however, could prepare me for what I saw and felt when I supervised my first execution. There is nothing commonplace about walking a healthy young man to a room, strapping him into a chair, and coldly, methodically killing him. I knew after the first one that if it ever did become routine, if I found myself no longer haunted by doubt, then I would know the time had come for me to leave corrections behind.[77]

---

68. Ibid.
69. Ibid., p. 15.
70. Ibid.
71. Ibid.
72. Ibid., p. 16.
73. Ibid.
74. Ibid.
75. Ibid.
76. Ibid., p. 17.
77. Ibid.

Cabana concluded, "I stood there, worried what my wife and children and my friends would think of me. But most of all, I wondered if my God would forgive me."[78]

Feeling Dirty and Like a Pawn

The final prison warden discussed in this chapter is Ron McAndrew, whose experience with executions converted him into an ardent death penalty opponent. Before his retirement in 2002, McAndrew had been involved in Florida corrections for twenty-three years, working his way up the ranks from entry-level correctional officer to warden. McAndrew was in charge of three executions—all of them electrocutions—and he also shadowed all aspects of five lethal-injection executions at the Walls Unit in Huntsville, Texas. He was sent to Texas to learn about lethal injection executions when the Florida legislature changed Florida's method of execution.

For the executions he supervised, McAndrew's responsibilities included choosing the execution team and training them daily prior to an execution. Before his first execution, however, he needed to know what to do. He explained how he learned the process:

> Initially I assembled the existing execution team and relied on each member to teach me their role as outlined in a secret instructional document. Then as a team, we would over a period of three or four weeks prior to executions have mock executions, as much as 40 times per day with actual use of electricity with the electrical connectors inside a five gallon bucket of saline solution. When the electricity was turned on, the [approximately] 2,200 volts and 13 amps would immediately boil this solution. We used volunteer officers to take the position of the condemned. There were a few men I immediately removed from this job, as I observed indications of trauma. Only when I knew the job of every member of the execution team did I proceed.

McAndrew related how he selected corrections officers to participate in executions:

> Carefully. Some would request to be on the team thinking perhaps it would further their career, while some wanted just to be in on the "action." I would review their personnel files and those with excessive uses of force, questionable uses of force, and serious discipline and/or acting out were not selected. Some, such as the [two] electricians ... had been on the team for many years, and although I wanted to change one of them, it wasn't possible as staff resources didn't have another who was qualified.

The execution team's training was described above. As far as how prepared they were to participate in executions, McAndrew noted, "No person is adequately prepared to kill another person. I learned this quickly and feel for those I subjected to this barbaric act." McAndrew had mixed feeling about how prepared he was at his first execution:

> Yes [he was prepared] in terms of my training. No [he was not prepared] in the sense that I realized that the Iron Triangle was filled to the brim with snakes lurking to strike out at me because I didn't "fit" their *persona* of a shotgun toting, tobacco chewing/spitting, "Cool Hand Luke" warden with soiled overalls who'd turn a blind eye to well known FSP [Florida State Prison] shenanigans. [The

---

78. Ibid., p. 18.

"Iron Triangle" refers to a cluster of prisons and lockups in rural north-central Florida that are linked by members of extended families who staff the facilities.] The shenanigans were of course the beatings, staged fights, torture and other forms of "pleasure" to break up the boredom of working on the "chain-gang."

In Florida, the warden typically selects the executioner from thousands of citizen volunteers. McAndrew related his method:

> When I first arrived at FSP, I was asked by my secretary if I wanted to meet the executioner. I asked if we'd ever had a problem with him/her, and if we had a backup. I was advised by the colonel that he had always been present and that his secrecy had been maintained. I stated that I did not care to meet him personally before an execution and for that matter as long as he did his job correctly, I did not need to even know his name. The shocker came after the second execution (by this time I'd gotten to know many of the staff members). After the execution, I gave the executioner (always in a black gown with a black hood … much like that of the KKK) his $150.00, and as I shook his small hand I looked at his eyes and realized that he was a member of my own staff. I never let anyone know that I knew.

As for the executioner's training, McAndrew revealed, "The process is so simple for the executioner that little if any training is needed. Five minutes only to explain that when he is told to turn a knob to the left by the warden he is to do so. If the executioner fails to turn the knob the warden will then become the executioner."

McAndrew described the experience of his first execution and the effect it had on him:

> I felt the operation was professional, and that we had done our job as required by law. Still, I had a knot in my chest that didn't want to go away. I just kept telling myself it was stress, and that the death penalty was proper. In those times, it was customary for the warden to take the execution team to breakfast (executions were at 7:00 a.m. then) following the execution. We all went to Shoney's in Starke. As we (all 8 of us) walked into the restaurant, it was instantly visible that we were all known and that everyone present knew who we were. There were even a few high signs. We ordered the buffet. Stirring my eggs into my grits, I looked over the shoulder of [one of my staff members] and I observed a woman turning her head in my direction. We locked eyes, and I recognized her as the defense attorney for the man we had just killed. Somehow I saw my own sickness on her face. It was a sight that'll never leave me.

Each subsequent execution had a profound impact on McAndrew:

> Each new execution brought me closer to the hearth in terms of disgust. Somehow I still supported the death penalty … or at least told myself to speak in its favor, but a sickening feeling of the act of killing itself was growing steadily. The second execution was difficult in that I didn't believe the jury in this condemned man's case had enough evidence to send him to his death. I had read all of the material, the investigations, the courtroom documents, and other so called evidence, and there simply wasn't enough there to vote for the death penalty. As I spoke with attorney friends at the time, I began to realize that "justice" is but a word and that the drama of the courtroom is all that counts. If the state has a flamboyant prosecutor with big political ambitions, and if this prosecutor is a great courtroom "actor," he can convince jurors of most anything. It was following this execution that I decided that most courtroom decisions on the death penalty involved theatrics and little other.

McAndrew then described what it was like to deal with the condemned's family members:

> This was very difficult. Once I had the mother and two sisters of a condemned prisoner in my office. I kept a small refrigerator in the office and offered them soft drinks and cold water. I moved from behind my desk, as I customarily did with all visitors, and joined them around a coffee table. The three were very nervous, and I was trying to make a horrible situation as bearable as possible. One of the sisters started out by saying that they really didn't know why they were there, that they'd never experienced anything like this, and simply didn't know what to do. I quickly let this family know that I'd do anything possible that was within the law … [that is,] I'd bend all local rules, whatever I could do to help make their lives as tolerable as possible during this process. I reminded them that the son/brother had an appeal under review. I likewise assured them that I'd make certain their son/brother was well treated by staff while in this particular status. It was near the end of the interview that the shocker awaited me. The mother of the condemned looked me straight into the eyes and said, "Warden, I just don't know what to do. I'm scared. But I just want to know one thing: will I be able to kiss my baby before y'all kill him?" I was able to hold back the tears until the three had left my office that chilly day in Raiford, FL.

He continued:

> It was difficult. It's important to note that when I first arrived at Florida State Prison I found that the warden's secretary had …"assumed [a] position of authority" and took it upon herself to tell such families that "the warden doesn't deal with such things," and that they should telephone the chaplain. My first confrontation at Florida State Prison was with my secretary, letting her know in plain terms that both of us were public servants, and that we served the public, and that the families of condemned inmates were innocent members of the public and thus were our actual bosses. I don't know if I was the first warden to take on this role. Throughout my career in corrections at whatever level of authority, I always accepted telephone calls and/or visits from members of the public and let my staff know the same was expected of them. This did not go over well at FSP initially, but like most change, it fell into place.

McAndrew also described what it was like to deal with the victim's family members:

> This was likewise difficult. All of the victim's families that I met both in Florida and in Texas were not vengeful and exhibiting anger, but were in fact doubtful of the killing of the person who had allegedly killed one of their own: WITH ONE HUGE EXCEPTION. At one execution the sister of the victim asked me if she could watch "this scumbag go to hell," and I agreed. From the moment I met this sister I never observed a smile or a soft gesture. She was an arms crossed, tight fisted woman with so much anger housed up inside that it was scary. She was strikingly beautiful and dressed in European fashion to the hilt. She asked if she could have a "front seat" in the death house directly in front of the condemned. I agreed. As we were about to execute the condemned, I looked through the glass at this very lovely woman sitting braced to the back of the chair with her left hand in a fist and her right hand clutching the fist. Her expression was one of hate as I'd never seen. As the electricity passed through the body of the condemned, her lips closed tightly and her eyes were glued toward this now charred body. Following the execution and back near the administration building

I saw the woman and her expression had not changed. The hate was still there, and I've pitied her since that time for the suffering she puts herself through.

He added, "It was difficult to have the same empathy for those carrying such hate."

As for the condemned inmates' behavior prior to their executions, McAndrew stated, "The inmates' behaviors were most always subtle and laid back. It was almost as if a resolve of some sort had taken over." He had this to say about his own behavior prior to the executions he supervised:

Professionally, for the larger part, following past and new procedures that I had laid down. There was one case where I sat on the bunk of a condemned inmate and began reading to him his "death warrant" signed by the governor and secretary of the state. I advised him that I didn't want to put him through this, but that it was required by law. He nodded his head affirmatively, and I began reading. Since I was about 10 minutes away from killing this man, I found the words a bit difficult. The condemned prisoner noticed my difficulty and with his left elbow nudged me in the side slightly and said, "It's OK boss-man. I'm ready."

McAndrew startled by the inmate's comment thought to himself: "I'm getting ready to kill him, and he's trying to make it easy on me."

McAndrew described his feelings about his executions: "Depending on the execution, feelings differed. The more of the killing I participated in the more disgusted I became ... first with the morbid act and finally with the moral issue of killing those who'd allegedly killed others. I say allegedly because I know in my heart that there are innocent people on death row."

In at least one case, McAndrew had gained the trust of an inmate he eventually executed:

Pedro Medina pretended he was insane weeks before his execution. This began immediately following a meeting with his attorney one day. He'd crawl around the floor barking as a dog, hanging from the bar stock and chirping as a monkey. After days and days of this acting out, I went into his cell ... sat down and told the officers to back off. Privately, I told Medina that I needed him to be sane long enough for me to get some important questions answered. I assured him that I'd not document it or tell the authorities, but that we needed to know what he wanted as a last meal and some other issues. For a few minutes he dropped the insane act, I got my answers and this continued on up until moments before his execution. I'd go down to see him, and he'd stop barking long enough for me to take care of business. This wasn't a "personal" relationship, but it was a feeling of "trust."

The "relationship" he had formed with Pedro Medina made Medina's execution especially difficult for the warden:

Following Medina's execution I began to feel dirty [because I] associated myself with the act. Moreover, I began to feel as a pawn for the filthy chest pounding politicians who had asked me to do this dirty work. I began [to] question why anyone would hide out in the governor's office with a speaker phone waiting to hear that the killing they'd ordered had been carried out. [Following his execution] [t]here was a serious psychological emptiness in my stomach. I began to go home, shower for a long time, change clothing, and try to send the guilt down the drain.

As for how Medina's execution affected McAndrew during the execution, McAndrew said, "During executions everything is very tense. Anxious feelings abound in terms of the team ... and certainly the condemned."

Executions also affect other death row inmates. Regarding those effects, McAndrew commented:

> Solemn. There is little to celebrate on death row during and following an execution. Note that the only "real people" death row prisoners get to know are those housed in the same vicinity. (Inmates on death row are confined 24/7 with the exception of one hour of exercise per day and showers on Monday, Wednesday and Friday.) Perhaps over a period of more than 20 years one prisoner plays chess with the person in the next cell (they have a method of laying the board on the floor between the cells and each can reach the board and pieces by pulling and pushing the board back and forth) and sharing inner thoughts one would only share with those closest to him … and then, suddenly his closest friend in the world is hauled down the hallway and out of sight. The only remaining contact for this friend will be to put his tiny battery operated radio to his ear on the morning of the execution to hear the sordid details from some network representative who'd attended the political killing.

As for the effects of an execution, and the hours leading up to an execution, on the general population inmates, McAndrew observed, "Thirty percent of those incarcerated at FSP are mentally sick people who should be in hospitals rather than in prisons. As a result, some actually celebrate the death, while the vast majority are likewise solemn. Total lockdown occurs before and after executions."

An execution, and the hours leading up to an execution, also affects other correctional personnel who are not involved with the execution. McAndrew explained their response:

> Apprehension. Correctional staff is apprehensive as they have been taught to be over the years. It's always suspected that "something" could go wrong and a riot or prison fire could erupt … or both. Things are generally very tense around the prison for a day or two before and after executions. I always tried to get a little something extra in terms of desserts or special foods on the trays at this time, much as a pacifier.

One of a warden's execution responsibilities is dealing with the media. McAndrew provided this anecdote about interacting with the media:

> A wonderful and extremely talented man by the name of Gene Morris was the media representative for the Florida Department of Corrections. Gene would meet with the media, give them my statement (that he had helped me draft), and set up interviews for me before the satellite dishes across the street from FSP. Without Gene's guidance I'd [have] probably waded into waters either too deep or too hot with the news crocodiles. One network asked me one day following an execution, "Well warden, how do you feel about putting this man to death?" I responded with "I earn my keep."

McAndrew provided another interesting anecdote about his dealings with the media following an execution: "Some were nice, and some were not so nice. Jane Pauley was the rudest person I ever dealt with as the warden at FSP. For years I'd admiringly watched this dainty little lady on TV and never would have believed the kind of language she would use over the phone when denied a media request."

For McAndrew, the most important aspect of conducting an execution was: "Safety of everyone and the prison as a unit. Security is paramount. Extra staff is available and well briefed. Outside security such as the Florida Highway Patrol is on hand to assist if necessary."

The most difficult aspect of conducting an execution for McAndrew was: "The final minutes of having the condemned stand in his cell, have the Assistant Warden for Operations and the Colonel snap stainless steel grips onto each of his wrists, and cup his armpit with the remaining hands as he's led down the 38-foot walkway to the death room."

"The barbaric act of killing a fellow soul in itself" was the worst aspect of conducting an execution, according to McAndrew. Asked whether he believed that he ever executed an innocent person, that is, a person innocent of the crime for which he was convicted and sentenced to death, McAndrew replied, "I believe there is a distinct possibility that we executed an innocent person. I can say this much ... that the man we killed was the victim of courtroom theatrics because the papers I read didn't have the hard cold evidence needed to send one to death row. His defense attorneys were inept in my opinion."

The executions that he supervised have affected him mentally and emotionally. McAndrew confessed, "I am scarred, but I'm in the healing process. Examining myself as a human being following Florida State Prison, I found that I didn't like myself very much. I felt hypocritical, shamed, and dirty for doing the filthy work of politicians." He added:

> Executions affect [me] terribly. Each time I fax a letter to a governor asking for clemency before an execution I wonder if it's another Juan Melendez. [Melendez was released from Florida's death row in January 2002, after serving nearly 18 years for a murder he did not commit.] Is Alabama, Virginia, or Tennessee killing an innocent person today? As one exoneree said to me in Nebraska sometime back, "Ron, you can pardon a man from a cell, but it's hard to do it from the grave."

McAndrew has experienced lingering effects from participating in executions, but they have given him direction: "[I]t's these 'effects' that prompt and excite me to fight the death penalty today." Finally, in response to the question of whether his opinion of the death penalty had been affected by his execution experience, he stated, "Absolutely."

Conclusion

That prison wardens, who are most familiar with the execution process, find it an abomination is telling. That their jobs require them to conduct executions despite their feelings about them is unconscionable. In the absence of capital punishment, the warden's job in prisons where executions are conducted would be lightened — no death row, no deathwatch, no executions. At the very least, the thoughts of prison wardens about capital punishment should be given serious consideration in debates about the subject.

Prison wardens do not supervise death row inmates and conduct executions alone. They manage death row corrections officers and execution team members, who assist them in their responsibilities. These employees also are affected by their roles in the capital punishment process, and it is to their stories that we turn next.

Chapter 11

Death Row Corrections Officers and Execution Team Members

Corrections officers have two distinct jobs in the capital punishment process. One is to guard death row inmates and tend to their needs; the other is to serve as a member of the execution team. As the name implies, these officers assist with executions. Rarely does a corrections officer perform both jobs at the same time. Also included on the execution team are prison chaplains.

The job of death row corrections officer has been described as stressful, frightening, boring, depressing, and thankless. Executions can be difficult for some death row corrections officers because they have shared the same environment with some inmates for many years and have sometimes developed meaningful friendships with them. However, most officers are careful not to become close with their wards. Many officers consciously remain emotionally detached from the execution; they receive neither pleasure nor pain from it. Most death row correctional officers support the death penalty.

The execution team—or deathwatch team, as it is sometimes called—is responsible for carrying out executions. In prisons that conduct executions, execution team members generally are considered "the cream of the correctional officer corps." An execution is a very ritualized process in which each team member has a specifically defined job to do. The division of labor makes the execution psychologically easier for the participants by making the execution a collective responsibility. Nevertheless, execution team members ride an emotional roller coaster during an execution, particularly when a stay of execution is granted.

Team members generally form a close bond with one another. Most believe that an execution "needs to be done," and they take pride in "doing it right," which means "doing it professionally," without emotion or sensation. However, some execution team members have been traumatized by their experiences.

Prison chaplains are an instrumenetal part of the execution team. Prison administrators believe that it is important to have the prison chaplain present during the deathwatch and execution to address any staff problems that might arise; to console victims' and offenders' family members, if needed; and to minister to the condemned inmate, if the inmate wishes. They also help make condemned inmates compliant for execution by offering them a way to salvation. This chapter investigates the roles of death row correctional officers and execution team members in the capital punishment process.

Preserving the Bodies of the Condemned

Work on death row has been described as follows:

> [A] stressful and often frightening assignment that too readily lends itself to in-different and even abusive treatment of the condemned prisoners.... Death row guards are enjoined solely to preserve the bodies of the condemned—to feed them in their cells or in common areas, to conduct them to out-of-cell activities, to watch them at all times. In large measure, the officers are reduced to intrusive waiters and unwanted escorts.... Not surprisingly, like the prisoners, the guards are bored and tense much of the time. Some even report being depressed by their circumscribed, thankless jobs.[1]

A female Texas death row corrections officer described how depressing her job was:

> It's not just tough, it's very depressing.... There are not too many people who can do this—who can walk in and see someone who you know has killed somebody or raped a child, who's not been out in the free world for ten or fifteen years. You have to get very callous, feeding a guy that spits in your face and says, "Yeah, and I'd kill *your* mother too." (emphasis in original)[2]

The number-one responsibility of death row corrections officers is security. As one officer put it:

> This is a security job: to keep them [the death row inmates] protected while they're here and to keep them from getting out. Anytime they go anyplace within the building or outside it, they have to have waist chains, leg irons, and all this stuff. So you have to act as a buffer between them and the inmates who are "free." So it's a form of protective custody. You have to protect them from the other inmates because they can't protect themselves.[3]

Death row inmates also need protection from one another. Because of the stress on death row, inmates sometimes act out; violent men become violent. Fights generally are broken up on command. However, when they are not, death row officers usually do not enter the fray but instead call on the prison tactical squad to break up the fight. That way, both the inmates and the death row officers are protected.[4]

The relationship between death row officers and death row inmates tends to vary between two ends of a continuum. On one end, the two parties are "overtly hostile, with harassment and counterharassment as a common form of exchange," and, at the other end, "impersonal, with little or no contact."[5] Most officers and their charges are able to reach an uneasy accommodation, and a few officers and inmates are even able "to transcend the limitations of their role[s] and develop normal, if generally superficial,

---

1. Robert Johnson (1998) *DEATHWORK: A Study of the Modern Execution Process*, 2nd ed. Belmont, CA: West/Wadsworth, p. 109.
2. Susan Blaustein (1997) "Witness to Another Execution," Pp. 387-400 in H. A. Bedau (ed.) *The Death Penalty in America: Current Controversies*. New York; Oxford University Press, p 391.
3. Johnson, op. cit., p. 113.
4. Ibid.
5. Ibid., p. 109.

human relationships."[6] However, as one death row inmate put it: "They [officers] don't make friends ... they just do their job and go home."[7]

Both officers and inmates feel vulnerable to violence, although the actual incidence of violence on death rows is quite low. This mutual fear of violence is said to cause hate, which, of course, elevates the chances of violence.[8] The long history of prison guard abuse of death row inmates is common knowledge among inmates and, thus, they are ever vigilant of violent confrontations with officers. Death row's custodial restrictions constantly remind both groups that inmate violence is expected. Officers know that inmates have proven they are violent (at least those who are not innocent) and have a great incentive to escape. Officers typically believe that because the inmates have nothing to lose and are forced to live in a prison's most deprived environment, they have no compunction about killing an officer.

On "reformed" death rows, where inmates are allowed to congregate out of their cells in small groups, the fear of violence is even greater. As one officer put it, "They will hurt you to get away. You've got to watch them all the time. You know if they get a chance, you're gone. They'll kill you. They've all killed before."[9] Another officer expressed a similar sentiment: "There was always that thought in your mind, 'If they ever get out of here, I'm as good as dead.' I feel they don't have anything to lose. If we get in their way, they just get rid of us quick."[10] One officer doubted that the custodial restrictions on death row inmates do much good: "If they want to escape, they can.... Somebody's going to slip up somewhere along the line."[11]

Officers differ in what they consider the most dangerous assignments on death row. One officer was most afraid of "taking inmates to recreation." Another officer most feared "counts," the security practice of physically counting inmates at certain times during the day. "I worry there'll be one hiding 'round the corner,'" he said, "and I'll have to go and find him."[12] A third officer remarked, "I'm uncomfortable working in the open area [in the hall] near the control station."[13] Still another officer, though he did not outwardly show it, was always afraid on death row because of knowledge of the inmates' crimes. That most death row inmates usually are docile made no difference. He maintained, "You can't judge a book by its cover. You've never seen him mad."[14]

Perhaps death row corrections officers' greatest fear, next to being killed, is being taken hostage. As one officer observed, "The inmates constantly threaten to take hostages.... Some of it is joking ... but the risk of one day becoming a hostage is very real."[15] Officers are fatalistic about this. They can envision a scenario where, one day, a preoccupied control room officer opens the wrong door at the wrong time and allows inmates to get the drop on an unsuspecting and defenseless hall officer. An officer had this to say about being taken hostage: "Anybody can get attacked or taken hostage at any time. But I just

---

6. Ibid.
7. Ibid.
8. Ibid., p. 110.
9. Ibid.
10. Ibid.
11. Ibid.
12. Ibid.
13. Ibid.
14. Ibid.
15. Ibid.

have a job to do, and I just go ahead and do it and hope that nothing will happen. I just try to do my job, be alert and observant, and nothing should go wrong. If it does, I'll just have to deal with it."[16] Another officer stated, "You know who you're dealing with, *what* you're dealing with, but you have to deal with it as it comes. You do what you have to do in the line of your duties, your job. You focus on what you're doing." (emphasis in original)[17]

A Missouri corrections officer remarked that he had a healthy fear of the inmates—not so much a fear of physical assault, though there was some of that, but rather a fear of being used by the inmates. (Missouri does not have a death row. Inmates sentenced to death are mixed with inmates sentenced to life imprisonment without opportunity of parole and life imprisonment plus fifty years at the Potosi Correctional Center.) The officer clarified what he meant:

> If you ever let your guard down, one time.... These inmates are in here twenty-four hours a day, figuring out a way to circumvent the system. And if they can use you as a correctional officer to do that, they are going to do it. And they are good at it. Their byline is con, and yeah, they can con you out of your shorts. They don't have to do it immediately; they can do it over the next ten years and do it so slowly, and so easily. It's kind of like the bullfrog in boiling water: He doesn't even realize he's in boiling water until he's dead. And that same thing happens in corrections. These guys are *so* smooth, and over a period of time they've got you doing things for them. (emphasis in original)[18]

Regarding fear for his physical safety, the officer stated:

> You know, people ask me, "Well, aren't you ever scared?" And I say, "Yes, sir. I'm scared every time I go in there." But it's the control of fear that makes the difference between a good officer and not a good officer. Some of the officers probably wouldn't tell you that they fear. They have fear at times, but I think they have good control of their fear. I think that makes the difference between a mediocre or a bad officer, and a good officer. He knows that he's scared, and he knows how to control it. And he knows how to keep himself out of a bad situation.[19]

The officer noted that fear can cause anger, which can lead to a bad situation:

> We had an incident here just in the last month or so where we had some fluids being thrown on officers and officers being spat on. There is no doubt in my mind that if someone spits on me, my anger is going to flare, because I'm a human being. And I'm afraid somebody is going to get the crap knocked out of them. It might be me but, hey, if somebody spits on me I'm just that type of guy. You don't spit on me and get away with it. So certainly those officers, in my mind, have the right to be angry when someone throws body fluids or spits on them. And, yeah, there's times when possibly there is an excessive use of force because of an incident where an inmate spits on someone.[20]

---

16. Ibid., p. 111.
17. Ibid.
18. Stephen Trombley (1992) *The Execution Protocol: Inside America's Capital Punishment Industry.* New York: Crown Publishers, p. 205.
19. Ibid., p. 206.
20. Ibid.

Fear of their charges affects the officers' job performance. Some fearful officers attempt to gain compliance by placating the inmates. These officers bend or ignore the rules "to keep it calm in there and to make their day go by."[21] As one officer remarked, "Anybody facing death, they gotta be dangerous. If he calls and he needs something, you got to try to get it for him."[22] Other officers "get too personally involved"; they are accused of "playing" with inmates instead of controlling them; of being "slap happy" and "sloppy" in following rules.[23] These officers slap inmates on the back and tell them: "'You're my buddy'.... 'You're my partner. I know you're not going to hurt me because we're stick buddies.'"[24] The problem with these fawning officers, according to one officer, is that death row "is no place to play. If you get that far gone, I think you better get out."[25] By catering to the inmates, these officers, in the minds of many of their colleagues, compromise their authority, undermine their ability to control, and jeopardize security.

Some officers respond to fear by becoming arrogant, domineering, and menacing. Such officers also are seen as a liability to their more humane fellow workers. As one officer related, "We have some hard cases. I could have everything calm, but this one guy wouldn't be there but two seconds and he'd rile 'em up so. When he left, you could hear the inmates down the hall, he'd rile 'em up so ... Just some small remark or something he'd know would get 'em riled."[26]

In some cases, officers are not mean *per se*, but, because of poor self-control, react inappropriately to the inmates' baiting. Inmates, after all, can be "impatient, touchy, demanding, and given to wide mood swings that sometimes end in tirades."[27] Whether officers are lax or abusive, both types of behavior can incite incidents that jeopardize the security of both the officers and the inmates.

As noted at the outset of this chapter, rarely do death row corrections officers participate directly in executions, yet most death row inmates view the officers as complicit. One death row inmate stated, "We know within ourselves that no matter how courteous a guard tries to be to us, we know what he will do in the end. And so that right there makes us guard against them."[28] A death row officer observed, "You can feel the tension in the air after an execution.... I think they are angry at anybody with a [correctional] uniform."[29]

Because of long stays on death rows, some inmates develop close relationships with their fellow captives. Executions can produce a complex set of emotions on the inmates left behind, including profound loss, powerlessness, and vulnerability. Of course, executions are also a grisly reminder of their own impending fate. Not surprisingly, then, some inmates direct their rage at death row corrections officers, even though they were not a part of the execution team. The reason is that the officers are the only people available to lash out at, other than other death row inmates.[30]

---

21. Johnson, op. cit., p. 111.
22. Ibid.
23. Ibid.
24. Ibid.
25. Ibid.
26. Ibid., p. 112.
27. Ibid.
28. Ibid., p. 114.
29. Ibid., p. 115.
30. Ibid.

Executions can also be difficult for some death row corrections officers. After sharing the same environment for many years, officers and inmates sometimes develop meaningful friendships. Thus, an inmate's execution can be a sad and depressing experience for an officer. However, most officers are careful not to develop close relationships with their wards. Many officers consciously remain emotionally detached from the execution; they receive neither pleasure nor pain from it. One officer commented, "You can't be buddy-buddy ... you've got to keep it business."[31]

In one of the few empirical studies of death row corrections officers, data were collected in 2002, in what the study's authors reported as an unnamed correctional facility in a Midwestern state that houses the state's death row.[32] However, from material in the article, it was apparent that Indiana was the Midwestern state. As of this writing, Indiana had executed only nineteen death row inmates since 1976. In 2002, when the study's data were collected, the state had thirty-eight inmates on death row.[33]

Death row corrections officers in Indiana were selected "via a union bid system or through a selection process initiated by the administration."[34] A total of forty corrections officers who had worked on Indiana's death row completed surveys, although only nine of the officers were working on death row at the time.[35] About two-thirds of the officers were male, approximately 56 percent were white, and 36 percent were black. A little more than half had some college education, and a little more than one-third had only a high school diploma or GED. Nearly half were married, and about 31 percent were divorced. The mean age of the officers was thirty-eight, but ages ranged from twenty-one to sixty-seven. Years of correctional officer experience ranged from less than one year to twenty-seven years, with a mean of nearly seven years. Officers worked on death row from one month to seven years, with an average of about sixteen months, although not all of that time was worked consecutively.[36]

Nearly 90 percent of the officers surveyed supported the death penalty, although white officers were more likely than black officers to support it. The death penalty was an "important" (61%) or "one of the most important" (17.9%) issues to almost 80 percent of the officers. It was "not very important" to only about 20 percent of the officers. More than 90 percent of officers had not changed their death penalty opinion as a result of their experiences supervising offenders sentenced to death, and approximately 90 percent of the officers were "somewhat unlikely" (23.1%) or "very unlikely" (64.1%) to change their death penalty opinion.[37] Only 7.5 percent of the officers had ever witnessed an execution, and only 30 percent of them had been required to participate in the execution process as part of their responsibilities as a corrections officer.[38] That may have been because so few executions had been conducted during the time they worked on death row, or the officers who participated were no longer working at the institution.[39]

---

31. Ibid., p. 116.
32. Kelly L. Brown and Melissa Benningfield (2008) "Death Row Correctional Officers: Experiences, Perspectives, and Attitudes." *Criminal Justice Review* 33: 524-540.
33. Ibid., p. 526.
34. Ibid.
35. Ibid., p. 527.
36. Ibid., p. 528.
37. Ibid., pp. 529-30.
38. Ibid., p. 532, Table 3.
39. Ibid., p. 532.

More than 80 percent of the officers believed that working on death row was different than working on other units in the prison. Officers described death row as having a different feeling. That compared to anywhere else in the prison, death row was "eerie," "scary," "depressing," and "too quiet at times"—a "scary silence." What gave death row that feeling, according to the officers, was that both staff and inmates knew why the inmates were there: to die.[40] Another distinctive feature of death row for the officers was that it is a "very controlled environment," that "every aspect of death row is strictly regimented." Rules are strictly enforced. For example, officers "can't be on the unit without another officer present," and "offenders are cuffed all the time when officers are present."[41] A related difference is that officers on death row must be more security conscious. On death row "security is at a higher level"; "security [on death row is] of the utmost importance."[42] Another difference is that officers on death row are under considerable pressure to "do it right" and to avoid mistakes. One officer commented, "Death row is safer if done right." Officers also are under pressure to "take care of each other." If the job is not done right or if mistakes are made, the consequences could be disastrous.[43]

Nevertheless, more than three-quarters of the officers considered work on death row less stressful than work with the general prison population. More than half of the officers preferred working with death row inmates than general population inmates, and only about a fifth of the officers were troubled being a part of a life-taking process.[44] Officers also considered work on death row less laborious, safer, and having fewer problems than working other assignments, especially the cell houses. The cell houses are much larger and have many more inmates than death row (it is common for cell houses to have one officer for every 100 to 150 inmates), and cell-house inmates have much more freedom and are less predictable than death row inmates.[45] Still, given the choice of job assignments, less than a third of the officers would rather work on death row. Nearly 38 percent preferred working the yard, the wall, or the perimeter; almost 20 percent preferred supervising offender workers; and about 11 percent preferred working the cell houses.[46] One officer said about death row: "less [sic] offenders, [but] more stress" working around death-sentenced inmates. Another officer remarked, "[it was] mentally more draining to work on death row" than elsewhere in the institution, because of death row's strict procedures and the possible dangers of working there. As one officer observed, "the offenders know they are in to die, it can be stressful having to work around them knowing they don't have much to lose and could take your life."[47] Interestingly, violent disturbances or assaults on death row are rare, so the stress and danger to which the officers refer is more about the potential than the reality of being assaulted or worse. As noted, many officers stated that death row inmates "are less trouble and easier to get along with than the [inmates] in the general population."[48]

---

40. Ibid., p. 533.
41. Ibid.
42. Ibid.
43. Ibid., pp. 533-34.
44. Ibid., pp. 531-32, Table 3.
45. Ibid., p. 534.
46. Ibid., pp. 531-32, Table 3.
47. Ibid., p. 535.
48. Ibid.

The Cream of the Correctional Officer Corps

The execution team, or deathwatch team as it is sometimes called, is responsible for carrying out executions. In U.S. prisons that conduct executions, execution team members generally are considered "the cream of the correctional officer corps."[49] They have been referred to as the "foot soldiers of execution."[50] Depending on the prison, either the warden or a team leader typically selects eight or nine carefully screened officers from among numerous corrections officer volunteers. California requires San Quentin's warden to select a minimum of 20 execution team members.[51] A Virginia team leader related his selection process:

> I would know what type of officer you have been, because I've been working with you and seen the way you conducted yourself. I'd sit down and talk to you and tell you what, what we gonna do and what's expected of you, and ask you, "Do you think you could handle it?" And if you told me you thought you could, why, I'd start training you. And then if I saw a weakness or something, that you're falling back, why then I'd ask you, you know, "Do you have a problem with it?" And then I would take you back and sit you down and tell you, if you did have a problem with it, had anything against it or you thought you had anything against it, you ought to just drop out. And nothing would ever be said. We'd just carry it on through.[52]

Being tight-lipped is a key quality for a team member. Team members do not want "outsiders" to know their business, because they assume that "outsiders" would not understand what they do. Stated a Virginia team member: "We look for a person who is very secretive, you know, and can keep things to himself. 'Cause this is very secretive, you know, what my part is and what his part is."[53] "Outsiders" include other corrections officers and sometimes their own family members. According to another Virginia team member: "Well, we, we were sworn to secrecy. When I first got on the team, I wouldn't even tell my wife what I was doing. The deal was, keep it among ourselves. Whatever we say or do down here had got to stay down here, you know."[54]

Zealots need not volunteer for the execution team, because they will not be chosen. The Virginia team leader described this important disqualifying criterion:

> I wouldn't want to put a man on the team that would like it. I don't want nobody who would like to do it. I'd rather have the person not want to do it than have a person who wants to do it. And if I suspected or thought anybody on the team really's gettin' a kick out of it, I would take him off the team.... I would like to think that every one of them on the team is doin' it, is doing it in the line of duty, you know, carryin' out their duties.[55]

---

49. Johnson, op. cit., p. 131.

50. Robert Jay Lifton and Greg Mitchell (2002) *Who Owns Death? Capital Punishment, the American Conscience, and the End of Executions.* New York: Perennial, p. 81.

51. "California Revises Lethal Injection Protocol," California Department of Corrections and Rehabilitation at www.cdcr.ca.gov/News/2007_Press_Releases/Lethal_InjectionFactSheet.html (accessed June 28, 2009).

52. Johnson, op. cit.

53. Ibid., p. 137.

54. Ibid.

55. Ibid., p. 131.

Thus, to be a part of the "team" requires a certain type of individual. As a Virginia prison administrator explained:

> What's the expression? "When the going gets tough, the tough get going." A certain amount of professionalism [is required] there.... An execution is something [that] needs to be done, and good people, dedicated people who believe in the American system, should do it. And there's a certain amount of feeling, probably one to another, that they're part of that—that when they have to hang tough, they can do it, and they can do it right. And that it's just the right thing to do.[56]

The belief that an execution "needs to be done" is a recurring theme among execution team members. As one Virginia member put it: "It was something, of course, that had to be done. We had to be sure that we did it properly, professionally, and [that] we gave as much dignity to the person as we possibly could in the process.... You gotta do it, and if you've gotta do it, it might just as well be done the way it's supposed to be done— without any sensation."[57]

"Doing it right" is another theme expressed by execution team members. Despite having doubts about the death penalty in general, one Virginia execution member emphasized the importance of carrying out an execution professionally:

> I've seen it. I know what it is. I've smelled it. I've tasted it. I've felt it.... I'm not sure the death penalty is the right way. I don't know if there is a right answer. So I look at it like this: If it's gotta be done, at least it can be done in a humane way, if there is such a word for it. 'Cause I know it can be a nasty situation. Executions have been here for a long time. And for a long time it's been done, you know, unprofessionally and for primitive reasons. The only way it should be done, I feel, is the way we do it. It's done professionally; it's not no horseplaying. Everything is done by documentation. On time. By the book.[58]

"Doing it professionally" also means doing it with a lack of sensation or emotion, which is still another theme among execution team members. A Virginia team member conveys this "emotionless" approach to executions: "I can take or leave executions. It's not a job I like or dislike. It's a job I've been asked to do. I try to go about every job in the most professional manner I can. If they would stop the death penalty, it wouldn't bother me. If we had ten executions tomorrow, it wouldn't bother me. I would condition my mind to get me through it."[59] Another Virginia team member expressed a similar view: "I look at it like it's a job. I don't take it personally. You know, I don't take it like I'm having a grudge against this person and this person has done something to me. I'm just carrying out a job, doing what I was asked to do ... This man has been sentenced to death in the courts. This is the law, and he broke this law, and he has to suffer the consequences. And one of the consequences is to put him to death."[60]

Being able to handle one's emotions includes being able to handle the stress of executions. A Virginia team member divulged why he was well suited for the job:

> I volunteered because of my [military] service background and my job background here. They were looking at experience, more or less, number one. And they were

---

56. Ibid., p. 128.
57. Ibid.
58. Ibid., pp. 130-31.
59. Ibid., p. 121.
60. Ibid., p. 129.

also looking for (pause) the people who had been through a lot of stress—stress from inside the institution—that could handle stress more. The overall thing was to deal with the stress and pressure.... As long as I've been here, I have been used, more or less, as the person to handle the big problems and straighten them out.[61]

A Missouri team leader also believed that his military experience prepared him for his role:

Certainly from the standpoint of protocol, of chain of command, it certainly aligns itself with the military chain of command. And I have heard [the warden] ... numerous times refer to it as a battle, or possibly preparing for a particular initiative, or a particular battle. And I think there's some validity behind that, even from my own standpoint, of when I went to Vietnam. I knew there was a job to do, and knew what job I had to do. And I knew that people were going to be killed. I knew that up front. So I think the preparedness that I go through might be somewhat similar.... I know where my chain of command lies. I know what is expected of me. I've prepared for it. I've practiced for it. And in order to make [the warden] look good, I'm going to do my job a hundred and ten percent. And I think all of that works together.[62]

About thirty minutes before the actual execution, the inmate is taken from the deathwatch cell to the execution chamber, where he is strapped down to the gurney. Strapping the inmate to the gurney, or the "tie down" as it is called in Texas, is one of the more ritualized stages in a ritualized process. Execution team members spend hours practicing the procedure. It's purpose, according to a 31-execution veteran Texas tie down team member, is "just [to] make sure he [the condemned inmate] is secure. That he won't be jumping up, that he won't be able to squirm out of the restraints themselves, and that the job can be done—the job being the execution itself."[63]

Each tie down team member has a specific assignment. Another Texas tie down team member, a veteran of approximately 120 executions, described the division of labor: "Each supervisor [In Texas, tie down team members were high ranking shift supervisors] is assigned a different portion—like we have a head person, a right arm, left arm, right leg, left leg. And the right leg man will tell him [the condemned inmate] 'I need you to hop up onto the gurney. Lay your head on this end, put your feet on this end.' Simultaneously while he's laying down the straps are being put across him."[64] One Texas team member described his specific assignment: "What I do, I will strap the offender's left wrist. And then there are two belts—one that comes across the top of his left shoulder—and then another goes right straight across his abdominal area."[65] Team members usually are cross-trained, so each member can perform all tasks. Nevertheless, when it comes time for an execution, according to the Virginia team leader, each team member performs only his assigned task.[66] The Virginia team leader explained why the operation is broken into small, discrete tasks:

---

61. Ibid., p. 132.

62. Trombley, op. cit., p. 216.

63. Transcript of a "Witness to an Execution" at http://sound portraits.org/on-air/witness_to_an_execution/transcript.php, Copyright © 2000 Sound Portraits Productions. All Rights Reserved (accessed June 25, 2009).

64. Ibid.

65. Ibid.

66. Johnson, op. cit., p. 133.

So people won't get confused. I've learned it's kind of a tense time. When you're executin' a person, killing a person—you call it killin', executin', whatever you want, the man dies anyway—I find the less you got on your mind, why, the better you'll carry it out. So it's just very simple things. And so far, you know, it's all come together; we haven't had any problems.[67]

Another unstated psychological reason for dividing the procedure into small, discrete tasks and making it a collective responsibility is to provide execution team members "plausible denial" to themselves and others that their role in executions is anything but minimal. This psychological dimension of execution protocols should not be underestimated. Killing other human beings does not come easily to most people, even when the killing is legally sanctioned. Research found, astonishingly, that during World War II only 20 percent of soldiers fired their weapons directly at the enemy on the battlefield; however, during the Vietnam conflict 95 percent of soldiers fired their weapons directly at the enemy.[68] What changed? Apparently, it was not that Americans had become more vicious since World War II. The research showed that only two percent of American soldiers in Vietnam could be considered "'eager' coldblooded killers."[69] What changed was training methods. The execution protocol components are some of the same enabling mechanisms used by the military since the Vietnam conflict to make soldiers into more efficient killers. Many prison officials involved with executions have military backgrounds.

A Texas team member conveyed how condemned inmates' respond to being strapped down: "Some of them are very calm. Some of them are upset. Some of them are crying."[70] A teammate added, "Some of them have been sweating. Some of them will have the smell of anxiety, if you will. Of fear."[71] When all the straps are secured, a curious response frequently occurs, according to one of the Texas team members: "[T]hey [the condemned inmates] will look at you and they'll say 'Thank you.' And here you've just strapped them into the table. And they look at you in the eye and tell you 'Thank you for everything that you've done.' And, you know, that's kind of a weird feeling."[72] He expressed how he felt about his role in executions:

It's kind of hard to explain what you actually feel, you know, when you talk to a man and you kind of get to know that person, and then you walk him out of a cell and you take him in there to the chamber and tie him down. And then a few minutes later he's … he's gone…. It's a very unique job. Very unique. Not many people are willing to do this or can do this…. I do believe in what I do. If I didn't and I felt that it was morally wrong or ethically wrong, then I wouldn't participate in it. And that's something we are not required to do—is participate in it. But I do this voluntarily…. You know, it's something that everybody has to deal with it in their own way. You know, some people they might like to drink and forget about it. I can take my mind off things when I go fishing. I like the outdoors and that's just how I cope with it.[73]

Another Texas team member related his feelings about his role:

---

67. Ibid., p. 132.
68. Lifton and Mitchell, op. cit., pp. 90-91.
69. Ibid., p. 91.
70. Transcript of a "Witness to an Execution," op, cit.
71. Ibid.
72. Ibid.
73. Ibid.

Just another part of doing what I do as a correctional officer. It's something that the vast majority of the people want done. And so I am one of the few people in the state that is able to play a part in the process. One thing I am glad of is that we're not using [the] electric chair. I don't think I would want to be part of that. This process here, it's clinical. The inmate, other than the fact that he's expired, you don't know anything has happened to him. And, you know, that's good.[74]

A Missouri death row inmate, who had received a last-minute stay of execution, provided an interesting description of the execution team's behavior on execution night:

I don't even know how to express what people do, but when they are about to kill you, they just seem very, very nervous. They seem like they can't stand still. They make idle conversation; you know, "How's the weather?" would be complex conversation for them. They seem very, very uncomfortable about what they're fixing to do. But, at the same time, they seem anxious to do it. I can't quite understand why these particular individuals seemed to take some satisfaction in thinking, "We are about to kill you." I don't know.[75]

His perception of the execution team's reaction to the execution stay also is instructive:

They said, "*Stand down from the exercise. Stand down from the exercise.*" That's how they referred to it, as an exercise. When they said stand down from it, that meant go back to normal status. It took almost an hour after my lawyer told me there was a stay for them to make that announcement. And there was obvious disappointment on their faces. (emphasis in original)[76]

Stays of execution are difficult for execution team members because it puts them on an emotional roller coaster. To do the execution, team members have to get "psyched up"; they have to get the adrenaline pumping. When a stay is received, team members experience an emotional let down, and when the stay is removed, they have to get psyched up again. A Virginia team member described the predicament:

If everything go when it's supposed to, then it's not too bad. But you get an on-and-off thing, like the court getting' involved, that's rough. Like with one fella, we's executin' him and, uh, that thing drug on. It be on one hour and off the next hour. And your adrenaline builds up. You have to build up, and then you get building up and then all at once they say, "Hey, it's not goin' to be tonight; it's off." Then you got to come all the way back down. And fifteen or twenty minutes later, they say, "It's back on again." And here you got to go up, pump back up, and it's really hard on ya. Courts, lawyers, and the governor—when they get into it, it's an unsure thing, and it's, it's pretty hard on ya.[77]

Another Virginia team member said the on-and-off of execution stays was like torture: "You crash. Your metabolism just drops. And then when it's back on, you got about a minute and thirty seconds to get up again. And you got to be professional about it and make no screwups. It's emotionally painful."[78]

---

74. Ibid.
75. Trombley, op. cit., p. 247.
76. Ibid.
77. Johnson, op. cit., p. 162.
78. Ibid.

Even when there are no stays and an execution goes relatively smoothly, team members experience mood swings that must be managed by an effective team leader. Talking about his team members, a Virginia leader related:

> They go up, and they come down. They get to talkin'—some of 'em will get to talkin' real fast, you know. Maybe you got a better word, but I call it climbing the ladder, you know, and I have to kinda talk 'em down, you know, get 'em settled down. And then I see 'em go down the ladder—they're way down here—and then I have to bring them up, you know, to a level. Yeah, they go through, they go through changes.[79]

At the same time the team leader is trying to keep his team members at an emotional level so they can do their jobs effectively, the leader and his team members are trying to keep the condemned inmate at an emotional level so that he creates no problems for them. The parallel amused a Virginia team leader: "They're trying to keep the inmate cool, right. (Laughing) So it's, it's challenging.... You don't know how your people gonna act during or after [the execution], so I'm not only watchin' the inmate, I'm havin' to watch my team, too. And so far we haven't had nobody [on the team] crack up, but you know it could happen, and I realize that it could happen."[80]

In the last few minutes after the execution warrant has been read, and the green light has been given to proceed with the execution, a Missouri execution team leader said it was quiet:

> It is *real* quiet. Probably, I could hear my own heart beating more than anything else that I'm conscious of.... [T]he individual normally looks at his visitors or just kind of looks around. It's very anticlimactic, and there's no convulsions, screaming, or paranoia. There's basically never been any of that. The individual, generally speaking, has accepted that they're sort of like a terminally ill person, and they have accepted their fate.... [T]he eyes just close, and they're dead.... It takes approximately four and a half minutes from the time that the first chemical is dropped until permanent death occurs. There's three chemicals that are dropped through IV tubes into the individual's body. It's basically very painless, very swift. The individual goes to sleep.... The doctor himself is behind a screen and he's constantly watching the heart monitor to pronounce the individual dead. It takes about four minutes, and as soon as that time arrives, he gives the word that the individual is deceased, and we close the blinds [to the witness area] at that time and disconnect the condemned inmate.... [81]

Once the inmate is pronounced dead and disconnected from the IVs, explained a Texas tie down team member, "the team members including myself, go in and unstrap him and then assist in putting him on the funeral home gurney until such time as he's wheeled out...."[82]

The Missouri execution team leader related that following the execution, members of the execution team were "very relieved." He added, they were:

> Very calm, cool, and collected. Very professional.... We anticipated a lot of stress in regard to executions. That has not been the case. People have met the challenge,

---

79. Ibid., p. 163.
80. Ibid.
81. Trombley, op. cit., p. 213.
82. Transcript of a "Witness to an Execution," op. cit.

if you will, and have taken the stress in stride and moved right along. Very professionally. And once an execution is over, people just basically go home. In regard to myself, I generally pack everything up and close my office about two in the morning, and go home. Normally, my wife is up, and we sit down, we talk and discuss, and I go to sleep. I don't have a problem going to sleep after an execution. [Actually, while the team leader goes home after an execution, the rest of the team holds a party.][83]

He said an execution did not bother him at all and explained:

I don't know if that's the calloused individuals in us, or what. I don't know. People say, "Well, you're right there in the execution chamber with them. I mean, you're the last person to see them draw breath. You're the last person that gives him a cigarette and lets him smoke. Does it bother you?" And I say no. And it doesn't bother me. Sure, I take it for what it is. And I *know* where I'm at. And as a professional in the Department of Corrections, I know my duty. These people killed somebody. I didn't. All I'm doing is a job that the state says I should do. (emphasis in original)[84]

A Virginia team member expressed a similar sentiment: "When I go home after one of these things ... I sleep like a rock."[85] Another Virginia team member spoke for his colleagues, "Nobody has any problems from this."[86] A third team member had a similar view, although it sounds as if he was in denial:

I don't think about it, you know. The man is executed, the body is gone, and I clean the place up and close the books out, and, hey, I go home and eat me a hearty meal. I just block it out, that's it. It all blocks out until the next time....
I say, "Hey, we got a job to do. We did the job. Let's go about our business, you know, go home." So that's the way I look at it, you know.[87]

The warden of the Virginia prison was convinced that his team members were able to handle their execution roles and avoid long-term adverse consequences: "It affects them, even if they don't let on, but they handle it. They're a strong bunch of men. They've come to terms with their conscience; they've been able to not get lost in the right or wrong of the situation here. And the cohesion of the team is good. They're not gonna be hurt; it's not gonna leave any scars."[88] However, one of his team members, who felt fine about the executions in which he participated, had his doubts about how he might feel in the future: "Sometime I might wonder whether some day, after I retire, this here might come back and hit me in the face. Religious like. When I'm an old man, ready to die, maybe this here will haunt me. I don't think it will, but it could.... I don't know how it will affect me in the future. Right now, I don't really think about it one way or the other."[89] Another Virginia team member was somewhat apprehensive when asked whether executions affected him:

That's a good question. That's a real good question. It do, in a sense, and it don't. It probably—if it do, it's cause every person that's put on this earth, I feel, is

---

83. Trombley, op. cit., p. 214.
84. Ibid., p. 205.
85. Johnson, op. cit., p. 183.
86. Ibid., p. 180.
87. Ibid., p. 181.
88. Ibid., pp. 180-81.
89. Ibid., p. 180.

created equal, you know, and they [are] put on this earth to do, to handle some
type of problems and whatever. They got to live to do that. But my old grandfather
had a saying, you know, "Do unto others what you want them to do unto you."
So when you kill somebody, you should be killed.... [But] the execution, the
killing itself, don't bother me. I was in the service eighteen months in Nam. I
was on body patrol, far as when they dropped napalm and you went in and
picked up dead bodies and stuff, put 'em in body bags. I guess another part of
it, I live in a ghetto. I see a lot of life and death over there, you know. It really
don't bother me, you know. Even inmates here get killed, you know. I've saved
a couple of inmates here who have been cut up real bad as well as taken the dead
bodies out from there that been killed. So the killing, it really don't bother me.[90]

Asked the same question, another Virginia team member responded a bit more intro-
spectively:

There is turmoil, even for someone that I didn't like per se and might not care
if he lives or dies, okay? But the violence doesn't bother me. Out in population,
you may have to subdue someone or whatever. Certainly, if you subdue someone
improperly, you could give them a lethal blow or whatever. So, then, you know,
working on the tower, we have firepower. Okay, push may come to shove and
we may have to use it.... [But with an execution] I ask myself, "Am I doing the
right thing? Is this just or unjust? So we have the right to take a man's life?"[91]

A Utah team member had second thoughts: "I used to be all gung-ho [for the death
penalty] but now I'm not so sure. It would be easier if he [the condemned inmate] were
a crud, but he is a nice, gentle person. I'm not sure we are doing the right thing by putting
him to death."[92] Some team members may be more affected by their execution roles than
others, as a Virginia team member asserted:

What I do, people don't wanna do that—physically have to touch this man after
sitting with him. We all be with him [on our shifts], but most of the team don't
actually have that much contact with him. But you be the one to sit with him
his last few hours of his life and you have to walk him in and you strap him in—
it takes a lot. And it's only a few others on the team that actually got to do that.
So they really don't get that touch, get all their senses involved; they can more
or less just cut themselves off from what's happenin'. Like they don't have a great
part in it.[93]

Contrary to the Virginia warden's belief, some team members suffer long-term damage
from their execution experience. One of his own team members reported suffering an
emotional numbness that affected his entire life:

I just cannot feel anything. And that was what bothered me. I thought that I
would feel something, but I didn't feel anything.... When I was small, I guess
about seven or eight, I used to spend time with my uncle and aunt. They ran a
funeral home service, so death to me was nothing new, being around death. But

---

90. Ibid., p. 130.
91. Ibid.
92. L. Kay Gillespie (2003) *Inside the Death Chamber: Exploring Executions.* Boston: Allyn and
Bacon, p. 49.
93. Johnson, op. cit., p. 181.

the actual participation of killing a person—I hadn't experienced that. And I didn't feel anything. That was the thing that bothered me.[94]

He added:

> It's laying over my whole life.... Ever since I joined the team. Very seldom do I get upset or get upset to a point where I would feel my voice rise. I just shut everything down.... I don't want to wake up tomorrow and recognize that my mind is gone, because I figure the stress will come later.... There's nothing to protect you from that. If it do come, like it's something that I'll have to deal with for the rest of my life. You never know when you might wake in the middle of the night in a cold sweat and you lost your mind.[95]

A Texas tie-down team member, who participated in approximately 120 executions before he quit, experienced even greater trauma. In his words:

> I was just working in the shop and all of a sudden something just triggered in me and I started shaking. And then I walked back into the house and my wife asked "What's the matter?" and I said "I don't feel good." And tears— uncontrollable tears—was coming out of my eyes. And she said "What's the matter?" And I said "I just thought about that execution that I did two days ago, and everybody else's that I was involved with." And what it was was something triggered within and it just—everybody—all of these executions all of a sudden all sprung forward.[96]

Three years after that episode, the team member could still see "the eyes of the men he helped tie down." He continued with his terrifying experience:

> Just like taking slides in a film projector and having a button and just pushing a button and just watching, over and over: him, him, him. I don't know if it's mental breakdown, I don't know if ... probably would be classified more as a traumatic stress, similar to what individuals in war had. You know, they'd come back from war, it might be three months, it might be two years, it might be five years, all of a sudden they relive it again, and all that has to come out. You see I can barely even talk because I'm thinking more and more of it. You know, there was just so many of 'em.[97]

He was so traumatized by his execution flashbacks, he resigned after serving 16 years in the prison system. He began working as a carpenter. His main concern now is his fellow team members: "I hope that this doesn't happen to them—the ones that participate, the ones that go through this procedure now. And I will say honestly—and I believe very sincerely—somewhere down the line something is going to trigger. Everybody has a stopping point. Everybody has a certain level. That's all there is to it."[98]

The team member's warden, Jim Willett (see Chapter 10), believes that his subordinate's case was exceptional, that few execution team members have the problems that this team member did. However, Warden Willett did admit: "I do worry about my staff. I can see it in their eyes sometimes, particularly when we do a lot of executions in a short period

---

94. Ibid.
95. Ibid., p. 181.
96. Transcript of a "Witness to an Execution," op. cit.
97. Ibid.
98. Ibid.

of time."[99] Perhaps the large number of executions in which he participated caused the damage done to the Texas team member. If that were the case, then similar damage to execution team members outside of Texas might be rare because Texas executes so many more inmates that any other executing state. Since executions resumed in United States in 1977, Texas has executed more than four times as many inmates as the next most executing state, Virginia (484 vs. 109, as of August 15, 2012).[100]

Some execution states provide psychological counseling for execution team members. Team members in Virginia, however, felt the counseling they received was inadequate on two counts. First, it was required of team members and not voluntary, and, second, it occurred following the execution rather than before it. Opined one team member:

> When I first began, we had one administrator who tried to make us go to a counseling session afterwards, far as debriefing, psychological support. You'll find a lot of resentment anytime it's not voluntary; it's not going to be that much of a help. First you gotta want help and accept help before you get it. If you just gonna like force it on him, you know, it's no good; you're defeating your own purpose.[101]

As for being offered help after the execution, he observed:

> It's almost degrading for anyone to tell us to go see a psychologist after the fact. After the fact! If you want me to see one, I think you should let me see one before I do it. 'Cause if anything was gonna happen, it was gonna happen while I'm in the process of doing this. I need to be prepared to do this. I need to know if I'm able to do this. After the fact, what's done is done, and if I need help, I can ask for help or I can go get help. And if you can see that I do need help, then come ask me and then give me the opportunity to volunteer for it. But don't put it to me that, you know, "I must do this," 'cause I may feel that I'm all right. Maybe I don't want to think about it; I don't wanna even bother with it; I don't wanna think about this. I wanna go ahead on livin', you know.[102]

Part of the appeal of being an execution team member is the cohesive bond that develops among team members. This bond is a function of their elite status within the institution; their isolation from the rest of the prison in the death house (or other remote location such as the infirmary in Missouri), where they practice; the long hours of practice; their reliance on each other; the trust they must have in each other; the camaraderie they share; and the support they receive from each other. An execution team has been likened to a family. As one team member stated, "We're not a team, we're a family. In the prison, we fuss, cuss, and threaten each other constantly. But down there [in the death house], we're family."[103] A team member conveyed the team's "closeness":

> The team is very close. I guess we're probably ... closer than any of the officers in here.... Comes from working close together. It's real, real close you know. We really don't have nobody [else] to talk to. And we'll share ideas and things, we'll go off and sit down and just talk and share ideas. How we feel or how it's affecting us. We, I guess, have confidence in one another, trust. Just a good group of people.[104]

---

99. Ibid.
100. Death Penalty Information Center at www.deathpenaltyinfo.org (accessed September 9, 2012).
101. Johnson, op. cit., p. 182.
102. Ibid., pp. 182-83.
103. Ibid., p. 135.
104. Ibid.

Another team member expressed a similar view:

> There's more closeness than in any other group I've seen in the system, as far as working together. And one thing we do—we got this thing with the team—we talk to each other. If we got a problem, we go and talk to each other *first* about it before we go off [and get upset].... Everything that we do stays there [and gets worked out], you know what I'm saying'? That's the way we operate.[105]

A fourth team member also emphasized the closeness of the group but, in doing so, revealed the strain experienced by some team members:

> We are very, very close-knit. When we got a problem from an execution, we all go down in the basement, the execution chamber—we call that our home—draw the curtains, and go in the back, and we'll talk. One guy may say, "I don't think I can make it tonight." And we'll sit down and say, "C'mon, what's the problem? Let's talk it out...." Then we have to remind him, "the law says that this is what has to be done, and we have to do it."[106]

The psychological support team members receive from each other is critical to doing the job. Team members bolster each other's confidence and assurance that they can do the job. As one team member recalled:

> When I first started, I was nervous. I told them I was nervous. I think they could sense it anyway, but I told them I was nervous. I was scared to death of my reactions, of how I was gonna react to seeing a man executed. Would I get so excited I might pass out, maybe embarrassing everyone? That would be unprofessional. I didn't know how I'd react. I didn't know once the switch threw whether I'd lose everything in my stomach or not.... I didn't [lose control], because I had the family. They were there. They gave me all the support I needed through the first one. Then after that it just became a job. It just became a normal job. You build up your self-confidence so that when the time comes, you just do what you got to do.... Now ... [executions] seem like something we do every day.[107]

Another appealing aspect of being a team member is the perks and privileges that come with the job. Although team members generally do not receive extra pay for their work on the execution team, they do get overtime pay for the long hours they work on the deathwatch and practicing and conducting executions. They also are freed for long stretches of time from the routine duties of the typical prison corrections officer. This is especially true in prisons that conduct a large number of executions. While isolated and alone in the death house practicing, they have time to smoke, have a cup of coffee, and socialize with their fellow team members.

For some team members, participating in executions provides them with helpful insights about life. A Virginia team member mused: "I know death is my destiny. I find that now I can accept death. I won't look for it. But if it, you know, if it happens, I'd rather die than suffer. I try to enjoy life more. I try to get the full meaning out of life. I try to learn more, as far as, not so much as just about living, but just being a person."[108] Another Virginia team member simply stated, "Learned something about life? Yeah. Get ready. Prepare yourself."[109]

---

105. Ibid.
106. Ibid.
107. Ibid., pp. 135-36.
108. Ibid., p. 183.
109. Ibid.

Most execution team members take pride in their special assignment. One Virginia team member confided, "It's an honor among ourselves to be on the team. I wouldn't go out on the street and broadcast that I'm on the execution team, but I'm proud of it."[110] One source of this pride is that team members work directly for the warden, so they are not subject to the often-conflicting demands of various supervisors. This relieves team members from a lot of stress, as a team member maintained:

> One thing that relieved us of a lot of stress was [that] we worked for the warden. When he activated us, we worked for him; that's who our orders came from. Came, you know, through the team leader and then to us. Anybody else, they couldn't come and, you know, disrupt you. So everybody knew what they had to do, and they just did what they had to do. You know, if you did it wrong, *you* did it wrong. You know what I'm sayin'? (emphasis in original)[111]

Working directly for the warden sometimes means working independently. One "hands-off" warden commented: "That team works on their own.... I never interfere. They know what they're doing. If they can't solve a problem, they'll bring it to me."[112] (Other wardens are much more "hands-on.") The pride that one team member takes in his job is clearly expressed in his boast: "We like to think we're the best in the nation.... Nobody ... does a better execution than we do."[113]

Offering a Way to Salvation

Prison chaplains are an instrumental part of the execution team, although generally they do not prepare for executions with the other team members. Prison administrators believe that it is important to have the prison chaplain present during the deathwatch and execution to address any staff problems, if they arise; to console victims' and offenders' family members, if needed; and to minister to the condemned inmate, if he wants. Importantly, they also help make condemned inmates compliant for execution. They do this by offering inmates a way to salvation, that is, "deliverance, by the grace of God, from eternal punishment for sin which is granted to those who accept by faith God's conditions of repentance and faith in the Lord Jesus."[114] Many condemned inmates find the kingdom of God preferable to life in prison.

Gary Tune was a prison chaplain at Missouri's Potosi Correctional Center. For the five years prior to his coming to Potosi, Tune had been pastor of a Baptist church in a small town about 40 miles south of the prison. He also had been a volunteer at the prison for six months before he was selected for the job. He believed that God was leading him to that position.[115] He said the reason he chose to work in a prison instead of a church was: "I've been pretty much a fighter for the underdog much of my life, and most of my

---

110. Ibid., p. 137.
111. Ibid., p. 138.
112. Ibid.
113. Ibid.
114. "What is salvation? What is the Christian doctrine of salvation" at www.gotquestions.org/Christian-doctrine-salvation.html (accessed August 8, 2009).
115. Trombley, op. cit., pp. 271-72.

ministry. I wanted to get out and minister with the nitty-gritty. Some of the church members, the ones with the suits and ties, didn't like that."[116] The reason he chose to work on death row was: "The Bible says that the healthy don't need a doctor. Those that are sick need a doctor. And that's my attitude on salvation and Christianity."[117] As for working on death row, he stated: "At first, there was a sense of intimidation. And then, as time goes on, you find out that they're just people. That in here, in this institution, it's a society all of its own. It's a different breed than what you're used to on the street. You tend to play by a little different rule book. They run games on you. But people on the street run games on you. It's just a different level."[118]

Chaplain Tune was one of the least liked staff members at Potosi. Prison psychologist Betty Weber noted that of the five men that had been executed at Potosi at that time, only one of them asked to see Chaplain Tune before his execution.[119] The chaplain admitted, "It is a job to establish credibility.... It's tough. You're staff, therefore you're a cop. Because you're part of the administration, you make decisions. And you make decisions they don't like."[120] He elaborated, "You've got a policy and procedure you go by; you've got rules you've got to go by. From time to time, an inmate does something he's not supposed to. And if you witness it, you end up having to write him a ticket. So you lose that credibility with them."[121] He acknowledged that the cop role he has to play compromises his ministry: "There's no way around it. What would be neat is if I had no authority. Then I could walk out and talk with the inmates, and they'd say, 'This guy has nothing to do with where I am or what's going on in here.' In here, they're quick to say, 'It's us against them.' And they say, 'Which side are you on, Chaplain?' But the very nature of the job demands that you've got to bide by the policy."[122]

Chaplain Tune described his role in the Missouri Protocol:

> I'll come in on that [execution] day and check on the inmate. And then, too, I'll look at staff. We will have, after our briefing meeting around six o'clock, a devotional time set aside for the staff who want to stay. We do it in the training room, in the assembly room. Of course, most of the staff don't stay. Only a handful will stay. And it's something I sometimes wonder: Am I being effective, or is there some other way I could deal with staff? After the devotional time, usually the inmate is visiting with his family. So usually the psychologist and I will just kind of roam around, from the housing units. We visit in the bubbles with the officers. We're looking at the stress level of the officers coming in. I asked one officer, "I don't feel like I'm doing anything." And he said, "You don't realize what your presence means." And I said, "What do you mean?" He says, "You walked by the office where I was with several other people, and just your presence seems to bring a sense of peace." Sometimes, some of the inmates themselves will be stressed out. And we have a couple that, at least every other time, they flip out. So we'll go visiting. We'll go out into the wings and visit with inmates. Those that want to talk. And some of them do. They're mellow. They're

---

116. Ibid., p. 272.
117. Ibid.
118. Ibid.
119. Ibid., p. 273.
120. Ibid.
121. Ibid.
122. Ibid.

depressed. Hey, some of them have been together for a long time. The older hands, they've been around for ten or twelve years, and they've developed relationships themselves. And so they realize, this is a friend of theirs that's being executed. And there's an emotional impact on them. So we're out there trying to deal with them, minister to them.[123]

As it gets closer to midnight and the execution, the chaplain and the psychologist go to the hospital area, where the death chamber is located:

As much as anything else, [we are] just on standby. Because that's when the element of the highest stress comes in, the highest emotions. To be there not only for the staff, but you're looking to be there for family. Maybe the family may need some help in some way. Part of the reason that Betty [the psychologist] and I run together is that sometimes people say, "I'd like to talk to somebody, but I don't want to talk to that preacher." The other individual may take it the opposite, and say, "I want to talk to somebody that is a minister."[124]

The chaplain discussed his first execution:

The first time we had a—I don't want to say a dry run, it was an aborted attempt, Leonard or George, one of them—anyway, we got within six hours of the execution, then we stood down. During that time I was very restricted in my access to the inmate. The security around here was just overwhelming. I could not go to the inmate unless that inmate requested me. There had been some lawsuits up in Jefferson City ... by inmates not wanting to be bothered by any spiritual individual, any religious individual. Some grievances had been filed saying, "Get that preacher man out of here," and I don't know what caused it.[125]

He then explained how participating in executions affected him:

Exhausting. You're running on adrenaline. You're stressed out. And when it's all said and done, because you're running on the adrenaline of stress, it's anticlimactic. And I've talked to some others. I've talked to [Potosi's then assistant superintendent/warden]. He and I are pretty close in our spiritual connections. I said, "How do you feel?" And he said, "Blank." I said, "Blank? That's it?" And he said, *"That's all I'm feeling. Blank."* There's nothing more. You keep thinking there's going to be some emotion. You're searching for something. *How do I feel?* It's just a blank. And we feel like we've determined that you're running at such a high level of stress that it just takes it all out of you. Reflection? I don't know. Stress takes the reflection out of it. (emphasis in original)[126]

Finally, the chaplain related how he was able to reconcile executions with his Christian beliefs:

Difficult. My personal belief is this. If you want to take the Old Testament, you can build a solid case for the death penalty. In the Old Testament it says, "Thou shalt not kill, but if you shed the blood of an innocent person your life shall be taken." So there is a good argument for it. You come to the New Testament, and the New Testament speaks of grace and forgiveness and whether we shall forgive

---

123. Ibid., p. 276.
124. Ibid., p. 277.
125. Ibid., p. 275.
126. Ibid., pp. 274-75.

an individual for whatever he has committed. And so there is another side to it. And, of course, you can become very liberal on that and say, "We should give him just a very light sentence"; or you can say, "Well, they should do something, but it should not be the death penalty." My personal belief is, and I base this biblically, the Scribes and Pharisees came to Jesus and they said, "Is it lawful to pay taxes?" And rather than answer their question directly, Jesus asked for a coin. They gave Him one, and He said, "Whose inscription is on it?" And they said, "Caesar's." And He said, "Render unto Caesar that which is Caesar's, render unto God that which is God's." So I've come to the conclusion that the death penalty is not a spiritual issue. It's not a Christian issue. This is our government, it's what our government has said we will do, and we will abide by that. And from that basis, I come over to Romans, where it tells us that we should render unto the higher authorities and higher powers over us. And if our government says it will go with a life sentence, I'll agree with that. If our government says, "Go with the death penalty," I must accept that.[127]

Jim Brazzil was prison chaplain at the Walls unit in Huntsville, Texas from 1995 to 2000. During those five years, he witnessed 140 executions. While serving as prison chaplain, Brazzil was interviewed about his job.[128] Following is from that interview. He was asked, "How did you feel about this job when you got into it?" He replied, "The chaplaincy is a very rewarding job. Even though it's a difficult job. It's a wonderful opportunity every day not just on the days there's an execution because that's a small portion of what I do. But the opportunity to work with the inmates who are being executed, the opportunity of working with these inmates in this unit, the officers, it's truly a wonderful job."

"When it comes to executions, what do you see is your job?" he was queried. His response:

I look at my job as strictly being there for the inmate. When I go back there I don't go back there with my own agenda. My opportunity is to go in there in the love of God and the name of Jesus. Regardless of whether he wants to receive that or not, that's my position. So I go in there simply to try and meet his needs. If he wants to sit and talk about football all day we just sit and talk about football. I just go in, and if he wants to tell jokes, we tell jokes. If he wants to sing, we sing. If he wants to listen to the radio, we listen to the radio. What ever he would like to do during that time it would help him prepare for his death. That's what we do.

Next, he was asked, "How do you feel about him or her [the condemned inmate]?" He remarked:

I look at this strictly ministerially. I don't go back with any political agenda or any other agenda. I look at that person as a dying person. I don't look at their background. I don't try to have an agenda with them. I try to keep myself away from the crime. I just try to go back there and meet that person's needs. To lead them to a peace with God. To help them find closure. I don't look at them with any kind of agenda whatsoever. Just in God's love. I guess that's a good way to put it.

The interviewer sought clarification: "I'm talking about personal feelings. Do you like him?" Chaplain Brazzil offered the following:

---

127. Ibid., pp. 278-79.

128. "Interview with Reverend Jim Brazzil," *Frontline* at www.pbs.org/wgbh/pages/frontline/shows/execution/readings/brazzil.html, web site copyright 1995-2008 WGBH educational foundation (accessed June 24, 2009).

It depends on the individual. But, yes, in a situation when you go back there, and you're dealing with people that are, how do you say it? Let's take it back into the death house. And all the avenues are already closed. Where there's nothing working in the courts, and they have no hope of walking out of that chamber ever again. And they know that in just a matter of a few hours they are going to die. All of the walls come down. You know, it's just that person. There's nobody else except he or she or myself, and we can talk without reservations, without any kind of holds barred, just an opportunity to let that person be that person. When you have that opportunity to get all the walls down, you have a tendency to bond very quickly. Of course I know some of the inmates that have been back there. I knew them before they came over here, because I used to teach Bible studies on death row. Some of them come over here, and they are really open, and an avenue of bonding comes real close, and they become a very real part of myself.

"Isn't that difficult?" was asked next. To which he said:

Very. Very difficult. It takes me about 3 days to really prepare for an execution. Psychologically, emotionally, spiritually. To really get myself in a position where I can minister to that man or that woman. And then it takes me about 3 days to get over one. And sometimes longer. You know, it's like any kind of pastor or chaplain who's working in a life or death situation, it becomes a very real part of who you are. And you can't go in there and not give of yourself and let the emotions come to you.

The interviewer wondered, "There aren't many tears are there?" The chaplain confided:

There's been a lot of tears. Back in the back. There haven't been a lot of tears in the chamber itself. Very few times that I can recall where there have not been tears. You know that's something. You know, that's a man thing. For all of our lives we've been taught, "Big boys don't cry." But when you come back there, you can let your emotions out. It's just that person and myself. Pastoral confidentiality kind a situation, tears come through. Tears for their families, tears because of frustration in their own life, true regret, true repentance in their life. Hating to say goodbye to a mom or having to say goodbye to a child. You know the grief process is very real and emotions are high, and there's a lot of tears.

Next he was queried, "Are some executions more difficult for you than others? I know you can't name names, but what can you say about that?" His answer: "Yes, I'd say that there are some executions that are more difficult. Circumstances, family members, yes, there have been a lot that have been difficult. None of them are easy, but there are some that are a lot more difficult than others." Asked to clarify: "What makes one difficult, more difficult that another?" He explained:

Generally speaking, hypothetically speaking, where you're dealing with a man who has small children, teenage children or young adult children, where they've never had an opportunity to be with that child, hold that child, hold his hand or let him sit on his lap, to be able to have that opportunity to touch them, to hear the pain in that child, the anger, the fear or why is this happening to me ... I guess those are the times that are more difficult for me. Just dealing with the families and the loss the families are feeling as much as dealing with the inmate themselves.

He then was asked, "Do you need counseling after these things?" He candidly replied:

Yes, I need somebody's shoulder to cry on. And I do cry. I have to express myself. My family's been extremely supportive, and other people, and the system who I can use as my confidant where I can go and unload on them. It's safe with them. I go home and talk, I write, I cry, I pray. Yes, I think anybody who deals with death on a routine basis realizes that it never becomes routine. It always becomes a part of you just as much as that person is going through a grief then so are you. So I'm not ashamed to admit that my emotions run high and low throughout my job relationships.

Queried about others: "Do some of the corrections officers, medics, whoever who takes part in the execution, need your counseling?" He commented:

We talk a lot, yes. You know so many people, I feel, have the wrong attitude about the officers, the people who work here. The people who work here are extremely professional. They are very sensitive. We talk, we cry, we laugh, you know, we work out whatever is necessary. Cause the tension is there, grief is there for everyone. And the tears are there. There's been many officers who've cried because of the experience they've gone through.

Finally, Chaplain Brazzil was asked: "Do you take a position on the death penalty?" He replied, "No, I do not." He then was asked, "Does the word neutral apply?"

I prefer not to even get into the political aspect of it simply because I feel that I can best meet the needs of these people that are coming through here, the best needs of me working with the inmates who live here on a daily basis for that not to even be a part of who I am. My position is I am a minister. I want to meet their needs whatever I can do to make their last hours meaningful and productive, and easy for everyone.

For prison chaplain Tom Feaster, who ministered to John Spenkelink before Florida's first post-*Furman* execution, coming to terms with his role in the execution was a disturbing revelation:

For a time, I felt nothing but anger at [the warden], at the governor, at the guy who pulled the switch—but finally I realized, hey, I'm a part of this, too. I sat outside the cell with the guards. I was a part of the system. I can't wash my hands of it. It comes down to what I said to the press after it was all over: "People who are of a persuasion to pray, don't pray for John. Pray for us."[129]

Conclusion

Death row corrections officers and execution team members, like so many of their counterparts in the capital punishment process, generally view their participation in the process as simply doing their jobs, being professionals. The job of death row corrections officers involves tending to the needs of death row inmates and keeping them alive until

---

129. David Von Drehle (1995) *Among the Lowest of the Dead: Inside Death Row.* New York: Fawcett Crest, p. 91.

their executions. This is no small feat because no one ever intended that condemned inmates would await their executions in miserable little cages for an average of nearly fifteen years, or, in some cases, for more than thirty years. Nevertheless, this has become the bleak, stressful, frightening, dangerous, and depressing environment in which death row corrections officers are required to work. Even so, many corrections officers consider work on death row less stressful than work with the general prison population and would prefer to work with death row inmates than with general prison population inmates.

Execution team members are specially selected corrections officers who conduct executions. The team also includes the warden, other prison officials, the prison psychologist, and the prison chaplain. Execution team corrections officers generally believe that an execution is a job that "needs to be done," "needs to be done right," and "needs to be done professionally, without sensation or emotion." They become a team, forming a cohesive bond and a closeness that is not duplicated anywhere else in the prison.

An execution is a very ritualized process in which each team member has a specifically defined job to do. The ritual with its division of labor makes the execution psychologically easier for the participants by making the execution a collective responsibility. Nevertheless, execution team members ride an emotional roller coaster during an execution, particularly when a stay of execution occurs.

Most execution team members do not appear adversely affected by their participation in executions, though some question what the long-term effects might be. Many team members take pride in what they do. Some team members, however, have experienced emotional trauma; in some cases, they have suffered serious emotional damage.

The role of the prison chaplain in the execution process is to be available to address staff problems, console victims' and offenders' family members, and minister to the condemned inmate. They also help make the condemned inmate compliant for execution by offering him a path to salvation. Most prison chaplains seem able to reconcile their ministerial roles with their execution roles.

In the absence of capital punishment, of course, death row corrections officers and execution team members would not be needed. Another group of participants in the execution process is execution witnesses. It is to them that we turn next.

Chapter 12

Execution Witnesses

Many death penalty states do not allow citizens to witness an execution unless they have a direct relationship to the case. However, in at least sixteen death penalty states, state law requires that a certain number of people serve as official witnesses to ensure that the execution is carried out in a dignified and humane way.

Witnessing an execution can have lasting and profound effects. People who have observed an execution report feeling fearful, sullied, degraded, dehumanized, ashamed, voyeuristic, complicit, detached, despair, and numb. They have experienced dissociative symptoms and have had difficulty sleeping afterward, but from what is known, few, if any, of them have suffered prolonged psychological trauma. This chapter examines execution witnesses and their roles in the capital punishment process.

Selecting Witnesses

As noted, at least sixteen death penalty states require that a certain number of people serve as official witnesses to ensure that the execution is carried out in a dignified and humane way. This is because, in some cases, condemned inmates were severely beaten the night before their executions to make them pliant. In a few cases, condemned inmates already were dead when they were brought forward to be executed, to prevent them from using their last statements to expose corruption or make incriminating accusations.[1] Currently, Pennsylvania and Virginia both require six witnesses, Missouri requires eight, Florida requires twelve, and California requires sixteen.[2] Official witnesses were unnecessary until the demise of public executions—the last ones occurring in the 1940s. In addition to official witnesses, many death penalty states allow many more "unofficial" witnesses.

Although California requires sixteen witnesses, it allows up to fifty witnesses to an execution, including the attorney general; twelve reputable citizens who are selected by the warden and who serve as official witnesses (these may include family members of the victim or victims); eight members of San Quentin's security staff; up to five inmate family

---

1. L. Kay Gillespie (2003) *Inside the Death Chamber: Exploring Executions*. Boston: Allyn and Bacon, p. 7.

2. Mark Hansen (2000) "Dearth of Volunteers: 16 States Require Civilian Witnesses to Ensure Dignity at Execution." *American Bar Association Journal*, www.abanet.org/journal/current/nwitns.html (July 21); Robert Johnson (1998) *DEATHWORK: A Study of the Modern Execution Process*, 2nd ed. Belmont, CA: West/Wadsworth, p. 167; Gary Taylor (2000) "Dozens Seek Front–Row Seat for Executions." *The Orlando Sentinel* (May 8), p. C–3; California Department of Corrections and Rehabilitation, "Lethal Injection Procedures" at www.cya.ca.gov/ReportsResearch/lethalInjection.html (accessed March 31, 2006).

members or friends, if requested by the inmate; up to two spiritual advisors, if requested by the inmate; up to seventeen news media representatives; and five members from the governor's office, which may include California Department of Corrections and Rehabilitation employees, California peace officers, and family members of the victim or victims. The warden following consultation with the assistant secretary, Office of Public and Employee Communications, and the San Quentin public information officer, selects media witnesses.[3]

The warden also selects the witnesses to an execution at Florida State Prison. He allows thirty witnesses, but usually only one or two of them is from the waiting list. A dozen places are reserved for the news media—six for the print media and six for television and radio. The warden lets trade organizations, such as the Florida Press Association, select the media witnesses. The warden also chooses the twelve official witnesses. His first priorities are victims' relatives and law enforcement officers and prosecutors who were involved in the case. Other witnesses include prison personnel, state officials, and a medical staff member to care for witnesses who need medical attention. Typically, an inmate's attorney and religious advisor witness an execution, but rarely are they counted as official witnesses. In Florida, the condemned inmate's family members are not allowed to witness the execution.

Currently, there is no shortage of volunteer witnesses. However, the Florida prison warden believes that with the state's recent shift from electrocution to lethal injection, interest in viewing an execution will drop substantially.[4]

Reasons for Witnessing an Execution

Unlike citizen witnesses in Virginia and other death penalty states, the few citizens selected from the waiting list in Florida do not have to provide a reason for why they want to witness an execution. One source suggests this is because Florida was having a hard time recruiting witnesses, but that no longer seems to be the case—assuming it ever was.[5] A study of thirty-five Virginia official witness applications, all of which were accepted, showed the following reasons given for wanting to observe an execution:

- Eleven applicants cited moral considerations: eight wanted "to reinforce or reaffirm" their belief in the "justice" and "rightness" of the death penalty and the American criminal justice system; two "hoped to educate and deter delinquent youth with whom they came in contact in their work" (one of the two also wanted to "scare himself straight"); and 3 wanted "to resolve their ambivalence about the death penalty."

- Nine applicants believed that witnessing an execution was their civic duty or an educational opportunity ("a case study of democracy at work").

---

3. *State of California San Quentin Operational Procedure Number 0-770 Execution by Lethal Injection* (May 15, 2007) at www.cdcr.ca.gov/News/2007_Press_Releases/docs/RevisedProtocol.pdf (accessed June 28, 2009).

4. Hansen, ibid.; Taylor, ibid.

5. Robert Jay Lifton and Greg Mitchell (2002) *Who Owns Death? Capital Punishment, the American Conscience, and the End of Executions.* New York: Perennial, p. 170.

- Seven police officer applicants viewed witnessing an execution as an extension of their general law enforcement responsibilities or their obligation in a particular case.

- Seven applicants stated that they were just curious about what an execution was like.

- One applicant had known the victims but did not give a reason why he should be allowed to attend.[6]

An informal review of witnesses' motives included:

- Victims' family members wanted to bring closure and complete the grief cycle. One designated family witness commented, "I'm not looking forward to watching him die. I want to see it as well as not see it. But the best step toward healing is if he gets executed." After witnessing the execution of her son's killer, one mother commented, "It was easy. I'm glad it's done and glad it's over and glad he's off this earth."

- Police officers wanted to close the case in which they had been involved. After witnessing an execution, one officer responded, "I just felt relieved. I waited for it three months short of ten years. I saw him kill a police officer, a friend of mine, not two feet in front of me."

- Curiosity motivated some. A Vietnam veteran who witnessed a Florida execution said, "You get up and walk away and he's just a lump of flesh without a spirit. Some of the [other witnesses] were overwhelmed. But I was somewhat prepared."

- Some criminal justice professionals wanted to know the consequences of their decisions. A member of the Parole and Probation Commission indicated, "I wanted to see what I was recommending. I thought I might have a better perspective. It was surrealistic. I was haunted for several days afterward.... The image froze of his breathing." After an execution, a public defender commented: "The ritual was the worst thing. I could just see somebody standing there saying the gods are appeased."[7]

Execution Protocol for Witnesses

Witnesses generally are asked to arrive anywhere from twenty minutes to two hours before the scheduled execution. Once they get to the prison, prison guards escort them into the witness room. In Oklahoma, for example, relatives of the victim are placed in a different room from relatives of the prisoner. In California, there are three separate witness areas: one for official/victim witnesses, one for media witnesses, and one for inmate witnesses. In other death penalty states, all the witnesses sit together. As noted, Florida does not allow family members to witness their loved one's execution.

Some execution chambers have a one-way mirror that allows only the witnesses to see the condemned. Others have a clear window that allows the condemned inmate to see the witnesses as well. Once the IVs are inserted into the prisoner's arms, the curtain or blind covering the window is opened. In California, a recent ruling by the U.S. Court of

6. Robert Johnson (1998) *DEATHWORK: A Study of the Modern Execution Process*, 2nd ed. Belmont, CA: West/Wadsworth, pp. 167-68.

7. Gillespie, op. cit., pp. 3-4.

Appeals for the Ninth Circuit allows witnesses to "view executions from the moment the condemned inmate is escorted into the execution chamber."[8]

Some states require complete silence in the witness area. In some cases, the witness room is not large enough to hold all the relatives who want to witness the execution, so an overflow room in another part of the prison may be used to allow them to view the execution via closed-circuit TV. Once the execution is completed, the curtain or blind is closed, and prison staff escorts the witnesses out of the witness room.

When outside the witness room, official witnesses are required to sign a document attesting to the fact that they witnessed the execution and that it took place. In some cases, members of the media and families may be taken to a media area for a press conference. The witnesses are then escorted out of the prison.[9]

Effects of Witnessing an Execution

Not much information is available on the personal reactions of execution witnesses. However, journalist Susan Blaustein witnessed a Texas lethal injection execution at Texas's Walls Unit and described her experience and insights in a 1994 *Harper's Magazine* article:

> The obliviousness of townspeople to the executions was notable, but more striking was the way in which career TDC [Texas Department of Corrections] employees involved in the work managed to keep it from impinging on their consciousness. "It's real simple: I either do my job or I don't eat," the assistant director for public information, Charles L. Brown, told me when I asked how he felt about witnessing every execution. "My position is purely defensible: if I'm going to have to answer questions about it, I ought to be there. It's got nothing to do with my feelings about the death penalty; I'm just doing my job professionally and to the best of my ability. It works perfect, in that regard. And nobody would know whether I'm for or against capital punishment." "You'd be surprised," Brown added, "how many people here are opposed to capital punishment."[10]

Blaustein's thoughts then turned to her own role in the impending execution:

> I was thinking about that evening's execution. I'd never even seen anyone die, and here I was, about to witness a man's death, to observe it without objection. Already I felt sullied, voyeuristic. Yet this is the law, I told myself. What's more, this one should be easy: this man *wants* to die. And he did pump four bullets into that poor law student's head. I kept this interior debate until it was time to report in at the TDC "Admin" building, just across from the Walls.[11]

---

8. Howard Mintz (2002) "Public has right to see executions, court rules," *The Orlando Sentinel* (August 3), p. A12.

9. Howstuffworks: "How Lethal Injection Works" (2002) www.howstuffworks.com/lethal-injection2.htm; *State of California*, op. cit.; L. Kay Gillespie (2003) *Inside the Death Chamber: Exploring Executions.* Boston: Allyn and Bacon, pp. 4-8.

10. Susan Blaustein (1997) "Witness to Another Execution," Pp. 387-400 in H. A. Bedau (ed.) *The Death Penalty in America: Current Controversies.* New York; Oxford University Press, p 390.

11. Ibid., p. 395.

A short time after she reported to the administration building, Blaustein and the other witnesses were escorted across the street to the death house. As the witnesses filed in, she recalled, "The other woman reporter must have seen the fearful look in my eyes. She told me that she couldn't sleep for three nights after her first execution. 'Just attend to the business at hand,' she advised."[12] As they waited to enter the witness room, Blaustein asked the public-information officer "whether it made any difference to him when the men whose death he witnessed were volunteers?" (A "volunteer" is a death row inmate who has given up all of his appeals so that he can be executed promptly.) The information officer replied, "I appreciate that they accept what they did and want to pay the penalty.... You gotta respect that."[13] The condemned inmate's defense attorney, who had overheard the exchange between Blaustein and the information officer, took issue with the officer's statement. Blaustein related the attorney's remarks:

> "Actually, [his client] was the perfectly rehabilitated prisoner," [the attorney] said, then mused about the fine theoretical line between the insanity plea of an inmate who claims to hear voices, and is therefore not competent to be executed, and a volunteer such as [his client], whose execution was expedited because he had heard the voice of Jesus promising him a heavenly escape from death row.[14]

The witnesses then were ushered into the witness room, where they "stood behind bars and a pane of thick glass." When the execution was completed, they filed out the same way they had come in, "more quickly this time, with little conversation."[15]

After attending the inmate's funeral, Blaustein drove out of town and "hoped the day's sharp rawness would clear [her] numbed senses."[16] She later wrote:

> That meticulous choreography had anesthetized me to the reality that a man was being killed before my eyes.... From what I'd read about the stench of electrocution and the vividness of public hangings, I imagined that witnessing deaths by these means would have an immediacy that would preclude numbness. The lethal-injection method ... has turned dying into a still life, thereby enabling the state to kill without anyone involved feeling anything at all. I wondered how viewing such a non-event could satisfy the desire for retribution so often expressed by death-penalty advocates and the families of victims. I wondered whether Huntsville's sterile, bloodless executions of the last twelve years might partly account for residents' wholesale disinterest and denial that what went on deep inside the Walls might have anything to do with them.... We have perfected the art of institutional killing to the degree that it has deadened our natural, quintessentially human response to death.[17]

Another journalist to report his reactions to an execution is Christopher Hitchens, who witnessed the September 24, 1997, Missouri execution of Samuel Lee McDonald. Hitchens wrote:

> In my time, I have seen people die and be killed, in sickness and in warfare.... It's all, in a manner of speaking, part of life. But I feel permanently degraded

---

12. Ibid., p. 396.
13. Ibid.
14. Ibid.
15. Ibid.
16. Ibid., p. 398.
17. Ibid., p. 399.

and somewhat unmanned by the small part I played, as a complicit spectator, in the dank and dingy little ritual that was enacted in that state prison cellar in Missouri. The medical butchery of a helpless and once demented loser ... made neither society nor any individual safer. It canceled no moral debt. It was a creepy, furtive, and shameful affair, in which the participants could not decently show their faces or quite meet one another's eye. I don't know that I shall ever quite excuse myself, even as a reporter and writer who's supposed to scrutinize everything, for my share in the proceedings. But I am clear on one thing. Death requires no advocates. It is superfluous to volunteer for its service.[18]

In the 2000 documentary *Witness to an Execution*, four other experienced media representatives described various aspects of the Texas lethal injection executions that they had witnessed.[19] The first was Michael Graczyk, an Associated Press bureau chief in Houston. He had sat through approximately 170 executions. He recalled, "I had a mother collapse right in front of me. We were standing virtually shoulder to shoulder. She collapsed, hit the floor, went into hyperventilation, almost convulsions."

John Moritz, a reporter with the *Fort Worth Star Telegram*, did not reveal how many executions he had witnessed but said this about his first execution: "The first execution I did, I was wondering how I'd react to it. But it's like any other unpleasant situation a reporter is asked to cover. At some point there's a detachment. You realize that it's not about you; it's about the guy who's about ready to be put to death." Inside the witness room, he observed, "The people inside the room watching it are invariably silent. Sometimes you find people holding hands, maybe a mother and father of a murder victim or friends of the condemned man."

Wayne Sorge, news director of the radio station KSAM in Huntsville had witnessed 162 executions. He provided the following justification for his participation:

> I wrestle with myself about the fact that it's easier now, and was I right to make part of my income from watching people die? And I have to recognize the fact that what I do for a living is hold up a mirror to people of what their world is. Capital punishment is part of that, and if you are in the city where more capital punishment occurs than any place else in the civilized world, that's got to be part of the job.

Sorge then commented about the mothers who witness the executions of their children: "I've seen them fall into the floor, totally lose control. And yet how do you tell a mother that she can't be there in the last moments of her son's life?"

Huntsville Item reporter Leighanne Gideon had witnessed fifty-two executions. She noted what being in the witness room was like for her: "It's very quiet. It's extremely quiet. You can hear every breath everyone takes around you. You can hear the cries, the weeping, the praying." She related, "I've seen family members collapse in there. I've seen them scream and wail. I've seen them beat the glass." She added, "You'll never hear another sound like a mother wailing whenever she is watching her son be executed. There's no other sound like it. It is just this horrendous wail. You can't get away from it. That wail surrounds the room. It's definitely something you won't ever forget." Regarding her first

---

18. Lifton and Mitchell, op. cit., p. 185.

19. Information about the four media witnesses is from the transcript of a "Witness to an Execution" at INK"http://sound"http://sound portraits.org/on-air/witness_to_an_execution/transcript.php, Copyright © 2000 Sound Portraits Productions. All Rights Reserved (accessed June 25, 2009).

execution, she remembered, "I was twenty-six years old.... After the execution was over, I felt numb. And that's a good way to explain it. And a lot of people will tell you that, that it's just a very numb feeling afterwards." She also observed, "I've walked out of the death chamber numb and my legs feeling like rubber sometimes, my head maybe not really feeling like it's attached to my shoulders. I've been told that it's perfectly normal, everyone feels it, and that after a while that numb feeling goes away. And indeed it does."

The numbness that Gideon and Blaustein reported has been considered a symptom of a dissociative state that occurs in people who experience psychologically traumatic events.[20] The symptom is believed to attenuate the immediate pain and emotional impact of the stressful event and to be a part of a larger pattern of symptoms called *acute stress disorder* or *acute anxiety and dissociative disorder*. In what may be the only empirical study of execution witnesses, subjects were fifteen of the eighteen journalists who witnessed the execution of Robert Alton Harris on April 21, 1992, in San Quentin Prison's gas chamber.[21]

Harris's execution was unusual not only because it was California's first execution following reinstatement of the death penalty in 1976, but also because Harris received four stays of execution between 6:30 p.m. on April 20 and 6:05 a.m. the following morning, when he finally was executed. The journalists had arrived at the prison during the afternoon of April 20 and stayed until Harris was executed. Study subjects completed a questionnaire, and twelve of the fifteen subjects participated in interviews.

The participants reported a median of five dissociative symptoms out of the thirty-five that were provided. The following shows the dissociative, anxiety, and other symptoms experienced by at least half the subjects during or shortly after the execution:

- Nine felt estranged or detached from other people.
- Eight felt distant from their own emotions.
- Eight felt that things around them seemed unreal or dreamlike.
- Eight felt a sense of timelessness.
- Eight tried to avoid thoughts or feelings about the execution.
- Eight felt other emotions to an extreme degree.

None of the journalists reported any severe or long-lasting psychological trauma as a result of witnessing the execution, which corroborates Gideon's experience. However, some of the journalists who reported no dissociative symptoms believed they may have been so dissociated that they did not recognize the symptoms. As one journalist asserted, "You click into another mode when reporting. I was so involved in my work that I wasn't aware of any emotions."[22] This may be why some execution team members also report being unaffected; they strive to intentionally dissociate themselves from their emotions.[23] Thus, dissociative symptoms may be an occupational hazard of being an execution team member or a journalist,[24] or they may be necessary qualities for successful participation. Also, because of the unusual length of Harris's execution, some of the journalists thought

---

20. Andrew Freinkel, Cheryl Koopman, and David Spiegel (1994) "Dissociative Symptoms in Media Eyewitnesses of an Execution." *American Journal of Psychiatry* 151(9): 1335-39.

21. Ibid.

22. Ibid., p. 1337.

23. Johnson, op. cit., p. 186.

24. Ibid.

that sleep deprivation caused their symptoms. Finally, though there is no empirical evidence to confirm it, other witnesses with less to distract them may experience more dissociative symptoms and experience them more profoundly and for longer periods of time than did the journalists in the study.

Attorney David Bruck, who witnessed the January 10, 1986, execution of his client Terry Roach in South Carolina's electric chair, provided another testimonial. Roach was seventeen years old when he committed the crime for which he was executed at the age of twenty-five. About Roach's execution, Bruck remarked that everything that transpired "made you think we ought not to be doing it. It's an ugly, very ugly ritual."[25] He added:

> I suppose it would be better to say that the actual killing was incredibly disgusting, painful, gruesome, and gory.... But, to me, the truth is, it was not as bad as that, and at the same time it was much worse. It was easy as shutting a drawer or snapping one's fingers. To me, what it said was that they take a living person, who took twenty-five years to create, and within just a few seconds they converted him into a piece of junk to be wrestled out on a stretcher and carted away. To me, the message was that human beings are junk and if you don't believe it — watch this. It is a completely incomprehensible miracle how a human being comes into the world ... but to snuff one out, it is nothing. It is the easiest thing. Murderers can do it, anyone can do it. We can do it. Watch this! It was banal. It was dehumanizing. Not only to him. It was a ritual which denied the importance and uniqueness of any of us.[26]

A few academics have also witnessed executions and reported on their experiences. One is L. Kay Gillespie, a criminal justice professor at Weber State University in Utah. He has witnessed six executions.[27] The following is his personal account of one of those executions:

> I was prepared for the execution. I had thought through what to wear (not too formal, not too casual). What to eat before the execution. (Would I get sick if I ate too much or if I ate certain foods?) The planning process had been formal and professional. There were neither jokes nor were there any indications of punishment or vengeance. As a matter of fact, the warden had made it clear to those involved in the execution that they were to act professionally. They were carrying out their duty and they were to be as accommodating as possible to all involved — inmate, victim's family, and all others. They were not there to punish anyone, only to do their duty. What I was not prepared for was the person next to me who was sobbing. Someone was grieving over the man being executed. It was raw emotion, something that had been left out of the planning process. Aside from the sterile setting of the actual execution, those involved — warden, staff, and inmate — had kept things on a level devoid of personal emotion and feeling. Those conducting the execution were expected to be "professional" and the one being executed was expected to "die game" — to go like a man. Everyone was "prepped" except the woman next to me. I remember my hands getting sweaty. I was trying to remain objective and detached. I was taking notes and "documenting" what I was observing. There was not much to observe. It was a

---

25. Lifton and Mitchell, op. cit., p. 185.
26. Ibid., pp. 185-86.
27. Gillespie, op. cit., p. 2.

lethal injection execution. The lethal drugs had been injected, I saw his stomach rise and fall, then nothing—no twitching, struggling, no deep sighs or tremors. He was there and then he was gone.[28]

So, based on his experiences, does Professor Gillespie support or oppose the death penalty? He writes:

I stand in the middle! I have no moral or religious code that requires me to oppose it. As a *sociologist*, I believe a society, particularly a democratic society, has the right to impose whatever sanctions it wishes so as to maintain social order. On the other hand, as a *criminologist*, I find the justice system too capricious and subject to manipulation and bias to be trusted with dispensing death in a fair and equitable manner. Perhaps my personal position is in actuality a nonposition. I have tried to immerse myself in as many aspects of the death penalty debate and the execution process as possible. I think it would be fair to say I have explored as many, or more, facets of the execution process from an academic and personal perspective as is possible. I am unimpressed with those who, on either side, make it such a simple matter—pro or con. How can anyone be either in favor of capital punishment or opposed to it? For me, it cannot be that simple.... I stand in the middle. My knowledge, observations, and experience have only made me more tentative about taking an absolute position for or against.[29]

Eight years after he witnessed his last execution—the federal execution of Timothy McVeigh in 2001—Professor Gillespie reported that he was unaware of any lingering effects from the executions he witnessed, although, periodically, he has a sense of how surreal the experiences have been. He did say that after witnessing an execution, his children observed that he was "a little testy."[30]

Another academic to witness an execution is Richard Moran, a sociology professor at Mount Holyoke College in Massachusetts. Professor Moran witnessed the lethal injection execution of Thomas Barefoot in Texas on October 30, 1984. In an editorial he wrote for the *Los Angeles Times*, Professor Moran described the drama: "The condemned man looked right at me. Only a few feet separated us. I was afraid he would try to touch me.... I was ashamed—ashamed of being there and afraid that he would ask something of me. I was an intruder, the only member of the public who had trespassed on his private moment of anguish. In my face he could see the horror of his own death."[31] Professor Moran experienced what has been referred to as "voyeur's guilt."[32]

As a postscript, twenty-five years after witnessing Barefoot's execution, Professor Moran reported no lingering adverse effects from the experience. However, he had made a concerted effort not to be consumed by it. Although he has always been leery about the death penalty, he is not firmly against it. If it could be shown that the death penalty actually deterred people from committing capital crimes, which Moran believes has not been demonstrated, he would probably accept the death penalty, albeit reluctantly. He does not believe there is any way to administer the penalty fairly.[33]

---

28. Ibid.
29. Ibid., pp. 9-10, 13.
30. L. Kay Gillespie, personal communication, August 12, 2009.
31. Cited in Lifton and Mitchell, op. cit., p. 184.
32. David Von Drehle (1995) *Among the Lowest of the Dead*. New York: Fawcett Crest, p. 369.
33. Richard Moran, personal communication, August 7, 2009.

Perhaps the execution witness with the most unique experience is Russell Stetler, who was the chief investigator for the Capital Defender's Office in New York.[34] In 1992, Stetler was living in Los Angeles and assisting the defense team for Robert Alton Harris. Judge Marilyn Patel had stayed the inmate's execution, ruling that death in California's gas chamber constituted cruel and unusual punishment. When another judge lifted her stay, Patel ordered that a member of Harris's defense team videotape his execution to provide evidence for future appeals. Russell Stetler was the defense team member selected. This is Stetler's account of what he saw and how he felt:

> It was hard to watch him struggling for air, for life ... so you want the suffering to be over—that is, you want him to be dead.... I suppose I could have feigned illness and left.... One of my friends had witnessed an execution and told me he threw up uncontrollably afterward. But I felt it was my job to be there, collecting important evidence. At the same time, however, I felt utter despair and a sense of failure, on multiple levels.[35]

Stetler had been a long-time death penalty opponent, but witnessing the execution significantly strengthened his view. He reflected: "I had opposed it mainly intellectually and philosophically and in the abstract.... I wasn't prepared for how horrific it was, my raw, emotional response. I went home feeling soiled."[36] Stetler had nightmares for months following the execution. In an interview six years later, he said that the memories of the execution were no longer so "intrusive" but that they could be triggered by reading about current cases that reminded him of Harris's case. He noted:

> Talking with my colleagues [in death penalty work] helps a lot, but it's sort of like those who survive combat.... You feel you can only talk to someone else who has witnessed an execution; no one else really knows what it's like. The gas chamber "visuals" may be particularly bad—it's what they call in veterinary ethics the "aesthetics" of euthanizing animals. But even talking to people who have witnessed lethal injections, the impact is still tremendous.[37]

Stetler's videotape, incidentally, was never shown; it was destroyed not long after it was made.[38]

Conclusion

People witness executions for a variety of reasons. For some of them, such as media representatives, it is a job assignment. Although not much information is available on the personal reactions of execution witnesses, what is known suggests that some witnesses feel fearful, sullied, degraded, dehumanized, ashamed, voyeuristic, complicit, detached, despair, and numb; experience dissociative symptoms; and have difficulty sleeping afterwards, From what is known, few, if any, witnesses suffer prolonged psychological trauma, but more research on the subject is needed. Without executions, of course,

---

34. Lifton and Mitchell, op. cit., p. 186.
35. Ibid., pp. 187-88.
36. Ibid., p. 188.
37. Ibid.
38. Ibid., pp. 194-95.

execution witnesses would not be needed. The last group of participants in the capital punishment process to be examined in this book is governors, who sign death warrants and have the power to grant clemency. Their stories are next.

Chapter 13

Governors

Governors have a critical role in the capital punishment process because they sign death warrants and can grant clemency. Both responsibilities require governors to make life-and-death decisions. They have the last chance to spare a death row inmate's life. Decisions about clemency are among the most profound and difficult a governor can make. This chapter examines the role of governors in the capital punishment process.

Three Types of Clemency

Clemency generally provides the final opportunity to consider whether a death sentence should be imposed.[1] All fifty states, the federal government, and the military have provisions for granting clemency.[2] In fact, every judicial system in the world except China's provides for clemency.[3] In the United States, clemency allows the governor of a state (or the president of the United States, when federal or military law is violated) to exercise leniency or mercy. Many states have specialized administrative boards or panels authorized to assist the governor in making the clemency decision. In a few states, the governor is not authorized to grant clemency unless an administrative body has first recommended it.[4]

Three types of clemency relevant to capital punishment are reprieve, commutation, and pardon:

1. *Reprieve* is the most common type of clemency employed in capital cases, and the most limited. A reprieve (or *stay*) temporarily postpones an execution. It is typically used to allow a death row inmate the opportunity to complete a pending appeal or to give the governor a last-minute chance to review questions about the inmate's guilt.

---

1. Unless indicated otherwise, material on clemency is from Daniel T. Kobil (2003) "The Evolving Role of Clemency in Capital Cases," pp. 673-692 in J. R. Acker, R. M. Bohm, and C. S. Lanier (eds.) *America's Experiment with Capital Punishment: Reflections on the Past, Present and Future of the Ultimate Penal Sanction*, 2nd ed. Durham, NC: Carolina Academic Press; James R. Acker and Charles S. Lanier (2000) "May God—or the Governor—Have Mercy: Executive Clemency and Executions in Modern Death–Penalty Systems." *Criminal Law Bulletin* 36:200–237; Austin Sarat (2005) *Mercy on Trial: What It Means to Stop an Execution*. Princeton, NJ: Princeton University Press.
2. Austin Sarat (2006) "Putting a Square Peg in a Round Hole; Victims, Retribution, and George Ryan's Clemency," pp. 203-232 in J. R. Acker and D. R. Karp (eds.) *Wounds That Do Not Bind: Victim-Based Perspectives on the Death Penalty*. Durham, NC: Carolina Academic Press, p. 204, n. 2.
3. Ibid.
4. Ibid.

2. *Commutation* substitutes a lesser punishment for the one imposed by the court. A sentence of life imprisonment without the opportunity of parole is the sentence most likely to be substituted for a death sentence. Sometimes commutations are contingent on certain conditions, such as the inmate waiving his or her right to a new trial or agreeing not to profit from the sale of an account of his or her crime. From 1976 through April 2012, 271 death row inmates had their sentences commuted. That represents about 3.5 percent of all death sentences imposed during the period. Illinois governors granted 69 percent of the commutations (187), including 167 in January 2003, by Illinois Governor George Ryan—now in prison himself—just days before leaving office. (More about this later.)[5]

3. *Pardon* is the most expansive type of clemency. With a pardon, the prisoner's crime is erased, and his or her punishment is terminated. A pardoned individual is freed entirely from the criminal justice system and is treated legally as if he or she had never been charged or convicted of a crime. Pardons are rarely granted to people convicted of capital crimes. From January 1, 1973, through April 2010, only seven pardons were granted to condemned inmates, including four by Illinois's Ryan in January 2003.[6] Also, between January 1, 1973 and April 2010, the Courts cleared 138 capital offenders of the charges that put them on death row, though exonerations by the courts are not "executive" pardons.[7]

The Fail-Safe of the Criminal Justice System

The late U.S. Supreme Court Chief Justice William Rehnquist considered executive clemency the fail-safe of the criminal justice system.[8] Theoretically, it serves as a safety valve and the last, best chance of rectifying miscarriages of justice. Ironically, the availability of clemency probably increases the number of death sentences because it gives jurors and the public greater confidence that any mistakes made earlier in the process will be eventually corrected by governors.[9]

Unfortunately, for those who would rely on clemency to correct errors made earlier in the process, recent experience contradicts the promise. In a bow to states' rights, the federal courts are increasingly deferring to governors the job of correcting substantive problems with death sentences. Yet governors are being effectively deterred from granting clemency. Few death sentences have been commuted under post-*Furman* statutes because of increased media attention devoted to capital clemency deliberations and the realization by governors that a decision to commute a death sentence is akin to political suicide.

A politically safer strategy for governors is to quietly *not sign* death warrants. The few commutations that have been granted have come mostly from governors not seeking re-

5. The Death Penalty Information Center, "Clemency" at www.deathpenaltyinfo.org/clemency (accessed April 29, 2012).

6. Richard C. Dieter (2010) Executive Director, The Death Penalty Information Center, Personal communication (April 23, 2010).

7. Ibid.

8. Cited in *Herrera v. Collins* (506 U.S. 390, 1993 at 415).

9. Robert Jay Lifton and Greg Mitchell (2002) *Who Owns Death? Capital Punishment, the American Conscience, and the End of Executions.* New York: Perennial, p. 132.

election.[10] This is a change from the past. Prior to 1970, governors in death penalty states "routinely commuted up to a third of the death sentences that they reviewed." Since then, however, only about two death sentences a year have been commuted in the entire country,[11] with four exceptions: the 167 death sentences commuted by Governor Ryan in 2003 (all death row inmates—does not include four pardons), eight commutations by Ohio governor Richard Celeste in 1991; eight commutations by New Jersey governor Jon Corzine in 2007 (all death row inmates); and four commutations by New Mexico governor Tony Anaya in 1986 (all death row inmates).

In the twentieth century, "the heyday of commutations was the early and mid–1940s, during which 20 to 25 percent of death penalties were commuted."[12] The most common reasons given for granting clemency during the post-*Furman* period are doubts about the offender's guilt, the offender's mental retardation or mental illness, and equitable concerns about offenders who have received harsher sanctions than other participants in the same crime.[13]

Granting Clemency

George W. Bush, in his autobiography *A Charge to Keep*, wrote that decisions about executions are "by far the most profound" that a governor can make. He should know, having presided over 152 executions during his six years as Texas governor—second most by a governor in the U.S. under post-*Furman* statutes.[14] (Bush's successor, Texas governor Rick Perry, has presided over more than 200 executions.) However, then governor Bush was not alone in his sentiment about clemency decisions in capital cases. For example, former governor of Pennsylvania Tom Ridge—like Governor Bush a death penalty proponent—stated about clemency decisions, "I think that's the toughest thing we do."[15] Likewise, former Maryland governor Parris Glendening, also a death penalty proponent, considered clemency decisions "probably the single most difficult type of responsibility that goes with the office."[16] He added, "No matter how comfortable you are philosophically

---

10. Stuart Banner (2002) *The Death Penalty: An American History*. Cambridge: Harvard University Press, p. 291.

11. See Death Penalty Information Center, op. cit.; David C. Baldus and George Woodworth (1998) "Racial Discrimination and the Death Penalty: An Empirical and Legal Overview," pp. 385–415 in J. R. Acker, R. M. Bohm, and C. S. Lanier (eds.) *America's Experiment with Capital Punishment: Reflections on the Past, Present and Future of the Ultimate Penal Sanction*. Durham, NC: Carolina Academic Press, pp. 388–9; Acker and Lanier, 2000, op. cit., pp. 212–13, Table 1 for the pre–1970's figure; also see Richard C. Dieter (1996) *Killing for Votes: The Dangers of Politicizing the Death Penalty Process*. Washington, DC: The Death Penalty Information Center. p. 26.

12. Victoria Palacios (1996) "Faith in Fantasy: The Supreme Court's Reliance on Commutation to Ensure Justice in Death Penalty Cases." *Vanderbilt Law Review* 49:311–372, p. 347.

13. Acker and Lanier, 2000, op. cit., p. 215. For additional reasons, see Cathleen Burnett (2002) *Justice Denied: Clemency Appeals in Death Penalty Cases*. Boston: Northeastern University Press, pp. 158 and 169, n. 7; Radelet, Michael L. and Barbara A. Zsembik (1993) "Executive Clemency in Post–*Furman* Capital Cases." *University of Richmond Law Review* 27:289–314.

14. Alan Berlow (2003) "The Texas Clemency Memos." *The Atlantic Monthly* (July/August), pp. 91-96.

15. Lifton and Mitchell, op. cit., p. 130.

16. Ibid., p. 131.

with the broad issue of the death penalty, when you are dealing with a specific person, it is very difficult. There is nothing as focused and immediate as deciding whether a person is going to die or not."[17]

Because Texas has conducted more than one-third of all executions under post-*Furman* statutes and more than four times as many executions as its nearest contender, an examination of its clemency protocol may prove instructive (though probably not representative).[18]

The state of Texas maintains the legal fiction that its governor, unlike governors of other states, does not have unfettered authority to grant clemency; he or she can grant clemency only to those inmates recommended by the eighteen-member Texas Board of Pardons and Paroles. Otherwise the governor must either approve the execution or grant a thirty-day stay. However, the governor can control the process because he or she appoints the board that is authorized to approve or deny all clemency applications.[19]

One good example of this legal fiction in action involves the case of infamous serial killer Henry Lee Lucas, the only person to whom Governor Bush granted clemency. Lucas, who had confessed falsely to hundreds of murders, had been convicted in the 1980s of nine murders for which he was serving six life sentences, two seventy-five-year sentences, and one sixty-year sentence. In yet another murder trial, Lucas was sentenced to death. After the trial and investigations by two successive state attorneys, it became apparent that Lucas had been wrongly convicted of the murder for which he was sentenced to death because he had not been in the state of Texas when the victim was killed. When Governor Bush became aware of this fact, he let the Board of Pardons and Paroles know that he would not allow Lucas to be executed for a crime he did not commit. The Board of Pardons and Paroles subsequently voted 17 to 1 to commute Lucas's death sentence to life in prison, which Bush approved.

Governor Bush used this process inconsistently, though. In 1998 he denied clemency for Karla Faye Tucker, citing Texas law that stated that he could not commute Tucker's sentence from death to life in prison without the recommendation of the Board of Pardons and Paroles—something he somehow was able to get in the Lucas case.[20] Tucker became the first woman executed in the United States since 1984 and the first in Texas since the 1860s.

The Texas Board of Pardons and Paroles does not meet to discuss applications. Instead, members review cases separately and fax in their votes from across the state. The board operates without guidelines and does not have to give explanations for its decisions. *The Dallas Morning News* described the clemency process in Texas as "shrouded in secrecy." In 1999, Federal District Judge Sam Sparks ruled that the clemency system in Texas had the "minimal procedural safeguards" required by the U.S. Supreme Court. He added, however, that

> [i]t is abundantly clear the Texas clemency procedure is extremely poor and certainly minimal. Legislatively, there is a dearth of meaningful procedure. Administratively, the goal is more to protect the secrecy and autonomy of the system rather than carrying out an efficient legally sound system. The board would not

17. Ibid.

18. For a description of the Missouri clemency process, see Burnett, op. cit., pp. 162–165.

19. Jim Yardley (2000) "On the Record: Texas' Busy Death Chamber Helps Define Bush's Tenure." *The New York Times* (January 7), www.crimelynx.com/bushdp.html.

20. Berlow, op. cit.

have to sacrifice its conservative ideology to carry out its duties in a more fair and accurate fashion.[21]

Before Governor Bush made a final decision on clemency, usually on the morning of the day of the scheduled execution, he reviewed a document prepared by his legal counsel summarizing the facts of the case. His counsel then briefed him on those facts. Alberto Gonzales, Bush's counsel and subsequently United States attorney general during the Bush presidency, prepared the first fifty-seven clemency memos given to the governor. An examination of those memos and Bush's handling of them is revealing about the clemency process in Texas at that time.[22]

The clemency memos, which were only three to seven pages long, were the primary source of information used by the governor in making his clemency decisions. Each memo contained a brief description of the crime, one or two paragraphs about the defendant's personal background, and a short legal history. Rarely were recommendations made about whether to grant clemency, but many memos reflected a clear prosecutorial bias and an assumption that the governor had no good reason to revisit claims already rejected by appellate courts. Conspicuously missing from nearly all of the memos was any reference to crucial issues in the case, such as ineffective counsel, conflict of interest, mitigating evidence, or evidence of actual innocence.

When speaking about the clemency process throughout his six years in office, the governor repeatedly made statements like "I take every death penalty case seriously and review each case carefully" and "Each case is major, because each case is life or death." Referring to his legal staff, he wrote, "For every death penalty case, they brief me thoroughly, review the arguments made by the prosecution and defense, raise any doubts or problems or questions." Bush touted the review as a "fail-safe" method for ensuring due process and certainty of guilt. During the 2000 presidential campaign, Gonzales was asked whether Bush ever read death row inmates' clemency petitions. He responded, "I wouldn't say that was done in every case … [b]ut if we felt there was something he should look at specifically—yes, he did look from time to time at what had been filed." However, a review of the clemency memos suggests that Governor Bush often allowed executions to proceed "based on only the most cursory briefings on the issues in dispute."

Former California governor Edmund G. "Pat" Brown probably allowed more inmates to be executed than any other governor who was personally opposed to the death penalty. During his eight years in office, thirty-six inmates were executed.[23] He also commuted the death sentences of twenty-three inmates.[24] Brown had not always been a death penalty opponent. When he became governor in 1959, he considered the death penalty a necessary evil. He believed that it might work as a deterrent and, at the least, served as "an emotional purge for society." As governor, he had sworn to uphold the laws of the state, and the death penalty was one of those laws.[25] Gradually, however, his position on the death penalty changed. In an interview, he bemoaned, "Nobody should be forced to do that [decide who lives and dies]. What did the good Lord give me that I should have the right to determine whether even the most abject, horrible character lives or dies."[26]

---

21. Yardley, op. cit.
22. Material on the Texas clemency memos is from Berlow, op. cit.
23. Lifton and Mitchell, op. cit., p. 133.
24. Ibid., p. 134.
25. Ibid.
26. Ibid., p. 135.

Later, in his memoirs, he confessed:

> The longer I live, the larger loom those fifty-nine decisions about justice and mercy that I had to make as governor. They didn't make me feel godlike then: far from it; I felt just the opposite. It was an awesome, ultimate power over the lives of others that no person or government should have, or crave. And looking back over their names and files now, despite the horrible crimes and the catalog of human weaknesses they comprise, I realize that each decision took something out of me that nothing—not family or work or hope for the future—has ever been able to replace.[27]

Conclusion

By virtue of their positions, governors in death penalty states are sometimes called upon to render life-or-death decisions. Those decisions about clemency, by all accounts, are among the most difficult that a governor is required to make. For some governors, those decisions haunt them the rest of their lives. In today's political climate, a governor's decision about granting clemency is a highly charged political action that could jeopardize his or her political career. That is why so few commutations and pardons are granted in capital punishment cases.

---

27. Ibid., pp. 135-36.

Conclusion

Capital punishment's collateral damage is widespread and, in many respects, unique to the people caught in capital punishment's web, as evidenced by the testimonials and other research presented in this book. Although caution should be exercised in making broad generalizations from the few participants examined in some of the chapters, important lessons still can be learned from them as well as from the larger number of participants in other chapters. In the language of science, consider the lessons hypotheses.

For example, and at the least, some participants in the capital punishment process are adversely affected by their participation. In fact, some are seriously damaged. Few participants are happy or satisfied with current death penalty systems. To be sure, many participants support the death penalty in theory, but a lesser number support the death penalty in practice. Few participants are enthusiastic about their roles. In fact, for some, such as execution team members, enthusiasm for the job is a disqualifying criterion. Many participants view their participation as simply doing their jobs or being professionals, something they are willing to do but would prefer not to do.

When speaking of participants, distinguishing between victims' and offenders' family members and criminal justice system personnel (including legal personnel) is important because the former have very little, if any, control over their participation, while the latter do have control. Unfortunately, with or without capital punishment, both murder victim family members and offender family members will suffer, albeit in different ways and for different reasons. Unlike murder victim family members and offender family members, criminal justice system personnel can always refuse to participate in the capital punishment process, which begs the question: Why do they participate, especially given the doubts that they express about the process and the collateral damage they suffer from their participation?

On one hand, the answer may be as simple as not wanting to lose their job, which may happen if they refuse to participate. Thus, keeping their job and the income and the perks that come with it are strong motivating factors to participate in a process about which they may have moral or utilitarian qualms and from which they may suffer collateral damage. In social-psychological terms, criminal justice system personnel are reinforced to participate in the capital punishment process. Strong reinforcers for execution team members, for example, are their elite status in the prison; the cohesive bond, the closeness, and the collective responsibility that team members develop for one another; the camaraderie that they share; and the support that they receive from each other. Reinforcement, however, is not the only or necessarily the most compelling theory to explain participants' behavior. A number of other theories—by themselves or in combination with reinforcement theory or with one another—might prove more compelling. Several of these theories attribute the willingness to participate in the capital punishment process to various psychological and social-psychological pathologies.

A second theory is that some participants, such as defense attorneys, prosecutors, postconviction attorneys, and some trial judges, make such a huge intellectual investment in becoming experts in the specialized area of capital punishment law and procedure that to not participate would be a waste of the expertise they worked so hard to achieve. The third and fourth theories may also explain both trial lawyers' and postconviction attorneys' willingness to participate in the capital punishment process. The third theory involves some attorneys' fervent belief in our adversarial system of justice. They take seriously their role to provide the best possible legal counsel and advocacy within the legal and ethical limits of their profession, regardless of their personal beliefs about the death penalty and despite the personal and financial sacrifices required. They believe that to refuse to defend unpopular clients renders the constitutional right to counsel and our adversarial system of justice meaningless. The fourth theory entails some attorneys' conscientious objections to the death penalty. Attorneys opposed to capital punishment seek to do everything legally permissible within their power to prevent their clients from being executed and to frustrate the operation of the death penalty process. Ironically, by participating in the process, even by fighting against it, attorneys opposed to capital punishment unwittingly help to legitimate the process.

A fifth theory is "obedience to authority."[1] Many participants in the capital punishment process state that they are simply doing their jobs, following orders, and/or respecting the chain of command. They also justify their roles by citing biblical commands, the "law of the land," patriotism, and/or an execution protocol. Each of these reasons belies a generally unreflective obedience to authority and desire to conform. That said, nothing is inherently wrong with following rules. What is wrong is not critically questioning the wisdom of the rules and the motives of those who made them.

Like "obedience to authority," a sixth theory imputes a willingness to participate in the capital punishment process to "an authoritarian personality." The concept derives from psychoanalytic theory, which locates an authoritarian personality's origins in early childhood experiences. An authoritarian personality has been described as "a mechanical surrender to conventional values; blind submission to authority together with blind hatred of all opponents and outsiders; anti-introspectiveness; rigid stereotyped thinking; a penchant for superstition; vilification; half-moralistic and half-cynical, of human nature; projectivity."[2] Reflecting characteristics of an authoritarian personality, many participants in the capital punishment process, as noted previously, unreflectively follow orders and frequently stereotype and vilify the capital defendant or death row inmate as an animal or monster — as something less than human.

A seventh theory attributes the ability to participate in executions to the psychological process of "doubling," which is the assumption of a "split personality" or the creation of "what is effectively a second self, a 'killing self.'"[3] This killing self, or execution self, does the dirty work and contrasts sharply with "the prior relatively nonviolent civilian [or everyday] self," which would never, or rarely, kill another human being, especially without provocation.[4] Only by deluding themselves by claiming to be "professionals doing their

---

1. Stanley Milgram (1974) *Obedience to Authority*. New York: Harper & Row.
2. Martin Jay (1973) *The Dialectical Imagination: A History of the Frankfurt School and the Institute of Social Research, 1923-1950*. Boston: Little, Brown, p. 240.
3. Robert Jay Lifton and Greg Mitchell (2002) *Who Owns Death? Capital Punishment, the American Conscience, and the End of Executions*. New York: Perennial, p. 77.
4. Ibid.

duty" are participants such as prison wardens able to effectively rationalize their behavior and become a part of the execution process.

Another plausible theory is "the Lucifer Effect."[5] The Lucifer Effect refers to the power of situational and systemic factors to induce good people to do evil things. This theory relegates dispositional factors, such as those described in previous theories, to secondary importance. In the context of capital punishment, the situational and systemic factors include legislative, law enforcement, prosecutorial, judicial, prison, and gubernatorial environments and the norms that regulate them. Each of those environments, with its attendant norms, provides the social circumstances in which the capital punishment process is allowed to exist and unfold.

A related theory suggests that "people tend to become what they do" because they must believe in what they are doing.[6] Thus, in the case of prosecutors, for example, who personally may have started out being opposed to the death penalty, their work can make them "execution oriented." This transformation enables them to maintain psychic equilibrium by reducing the cognitive dissonance that would otherwise exist between their own feelings against the death penalty and their job to prosecute capital cases.[7]

Another related theory involves "moral disengagement,"[8] which was discussed at length in Chapter 7 on capital jurors. Moral disengagement, accomplished primarily by the dehumanization of the capital defendant and eventual death row inmate, enables participants in the capital punishment process to play their roles in the condemnation and execution of a capital offender. Dehumanization of the capital defendant generally starts with typical media portrayals of the capital offender as a monster or an animal. Prosecutors continue the process by reinforcing the media's image at trial. The trial's structure and rules facilitate the process. Killing a monstrous offender is easier to justify than the killing of a flawed human being.

An eleventh theory attributes the willingness to participate in the capital punishment process to the "banality of evil."[9] The concept applied to capital punishment suggests that the participants in the process (for example, execution team members) are neither malevolent nor psychologically disturbed but unexceptional individuals who follow orders without thinking about the human and moral ramifications of what they do. Their primary focus is attempting to carry out their orders as efficiently as possible.

A final theory to be considered here imputes the willingness to participate in the capital punishment process to "false consciousness" about what capital punishment is believed to accomplish. Unlike some of the aforementioned theories that view capital punishment participants as unreflective or unthinking bureaucrats, this theory emphasizes the cognitive dimension to their participation. A theory of false consciousness presumes that participants in the capital punishment process have what they believe to be good reasons or sound arguments for capital punishment and their roles in the process. The problem for such individuals is that what they believe to be true about capital punishment—the arguments

5. Philip Zimbardo (2008) *The Lucifer Effect: Understanding How Good People Turn Evil*. New York: Random House.

6. Lifton and Mitchell, op. cit., p. 117.

7. Ibid.

8. Craig Haney (2005) *Death By Design: Capital Punishment as a Social Psychological System*. New York: Oxford University Press.

9. Hannah Arendt (1963) *Eichmann in Jerusalem: A Report on the Banality of Evil*. New York: The Viking Press.

they use to justify their behavior—is false and the product of propaganda. Despite substantial evidence to the contrary, many participants continue to believe, for example, that capital punishment deters would-be capital offenders better than long-term imprisonment, prevents vigilante justice, is the only legitimate way of achieving retribution for the most heinous crimes, provides comfort and closure for victims' family members, is administered fairly (that is, not in an arbitrary and discriminatory way), is not plagued by miscarriages of justice (such as wrongful convictions and executions), and is cost-effective compared to a process that results in lifelong imprisonment.

If any of those beliefs about capital punishment were true—if capital punishment was the only way of achieving a greater social good or social advantage—then the collateral damage to the participants in the capital punishment process could be justified, at least from a utilitarian view. However, an enormous body of research shows that the claims made about capital punishment's unique utility are false. Perhaps the strongest evidence is that seventeen states and the District of Columbia, as well as two-thirds of the world's nations, are able to achieve the utilitarian (and moral) goals of capital punishment with an alternative noncapital punishment at least as well as states and countries with capital punishment. Thus, capital punishment is unnecessary to accomplish any utilitarian or moral goals, which begs the question: Why incur capital punishment's collateral damage?

No doubt, any alternative to capital punishment will produce collateral damage, too, but that alternative, whatever it is, is less likely than capital punishment to be used by politicians for political gain, needlessly divert scarce resources from efforts to reduce violent crime, force participants to navigate a complex and chaotic capital punishment process, subject victims' family members to the secondary victimization caused by the capital punishment process, burden defense and postconviction attorneys, damage offenders' family members, wreck havoc with trial judges' court dockets, and cause appellate court judges to expend a disproportionately large share of their resources on a very small percentage of their caseload.

The replacement of capital punishment with an alternative punishment would also eliminate entirely the need for defense attorneys, prosecutors, and judges to expend time and resources on capital punishment; for jurors and governors to make life-and-death decisions; for prison wardens, death row correctional officers, execution team members, and execution witnesses to participate in executions; and the ultimate horror of executing an innocent person.

The arguments in support of capital punishment do not hold up well to critical scrutiny, while the arguments in opposition to it seem compelling. Capital punishment's collateral damage is another good argument for rethinking the wisdom of the ultimate sanction.

Index

Note: *n* designates footnote.